Also by
JONATHAN M. HANSEN

Guantánamo
The Lost Promise of Patriotism

YOUNG CASTRO

The Making of a Revolutionary

JONATHAN M. HANSEN

SIMON & SCHUSTER
New York London Toronto Sydney New Delhi

Simon & Schuster
1230 Avenue of the Americas
New York, NY 10020

First Simon & Schuster hardcover edition June 2019

SIMON & SCHUSTER and colophon are registered
trademarks of Simon & Schuster, Inc.

For information about special discounts for bulk purchases, please
contact Simon & Schuster Special Sales at 1-866-506-1949
or business@simonandschuster.com.

The Simon & Schuster Speakers Bureau can bring authors to
your live event. For more information or to book an event, contact
the Simon & Schuster Speakers Bureau at 1-866-248-3049
or visit our website at www.simonspeakers.com.

Interior design by Lewelin Polanco
Maps by David Lindroth

Manufactured in the United States of America

1   3   5   7   9   10   8   6   4   2

Library of Congress Cataloging-in-Publication Data

Names: Hansen, Jonathan M. (Jonathan Marshall), 1962– author.
Title: Young Castro : the making of a revolutionary / Jonathan M. Hansen.
Description: First Simon & Schuster hardcover edition. | New York :
Simon & Schuster, 2019. | Includes bibliographical references and index.
Identifiers: LCCN 2018034853 (print) | LCCN 2018041173 (ebook) | ISBN
9781476732497 (Ebook) | ISBN 9781476732473 (hardcover : alk. paper)
Subjects: LCSH: Castro, Fidel, 1926–2016. | Cuba—History—1933–1959. |
Heads of state—Cuba—Biography.
Classification: LCC F1788.22.C3 (ebook) | LCC F1788.22.C3 H36 2019
(print) | DDC 972.9106/4092 [B] —dc23
LC record available at https://lccn.loc.gov/2018034853

ISBN 978-1-4767-3247-3
ISBN 978-1-4767-3249-7 (ebook)

For Nathalie, Julian, and Oliver

History is a product of so many different interpretations and points of view that it's hard to be sure that true history exists. . . . Years from now, if historians describe what happened in Cuba today, what will they say? How close will they get to the facts? What will they get wrong?

FIDEL CASTRO, 1992[1]

CONTENTS

PREFACE

Tengo material abundante para el estudio de los grandes mov-
imientos políticos contemporáneos: Socialismo, Fascismo y Na-
zismo," Fidel Castro wrote Naty Revuelta in April 1954,
"*pero no tengo nada del New Deal de Roosevelt*" (I have plenty of material about the great political movements—Socialism, Fascism, and
Nazism—but nothing about Roosevelt's New Deal). At the time,
Castro was serving the ninth month of a twenty-six-year sentence
for his leadership in an attack on the Moncada military barracks in
Santiago de Cuba and was looking to expand his library. Revuelta
was a friend and fellow rebel. The two were in the early stage of
an epistolary love affair. When Revuelta suggested a book about
Roosevelt's foreign policy, Castro demurred. "What I really want to
document," he explained, "is FDR's program of raising agricultural
prices, promoting and preserving soil fertility, providing credit, forgiving debt, expanding internal and external markets; creating jobs,

reducing working hours, lifting wages, assisting the unemployed, aging, and infirm; reorganizing industry, revising the tax code, regulating trusts, and reforming banking and monetary policy"—in short, just about everything he himself wanted to do for Cuba.[1]

Castro's romance with Revuelta, which lasted just shy of six months, produced over one hundred letters, only a handful of which have ever been published (in radically abridged form). The available excerpts are tantalizing, revealing a prisoner wrestling with the future of Cuba while immersed in world history and literature and contemplating the meaning of life. Sensing that the letters could help me round out the caricature of Castro that passes for authoritative biography, I reached out to Revuelta in 2014 in much the same way that Castro himself had done a half century earlier: I had *material abundante* consistent with existing stereotypes, I explained; could she help me with evidence to illuminate the real man? Cubans are wary of U.S. writers revisiting the life of a figure they continue to admire despite his own and the Revolution's deficiencies. When a friend reported that Revuelta was willing to meet me, I was hopeful if somewhat shy of optimistic.

Gazing out at me from her shaded entryway as I stood in the blazing sunshine atop the steep front stairway of her home in the New Vedado neighborhood of Havana, Revuelta had the caution of an aging beauty accustomed to sizing up approaching predators. *Bienvenido*, came a low, raspy voice from out of the shadows. I extended my hand, which she graciously accepted, her cold, bony clasp reminding me of my late grandmother. Before my eyes could adjust, she led me onto a sun-dappled terrace, its green wicker chairs surrounded by tropical plants—palm, ficus, philodendron, bird of paradise. A small electric fan whirled futilely nearby, the faint tropical aroma overwhelmed by a cigarette smoldering in a nearby ashtray full to the brim. A glass coffee table was strewn with the day's newspaper, various magazines, and books, along with a few articles and photographs that seemed to have been cobbled together for me. The letters were nowhere to be seen. Clad in a sleeveless flower-print dress and sandals, the once voluptuous, now reedlike Revuelta seemed to float above the tile floor. "*Siéntate*," she said, before continuing in perfect English, "so you're writing a book about young Fidel." Sitting down herself, Revuelta erupted in a violent cough, her frail body racked to the bone. Waving away my look of concern, she ordered an assistant to bring us coffee. "Yes," I said, as she looked at me through emerald eyes with a skeptical smile and characteristic cock of her head. "I want to get this story right, and I'm told you can help me."

Several months and a few leisurely visits later, I heard that Revuelta was ready to share her letters with me, only to learn upon arriving at her home one afternoon that she had changed her mind. "*No hay problema, Naty*," I said, pulling out a letter Castro had written his father from Bogotá. "Let me show you something I just discovered in the archives." The letter, which few have ever seen, brims with youthful innocence and detailed descriptions of the physical landscape and political economy of Panama, Venezuela, and Colombia. "These voyages impart great wisdom and experience, at the same time that they open up great horizons and perspectives," Castro told his father.[2] Revuelta read on silently, her eyes welling with tears. "That's so Fidel," she murmured, "that's so Fidel." She then stood up, entered her library, and returned with a thick stack of paper which she plopped down on my lap, punctuating the moment with a single, unceremonious word: "HERE."

———————

This book is not a defense of Fidel Castro. My aim is to re-create his life as he actually lived it, moving forward, without the benefit of hindsight. With this in mind, I ask a favor of the reader: suspend for a moment the image you have of a bearded revolutionary clad in green fatigues, communist at conception, anti-American in utero, bilious at birth, and harken instead to a saga that begins in a small stone farmhouse in northwest Spain at the end of the nineteenth century. The reward for doing so may not be a more likable Castro, but one whose aspirations, accomplishments, and failures make sense in light of the political and economic conditions that inspired and constrained them.

Readers willing to take this leap will learn a few things that may surprise them. Castro did not commit himself or Cuba to communism until after the triumph of the Revolution in January 1959. He did so, ultimately, not as an end in itself, but as a means to the end of securing the Revolution from domestic and foreign opposition, including the United States government. This argument holds both for Castro's embrace of the Cuban Communist Party in 1959 and for his alliance with the Soviet Union in the aftermath of the Bay of Pigs invasion. Had Castro been more successful in building a disciplined political party to match his guerrilla army before he came to power, his turn to the PSP (which had never demonstrated much interest in him or his armed struggle) would not have been necessary.

Castro grew up a liberal nationalist, inspired by the unrequited dream of Cuba Libre—a Cuba free and independent of foreign rule and dedicated to the well-being of all its people. This program comprised both constitutionalism and civil rights, along with a set of social entitlements that included access to education, health care, employment, and a decent standard of living (common in Cuban cities but harder to find in rural areas[3]). In his late twenties a maturing Castro tied Cuba's struggle for sovereignty and independence to a liberal tradition that encompassed the English Civil War and the American, French, Haitian, and Latin American Revolutions, at the same time that he insisted that Cuba had a unique contribution to make to social and political science. Citing both Montesquieu and Simón Bolívar, he imagined Cuba charting a third way, at once democratic and socialistic.

Castro's rise is incomprehensible without an understanding of Cuban history and the history of U.S.-Cuban relations, which he knew like the back of his hand. The dream of national sovereignty and self-determination was hardly unique to Cuba, but Cuba waited an especially long time for independence. When Cubans thought they had it in their grasp in 1898, the United States snatched it away, inaugurating six decades of political and economic subservience that haunts Cuba to this day. Throw in the constraints of the Cold War, and the fate of the Cuban Revolution seems overdetermined. Despite arguments to the contrary, the U.S. government was never prepared to recognize the Revolution on Castro's original terms, making his alliance with the Soviet Union all but inevitable.

Castro's liberal nationalist agenda was neither original nor inherently revolutionary. Cuban politicians had been espousing this platform since the founding of the Cuban Republic in 1902, only to become distracted upon taking office by the opportunity for financial gain. By contrast, Castro meant it when he said it, making him not only radical but dangerous to establishment politicians, left, right, and center, as well as to the outside banks and corporations, many of them North American, which pulled the strings. Call it a fixation, call it an obsession, call it what you will: Castro experienced Cuba's subservience to the United States like a scarlet "S" tattooed on his chest, resolving at a remarkably young age to once and for all win Cuba's liberty even at the cost of liberty itself.

Castro regarded the struggle for Cuba Libre as part of a larger anticolonial project that encompassed not just the rest of Latin America but much of Africa and Asia besides. To critics, Castro's internationalism appeared at once dangerous and grandiose. U.S. officials accused Castro of meddling in other countries' affairs, as if the United States alone was authorized to do so. To Castro, as to Guatemala's Jacobo Árbenz, Egypt's Gamal Abdel Nasser, Vietnam's Ho Chi Minh, and countless other revolutionaries fighting to rid their nations of colonialism, it simply made sense to combine forces. There was strength in numbers. Again, this idea was hardly new at the time. Simón Bolívar and José Martí had seen it much the same way a century before.

Castro was not motivated originally by money or power. He grew up on a plantation in eastern Cuba owned by his parents, which stretched forty-two square miles across some of Cuba's most valuable farmland. By the time he was old enough to choose a vocation, his parents' enterprise included not only sugarcane production, but lumber, cattle, and mining operations besides. If it was money or influence he was after, he did not have to take on a U.S.-backed military dictatorship to get it. As a newly minted lawyer in 1950, he was practically granted the keys to his parents' kingdom only to look the other way. He simply would not be domesticated. He spent much of his mid-twenties making common cause with the men and women who first put their lives on the line for independence from imperial Spain. Their work remained unfinished a century later, and Castro worried that they were being forgotten. Much of his quixotic (some would say reckless) behavior represents his attempt to reacquaint Cubans with this revolutionary tradition.

Castro's solicitation for Cuban peasants and workers was deep-seated and sincere. Growing up on his parents' plantation, Castro's playmates were invariably the children of peasants and farm laborers. Returning home on school holidays, he easily fell back in among them, cherishing the local ways even as he became increasingly worldly. Crucially, his own parents were born and raised in peasant households, his father amid crushing hardship, a fact which no amount of new wealth could disguise. Observers later remarked that Castro always seemed at ease when engaging peasants and workers. This comfort was literally in his blood. As a young boy joining his father on his rounds of the cane fields, Castro witnessed more than just a conventional encounter between labor and management; these were also, at some level, exchanges between peers, his father's economic mobility providing fodder for his own Pan-American Dream.

Castro grew up feeling like an outsider, not an outcast, exactly, but an island, vulnerable and alone. Old schoolmates describe him as preoccupied at times, even detached. During the Great Depression and periodic price collapses that afflicted Cuba's sugar economy the Castro children never remember going hungry. This could not be said of their neighbors, and Castro recalled often scraping together leftovers to share with friends. At boarding school in Santiago de Cuba and Havana, he was greeted as a hick. Later, at the university, he described feeling isolated and exposed. Later still, he grew frustrated by Cubans' passivity in the face of a stultifying status quo, as if he were the lone voice in the wilderness calling the people to a higher end. He wasn't, of course, but he saw it that way, a fact that would become increasingly important as he began to attract followers and build a movement whose outcome would depend on his ability to work productively with others.

Castro believed his record of sacrifice and single-minded dedication to the cause of Cuba Libre gave him (and him alone) the legitimacy to lead the revolutionary struggle and, eventually, the revolutionary government. This, too, is debatable as there were many capable opposition leaders pushed aside by fate, accident, or by Castro himself. The last man standing is not necessarily the most deserving or most qualified. Still, Castro could be excused for thinking the Revolution would not have been waged, much less won, but for him. His extravagant claim to be the embodiment of the Revolution stems partly from the unlikelihood of his family's rise from rags to riches and of his surviving innumerable mishaps and setbacks, including sepsis at age seven, gang warfare at the university, a foiled invasion of the Dominican Republic, revolutionary upheaval in Colombia, and the Moncada Barracks attack, just to name a few.

The odds against Castro surviving to win and lead the Revolution appear preposterous in retrospect. Once captured after Moncada, he should never have been brought in alive; once jailed, the key to his cell should have been thrown away; once freed, he should have been eliminated while in exile; once bound for home with eighty-two men aboard a boat built for eight (including crew), he should never have survived a botched landing; once ashore he should never have eluded the government ambush that reduced the eighty-two men to fourteen; once in the mountains, he should never have outfought Batista's military; once victorious, he should never have outlasted innumerable U.S.-backed plans first to deny him victory, then to overthrow his government, finally to assassinate him. Considering all the pawns in the Cold War who have come and gone over the years, he should never have outlived nine U.S. presidents, while vexing a tenth, if only posthumously. Cats have nine lives, Castro had nine times nine. But we make our own luck, the saying goes, and Castro was a maestro. He believed he was chosen. Given this litany, it's hard to argue with him. This does not justify many of his actions or excuse his seizing power for half a century, but it helps explain them. *Only I could have done this; only I can see this through.*

Finally, as with so many world historical figures, Castro's strengths were the source of his greatest weaknesses. He was at once brilliant and arrogant, charismatic and overbearing, courageous and reckless, pragmatic and quixotic. He had a killer instinct, as those in his line of work always do. Capable of real affection, he possessed a coldness at the nether reaches of the Kelvin scale. In the end, he was able to love one thing and one thing only—not his first wife, Mirta, not his son, Fidelito, not even himself. He loved the Revolution. At the height of his powers, he was said to have been able to tolerate one person on a day-to-day basis, Celia Sánchez, not a lover exactly, but someone whose commitment to the Revolution rivaled his own. In waging and defending the Revolution, he could be simultaneously stoical and self-pitying, forgiving and vengeful, solicitous and autocratic. Not all of these characteristics are easy to explain. Many are hard to defend. This book attempts to account for as many of them as possible.

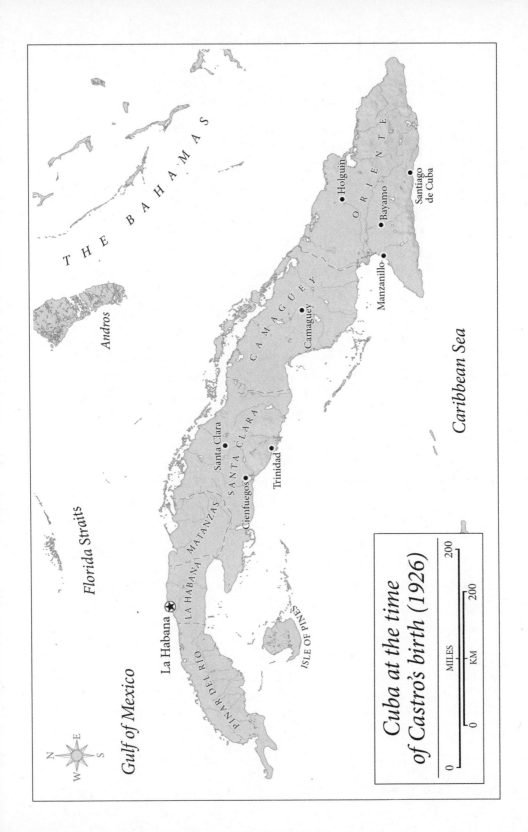

Cuba at the time
of Castro's birth (1926)

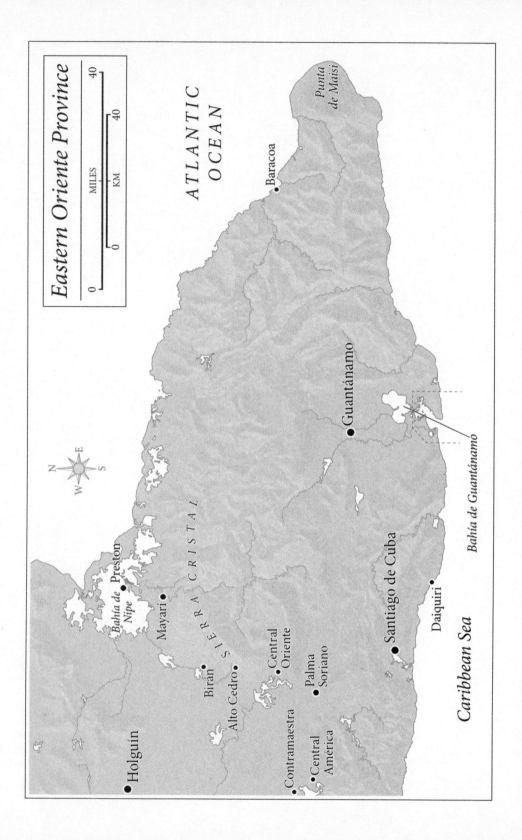

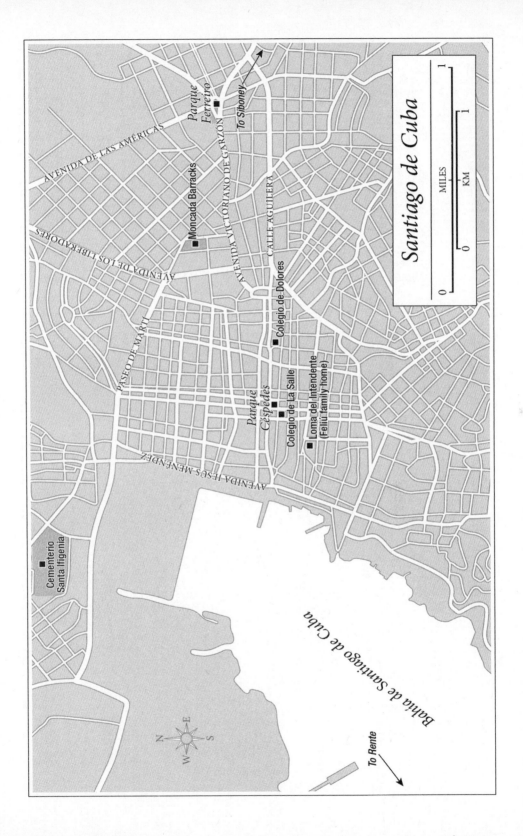

Santiago de Cuba

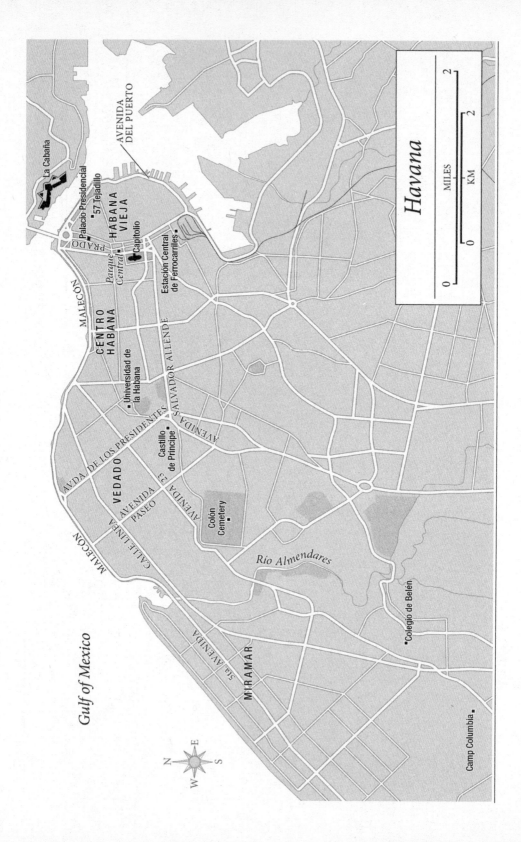

chapter one

LIKE FATHER

Like the fieldstone farmhouses of_ Láncara, Galicia, the boy
born the night of December 5, 1875, to Manuel Castro
Núñez and Antonia Argiz Fernández was made to last. _Castro_, from the Galician _castrexa_, Latin _castrum_, means castle or fort.
Ángel Castro Argiz, Fidel Castro's father, had the build and bearing
of the granite lintel that framed the doorway of his parents' low-slung home. First and last surviving photographs reveal a figure as
unyielding as inland Galicia itself: short, stout, chiseled, severe, with
sagging eyelids and furrowed brow—a walled city, a _castro_, of one.[1]

Ángel was the couple's second child, the first to make it through
a night. A survivor by sunrise of his natal day, Ángel embodied his
parents' faith not that things would be good in Láncara, exactly, but
that things could be better.[2] All infants did not die in childbirth.
All livestock did not succumb to wolves. The rain would cease. The
cold would ease. The restoration of King Alfonso XII would end

the chaos unleashed by twenty-two months of republican government. For eleven years, the family's fortune held. Then the latest
child went the way of the first, this time taking her mother, Antonia,
along with her. The couple had lost its hedge with fate and the family quickly disintegrated. Two surviving daughters were sent to live
with a nearby aunt. The father remarried the next year. The boy, just
twelve, quit his sad and broken home in search of something better.[3]

He did not wander far at first, taking up with two sausage-mak-
ing uncles in the nearby village of Armea, a patchwork of pastures,
fields, and woods from Láncara, on the south bank of the Neira
River. Three years later, having tired of sausage making, Ángel left
home again, this time for Madrid, the nation's capital, 470 kilometers southeast of Láncara, where he called on a distant aunt. Descending Spain's Cordillera Central onto the outskirts of Madrid
on day ten or so of what would become a decades' long pilgrimage,
Ángel would have sensed the city long before arriving in it. By
1890, Madrid was enjoying the fruits of a commercial revolution
two generations old that had swept south and west into the heart of
the Iberian Peninsula from the port cities of Barcelona and Bilbao,
and which introduced new industries and markets, new legal and
political institutions, new social and civic allegiances.[4] The revolution was surely palpable in the vibrant colors and commotion, the
unfamiliar smells and tastes, which greeted Ángel as he approached
the city. It was present, too, in the curious confidence and careless-
ness of the young boys and girls he met along the way who must
have regarded the country bumpkin with bemusement.[5]

This new world would prove as cruel as it was exhilarating, but
its downsides would have been easy to miss as Ángel crossed the
Puente Segovia and disappeared into the heart of the old city. Any
one of Madrid's great public squares could absorb more visitors than
populated all the little villages along the Neira. The Plaza Mayor,
its stalls bursting with luxuries, the Puerta del Sol, with its opulent
town houses, the spanking new Jardines del Buen Retiro, where
the city elite frolicked, boated, basked, and bowled made Madrid

seem less a distant metropolis, in Ángel's eyes, than a foreign country, with its own moral and political economy. Everything the boy had learned from his parents about virtue and self-discipline toppled head over heels with the nimble acrobats, spoiled children, and brazen couples on the sumptuous lawns of Buen Retiro. With time, Ángel would learn to manipulate the economic levers of the new liberal order, but there is no record of him ever succumbing to its hedonism.[6]

Years later, with a family of his own, Ángel insisted that his children pursue higher education. The cost of his own illiteracy was everywhere apparent in Madrid, where he found himself shut out from the lucrative clerical and administrative jobs that characterized the new commercial economy. Unqualified for meaningful work he was cut off from the pleasures that went with it. The elegant restaurants, the hypnotic music, the coded flirtation, the casual strolls, even the rough-and-tumble world of sport were the province of a class above, and no amount of backbreaking work in a butchery here or bakery there could win him elevation. For four years Ángel toiled in vain to amass the savings that might alter his fate. Relief came not in a lucky break, but in a note from home when, in 1894, with Spain on the verge of war in Cuba, the government issued a draft decree. Ordered to attend a lottery in the Galician town of Carracedo, Ángel, now eighteen, retraced his steps across the city, behind him a beguiling but unforgiving capital, ahead a tedious ascent up the Cordillera Central toward a future no more promising than when he first departed Láncara.[7]

Unable to read or write, Ángel made his mark on the world with his hands and feet. His mother's death launched him on an extended journey that took him to Madrid and back, to Cuba and back, then back to Cuba again, finally to Oriente Province in far eastern Cuba to stay, where, despite long odds, he managed to establish a toehold and, eventually, the financial footing that allowed him to settle down. The man who emerged from this pilgrimage was not a cultured, playful, adoring father or spouse, as we shall see. But he was a dogged worker, a reliable neighbor, and a generous benefactor, determined to provide his children the stability and education he lacked. As befits the surname *Castro*, Ángel was resolutely self-assured, able to get along with others when necessary, but ready to go it alone—a characteristic he passed on to his famous son.

———————

To be drafted into Spain's army in 1894 was inauspicious, even for a luckless Láncaran. Decades of corruption and neglect had rendered the Spanish army less an effective fighting force than a gentleman's club, bloated at the top, rotting at the bottom, good for little more than keeping Spaniards themselves in line. A people's army, the saying goes, is dangerous to its neighbors. A professional army is dangerous to its own people.[8] By the time Ángel was summoned to Carracedo, Spain's army had long since ceased to provide the rank and file with decent housing, diet, sanitation, medical care, even adequate training. These are requisites not only of an effective fighting force, but of life itself. Deprived of these, Spanish soldiers expired in astonishing numbers: 10 percent in their first year of service, 25 percent over their next four years, bringing the toll to nearly four deaths for every ten soldiers over a five-year enlistment—and this not in war but in peacetime, and on the Iberian Peninsula itself.[9]

To make matters worse, the nation's draft laws encouraged wealthy citizens to buy their way out of military service. This created a caste system in which regular enlistees were treated as common criminals, deployed as strikebreakers, and forced to work the fields. The Spanish public was powerless to do much about the corruption and abuse. New laws forbade criticism of the army and restricted freedom of the press. Individuals who defied the laws were made to answer in military courts. Opponents of the regime, like Carlists (archconservatives) and Republicans (leftists), were posted to remote and undesirable settings. The result was a rank and file populated by the most desperate and defenseless Spaniards—in short, by the likes of Ángel Castro.[10]

Ángel's draft number was not called at Carracedo. A year later, he got the opportunity to leave home again, when, for the third time in a generation, Cuban separatists led by an exiled nationalist named José Martí, declared independence from Spain on February 24, 1895. Desperate to attract recruits to fight in a climate Spaniards had learned to loathe, the government offered stipends payable at the stroke of a pen. Ángel promptly signed on, concluding that if things might not be better in Cuba, they could hardly be worse.

By the time Manuel Castro delivered up his eldest son to the Spanish Army at the port of A Coruña in August 1895, the Cuban War of Independence was six months old. A conflict that had elicited only the most casual shrug from the Spanish government initially had become a source of consternation across the land. For decades, senior army officers had refused postings to the Antilles, so notorious were the islands for heat, humidity, and tropical disease. In the latest flare-up, their intransigence led to the hasty promotion of reserve officers and ordinary enlistees with no experience in command of men. Combined with preexisting problems, the inexperience proved immediately calamitous, and word reached home of skyrocketing fatalities in Cuba just as Ángel's ship set sail. Public disquiet about these developments was palpable in the grim countenances of locals who lined the lanes to the nation's seaports for one last glimpse of the flower of Spain. Mothers and sons, sisters and brothers clung to one another in scenes of desolation. "When Spanish parents said goodbye to a beloved son drafted into the army," one historian has observed, "they really meant it."[11]

Ángel departed A Coruña on August 24, 1895, arriving in Cienfuegos on September 8, after sixteen topsy-turvy days at sea. He was posted to Remedios, in central Cuba, just northeast of Santa Clara, headquarters of Spanish forces in a region identified as Cuba's Rubicon. Should the Cuban guerrillas penetrate west of there, Spanish officials believed, there would be no stopping an advance on the capital Havana. Very little is known about Ángel's day-to-day experience with the Regimento Isabel II, but there is a good chance he never fired a shot.[12] A disciplined guerrilla force is notoriously difficult to engage, and the Cuban general, Máximo Gómez, marshaled his resources shrewdly. Outnumbered by more than five to one, the insurgents avoided face-to-face combat, striking from cover and under cover of darkness, while relying on local knowledge to dodge their adversary at lightning speed. Spain's strategy played into insurgent hands. Abandoning the countryside to the enemy, Spanish forces busied themselves protecting property, cities, and towns, as well as the *trochas* (trenches) that carved the island into thirds. Meanwhile, Spanish officers hired out troops on private terms to guard the great plantations, just as they had done back home in peacetime. The strategy made Spain's soldiers sitting ducks, easy to pick off as they stood rooted to their garrisons, easier to evade as the rebels knew their every whereabouts. It all made for a very curious kind of war. "The countryside is ours," a rebel leader wrote home in August 1895. "There is hardly any fighting in this revolution; it has been two months since I have had serious battles." A month later little had changed. "We have crossed all of Camagüey without firing a shot."[13]

An onslaught of tropical disease exacerbated Spain's misguided strategy. By the time the war ended in summer 1898, Spain had dispatched nearly 200,000 thousand men to Cuba, a record in colonial warfare to that time. Spain's losses throughout the war are conservatively estimated at 42,000 killed. Of these some 4,000 died in combat, the remaining 93 percent from disease. At any one time during the war, more than half Spain's soldiers were incapacitated due to illness. Midway into the four-year war illnesses climbed above 230,000 for two years in a row. Virtually every Spanish soldier became sick at least once during the war.

Ángel joined this wretched host just as the insurrection gained strength. Accompanying him were 40,000 new recruits, many of them teenagers far younger than he. Novices were given no training, granted no period of acclimatization. It took a little over eight months for mosquitoes, gnats, fleas, flies, lice, and poor sanitation to break down Ángel's natural defenses, remarkable in a theater that saw one in two soldiers incapacitated in their first two months in Cuba. In June 1896, Ángel was hospitalized for the first time with fever, chills, and delirium. The following December, he was admitted for eleven days with stiff and swollen joints. Out of the hospital, soldiers were hardly safe, as the garrisons to which they returned resembled hospital wards only without the medical staff. Once sick, Ángel could not dodge the microbial bombardment. In 1897, he was hospitalized seven different times for typhus, rheumatism, ulcers, malaria, diarrhea, lesions, and general fatigue. One hospital stay lasted an entire month. The end of the war brought no relief. Ángel returned to hospital on the eve of the armistice in July 1898, then again early the next year while awaiting transportation home.[14]

Together with Spain's garrison strategy, the rampaging disease leveled the playing field. The few times Spain sallied forth to engage the foe directly it did so with more or less equal numbers and the results were catastrophic. At the aptly named Battle of Mal Tiempo in December 1895, a Spanish regiment stumbled headfirst into a trap set by the guerrillas. In the ensuing melee sixty-five Spaniards were hacked to death by machete, forty grievously wounded. The role of the machete at Mal Tiempo inspired the legend that the guerrillas were amateurs who fought this war by hand. In fact, they were battle-tested marksmen who used the machete as their principal weapon as a last resort. One need not have survived Mal Tiempo to suffer its effect on Spanish morale, as fear of the machete won permanent lodging in the minds of greenhorns like Ángel. Still, the significance of the battle lies elsewhere, namely, in the lesson it suggests that on a level battlefield the advantage goes to the side that knows what it is fighting for.[15]

The rebels' success in taking the battle to the heart of Cuba brought turnover atop the Spanish command. In February 1896, Valeriano Weyler replaced Arsenio Martínez Campos as captain-general of Cuba. Weyler is said to have greeted his latest appointment with the remark that "war should be answered with war."[16] Cubans interpreted Weyler's appointment as prophesy of mayhem. Weyler did not disappoint, corralling peasants into concentration camps, destroying the homes and fields they left behind.[17] Weyler's destruction of the rebel's food supply cleared western Cuba of insurgents but did nothing to end the insurrection. Less than a year after his arrival, the number of rebel troops in the country had swollen from a mere three thousand at the start of the conflict into the tens of thousands. By summer 1897, the war reached a stalemate not so different from the one that Weyler inherited, with Spaniards protecting the cities and insurgents ruling the countryside.

As Weyler waged war on unarmed peasants and as Ángel fought off infection, forces stirred in the goliath to the north that would shape Cuba to the present day. The conflict in Cuba had not gone unnoticed in Washington, D.C., where for over a century U.S. officials had kept a jealous eye on Cuba, which they regarded as the heart and filter of Atlantic commerce, hence essential to the welfare of the young republic.[18] Over the course of the nineteenth century, U.S. merchants, slaveholders, and diplomats talked endlessly about buying or seizing Cuba from Spain. Only the perfect opportunity eluded them. Most Americans were content to leave Cuba in Spain's hands so long as it did not threaten U.S. interests or invite British or French intervention. Weyler's brutality and the destruction of private property during the war refocused Americans' attention, with some calling on the government to intervene on the side of the Cuban independence, others for outright annexation.

If the United States intended to intervene in the conflict, it would have to hurry. By late 1897 the war favored the insurgents, who began to target the cities just as Spanish troops began to lay down their arms. Through late 1897, talk of U.S. intervention in Cuba remained hypothetical. On New Year's Eve, a correspondent of the *New York Herald* visited General Gómez in his camp to see whether he still opposed U.S. intervention. Not necessarily, Gómez replied, so long as intervention did not mean "annexation." With this distinction, Gómez struck preemptively at U.S. officials who insisted that Cubans were incapable of self-government. How could anyone be sure just what Cubans were capable of, Gómez wondered, before they had been given the opportunity to prove themselves? Cuba's only objective was independence. "We have among us young men who have sacrificed everything to this sacred cause," he said, men who had "but one goal in life, and this is to see the flag of Cuba supreme from Cape Maisí to San Antonio." Worried lest Cuba "be robbed of any share in the honor of the expulsion of the Spaniards," Gómez was confident that "the people of the United States will never balk us in this, our hour of victory."[19]

An insult and an explosion catapulted the United States into the Cuban conflict early the following year before Gómez or anybody else anticipated. On February 11, 1898, the pro-intervention *New York Journal* greeted readers with a letter by a Spanish official describing U.S. president William McKinley as a "weak and popularity-seeking . . . hack politician." Though few Americans regarded these remarks as "the worst insult" in U.S. history, as the *Journal* declared, the slur brought cries for U.S. intervention to a fever pitch. The explosion of the battleship *Maine* in Havana Harbor four days later sealed the debate. A nation hungry for adventure needed no judicious weighing of the facts to discern the source of the *Maine's* destruction. "The Maine was sunk by an act of dirty treachery," Theodore Roosevelt, assistant secretary of the navy, concluded the following day. The *New York Journal* blamed "an enemy's secret infernal machine."[20]

On April 11, President McKinley petitioned the United States Congress for authorization to intervene in Cuba. On April 19, Congress passed a war resolution, which the president signed the next day. On April 21, the president ordered a naval blockade of Cuba. On April 25, the United States declared war on Spain. The most significant aspect of these preliminaries went virtually unnoticed.

Attached to the war resolution was a legislative rider introduced by Republican senator Henry M. Teller, known as the Teller Amendment, which in one sentence seemed to repudiate a century of U.S. policy toward Cuba. Clause one of the resolution asserted Cuba's independence. Clause two demanded Spain's withdrawal from Cuba. Clause three authorized the president to use the military to effect these ends. Then came the kicker: "the United States hereby disclaims any disposition or intention to exercise sovereignty, jurisdiction, or control over said Island except for the pacification thereof, and asserts its determination, when that is accomplished, to leave the government and control of the Island to its people." [21]

Historians disagree about how to account for the Teller Amendment. Its passage followed the withdrawal of a more radical resolution granting immediate recognition to the revolutionary government, suggesting that a bargain had been struck.[22] Senator Teller hailed from Colorado, home to a lucrative sugar beet industry reeling from new European competition; the introduction of Cuban sugar into the U.S. sugar market duty-free could potentially ruin U.S. beet growers.[23] Then there was the roughly $1 million in cash that Tomás Estrada Palma, exiled leader of the Cuban Revolutionary Party in New York, handed to Samuel Janney, a Cuban lobbyist in Washington, to distribute among U.S. congressmen.[24] Finally, there was widespread and sincere support for Cuba Libre among the American people and some elected officials.[25] Whatever the explanation, there could be no doubting the amendment's effect: for the first time in U.S. history, American officials had elevated the cause of Cuban independence above American interests on the island. Americans were heading down to Cuba to help remove the Spanish. With that mission accomplished they would leave Cuba in the hands of its people.

———————

U.S. marines came ashore at Guantánamo Bay on June 10, 1895, quickly converting the bay into a coaling facility and staging ground for an advance on Santiago de Cuba, thirty miles up the coast. In early July, U.S. forces launched a series of attacks on Spanish garrisons protecting Santiago, which included the Rough Riders' celebrated charge up San Juan Hill. In mid-July, Santiago capitulated to the United States, more or less bringing the Cuban conflict to a close. U.S. accounts of the victory ignored two salient aspects of the battle: first, how valiantly depleted Spanish forces rallied to meet the American attack; second, how readily U.S. publicists transformed a brief intervention in a generation-old colonial conflict into a smashing American victory. With that victory came the right not only to rename the conflict "The Spanish-American War" but to determine Cuba's future, notwithstanding the solemn promise of the Teller Amendment. U.S. military officials and journalists wasted no time making the case for annexation. Discussion centered on the question of Cubans' capacity for self-government, with U.S. officials ultimately deciding that Cuba could not be left to its own devices. A solution would have to be found for Teller.

Ángel Castro remained posted in central Cuba through the end of hostilities in mid-July. The armistice might have made things worse for Spanish soldiers, who could expect little sympathy from an adversary that Spain had exploited for centuries. In fact, it proved more punishing to the Cubans. Besides providing Spaniards food and medicine as the fighting came to an end, U.S. generals deployed Spanish troops throughout the country to maintain order, as if regarding the people they had come to liberate as more menacing than the enemy itself.

On July 17, 1898, Spain surrendered Santiago not to the Cubans who had been waging this war for thirty years, but to the Americans who had arrived weeks earlier. On what might have been a day of celebration among victorious allies, U.S. General William Shafter refused to let the Cubans partake in Spain's surrender. Cuban General Calixto García had fully expected U.S. forces to commandeer Santiago, its garrisons and forts. He was eager to cooperate with Shafter to preserve order until the time came for the U.S. to fulfill

its pledge to establish a free and independent Cuban government.
What could explain this official snubbing? Rumor had it that the
Cubans planned a massacre. This was calumny, García responded.
"We are not savages ignoring the rules of civilized warfare. We are a
poor, ragged army, as ragged and poor as was the army of your fore-
fathers in their noble war of independence, but like the heroes of
Saratoga and Yorktown, we respect our cause too deeply to disgrace
it with barbarism and cowardice."[26]

Shafter's humiliation of his Cuban hosts was the first in a long
series of indignities visited on Cuba in the aftermath of the Spanish-Cuban-American War as the United States struggled to reconcile its pledge, as stated in the Teller Amendment, "to leave the
government and control of the island to its people" with the centuries old conviction that Cuba was essential to U.S. prosperity. As
Ángel Castro awaited transport home in autumn 1898, the United
States recapitulated Shafter's snubbing of García on a grand scale.
When American and Spanish officials descended on Paris in early
October to work out the details of the transfer of Spanish sovereignty over Cuba and its other colonial possessions to the United
States, not a single Cuban representative could be spotted in their
midst. Like Shafter, the U.S. government simply assumed that Cuba
had no role to play in negotiations about its future.

———————

Ángel Castro said little or nothing in later years about the North
Americans' behavior at the end of the war. His son would make
this history a cornerstone of the Cuban Revolution. The war itself
could not have been much crueler to Ángel had it taken him to
the grave. Dispiriting news from Láncara punctuated his recurring
hospital visits. In November 1896, one of two surviving sisters died
(the last would follow a few years later); the next year he lost a
beloved grandfather. The news from home dispelled illusions that
things would be better if he could only make it out of Cuba alive.
He eventually did so in January 1899, exchanging his hospital bed

for a musty hammock aboard the steamship *Ciudad de Cádiz* just as the U.S. occupation formally began.

There was scant rejoicing in the floating hospitals that creaked home after the war, their passengers, like the once formidable empire itself, in tatters. In a belated act of sympathy, the government handed the soldiers 20 pesetas each as they set foot on Spanish soil, enough to get by for a few months at most.[27] No handout could rectify successive years of capital neglect. Journalists struggled for words to describe the human wreckage that tumbled down the gangways ("Like Christ coming down from the cross," one wrote) and dotted the dusty roads that fanned out from Spain's seaports ("the light gone from their eyes, the blood from their cheeks, their bodies resembling scarred meat").[28]

The shame of arriving home in ruin was magnified by the soldiers' knowledge that nobody had cared enough to increase the odds of their success. The first boats pulled into Spain's seaports in autumn 1898 in the midst of a self-serving debate over who was to blame for the Cuban debacle. To be fair, the war had not been kind on the home front. War can spur economic growth, but only where governments possess the legitimacy to put the nation on a war footing, decidedly not the case in late-nineteenth-century Spain. Amid the void of leadership and solidarity, the nation's economy ground to a halt. Capital froze up, contracts lapsed, factories shuttered their doors. Hunger stalked the land. "Bad now," *La Correspondencia Militar* wondered, "what will happen next winter . . . with competition from soldiers returning from Cuba and Puerto Rico?"[29]

There is an old fountain in the town square in Láncara that brims with water all year round, as inland Galicia has no dry season to speak of. Framing the square, which opens to the main road, are three stone barns, one of them cloaked in chipping stucco. Into that square one cold, clammy day in early February 1899 marched a solitary figure, thin, disheartened, ground down. A quick right down a narrow lane, first building on the left, and there stood Ángel Castro, face-to-face with the heavy farmhouse door, guardian of

his family's grief, for the second time in four years with nothing
but fresh scars and a meager government handout to show for it.
A son's return from war in Cuba might have been greeted as auspicious, what with the odds against him and the time he spent in
hospital. But the Castros of Láncara had long since lost their faith
in auspices, just as Ángel himself had long since lost his love for
home. Stingy from the first, fate had tightened its grip inexorably
in his absence: another little sister gone, a grandfather, too. Even the
warmest greeting could not allay Ángel's growing conviction that
his future lay outside Spain. For several months, he tried to make
a go of it in Láncara. In contrast to many of his fellow veterans, he
still had his wits about him, along with two stout arms and legs.
Not liking his prospects, he resolved to cross the sea once more,
committing his future to a country whose dream of independence
he had only recently set out to crush.[30]

On December 3, 1899, Ángel arrived in Cuba for the second time,
disembarking at the port of Havana and clearing U.S. customs the
next day. By this time, the U.S. military occupation neared the end of
its first full year, with the occupying forces at work improving sanitation, wiping out disease, creating municipal government, erecting
infrastructure, building schools—in short, providing a climate favorable to U.S. investment. Asked for his thoughts about a stable Cuba,
Military Governor Leonard Wood, the man in charge of the U.S.
occupying force, took the mercenary view: "when money can be
borrowed at a reasonable rate of interest and when capital is willing
to invest in the island, a condition of stability will be reached."[31]

U.S. citizens of all stripes flocked to Cuba in the aftermath of
the war as if to a new frontier. Real estate, agriculture, mining, finance, engineering, construction, education, the professions, gambling, prostitution, you name it—all were overrun by opportunistic
Americans arriving on the island often with extended families in
tow. It is hard to exaggerate the scale of the migration. By 1905,

some 13,000 Americans had purchased land in Cuba valued at $50 million. By 1919, 44,000 Americans had relocated there, prompting one Southern journal to remark, "little by little the whole island is passing into the hands of American citizens." And why not? U.S. newspapers and magazines depicted Cuba as "a land of perpetual sunshine, flowing with milk and honey"—"a year-round country," with "no unproductive season."[32]

By contrast, Cubans found it difficult to square the talk of liberty and opportunity with the fact of U.S. domination. "There is so much natural anger and grief throughout the island," General Gómez noted in his diary in January 1899, "that the people haven't really been able to celebrate the triumph of the end of their former ruler's power."[33] The end of the U.S. military occupation did not improve things from Cubans' perspective. Obligated by the Teller Amendment to uphold Cuban independence after the war, U.S. authorities came up with a legislative vehicle known as the Platt Amendment to render the new Cuban Republic a U.S. colony in all but name. Among other things, the Platt Amendment compelled Cuba to lease Guantánamo Bay to the U.S. Navy and to concede the right of the United States to intervene at will in Cuban affairs. When Cubans cried foul, they were told that adoption of the Platt Amendment into the new Cuban Constitution was the condition of U.S. withdrawal. The logic of Platt was undeniable. "There is, of course, little or no real independence left Cuba under the Platt Amendment," a triumphant Wood wrote the new U.S. president, Theodore Roosevelt, in October 1901. "The more sensible Cubans realize this and feel that the only consistent thing now is to seek annexation."[34]

That was not the end of it. Two years later, these unequal partners signed a trade deal that ensured that Cuba would remain as economically dependent as it was politically subservient. The so-called Reciprocity Treaty of 1903 granted Cuba a 20 percent reduction in the U.S. sugar tariff in return for a still larger reduction in Cuban tariffs on a range of U.S. products. The treaty set off a sugar bonanza, increasing U.S. investment in Cuba from $80 million to $220 million in the decade after independence. By 1923, U.S. investment reached a staggering $1.3 billion, over half of it devoted to sugarcane production. The sugarcane industry employs its workers for at most four months a year, often as little as two (the rest of the year is called the *tiempo muerto*, or "dead season," a term that speaks volumes to the ravages sugar has wrought on Cuban society). The trade agreement drained Cuba of capital that might have promoted new agricultural and industrial development along with jobs and markets. A mixed economy might absorb laid off workers. Cuba's sugar monoculture could not. By inflating the price of sugar, the Reciprocity Treaty triggered the conversion to cane fields of land formerly devoted to other agricultural commodities. Cuba struggles with the effect of these policies to this day.

Strolling the streets of Havana in December 1899, Ángel could be excused for missing Cubans' simmering resentment. Having emerged from the war relatively unscathed, Havana bustled with businessmen, peddlers, immigrants, and hucksters of every shape and color, all vying for a piece of a country suddenly awash in U.S. capital. The North American presence was visible everywhere, from the steamships lined up outside the port of Havana, to the seawalls sprouting up across the city, to the work crews repairing bridges, dredging waterways, and laying rail. U.S. advertising dominated the front pages of the leading dailies, with McCormick Harvester, New York Trust, Iris Insurance, New York and Cuba Mail Steamship Authority (to name but a few) all promising to provide whatever anybody wanted faster, cheaper, better, and stronger than the competition, at very low interest and with minimal strings attached.[35]

Those tired of work could make their way to the New Cuba Theater ("the proper place for American visitors to Havana to fool away their time and spend their money"), or catch *Rigoletto* or *Aida* at the Gran Teatro Tacón, the city's oldest playhouse. If Verdi was

not your thing, you could cross the Prado to the still grander Teatro de Albisu, with its full card of one-act comic operas. There was
money for this, credit for that, cheap land here, ready labor there,
even books promising to educate Cubans about the history and
customs of their new benefactor to the north. Truly, a phoenix rose
from the ashes of decrepit Spain. Those with initiative and daring
might come along for the ride. Only the timid and tentative would
be left behind.

And yet resentment festered. Just the week before Ángel's arrival,
city papers reported a rally at the University of Havana commemorating the murder of eight Cuban medical students by Spanish
soldiers in 1871. Fifty thousand *habaneros* joined the procession, including students, doctors, "civil and municipal authorities, the city
police, firemen, and various friendly corporations." Journalists described the crowd as restive and edgy. One speaker warned listeners
not to lose sight of the nation's sacred and unequivocal commitment
to "Independence or Death," as if the struggle for Cuba Libre was
not yet over.[36]

If Havana bustled, much of Cuba lay in ruin. The country lost
an estimated 100,000 to 400,000 dead (depending on whether one
counts noncombatants), as well as countless injured, maimed, and
incapacitated by war, disease, and malnutrition. Private property suffered, too, with some 100,000 small farms, 3,000 cattle ranches, 800
tobacco plantations, 700 coffee farms, and over 1,000 sugar mills
completely destroyed.[37] Terrible as it was, destruction created opportunity in a country with an acute labor shortage. The problem of
labor on the island went back to the sixteenth century, when Spain
turned to Indians to work the mines. When the Indians succumbed
to abuse and disease, Spain imported African slaves, continuing to do
so until long after the slave trade became illegal in the Spanish Caribbean in 1820 (slavery was abolished in Cuba in 1886). The formal
end of the slave trade compelled Spain to look to China for labor,
which it did until the "coolie trade" itself was prohibited in 1875.[38]

With the Indians annihilated, slavery abolished, and Chinese

importation banned, there was renewed demand for labor at the end
of the war. This was especially true in rural areas, and above all in the
east, where violence and Weyler's reconcentration policy drove men
and boys from the countryside. Part of the postwar negotiations between the United States and Spain, from which Gómez, García, and
their fellow Cubans were excluded, concerned the number of Spanish soldiers that would be permitted to remain in Cuba. Naturally,
Cubans looked on Spaniards as competition. By contrast, U.S. investors viewed Spaniards as ideal workers. According to William Jared
Clark, author of a primer on business opportunities in postwar Cuba,
Cubans, whether "white, black, or medium-colored," eschewed
wage labor, preferring to work their own plots despite competitive
disadvantages. Years later, Cubans' commitment to private property
would bedevil Fidel Castro's collectivization campaign. At the time
of Ángel's return to Cuba, it contributed to the underdevelopment
of Oriente Province, especially, making the region ripe for Wood's
economic modernization. The worker of choice from the planters'
perspective was a former Spanish soldier followed closely by Cata-
lan and Galician immigrants. Where the former worked "faithfully
at any place or under any conditions," according to Clark, the latter
distinguished themselves by "their industry and other commendable
qualities." All of which augured well for Ángel Castro, until now the
embodiment of the dispensable man.[39]

Ángel did not remain long in Havana. After a few days exploring the capital and consulting fellow Galicians, he left for the town
of Camajuaní, in Las Villas Province,[40] which Clark described as
"a small unimportant station" on the railroad line linking the region's north coast with its sugarcane fields. Ángel did not linger
there either, soon departing for Oriente Province after a brief stop
in Cayo Romano, off Cuba's north-central coast.[41] For a stranger in
search of work, Oriente was a sensible destination. Nowhere did the
milk and honey inundating Cuba flow more abundantly than there.
Contemporaries spoke of the "Americanization" of Oriente Province, historians of an "invasion."[42] By the early 1920s, this invasion

made Oriente, long the least developed, least populated part of Cuba, the country's most densely populated province and second leading sugar producer. By 1929, foreign sugar growers, most of them American, had bought up 64 percent of the province.[43] Three quarters of this investment was devoted to large-scale sugar production, which crowded out smaller coffee and tobacco enterprises, displacing Cuban farmers and replacing them with cheap Haitian, Jamaican, and other migrant labor.

The transformation of Oriente was spurred by Civil Order No. 62 of the U.S. military government. Announced in March 1902, the order promoted the zoning and sale to American and other foreign investors of vast properties owned or occupied by small farmers. The small farms of the east had their origin in a system of communal landholding that developed in the eighteenth and nineteenth centuries on unoccupied royal estates. The *hacienda comunera*, as they were known, were divided into shares (*pesos de posesión*) representing the value of the original estate. To own a share of the value of the entire estate was not the same as possessing the title to a specific parcel of land, making property claims elastic. The informality functioned more or less effectively in a traditional setting. It became strained in the face of the American-led modernization, as the war destroyed public records and property titles, thus depriving small farmers proof of their proprietorship. In the end, farmers were left at the mercy of powerful forces bent on their demise.

Legitimate owners of *pesos de posesión* were not the only ones who suffered. Oriente had long served as Cuba's safety valve. The teams of foreign developers that descended on Oriente after the war found much of the land occupied by squatters, some of whose families had been there for decades, even centuries, as well as by displaced veterans. Civil Order No. 62 ripped through this traditional landholding system like a locomotive tearing up Cuba's virgin forests, dispossessing legions of small farmers while disposing of their land for the scandalously low price of between one and two dollars an acre. In short, conditions in Cuba were ripe for U.S. capital under the military occupation. U.S. capital arrived in abundance unequaled before or since—unhampered, Cuban scholars are quick to point out, by regulations in place in the United States.

Oriente Province consists essentially of two great mountain chains, the fabled Sierra Maestra and the no less formidable Nipe-Sagua-Baracoa massif. The mountains dominate the province's southern coast, north of which lies an extensive plain. These mountains, valleys, and plains endow Oriente with tremendous agricultural and mineral diversity, made accessible by miles of seacoast, navigable rivers, and generous bays. Elevations in the province range from sea level to over six thousand feet atop the Sierra Maestra, thus supporting a variety of valuable timber (mahogany, majagua, cedar, lignum vitae, lancewood, and ebony) and agriculture (sugarcane, bananas, pineapple, tobacco, rice, and citrus, on the plains, cocoa, café, and indigo, higher up). Blessed by rich, alluvial soil, the mountains are ringed by grassy foothills suitable for large-scale ranching. The mountains are home to rich mineral deposits, including gold, copper, manganese, mercury, zinc, nickel, asphalt, coal, marble, alabaster, rock crystal, and precious gems, considerably adding to Oriente's commercial potential.[44]

After leaving Camajuaní, Ángel tried his luck in the mining town of Daiquirí, east of Santiago, run by a subsidiary of Carnegie Steel. He found work as a night watchman, a job for which the war had left him overqualified. Carnegie paid the miners one U.S. dollar per day. As a guard, Ángel probably made a little more. A few dollars a day does not sound like much until you remember that land in north Oriente was going for just over a dollar per acre at the time of Ángel's arrival. There is scant evidence of his life among the miners. Many of them hailed from his native Galicia; he would have recognized the dialect and understood the references. There were few distractions in these mountains, and Ángel seems to have succeeded in setting aside a small savings for the first time. He did not drink much, but he was a natural gamer with a memory for cards and the good sense to quit when he was ahead. For much of the year Oriente is scorching hot and humid, even by Cuban standards. Miners lived in squalid quarters not so different from those Ángel had occupied as a soldier. It was not long before talk of cool breezes and greener pastures drew his attention to the rich, untapped country north of the Sierra Maestra in the vicinity of the Bay of Nipe. Collecting his few belongings, Ángel departed the south coast, not knowing that his decades-long pilgrimage was nearly over.

The Bay of Nipe sits atop the large shark tail that is southeast Cuba. Surrounding the bay on the north and west are fertile plains suitable for grazing and agriculture. To the south and west of the bay lies the Sierra Cristal, with its vast forests and mineral deposits. Up to the time of the U.S. occupation, the region was occupied by the sort of independent farmers whom Wood, Clark, and others regarded as an impediment to the region's economic development. In 1885, a man named Hipólito Dumois, son of French émigrés from Haiti, established a banana, citrus, and pineapple plantation just north of Nipe Bay, near the future town of Banes. In 1899, Dumois sold his land to Andrew Preston, owner of the Boston Fruit Company, which owned banana plantations across Latin America and would soon change its name to the United Fruit Company. In a few short years, Preston erected a new sugar mill called Boston, which spurred the transformation of Nipe Bay into one of Cuba's top sugar-producing regions. A few years after that, United Fruit purchased 200,000 more acres around the south coast of the bay, erecting yet another massive mill named Preston.

The rise and consolidation of United Fruit Company in Cuba coincides with Ángel's arrival in the region. His first stop in north Oriente seems to have been at or near the town of Mayarí, not far from Preston. Mayarí was a hub of the region's new development, and Ángel would have collided there with labor drawn from all over Cuba and the Caribbean, as well as from China and the United States. American capital was on the march across the region, buying out small landholders, razing virgin forest, and converting a diverse agricultural base into sugarcane fields. This process entailed much dispossession and misery, as well as environmental degradation, but it also created jobs. New mills and mill towns needed constructing. Mills, warehouses, shipping ports, stores, factories, restaurants needed staffing and provisioning. This labor force needed direction. Resilient, disciplined, and enterprising, Ángel recognized in these necessities the chance of a lifetime. "There are doubtless tremendous possibilities in store for those who will purchase and concentrate such properties, erect modern mills, and manage them according to the most improved methods," William Clark observed. There was also opportunity down the line, and it was there that Ángel proved his usefulness as a medium between men looking for work and owners and managers in search of labor.

As a former Spanish soldier and native of Galicia, Ángel would have been given the benefit of the doubt in head-to-head competition for jobs, and he soon distinguished himself as a reliable foreman. Having worked for others all his life, he took his first step toward independence by purchasing a team of oxen, hiring himself out, then hiring other men to lead his team, before acquiring more oxen and still more men, and so on, until he commanded some three hundred workers. With these teams of men and beast, Ángel crisscrossed the Nipe region, draining swamps, cutting and burning forests, transporting timber, and planting and harvesting sugarcane. In an era of rampant speculation, nothing is more valuable than a contractor who can deliver the right men for the right job at the right time, and Ángel soon amassed substantial savings.

"It is impossible to exaggerate the prosperity and progress in evidence in the Nipe Bay district," observed a leading trade magazine in 1905.[45] That same year, Ángel invested 200 pesos in a small inn located in the town of Guaro, down the road from Mayarí, along the thoroughfare linking the United Fruit enterprises at Boston and Preston. He named the inn El Progreso, an understated acknowledgment of his recent turn of fate. With its favorable location and ample shade, the inn provided much needed respite from the blistering sun that scorched the east nine months a year. The inn doubled as a country store, providing a burgeoning local population with cheese, olives, hazelnuts, honey, candy, sausages, flour, chestnuts, oil, wine, newspapers, and other sundries.[46]

Four years later, on the verge of thirty-five, Ángel met the first woman to play a significant role in his life since the death of his mother. The woman's name was María Luisa Argota Reyes. Born in the port town of Gibara, thirty miles west of Banes, María Luisa grew up in Guaro under the supervision of her father, a manager at United Fruit. The couple married on March 25, 1911, and settled in Mayarí, where Ángel erected a spacious house on Avenida Leyte Vidal. With decorative arches, high ceilings, paneled walls, and mosaic tile floors, this residence provided quite a contrast to the last place Ángel had dared to call home. The willingness of María's father to allow Ángel to marry his well-heeled daughter suggests the remarkable distance the illiterate peasant had come.

For five years, Ángel and María Luisa got along well enough. María liked the city life and hoped one day to trade Avenida Leyte Vidal for a home on one of the broad squares of Santiago de Cuba, the provincial capital, a hundred kilometers to the south. The couple named their first-born son, Manuel, after Ángel's father, who died in 1903. Summoning the ghosts of Galicia proved inauspicious, and the boy did not make it to his first birthday. The next three children, two girls and a boy, survived. The fifth and final child, a daughter, did not, and the infant's death seems to have sunk a permanent wedge in the couple's relationship.

Ángel spent very little time at home. Running teams of men and oxen around the bay, managing his inn, training champion fighting cocks, he came to know and be known by owners, managers, administrators, and workers of the vast U.S. enterprises in the region, as well as by local Cuban businessmen and politicians. Greater and wider opportunities began to fall in his direction. In this way, he met an entrepreneur named Fidel Pino Santos, who was based in

Santiago de Cuba, but who had business throughout the province, including with United Fruit. The men became friends, with Pino Santos playing the role of confidant and private banker, eventually becoming the namesake of a future president of Cuba.

In 1915 Ángel learned of a parcel of land for sale thirty miles south of Nipe Bay in prime cane-growing country. The world war was in its second year, and European beet production had ground to a halt, significantly elevating the price of Caribbean sugar. Meanwhile, the price of land throughout Oriente remained ridiculously low. With his modest savings and a 6 percent loan from Pino Santos, Ángel purchased the 660-acre parcel known locally as Manacas for a little over a dollar per acre. Located near the small town of Birán, the parcel became the foundation of Finca Manacas, the Castro family home. In succeeding years, Ángel acquired 2,000 additional acres of his own while leasing another 22,000 acres from neighboring U.S. and Cuban planters. By the time he was done, his plantation comprised forty-two square miles of some of eastern Cuba's richest farmland.[47]

Prosperity did not bring marital bliss to Ángel and María Luisa. María Luisa never saw herself as a plantation mistress. Ángel preferred the farm to the city. With the purchase of Finca Manacas, Ángel came to spend more time at Birán than in Mayarí, and the couple drifted apart. Lidia Castro, one of the couple's three surviving children, once asked her mother why she and Ángel separated. "Live in the countryside?" María gasped. "No thanks. The countryside is for birds and other animals."

In 1920 Ángel met the woman, the girl really, who would become his soul mate. Lina Ruz González made quite a contrast to María Luisa. Ángel was forty-five, Lina was seventeen.[48] Lina's family were sugarcane and tobacco farmers from Pinar del Río in far western Cuba. Her family left home in 1910 after a cyclone destroyed their crops. They moved first to Camagüey, then to Oriente, where her father and uncle came to the attention of Ángel. Being married (if separated) from María Luisa did not deter Ángel from adopting

Lina as a second wife, and the two began to produce a family of their own. They would have seven children total, all of them born before Ángel divorced María Luisa in 1941, and long before they themselves finally wed two years later. Ángel and María Luisa's divorce seems to have been motivated by convenience rather than conviction, as he had to appear that day in court anyway (to renounce his Spanish citizenship).[49] Ángel produced yet another child, Martín Castro, in 1930, with a local peasant named Generosa Mendoza, the informality of these relationships of little concern to him.

The years immediately following the world war were difficult for Cuban planters. In May 1920 an extraordinary spike and vertiginous collapse of sugar prices, known colloquially as the Dance of Millions, imperiled the entire Cuban economy, causing banks to default while bankrupting U.S. and Cuban plantation owners alike. Ángel managed to survive the crisis thanks to his constitutional restraint and to the generosity of his friend Pino Santos. Surveying the damage of the Dance of Millions, Ángel recognized that the widespread bankruptcies left American lenders with more property than they could possibly take advantage of. He also knew from experience that the Americans could not run their Cuban enterprises singlehandedly. Banks need borrowers, farmers could not borrow if they did not stay afloat. As the frenzy of speculation came to a halt, Ángel provided evidence of his farm's profitability, asking his U.S. lenders to freeze his loan payments for three years in exchange for a higher interest rate. The North Americans agreed, Pino Santos offered to back him, and Ángel survived to farm another day.

Ángel Castro makes a curious subject of historical investigation. As the father of one of the twentieth century's most controversial figures, Ángel has many detractors. He has been accused of moving fences to increase his landholdings (a charge first made by a U.S. surveyor against the North American companies that surrounded his land).[50] He has been described as domineering and abusive and labeled a philanderer. Such charges are difficult to deny or confirm. Amaury Troyano, a former acquaintance (and a critic of Ángel's son), who fought in the Cuban War of Independence, suggests Ángel's faults have been exaggerated. His daughter, Juanita, insists that this has been the case. A childhood friend of Fidel, whose entire family worked for Ángel in many different capacities, says that this was not Ángel's reputation at the time.[51]

But for being the father of a future revolutionary, there is much in Ángel's story for a U.S. audience to admire. He seems the very embodiment of Yankee ingenuity, the subject of one of the most improbable rags-to-riches tales of all time. He was a first-generation entrepreneur and capitalist who pulled himself up, borrowing money where he could find it, tapping political connections when needed, concentrating not on the hour-to-hour, day-to-day happiness of his family, as we shall see, but on how to ensure that his children never had to suffer the hardship he endured. In a one-way world in which U.S. politicians, bankers, and managers typically called the shots, Ángel got along with his U.S. neighbors. The penniless laborer turned successful teamster become enterprising farmer did not regard the North Americans as adversaries. The North Americans, in turn, regarded him as somebody they could do business with. If less than warm, this relationship was civil and respectful, providing the Castro children a lesson in dignity and reciprocity that they would never forget.

chapter two

MORNINGS ON HORSEBACK

A *young boy lies awake in* bed before sunrise, alert to the first stirrings of the family farm. Home for school vacation, he listens intently as the rustle of leaves and breathing of animals yield to the chirping of birds, cry of the rooster, and howl of a dog, followed by foot falls and the murmur of his father doling out the day's instructions to the farm manager. Accustomed now to the noise of the city, the boy never ceases to wonder at how quickly the predawn quiet yields to the cacophony of an awakening barnyard.[1]

With big plans for the day, the boy does not dally. He rolls out of bed, pulls on a pair of worn trousers, a comfortable shirt, and sturdy shoes. He is going riding. Ever since he can remember, he has been comfortable on a horse. At age six or seven, his parents gave him a horse of his own, named Careto, on which, with shotgun in hand, he explores the vast property. Sometimes he rides in the company of friends or siblings. Sometimes he rides alone. Today, he is going solo. In recent years, his parents have granted him increasing leeway, asking few questions as he packs a lunch, saddles Careto, and heads off past the barns and outbuildings at the north end of the property, before cutting east in the direction of the foothills and, ultimately, a favorite hideout named Pinares de Mayarí high atop the Sierra Cristal. He has promised to be home by nightfall.

Pinares de Mayarí sits about four and a half miles and two thousand vertical feet above the heart of Finca Manacas. For the first mile or so, the going is easy, as horse and rider leave the fields that girdle the farm and mount the grassy foothills where his father grazes his cattle. On this part of the journey, the boy has few decisions to make, and Careto proceeds unguided. "I loved that horse," the boy told an interviewer years later. Careto was "smart and surly, restless, lively, and fast," and liked to escape his minders. In retrospect, horse and rider seem a good fit. "When Careto saw me coming, he would run away. I'd have to get one of the men to corral him."[2]

There is no well-worn route to Pinares de Mayarí. The boy relies on a natural sense of direction to guide them. The going gets steep between miles two and three as the grassland yields to cedar, pine, caguairán, and mahogany forest. The boy eyes a shortcut, which increases the risk as an errant step now could result in calamity. On summer days, the temperature down below can reach the 90s by mid-morning. Up here in the hills, it is considerably cooler, but even so Careto's hide is spotted with sweat. After several hours, the ground levels, and the pair emerge onto a mesa covered in red soil from local nickel deposits and topped by a thicket of pine.

Alone with his horse, the boy gazes down on the plains below and experiences something close to bliss. He loves this place. There is always a cool breeze, and the trees provide relief from the blistering sun. There is also plentiful water from local streams ("ice-cold, pure, and delicious"). The boy might stop there or proceed to lumber and mining camps deeper into the mountains, further evidence of his father's extensive enterprise. But he has already achieved what he came for. "Up there in the woods and mountains, I experienced real freedom," he noted later; "there was nobody telling me what to do; I traveled for miles and scaled mountains."[3]

Freedom and independence were but two of the incalculable gifts bestowed by a childhood at Finca Manacas. A mature Fidel Castro once told an interviewer that having grown up as the son, rather than the grandson, of a rich landowner, he was unafflicted by "the sense of superiority" that comes to those of "aristocratic birth." The Castro farm straddled two worlds, the world of privilege that allowed a young boy to attend faraway schools and own his own horse, and the world of menial labor from which his parents delivered themselves and the source of his earliest friendships. The local children were his "*compañeros* in everything," he said. "We went to the river, the woods, and the fields together to hunt and to play." Jealous of his own freedom and aware of the inequality around him, Castro came to understand from an early age the arbitrariness of class and racial distinctions. Years later, while representing the down-and-out in his Havana law office or waging guerrilla war in the Sierra Maestra, Castro would be commended for the sympathy and sincerity he exhibited in conversation with peasants and common laborers. This, too, was a legacy of Finca Manacas, where he learned not to confuse social status or material possessions with merit.[4]

Castro entered the world on August 13, 1926, his birth supervised by an American physician from the United Fruit Company town of Preston, located on the eastern shore of the Bay of Nipe. In the decades before setting up shop in Birán, his father helped build Preston and clear the forests to make way for its cane fields. Ángel remained on good terms with his former bosses, availing himself of their resources when necessary. This was his third child with Lina Ruz González. He had lost two young children with his former wife. Wanting to take no chances with Lina's babies, he sent for the nearest doctor.[5]

The doctor arrived at Finca Manacas in the dry season, but the farm is located in such a way as to have access to water year round while remaining functional in the drenching rains of May and October. Arriving on the scene a decade earlier, Ángel found well-drained soil suitable for a farmhouse, barns, warehouses, shops, and other buildings. Its elevation above the surrounding fields left it open to the prevailing breeze, and the doctor may have noticed the large citrus grove at the north end of the property situated to take advantage of the natural ventilation.

With its back to the foothills of the Sierra Cristal, its front gazing out over the Holguín plateau, the location of the Castro farm is spectacular. Those who like mountains will feel the tug. The Sierra Cristal is grand without being forbidding, providing solitude, relief from the heat, and a panoramic view of the neighborhood. But the mountains are more than inviting. They are suitable for grazing and home to rich timberland, as well as to valuable iron and nickel deposits. This is what prompted Ángel to establish his farm there in the first place. Though devoted to sugarcane production, he would not leverage his family's fate on a fickle market. When sugar prices plummeted, he turned to other things, managing to keep afloat while many surrounding farms went under. In a region of Cuba dominated by foreign corporations and run by professional managers, Ángel was unusual for being self-made, self-taught, and all but self-sufficient. He was more than a curiosity, but he was that, too, and it was surely with bemusement and at least a little admiration that the doctor, spinning his wheel to the right, pulled into the lane of Finca Manacas and made for the farmhouse, where his patient, Lina Ruz González, was in labor.

Finca Manacas is said to have been an unusually clean farm, which sounds like a paradox to anyone who has tried to scratch a living from the earth. The cleanliness was not for want of real work going on there. Sugarcane, lumber, citrus, coffee, cocoa, bananas, mango, papaya, guava, passion fruit, potatoes, wheat, cabbage, carrots, beans, lettuce, tomatoes, and indigo were grown and harvested on the property. A dairy provided milk, cream, and cheese from cows, sheep, and goats. A bakery turned out fresh bread. An apiary produced fragrant honey. Owners, managers, clerks, and mechanics shared the grounds not only with the myriad neighbors who showed up to buy groceries, go to work, attend school, use the telegraph, mail a letter, have a drink, play ball, or see a cockfight, but also with horses, mules, cattle, pigs, sheep, goats, dogs, cats, chickens, guinea hens, carrier pigeons, parrots, turkeys, and champion fighting cocks. When it rains in eastern Cuba, it pours, turning roads into rivers, fields into lakes. And yet the Castro farm sparkled, so everybody says.

Immediately to the doctor's left on entering the Castro farm lay a sparsely wooded field scattered with thatched huts occupied year-round by Haitian workers. Many more Haitians arrived at the farm during the *zafra*, or sugarcane harvest, joining a collection of Cuban, Jamaican, and other West Indian migrants who wandered the island season after season looking for work. The Haitians who occupied these *joupas* were regulars. Some of them had families. The ones that did would come to know the Castro children, who showed up on a daily basis looking for playmates and occasionally the forbidden fruit of the aromatic *maíz asado* (roasted corn), which the children considered a delicacy, but which their mother believed would be the end of them.

"The countryside was freedom," Fidel Castro told an interviewer.[6] Not for these Haitians. If welcome on the Castro farm, they were better off than their compatriots only by degree. Castro the revolutionary leader would come to adopt the Marxist critique that labor under capitalism is scarcely better than slavery (slaveholders were at least responsible for ensuring the survival of their property, the argument goes). These Haitians migrated to eastern Cuba during the American-led sugarcane expansion that peaked during the First World War and the Dance of Millions. Many came without spouses or families, not expecting to stay. Some of the Haitian men shared a single woman in a local form of polyandry. This was not "prostitution," Fidel Castro later insisted, just a practical response to an obvious problem. The Haitians were reliable workers. Ángel paid them what his son considered a "very low wage." No one gave much thought to Haitians' clothing, food, or health care, he said; "they were abandoned to their luck." And this on Ángel Castro's farm, reputed to be the most forgiving in the region.[7]

Which gets us back to the farm's legendary cleanliness. This was not a product of the boss's fussiness, Pedro Pasqual Rodríguez Rodríguez explains, but of his "big heart," of his willingness to provide work that was not strictly necessary. "Paquito" Rodríguez is the youngest of twelve children from a peasant family that arrived in the region in the 1920s after his father and older brothers were laid off by another plantation. They found work in Birán, where members of the family remain to this day. Born in 1925, a year before Castro, Rodríguez grew up alongside the Castro children, attending the primary school on the property and accompanying the Castro children at play. There are plenty of people in Cuba ready to tell a visitor what they think he or she wants to hear about the Cuban Revolution. Rodríguez passed a preliminary test of veracity when, asked whether he knew that the young Castro was destined for the presidency of Cuba one day, answered, effectively, "Hell no. He was a normal kid, like the rest of us, only a little different."[8]

Asked to explain that difference, Rodríguez said that the first thing people needed to know about Castro's life was that "Birán Castro," as locals knew the place, "was no ordinary farm, Ángel no ordinary owner," an answer that presupposes a little historical background about early-twentieth-century Cuba.

––––––––––––––

In the decade of Castro's birth, Cuba continued to struggle with the economic and political distortions introduced by the Platt Amendment, the Reciprocity Treaty, and prioritization of U.S. over Cuban interests at the time of the early Republic. The U.S.-funded re-capitalization of the island's sugar industry created insurmountable barriers to entry for farmers shy of capital, effectively shutting out the middle class while creating a demand for cheap labor. With sugar production dominated by foreigners, and lacking an industrial base, Cuban professionals turned to politics as a way to make a living. As a result, government became an instrument not for solving the nation's problems but for distributing political spoils. By the mid-1920s, Cuba's federal bureaucracy and payroll swelled to unimaginable levels as the island became a welfare state for displaced elites, channeling the island's resources into the pockets of professional politicians.

These political and economic distortions were embodied in the person of Gerardo Machado, elected president in 1924 on a platform of public works, anticorruption, and political and economic independence, but who quickly revealed himself to be a shameless, even sadistic, power monger. Combined with U.S.-funded public works projects, Machado's bullying might have kept a lid on Cuba. But 1926 marked the beginning of a protracted slide in Cuban sugar prices that would grip the country for the better part of a decade. As sugar goes, so goes Cuba. The falling prices reverberated up and down the nation's economy, with planters laying off workers and the federal government suspending the salaries of schoolteachers and other public servants, just as protests erupted across the country.

Machado's response to the protests was clumsy and self-serving. With a pliant Congress executing his will, Machado jiggered Cuban election law to give himself the potential to remain in office through the mid-1930s, while outlawing public demonstrations and suspending constitutional guarantees. Make political opposition illegal, future president Carlos Mendieta warned at the time, and all you have left is violence. Violence ensued. In May 1930, Machado's police stormed an opposition meeting attended by the war hero Juan Gualberto Gómez, killing eight and wounding dozens. In September, the university erupted, with a student named Rafael Trejo killed by police. Inevitably, Machado's heavy-handedness provoked further violence. Statues of Machado and other political leaders were torn down. Protesters and police exchanged gunfire. The ranks of martyrs swelled. By the end of the year, schools across the island were shuttered, and the army patrolled the streets.

Machado hung on for another three years, unleashing his police and military, along with a gang of private thugs known as the Porra, on opponents left, right, and center. The opponents responded in kind as the country descended into armed conflict. Always wary of unrest in Cuba, the United States government dispatched a special ambassador to Havana in May 1933 in the hope of establishing a truce and finding a replacement for Machado. Amid escalating violence and with the United States pulling the strings, Machado was replaced in mid-August by Carlos Manuel de Céspedes, son of the War of Independence hero of the same name. Unable to restore peace and lacking legitimacy, Céspedes was deposed by a military coup known as the Sergeants' Revolt on the evening of September 4, 1933.

As if surprised to find themselves in power, the sergeants formed an unlikely alliance with a group of leftists (led by Antonio Guiteras) and moderates (led by Ramón Grau) determined to end Cuba's dependence on the United States. In late 1933, the so-called revolutionary government abrogated the Platt Amendment, outlawed the importation of foreign workers, distributed land to peasants, granted women the vote, and reduced utility rates, popular measures all. Subsequent measures—the suspension of payments on U.S. loans, the seizing of U.S. sugar mills, land appropriation, and the nationalization of private utilities—robbed the government of moderate support and further alarmed U.S. officials and businessmen, with some branding the revolution communist and asking Washington to send in the Marines. Ultimately, the United States used the question of recognition as a trump card, refusing to recognize the new government until Guiteras and Grau were replaced by State Department favorite Carlos Mendieta.

The one survivor from the revolutionary government was the leader of the Sergeants' Revolt, Fulgencio Batista, who studiously bided his time as Guiteras and Grau flamed out. Handsome, articulate, and charismatic, Batista was neither ideological nor idealistic. But he was a keen reader of the political winds and a shrewd strategist and tactician. He had a killer instinct and had no compunctions against using violence to achieve his ends. The more unstable Cuba became under Guiteras and Grau, the more Batista liked his chances. Cozying up to U.S. officials, Batista presented himself as the vehicle of order on the island. In late October 1933, with the blessing of the U.S. ambassador, Batista had warned Grau to slow down with the social and economic reforms or be removed; the Cuban people did not want revolution, he said, but a return to normalcy. The old officer corps regarded this as treason and Batista was on the verge of being arrested. Pleading for forgiveness, he survived to fight another day. When Mendieta replaced Grau as president on January 22, 1934, Batista and his army occupied pride of place beside the rostrum.

"American diplomacy has many resources," writer Julio César Fernández observed at the time; "when the steel of her warships is not convenient, she uses the docile backbone of her native lackeys."[9] Later that year, the U.S. Senate formally abrogated the Platt Amendment, replacing it with a new Treaty of Relations, which increased Cuba's economic dependence on the United States.

Thanks to Ángel Castro's ingenuity, Finca Manacas was insulated from some, if not all, of the fallout from these developments. In 1926, the year of Castro's birth, the Cuban government passed a series of laws designed to stabilize a volatile sugar market. The signature piece of legislation, the Verdeja Act, reduced the country's sugar production by 10 percent, unintentionally making the problem worse by stimulating foreign competition. The ensuing depression lowered agricultural wages between 50 to 75 percent. The value of Cuban exports dropped by as much as 80 percent, inevitably cutting short the harvest, which in the year of Castro's birth lasted a mere two months.[10]

Sugar was the foundation of the North American plantations that surrounded the Castro farm. Owned by joint stock companies headquartered in Boston, New York, and Chicago, these farms were run by professional managers with little stake in their employees' lives. Falling prices cut their profits, forcing them to lay off thousands of sugarcane workers.[11] Ángel Castro was an anomaly in the neighborhood. Having lived for years on the edge of ruin, he knew that all that distinguished him from an unemployed worker was persistence and a bit of luck. He was a capitalist and entrepreneur, but of an unusual sort. His principal aspiration was not to amass a great fortune but to provide his children (and some of his workers) opportunities he himself never had. When the Depression hit, he was not responsible to absentee landlords or outside stakeholders. Profit was very much his goal, but not for profit's sake. This made for curious behavior, Rodríguez explains, like Ángel regularly ripping up IOUs at the company store (where Rodríguez worked as a clerk) and hiring unemployed workers to clean the farm in the dead season.[12]

One big-hearted farmer could not redress the structural flaws that undermined Cuba's economy. Ángel could come up with only so much make-work for so many needy people. As word of his largess got around, Birán became overwhelmed with solicitations. Countless workers were turned away. Still, the boss's reputation held to the end of his life, Rodríguez says, his popularity confirmed by the stream of mourners that snaked its way down the Camino Real one heavy afternoon in autumn 1956, accompanying Ángel's casket home for burial.

Fidel Castro's younger sister, Enma, once asked her mother about life during the Depression. Those were difficult times, her mother acknowledged, but never truly threatening. "Of course, it's easier for those with means," her daughter observes, "and for those with plenty to eat."[13] Which was precisely the point. Experience taught an aspiring businessman not to bet on one crop. When sugar prices fell and the *zafra* was cut back, Ángel cranked up production of lumber and cattle, whose markets remained comparatively stable during the downturn. Ángel also made land available to enterprising employees to grow their own food. When the price was right, some even grew their own sugarcane. These *subcolonos* (small-scale planters) turned over a percentage of their crop to Ángel (who used the money to pay off his own debts). The balance was theirs to keep, and a few managed to amass a small savings.[14] The farm's self-sufficiency ensured that the supply of food remained stable ("I never knew hunger," Castro later testified), while its cattle and lumber enterprises enabled Ángel to meet his interest payments. This was the secret of Birán Castro, an agriculturally diverse, economically self-sufficient microsystem, a drop of perspicacity in a sea of single-mindedness, a model, if anybody was looking, of what a fertile Cuba might become.[15]

Past the Haitian "ghetto," as Castro called it, sits a large circular building with a conical tin roof. A circus tent? No, a cockfighting ring, complete with bleachers capable of accommodating up to a hundred guests. Like everything else on the Castro property, this was a business proposition. With money scarce, the cockfighting took place on Sundays during the *zafra*, one of the few times when locals could boast discretionary savings. The week between Christmas and New Year's was chock-full of cockfights, Easter, too, along with a few other holidays. The boisterous, mostly male audience drawn from the property's forty-two square miles paid a small entrance fee (along with a 10 percent tax on winnings). On match days, cocks battled from sunup to sundown, with as many as fifteen contests on a good day. As night fell, spectators headed home hoarse, hungover, exhausted, many lucky to escape with the shirt on their back.

Cockfighting became popular in Cuba during the War of Independence. Ángel was an aficionado, supplying not only the venue but also a roost of champion fighting cocks. His boys grew up with cocks of their own, and his son testified to the cost entailed in raising a winner. Cocks had to be strong, obviously, hence well fed. Their diet included not only grains and leavings, but fresh eggs besides. They needed stamina as well as pecking power. Abstinence was thought to be essential to both, with the cocks isolated from the obstreperous hens that ruled the farm. By big-city standards, bets were low, 5, 10, occasionally 15 pesos per fight. Guests could bet on individual fights or by the card.

The level of competition mounted through the day in lockstep with blood alcohol levels. Castro remembered contests so boisterous they bordered on mayhem. An epic fight, a remarkable comeback, a showdown between a callow David and an aging Goliath sent the spectators into a frenzy, the banging of bleachers and roar of the crowd making neighbors fear that war had broken out. In truth, little distinguished this from war. This was "no place for kids," Castro said. The kids loved it. Years later, the Revolution would ban cock-fighting as part of a campaign to eradicate gambling. The social cost was too grave, the revolutionaries concluded, what with the alcohol, lost wages, and time and money spent on raising cocks. Cockfight-ing strained marriages and promoted the misconception that one could improve one's lot in life through gaming.

Castro once described his father as "paternalistic." This needs qualification. Ángel could not have cared less what people did with their money. He liked playing cards and knew when to quit. He liked cockfighting. If people wanted to bet their last cent at his ring, that was fine with him. If people needed work, there was work to be done, and they could take or leave the salary he offered. If Haitians wanted to live on his property, they were welcome so long as they did good work. Cubans likewise. Spaniards the same. Money was money to him, the great equalizer, the price of entry, the reward if you were lucky, the cost if you were not. The color of your skin did not matter, less so your political or religious beliefs. So long as you were not communist.[16]

Paquito Rodríguez found this last bit out the hard way. On the verge of twenty, owing partly to the example of Fulgencio Batista, who as the man behind the throne in the mid-1930s cultivated communists as a way of controlling the labor force, Rodríguez joined the Communist Party and thought to organize the workers at one of Ángel's stores. The manager found out and gave Rodríguez a good chewing out. He would keep his politics to himself. "Ángel and Lina had no tolerance for communism," Rodríguez told an interviewer, a twinkle in his eye.[17]

Lina gave birth to a baby boy. This was the couple's third child, after Angela (born 1923) and Ramón (born 1924), with four more to follow: Raúl (born 1931), Juanita (born 1933), Enma (born 1935), and Augustina (born 1938). The parents named the child "Fidel," after Ángel's mentor, banker, and friend. Fidel Pino Santos was expected to be the boy's godfather, but there was no church in Birán, hence no priest, and Pino Santos was very busy. It took over eight years, until January 1935, for parents, priest, child, and godfather to unite and so consummate the boy's baptism, though by this time Pino Santos's honor had passed to a man named Louis Hibbert, the Haitian consul in Santiago de Cuba, a long story. Castro was never religious, and as a child is said to have exuded great confidence. He seems to have borne the stigma of his belated baptism like a curse. When word got out that he had yet to enter the kingdom of God, he was teased and labeled "a Jew," the sting of the epithet softened slightly by the ambiguity that "Jew" was also the name of a local bird, enabling him to conclude, almost plausibly, *they can't be referring to me.*

Castro once described his parents as "isolated landowners." This needs some explaining, as witnesses portray Finca Manacas as a whirlwind of activity. The large sugar *centrals* of eastern Cuba stretched over tens, sometimes hundreds of thousands of acres. The mill itself constituted the heart of a plantation community. Adjoining it were administrative headquarters and somewhat further away housing for managers, staff, and year-round workers. Many of these plantations (Banes and Preston on Nipe Bay, Miranda to the south, Alto Cedro to the west, Marcané to the north) spawned their own towns, with churches, parks, shopping centers, hospitals, golf courses, and distinct neighborhoods. With Finca Manacas at its center, Birán functioned as a microcosm of these larger *centrals*. Castro often accompanied his father on business trips to the nearby U.S.-owned plantations, noting their "special neighborhoods, beautiful houses, formal gardens, metal screens, electricity, refrigeration, nice furniture, exotic food, and fancy stores full of imported goods."

A vast cultural chasm separated Ángel and Lina from the university-trained administrators, scientists, and managers who ran the neighboring estates. "My parents did not go out to visit people and only rarely had visitors," Castro said, by which he meant visitors from the neighboring U.S.-owned plantations. "They didn't have the culture or the customs of a family from the wealthy class." Still, if isolated from the North American social scene, Ángel and Lina were far from lonely, as the doctor could attest. Castro was born in the middle of the night, which meant that the doctor did not depart until morning. He awoke in a household that buzzed with activity from sunup to sundown. The town of Birán comprised a steady population of several thousand people. The *zafra* raised the population by another thousand. The farm's store and diverse enterprises brought laborers, contractors, and businessmen of all sorts to the Castro home and office. The post office and especially the telegraph office attracted visitors and managers from nearby plantations. There was no dispensary on the grounds, which meant that the Castro home doubled as a clinic, with Lina serving as paramedic, nurse, and occasionally doctor, bandaging and sewing wounds and caring for the sick. Severely sick or injured family, friends, or workers were taken straight to the nearest hospital, always a long way off.

Rodríguez describes the Castro home as a welcoming place. As a young child, he often dropped by the house to play ball, go swimming, or ride horses with his friend Fidel. He never once set foot inside the Castro house, he insists, but others did, including Cuban and Haitian workers. The family was always kind to him. "You need to wait," they would say; "Fidel will be out in a minute."

The Castro home was never busier than at election time. In pre-revolutionary Cuba votes were openly bought and sold, especially in the rural areas where illiteracy was high and candidates little known. Ángel Castro had something everybody wanted, namely, work, hence he exercised political influence in the region, serving as a middle man between candidates and voters. In exchange for Ángel's patronage, local residents voted for his favored candidate. Ángel commanded a team of ward heelers, influential neighbors whose job it was to round up votes for local, provincial, and national offices. In the mid-1930s, Fidel Pino Santos, Ángel's friend and private banker, ran for election to the Cuban House of Representatives. Ángel disbursed funds from his front porch to secure his friend votes. During that campaign, Fidel Castro remembers traffic so heavy in the house that it was sometimes difficult to sleep. "The safe was constantly being opened and closed," he recalls, "making an inevitable metallic bang." This was all done in a spirit of innocence and altruism, Castro explained; it seemed perfectly natural to all concerned. What was good for Pino Santos was good for Ángel, and so good for Ángel's workers.[18]

Political corruption is capricious, as likely to impede as advance the cause of those caught up in it. Castro learned this lesson firsthand, now watching his father lasso votes for a favored candidate, now seeing him fall prey to the machinations of local government officials. Eastern plantations were monitored by municipal and state authorities who collected taxes, enforced health and safety codes, and, starting in the 1930s, upheld an expanding array of labor laws. Visits by these officials were stomach turning, Enma Castro recalls, with much hemming and hawing and double speak until owners came up with the cash sufficient to speed the swindlers on their way. Enma remembers one such episode coinciding with her brother's return from university. Coming upon a father recently bilked by two inspectors, Castro pursued the men to a nearby town, where he threatened them with legal action if they did not fork over Ángel's money. Hours later he arrived home money in hand, turning it over to a humiliated Ángel.

The Castro kids remember Ángel as hardworking, serious, unaffectionate. Enma Castro recalls seeing her parents hold hands exactly once in her lifetime—while riding in the family car. Fidel Castro describes his father exhibiting his fondness for his children by occasionally patting their heads or running his fingers through their hair. No one remembers him picking them up in his arms or hugging them. Like busy fathers everywhere, Ángel talked from time to time about taking the family on a visit to his native Galicia. But the Castros rarely if ever traveled together, and they never went away on holiday. As the family grew and became increasingly rambunctious, Ángel dined alone in his office at the back of the house, a small shortwave radio his preferred company. On Sundays and holidays when the family ate together, Ángel's presence imparted an air of soberness. When he retired to his office, the table erupted. Ángel "wasn't much for words," his son remembered. "He spoke rarely, as least in the period in which I knew him." It was as if he never learned the meaning of the word play—not as a child in Láncara, not as a stowaway in Madrid, not in the war, not on the hospital ward, not when setting himself up in Birán, not even when entertaining his own children.[19]

Ángel's satisfaction in life derived from work. Castro describes his father coming alive during business interactions. "I always noticed that when he left on a trip to whatever place, the central, Santiago, his demeanor changed." In work settings, Ángel seemed unrestrained, sharing stories and bits of his past that the children never heard about at home. "Perhaps he thought I wasn't paying attention," Castro remarked, "but I was."[20] Paquito Rodríguez says that Ángel regularly engaged his workers on his tours of the cane fields. In a country full of absentee landlords and condescending managers, "Ángel worked as hard as anybody on the property. He was not proud. He was plain spoken and intelligent." Rodríguez says that Ángel welcomed his workers' opinions and helped resolve their problems, which "made him both unusual and popular."[21] Which is not to say that Ángel was altruistic or blind to the conflict between labor and management, simply that he seems never to have forgotten his peasant roots.

Not all accounts of Ángel are glowing. One of Castro's former schoolmates, an exile and sworn enemy of the Castro regime, tells a damning story, unsubstantiated by evidence, of Fidel Castro once beating a striking worker with the flat blade of a machete, while his father looked on approvingly.[22] The story is apparently meant to convey a father's cruelty and a boy's bullying: like father, like son, the dictator to be. It is hard to know what to make of such accounts. The story contradicts the testimony of all who knew Ángel, whether intimately, as a family member, or impersonally, as a boss or colleague.[23] Such stories defy the logic of the father's life. It seems hard to imagine him succeeding in eastern Cuba as a teamster, contractor, storeowner, manager, planter, ward heeler, and king maker, hemmed in by U.S.-owned plantations, while relying on others' good will for his survival if he bullied, intimidated, and abused his workers. But what do others say?

Enma Castro says that Ángel had an experienced team to deal with wayward workers. Most of the policing among the workers was carried out by workers themselves. "Fool," a disgruntled worker would be told, "do you think things are better at United Fruit?" Why, Enma asks, would a successful businessman delegate the punishment of a worker to an ignorant son? On school break, the Castro kids were expected to contribute on the farm—in the office, sometimes in the store, "never in the fields," Enma says. Finally, the *zafra* did not coincide with the children's school vacations. Since age seven, her brother was away at school during the *zafra*, she observes. "That story is preposterous."[24]

Rodríguez concurs. If that episode were true, he says, he would have known about it, and he never heard talk of such a thing. If

anything, he said, the Castros went out of their way to protect workers from the rural guards introduced by the U.S. military government
at the turn of the century and whose job it was to keep order in
sugar country. One year, there was a rash of cane burnings in the region around Birán. The guards accused Rodriguez's older brothers of
perpetrating the acts. Hearing that the boys had been arrested, Lina
rushed to their defense. "They didn't do it," she told the guards; the
Rodríguez boys would never do that. "These are my fields," she said.
"These are my workers. I know what goes on here." Despite her protest, the guards took the boys in for questioning, but not before Lina
sent along her eldest daughter, Angela, to ensure the boys' safety.[25]

With Ángel focused on the business, Lina functioned as the
family's center of gravity, guiding and correcting the kids and managing the household staff. The house had a cook and two maids
who cleaned and did the laundry. Serious (if not somber) in photographs, Lina was the life force of the Castro farm. Twenty-eight
years Ángel's junior, she had her first child with him when she was
nineteen, leaving her closer in age (and spirit) to her children than
to her husband. Children and neighbors describe Lina as playful and
full of life, with a sailor's tongue. She was known to fire a rifle to
alert the family that it was suppertime. She kept a personal flock of
sheep, which accompanied her around the farm. When the children
needed medical care or a shoulder to cry on, she was there. And
not just for family. Paquito Rodríguez remembers Lina plunging a
bleeding hand in hot water, greeting his howls of protest with the
admonition to "stop his bleating and be a man!"[26]

Lina also ran the company store and assisted Ángel with book-
keeping. Indeed, Castro credits his mother with keeping the farm
afloat. Ángel was only partly literate and entirely self-taught. Lina, an
autodidact herself, was good with numbers. She was also a stickler
for discipline and order, a characteristic she passed on to her son,
Fidel. Castro described her as both the farm's "overseer" and "the
family economist." The Castro siblings respected their father. They
worshipped their mother. "Nobody ever knew where she got the

time and energy to do everything she did," Castro said; "she never sat down, I never saw her rest one second the whole day." Lina gets more credit for providing her children an education than her husband. "Without her," Castro remarked, "I assure you that I—who always loved to study—would be a functional illiterate."[27]

Despite rarely receiving formal visitors, Ángel and Lina regularly entertained their immediate neighbors. A typical evening found the parents perched in the living room or on the veranda in the company of the fellow Spaniards who helped run the place, playing cards and dominoes, listening to the Victrola, talking politics. The group included an Asturian bookkeeper, a telegraph operator named Velero, and García, the cook, who moved from the machine shop to the kitchen on account of rheumatism, and who was said to have been hopeless culinarily. Fidel Castro was attracted to the bookkeeper, who spoke many languages and translated the news of the world to assembled guests. Trained in the classics, this man regaled Castro about the Greek orator Demosthenes, "who put a little stone in his mouth to cure his stuttering."[28] Home from school in summers, the growing Castro would pay this favor forward, reading news of the Spanish Civil War to the illiterate García and fellow members of the cosmopolitan microcosm that was Finca Manacas. Constitutionally conservative, Ángel (and García) sided with the Nationalists in the conflagration consuming Spain. But there were few barriers to entry in the Castro sitting room. Lina and Ángel were open-minded and ecumenical and did not let ideological differences get in the way of the camaraderie.[29]

Besides the post and telegraph office, the one other public building on the Castro farm was Escuela Rural Mixta, No. 15, a one-room primary school. Constructed of local lumber, it was painted a cheerful blue, topped by a red metal roof, and had the charm of a little church. Its doors and windows were hung with heavy wooden shutters that could be thrown open to the breeze. Its interior was simple, with a polished wood floor, gray walls, and a large slate chalkboard. There were desks for thirty students, with a few desk-less seats at the front of each row reserved for pupils too young to write. It was on one of these front row seats that Fidel Castro began his education long before officially matriculating in January 1932. With his older siblings ensconced in class, there was little else for him do, and he simply refused to be excluded.

At the time of Castro's birth, Cuba had the highest literacy rate in Latin America. According to a government pamphlet from the era, the aim of education was to prepare students to fulfill the obligations of citizenship, while giving them "the confidence to cling to what they know is right." More than a mere physical space in which stilted professors enforced a fragile order, the Cuban primary school was said to comprise a "living spirit" in which students experienced "the joy and contentment of a free and secure life," while mastering an array of subjects that included Spanish, reading, writing, arithmetic, biology, geography, history, civics, morals, agriculture, physical education, music, and art.[30]

Looking back on his introduction to primary school, Castro said that few if any of the rural schools realized this mandate because of a lack of resources and social inequality. "My classmates, the children of humble farmers, generally used to go barefooted to school and they wore very bad clothes," he told Naty Revuelta. Despite being bright enough, his neighbors did not have the support required to succeed at schoolwork. As a result, most dropped out. This "social fatalism," as Castro called it, was only magnified later in life.[31]

Castro's observations on the state of primary education in rural Cuba are confirmed by a study made a few years after his birth by a team of visiting U.S. scholars known as the Commission on Cuban Affairs. The Cuban Republic had not met its ambitious goal of extending primary school education to all its children, the commission observed. Nationwide, less than half of eligible children were enrolled in school, and most of these in the first two years. Though modeled after the U.S. school system, Cuba spent a meager $13.90

per pupil per year in primary schools, less than one third of the money allocated by the most cash-strapped U.S. states at the time. Cuba's primary school curriculum was outdated and "irrelevant" to the lives and needs of rural students especially, the U.S. commission reported. As a result, illiteracy remained a problem throughout the country. In 1932, nearly one in four pupils were enrolled for less than a full school year; average daily attendance was estimated at 77 percent. In a single month (November 1933, for instance), over half of school-age children were not enrolled in school. These numbers, skewed in favor of the cities, did not begin to tell the story in the rural areas, which the commission labeled "a calamity," and where illiteracy exceeded 50 percent. Castro estimated illiteracy in the Birán of his youth to be as high as 80 percent.[32]

The student-teacher ratio in Cuban primary schools was roughly forty-five to one, with teachers responsible for classrooms packed with students ranging from kindergarten through sixth grade. Statistics do not tell the whole story. There was a lot of turnover in the teaching profession and sometimes no teachers at all. In 1930, when a woman named Engracia Perrand showed up in Birán, she was one of three teachers to come through the school in a single year. Moreover, it was not so much the class size that impressed Perrand (the number of pupils hovered around twenty or so throughout the decade) as the students' range in age and ability, "with all but fully-grown men occupying the first-grade row."[33]

Conditions such as these led a maturing Castro to conclude that justice in the realm of education would depend on deep-rooted political and economic reform. "Everything that might be done relative to technique and organization of teaching won't be worth a damn," he told Revuelta, "if the status quo of the nation is not profoundly altered where the root of the tragedy lies, from the bottom up." He had come by this conclusion not through reading Marx and others, but by "the palpitating reality of life." No amount of "great teachers or resources" could "prevent the son of a humble peasant from drowning sooner or later."[34]

The woman Perrand replaced was named Eufrasia Feliú. Feliú arrived in Birán in spring 1927, nine months after Castro's birth. Feliú was Haitian, of "mixed-race," in Castro's words, which in Cuban parlance meant light-skinned.[35] Perrand lived in one of the outbuildings on the Castro property and ate with the family. Castro's name formally appears in her ledger in January 1932, when he was five. Though modeled on U.S. elementary schools, which at this time began with kindergarten, most Cuban primary schools began formal teaching with first grade. Like Perrand, Feliú remembers a four-year-old Castro occupying the middle seat in the front row. Curiously, the Castro kids, surely the most privileged at the local school, did not progress systematically from grade to grade. The 1933–34 school ledger reveals eleven-year-old Angelita enrolled in third grade (one would expect her to have been in sixth), eight-year-old Ramón enrolled in second grade (instead of third), and the seven-year-old Fidel's grade unspecified, as if, six months after completing his first semester (January–June 1932), he had yet to make it to the first grade. This delay would later give Castro an athletic advantage over his fellow classmates.[36]

During her brief spell at Escuela Rural Mixta, No. 15, Perrand boarded with the Castro family. Perrand confirms accounts of the Castro household as open and inviting, recalling long evenings of dominoes surrounded by family, friends, and even the rural guards. At night Perrand entertained the Castro children with tall tales, which she made up as she went along, passing them off as gospel. The Castro children delighted at exposing inconsistencies in her stories. It often fell to Perrand to put three-year-old Fidel to bed. "Engracia, you sleep with me," the boy would plead. She escaped his clutches only after more stories and favorite lullabies. The children insisted she share whatever they themselves enjoyed. "They tried to give me the best of everything, games, dolls, fruit, whatever. Fidelito would run up to me and say: 'take it Engracia, it's for you!'"[37]

Perrand provides the earliest descriptions of the young Castro. Three-and-a half-years-old at the time they met, Castro was plump and heavy. "I could scarcely lift him. He had rosy skin and was very cute. His hair was dirty blond. He was playful, fiddling around with this and that just like any child." Mimicking the students around him, Castro taught himself the alphabet. By the time Perrand departed that June, he could write his name, "Fidel." Perrand described a lively, mischievous boy, who addressed the school janitor as "Old Woman." Perrand chastised him whenever he did so, prompting him to smile at her and ask, "When you grow old are you going to be like her?"[38]

The next earliest description of the boy comes from a carpenter who worked on the estate named Juan de la Cruz Mugelsia Labañedo. There was always some fence, building, or piece of furniture in need of repair, and Ángel liked to turn to Spaniards, better still Galicians, for skilled labor. De la Cruz and several fellow Galicians were felling a tree one day, when one of the men, high atop the branches, began to holler, "Boy! Get away from there! Get away from there!" The boy in question was the young Castro. The danger was a ditch that bisected the farm and ran down toward the orchard. A tropical storm had just plowed through the region transforming a trickle into a torrent, which proved too tempting for a four-year-old to resist. Rather than crossing the stream over a nearby bridge, the boy waded in, misjudging the strength of the current, and was swept away.[39]

The boy's head disappeared as the warning cry rang out across the property. Recognizing the danger, de la Cruz dashed downstream, plunged into the water, and thrashed about, praying his hands would hit on an arm or a leg, a piece of clothing, a lock of hair—anything. To his relief, the boy bumped into him, and he pulled the youngster from the water, blue in the face and scarcely breathing. "I took him by the feet and hung him upside down," de la Cruz recounted. "Then I thumped his chest, and he sprang to life, coughing out a bit of water." De la Cruz described Castro's fearlessness that day as typical. Castro was confident and matter-of-fact, de la Cruz said, socially as well as physically. He never sought others' approval before acting, always plunging in headfirst. They boy was also defiant. When summoned by his father to do this or that, the boy would often answer simply, "no."[40]

Boarding school eventually robbed Paquito Rodríguez of his childhood friend. When Castro returned from school on holidays, the boys renewed their camaraderie, playing sports, exploring the countryside, climbing mountains, chasing girls, riding horses high into the hills to go hunting. Castro always prided himself on his swimming ability. Rodríguez claims he could outswim Castro any day. Rodríguez and Castro also liked to box. Castro wore thick-soled shoes and would step on his opponents' foot to immobilize his adversary and gain a tactical advantage. The young Castro was tall, making him a fierce opponent in the ring. "Fidel could beat his older brother Ramón." Rodríguez describes Castro as very social, but also as someone who enjoyed solitude and reading, which set him apart from the neighborhood kids. "We'd be walking around somewhere and he would stop suddenly and come up with the craziest questions," Rodríguez said. "He was always asking about things I never understood. I'd say to myself, 'where in the world did that come from?'"[41]

Enma Castro confirms Rodríguez's account of his brother's curiosity. "He would follow my dad around constantly asking questions: 'what's this?' 'what's the point of that?' 'how does this work?'" This, along with the visits to the American plantations, may have been the closest Fidel Castro came to developing an emotional attachment to his father. Both were inquisitive and mechanically minded. Both liked to know how things worked. The father seemed to recognize something of himself in his emerging son. There was another thing Rodríguez remembers that set Castro apart. Though a gamester, as quick as any to seize the advantage in a running race, swimming contest, or boxing match, "he hated bullies, liars, and crooks." If he saw somebody picking on a weaker kid or one of the rural guards abusing a worker, "his mood would change instantly, and he would take action."[42]

These anecdotes from Perrand, de la Cruz, Rodríguez, and others match the account that Castro provided about his childhood over the years. Castro speaks of playing with his brother and the local kids, going swimming, hunting with slingshots, bow and arrow, and rifles, and riding horses in the mountains. "On vacations, I kept in permanent contact with nature," he said. Like boys everywhere, the kids from Birán were constantly getting into trouble—and constantly worming their way out of it. The most penalized transgressions involved barnyard animals. The boys apparently liked to not only target but inebriate their parents' chickens, turkeys, and waterfowl. They bombarded the schoolhouse with a homemade mortar cannon, and they were regularly called out for their foul language or disrespect. Boys will be boys. Ángel was the symbol of authority, Lina the disciplinarian. The threat of punishment was always worse than the fact. When occasionally sentenced to their father's belt, the boys simply hid it or stayed out of sight until the storm had blown over.[43]

chapter three

SCHOOL DAYS

One day the head of the athletic department at Colegio
de Dolores, the Jesuit secondary school in Santiago de
Cuba, was asked to select a basketball team to represent
the school in a regional tournament. These selections tended to
favor the kids from wealthy families. "You know how that goes,"
a former classmate remarked, "the more you have the more you're
worth." Fidel Castro loved basketball and considered himself a superior athlete. The stakes were high, made higher on account of the
fancy uniforms supplied by the school, along with the team's official
name, San Ignacio de Loyola, a title reserved for illustrious occasions. Castro expected to be named to this team. He was not. Nor
was "a mulatto" who many knew to be the best basketball player at
the school.[1]

Indignant at the snubbing, Castro and the others decided to
form their own team. Short of money, they cut the legs off pants to

make shorts and bought cheap T-shirts and tennis shoes. They took up a collection to buy a basketball. In a sign that they had not lost their sense of humor, the boys named their team Los Ripieras (the Lowlifes) and set to work, determined to provide their teachers a lesson in homespun meritocracy. When the long-awaited game day arrived, Castro threw himself against the opposition with complete abandon. It was "one against five," a teammate recalled. "Fidel pass," his teammates cried, "here Fidel, pass Fidel, Fidel!" Nothing. "At the end, as you might suppose, we lost the game. Basketball requires teamwork."

Castro was a pillar of the team. This was awkward to say the least. The boys pulled themselves together and prepared for the next opponent. "Gentlemen, this time we are not losing," Castro announced. Well and good, thought the others, imagining that Castro had learned a lesson. The whistle blew. Then more of the same: "'Fidel pass,' 'pass Fidel,' 'here Fidel,' and nothing." The boys called time-out and kicked Castro off the team. "What do you suppose he did then?" another former classmate asked. "He bought a ball of his own and spent the rest of that term practicing." Friends describe Castro in mortal combat with himself, right hand against left hand, left against right. When one or the other failed him, he would castigate the offender. "Everyone thought he had lost his mind," said one witness; "no one could conceive of it." In the end, Castro acquired competence with both hands and the coach noticed, eventually adding him to the roster. He continued to play "an annoying style of basketball."

Despite growing up surrounded by family and friends, a mature Castro told a confidant that it had been his "destiny . . . to be alone in everything."[2] This can be read as both a point of pride (he knew what was right and was self-reliant) and a source of hurt (he felt abandoned). This emotional insecurity was honed in childhood and adolescence, as Castro moved from the one-room schoolhouse in Birán to one elite boarding school after another. Though a child of privilege, especially in comparison to his early friends, Castro continued to see himself as an outsider, never sure exactly how he fit in. If this made him insecure at times, it also motivated him to be the best at everything, as he became an island to his father's walled city.

––––––––––

In January 1934, Eufrasia Feliú convinced Ángel and Lina Castro to send Fidel and his older sister Angela to Santiago de Cuba for private tutoring. Eufrasia had a sister named Belén who taught private piano lessons. Belén could provide the children a better general education than they could receive in the chaos that was Escuela Mixta Rural, No. 15, her sister said. In counseling such a move, Feliú was not thinking entirely about the good of her charges. The political upheaval and economic downturn that gripped Cuba in the early 1930s all but ended luxuries like private piano lessons at the very moment the untimely death of another sister, a physician, deprived the family of income. These twin blows, combined with a schoolteacher's inconsistent paychecks, pushed the Feliú family to the brink. Something had to be done. By Christmas 1933, when this arrangement was broached, the Castro family was struggling to keep up with two new arrivals, Raúl, barely two, and Juanita, an infant. To have the older children safely out of the way could make things easier.

Ángel and Lina did not know what they were getting their children into. Had they seen the Feliú household firsthand, they might have changed their minds. The Feliú sisters shared a home with their elderly father on Intendente Hill in the Tívoli neighborhood of Santiago, a few blocks down from Parque Céspedes, the city center. Still standing today, the house is located on a small plaza across from what used to be a public secondary school, but which was later converted into a military barracks, and still later a museum. The Feliú house looks a lot like an old saloon. It consists of a single story fronted by a shallow portico supported by thin timbers that reach from floor to ceiling, roughly ten feet high. Three tall, slim doorways face the front, which measures roughly twenty feet across. At the time the Castros arrived, the house had a small living room (with a piano) and two small bedrooms divided by bead-board walls. In one of the bedrooms, the girls' elderly father, Néstor Feliú, occupied "a rickety old bed." Attached to the back, with a sweeping view of the city and Santiago Bay, was a bathroom and an outdoor kitchen, as well as a small balcony where Fidel Castro used to take in the sights.

Though small and crowded when the Castro children arrived, the tile floors, decorative appliqués, and panoramic view made this a potentially nice home for a small family capable of keeping up with the maintenance. This was not the Feliús by late 1933. Fidel and Angelita joined a family already swelling with Belén (the piano teacher and would-be tutor), her father, her sister Eufrasia (during school vacations), a recently orphaned girl (whom the family adopted as a maid), and, eventually, Ramón Castro—seven people in all. Where they slept is anybody's guess. Privacy was out of the question. When it rained, the house leaked.

Castro told more than one interviewer that he was five years old when he left Birán for the big city. The Birán school ledger refutes this. In January 1932, Castro formally began school in Birán at age five. He remained there through December 1933, after two full years of education. In January 1934, Castro, now age seven, moved to Santiago. Ramón Castro joined his siblings in April for the last third of the 1933–34 academic year, which ended in June. Castro also reported that his matriculation at the Feliú home lasted two years. In fact, he boarded with the Feliús on two different occasions, each for a maximum of six months. The first stay lasted from January to June 1934, after which he and his siblings returned to Birán through the end of the year.[3]

Besides clearing up the historical record, the Birán school ledger reveals the vulnerability of the Cuban educational system to political and other vicissitudes. The upheaval surrounding the dictatorship and fall of Gerardo Machado closed secondary schools and the University of Havana for three years from December 1930 to December 1933. Primary school students posed no threat to the regime, hence many remained open during much of that period. Still, Machado's fall in August 1933 delayed the opening of Escuela Rural Mixta, No. 15 by a month. The following year, opening day was delayed by two months due to a polio epidemic in Oriente Province. When the school year finally began in mid-November 1934, the three eldest Castro children were back in Birán and in attendance, suggesting that the Feliú experiment had been less than successful.

The Feliús were descendants of Haitian farmers who came to Cuba in the late eighteenth century to escape the Haitian slave revolt led by Toussaint L'Ouverture. They were cultured people who spoke perfect French. They also observed rigorous social etiquette that Castro associated with French customs and upbringing. By the time the Castro kids moved in with them, the family could barely feed itself, despite the fact that Ángel paid the schoolteacher 40 pesos (roughly $1,000 U.S. in 2008 dollars) per child per semester. When Ramón joined his siblings, in other words, the Castros were supplementing the Feliú family's income by $3,000, not a lot by North American standards, but a windfall in eastern Cuba at the time.

It is hard to say where the money went. Eufrasia Feliú took a lavish trip to Niagara Falls the summer after the three kids returned to Birán. The money did not go into food or education, that much we know for sure, as Castro's memories of the period consist essentially of hunger and ennui. The six or seven members of the household ate from the *cantinita*, Cuban for a stack of metal plates consisting of rice, boniato, vegetables, sometimes a bit of meat sauce, brought to the house each day by a cousin, who functioned as the family cook. Castro remembers never once feeling hungry in Birán what with abundant food and ubiquitous sweets and delicacies produced on the farm and available at the company store. This was not the case at the Feliús', where he could have devoured the entire *cantinita* by himself. The *cantinita* was meant for the household to share, and not for lunch alone, but for dinner besides. Castro remembers scouring his plate for the last kernel of rice, smashing it with the tines of his fork before transferring it to his tongue where it remained until it melted away. No wonder he remembered these six months as two years. It took a visit by his father later that May or June to confirm what the boy did not know how to articulate in letters home: he was starving, losing so much weight that his shocked father was told upon setting eyes on his emaciated son that the boy had recently been ill.

His mind fared little better. When Castro enrolled in a private school in Santiago de Cuba the next year at age eight, he began as a first grader. Two years of schooling in Birán plus half a year of private tutoring left him functioning at the level of a six-year-old. However gifted a piano teacher, Belén Feliú was unqualified to tutor the kids in even the rudiments of early primary school education, never mind the astonishing array of subjects on the Cuban government's course list. In fact, Castro recalled, Belén made no effort to teach him anything, leaving him to his own devices, which included memorizing multiplication tables and long division from the front of a spiral notebook. He also read comic books during this period when he could get his hands on them, borrowing from neighborhood kids or reading them on trips to a local market.

Hunger and boredom do not make for a happy child. When Castro pushed back, he was verbally, sometimes physically, chastised. The Feliús were notorious in the neighborhood for their strictness. The local boys (Castro speaks of "friends" here) used to try to bait him into breaking house rules by eating forbidden delicacies. One day, out of the grasp of the Feliús, Castro asked his sister why, able to write with the confidence of a fourth grader, she had not informed their parents about their plight. She had tried, Angela assured her brother, but the Feliús seized her letters and scolded her for informing on them. Which raises the question of abuse. In 1933 Cuba, it did not take $3,000 to put a decent meal on the table twice a day, much less deliver on the promise of giving the kids a minimal education. Years later, Castro told a skeptical interviewer that he harbored no ill will toward the parsimonious Feliús. He said they were victims of a corrupt social system.[4]

Ángel's description of his children's appearance at the Feliús' inspired Lina to depart for Santiago the next day. Setting eyes on the three, she immediately marched them to a local restaurant, watching as they gorged themselves on ice cream and mangoes. They then all promptly returned to Birán, where they remained through the summer and a politically truncated fall semester. Thereafter there was a noticeable coolness at the family dinner table toward Eufrasia Feliú, who continued to command the Birán schoolhouse. The contrast between how she ate at the Castros and how the Castro kids had eaten with her family was lost on nobody.

That same summer 1934 Belén Feliú married Louis Hibbert, the Haitian consul in Santiago de Cuba. Once united with Hibbert, the Feliú family moved from their cramped saloon to a larger house next door with more space, a little privacy, and plenty to eat. In January 1935, in what seems an act of criminal negligence, the Castros returned Angela, Ramón, and Fidel to the Feliú home as borders in order to enroll them in private school. It was at this time that Castro, now age eight, was finally baptized, the honor of godfather going to Louis, the Haitian consul.[5]

Looking back on his initial encounter with Santiago de Cuba, Castro retained some indelible impressions. First there was the never-ending commotion of a boisterous commercial center—the crowds of people, the numerous shops, the dazzling array of merchandise. Then there was the arbitrary force exercised on *santiagueros* by Machado's police and soldiers. The Feliús' homes old and new faced a small square on whose opposite side sat the large Instituto de Segunda Eneseñaza (secondary school institute), seized by the Machado government in December 1930, and converted into a military barracks. Castro grew accustomed to seeing alleged criminals dragged through the square and into the building, their cries echoing across the public square.

Castro also recalled instances of xenophobia and scapegoating. In autumn 1933, the revolutionary government issued a set of decrees designed to improve the plight of Cuban labor. One of the laws ordered the expulsion of all unemployed Haitians. Given the seasonal nature of work in the sugar industry, it was not easy to distinguish an unemployed from an underemployed Haitian, and the legislation created turmoil in a Haitian workforce already poised on the edge of the abyss. The job of deporting indigent Haitians fell to the Cuban Army, which exhibited little sympathy and less discernment in identifying targets.

Growing up among Haitians in Birán and living with them on Intendente Hill, Castro witnessed the cost of this supposedly progressive legislation. In Birán, Haitians were rounded up and herded to the ports at Santiago and Nipe. In Santiago, Louis Hibbert, the Haitian consul and Castro's host and godfather, took the boy down to the harbor to witness heartbreaking scenes of Haitians being packed ("like sardines in a tin") onto waiting boats as stricken family members looked on. The Haitian exiles, many of whom had been on the island for over a generation, went from "one terrible life of misery and poverty, to another even worse one," Castro told an interviewer. And nobody seemed to care. Combined with evidence of arbitrary violence on the city streets, scenes like these helped a young boy "understand the world."[6]

———————

When Ramón and Fidel returned to the Feliús for the second time in January 1935 (now in the company of their younger brother, Raúl), their parents enrolled them in one of Santiago's most prestigious boys' schools, Colegio de La Salle. Founded by the Christian Brothers in 1908, the school was located on the site of what had been the island's first institution of higher learning, the Seminario San Basilio Magno, established in 1722. La Salle was of French rather than Spanish affiliation. Most of its business was conducted in Spanish, but it taught French rather than English as a second language, and it followed a French schedule, with classes on Monday, Tuesday, Wednesday, Friday, and Saturday, with Thursdays and Sundays off. La Salle differed from its nearby rival, Colegio de Dolores, a Jesuit school where Castro moved three years later, in being low-key and ecumenical. Unlike the Jesuits, few of the La Salle brothers were or expected to be ordained. Established partly to meet the needs of migrants fleeing the Haitian Revolution, the school did not discriminate racially. This did not mean that there were many black kids in Castro's classes (there was one in his grade), only that blacks were welcome if they were deemed to have the proper background and could come up with the tuition.[7]

Castro began the year as a day student, returning to the Feliús' in the afternoon. Castro experienced his entry into a real school as "a big step forward."[8] Still, his country ways, advanced age, and lack of preparation distinguished him from his classmates for all the wrong reasons, and it took him a semester or so to get comfortable. Meanwhile, he continued to bridle under the "feudal discipline" of his godparents. One minute he had no food and dared not complain about it, the next minute he had to eat whatever was put in front of him. "I was bored by all those French rules, that French way of living," he recalled. Along with the tight leash and occasional spankings, one favorite refrain of his hosts particularly irked him: they would send him away to boarding school if he did not watch himself.

It was not long before Castro resolved to test that threat, erupting in fits of pique and misbehavior that convinced his godparents to call it quits. Castro remembered his liberation from the Hibbert-Feliús as one of the happiest moments of his life. He took to boarding school like a starving kid to mangoes, relishing the opportunity simply to fit in. Like schoolboys everywhere, he enjoyed recess and weekend excursions to various points on the bay best. Schoolwork was a blur of catechism and Cuban history, recess a whirl of sports, games, and wilderness adventures. The new camaraderie made for lasting contentment. "I was happy, because I was with all the other boys. We'd play, and on Thursday and Sunday, they'd take us to a place down by the ocean where there was a big area where there were all sorts of places for sports and adventures."[9]

The name of the place Castro loved so much was Rente, a spit of land that juts out into Santiago Bay (and which is now home to a sprawling oil refinery). Arriving at the port of Santiago, the boys would clamber aboard the school launch, *El Cateto*, for the twenty-minute trip ("pum, pum, pum") across the bay. Castro fondly remembered the sweet smell of sea air. At Rente, the boys could swim, play ball, and explore sunken ships. Castro and his friends liked to fish and sometimes returned to school with their catch, which would then be prepared for them by the school staff. In retrospect, he described spending four happy years at La Salle, but they were not without conflict. Once comparing La Salle, a Christian Brothers school, to Jesuit schools in Santiago and Havana, Castro noted that the La Salle brothers were less disciplined, less professional, less committed to their work. Some physically abused the boys.

One teacher stood out from the rest, Brother Bernardo, the man in charge of boarding students. It is not uncommon for teachers in such settings to succumb to favoritism. Brother Bernardo took this further than the rest. Bernardo betrayed an unusual fondness for a young boy from Baracoa, not some vulnerable or unhappy kid, Castro noted. One day Castro and this boy got into a dust-up on the launch back from Rente. The boys separated but the conflict remained unresolved as they climbed the hill back to school. Typically, the boys' route of choice passed through the heart of the city's red-light district, and they delighted at seeing their teachers blush at the siren calls of the working women. A favorite prank was to ring the bell of these establishments and run away just as one of the brothers approached the entrance. On this particular evening, Castro was in no mood to play. Arriving back at school first, he laid in wait for his nemesis, jumping him and then delivering "a jab" into his eye.[10]

Castro imagined the episode over. But he had picked a fight with the wrong boy. Brother Bernardo was not happy. At vespers that evening, Castro sensed that he was being hunted, and headed for the chapel gallery, the better to keep an eye on a predatory priest. It wasn't long before Brother Bernardo appeared at the gallery door and beckoned Castro with a chubby finger. "We walked down a hallway," Castro recalled, "turned a corner, and after a few steps he asked me, 'what happened?' I started to explain, but he didn't let me finish." The brother "walloped" Castro on his left ear, then followed that up with a blow to his right ear. "A grown man struck me as hard as he could!" Castro told an interviewer, still ringing with indignation. "This was unjust, humiliating, abusive." No one saw the brother hit the boy; there was nobody for the boy to turn to. He had to swallow the humiliation.[11]

This incident occurred toward the end of third grade. Castro was ten at the time, bright, but old for his grade. Castro skipped fourth grade, putting him in fifth grade (age eleven) when he next caught Brother Bernardo's attention the following fall. The second episode occurred in public one evening when the boys were lining up after study hall before making their way upstairs to their bedrooms. Boys are not made for waiting in lines. On this evening Castro was conversing with another student when yet another blow, lighter this time, on the side of his head took him by surprise. Bernardo had struck again, and though this blow hurt less than the first, it stung more on account of its being witnessed by his peers.[12]

At La Salle, lunch was followed by a short recess that preceded afternoon classes. The boys moved from lunch to recess as quickly as possible, often taking their food with them. Lunch itself did not amount to much: coffee with milk and *pan rapido* (a muffin with butter). Recess, by contrast, was high-stakes—a baseball game in which not everybody got to bat, with batting determined by one's place in yet another dreaded line. One day later that fall, Castro found himself toward the front of the line where a struggle ensued between a couple of boys determined to be the first batter. In this case, Castro himself was not involved. But from Brother Bernardo's perspective, proximity was proof of guilt, and "Paf! came yet another smack on the head." What was a boy to do? Absorb yet another humiliation and walk away? Castro threw himself on his elder, biting, punching, and kicking, until he was pulled away. Once separated from Bernardo, Castro approached the headmaster, who naturally sided with his colleague but took no action, or so it appeared.[13]

But just before Christmas holiday, when Ángel and Lina came to fetch their three boys, they were greeted by news that their sons had become demons—"the worst bandits that had ever passed through the school," the headmaster said. The news about Ramón and Raúl came as a surprise, as both were known to be courteous and obedient. Suspicion naturally fell upon Fidel. Mortified by his sons' behavior, Ángel repeated the headmaster's charges to anyone who would listen back in Birán, even sharing the story with friends and family over the dining room table at Christmastime. Fidel, aware that he was being blamed for what seemed to him to be Bernardo's bullying, felt hurt and resentful.[14]

The conflict did not simply blow over. In Cuba, the biggest day of the Christmas holiday is not Christmas itself but Three Kings Day, the twelfth day of Christmas, which falls on January 6. On that day, Cubans exchange gifts and enjoy a celebratory feast. The following day, January 7, life returns to normal, with schoolage children heading back to their classrooms. This January 7, nobody left the Castro house. Ángel had resolved to punish his children by withdrawing them from La Salle. Ramón, never one for school, was delighted (he had always wanted to become a mechanic). Raúl was confused, as if too young to comprehend what was happening. Castro was apoplectic. "I would have become a cattle farmer," he later remarked, if his father had had his way. Castro begged and pleaded, ranted and raved, even threatened to burn the house down if his parents did not return him to Santiago. "I loved school," he said. "School freed me." His parents eventually relented. Years later, a reflective Castro suggested that his parents were simply testing his commitment. How hungry for education was he *really*?[15]

———

Colegio de Dolores, where Castro enrolled as a fifth grader (age twelve) in January 1938, after being effectively expelled from La

Salle, was one of the country's most prestigious private schools. Castro entered Dolores as a day student, staying in the home of Martín and Carmen Mazorra, business associates of Ángel, who owned a department store in the city called La Muñeca (the Doll). The Mazorras were social climbers, Castro later charged, eager to take on a student enrolled in a school that would allow them to "rub elbows with all the rich people who also sent their sons there." Carmen Mazorra had peculiar ideas about what she might demand of someone else's child. She told Castro that in order to access the petty cash his parents had set aside for him, he had to get exemplary grades. That was all well and good, Castro thought to himself, for a student used to the rigor and ways of the school. But this wasn't him initially and his first semester marks showed it. Rather than sacrifice the sweets, ice cream, movies, and "little pork sandwiches" he so enjoyed, Castro doctored his report card to reflect outstanding grades. At the end of the first school year, when the school doled out prizes, Castro was conspicuously absent from the list of honorees. He told his surprised hosts that only year-long students were eligible. The Mazorras were just credulous enough to believe him. Asked later what he thought of his deceit, he replied that deceit is in the eye of the beholder, spinning his behavior as another example of his innate rebelliousness.[16]

Castro spent the summer of 1938 in Santiago de Cuba in the company of his older sister, Angela, who was preparing for the secondary school entrance exam. That summer, Angela studied under the supervision of yet another Haitian teacher named Emiliana Danger. With little to distract himself, Castro eavesdropped on the lessons. Impressed by the boy's curiosity, the tutor sometimes included him in the instruction. Looking back on this stage of his life, Castro told an interviewer that he had never had a mentor or a true role model as a child. For a few months that summer, Danger appears to have approximated that description, affording Castro some relief from the echo chamber of his own mind. Danger delighted in his ability to answer questions intended for students far older than he. He credits her with being the first person to ever really challenge him, the first to make him "enthusiastic" about the life of the mind.[17]

Late that summer, Castro was stricken by appendicitis, keeping him out of school the following autumn just as he was hitting his stride. The surgery went satisfactorily, but the incision became infected, leading to a prolonged and solitary stay in hospital. The previous month, Lina gave birth to the couple's seventh and final child, a girl named Augustina. Together with the three other little children (ages three, five, and seven), the new arrival left the parents tethered to the farm and Castro more or less fending for himself on the hospital ward. Ramón visited occasionally and the monks checked in from time to time. "I spent almost the entire time alone," Castro said, insisting that he did not regard his hospitalization with bitterness. He made friends "instinctively," working the wards like a politician, befriending old and young alike.[18]

The intellectual sparkle that Paquito Rodríguez recognized in his childhood friend began to exert itself in public around this time. The young patient was as curious as he was social. "I passed hours simply observing my surroundings," he wrote. He became fascinated by seemingly trivial things—like the ability of the ants on the floor of his room to work together to move bodies thousands of times bigger than their own. He paid rapt attention to the medical care going on around him, conducting his own operations and anatomy class on the lizards and myriad insects that shared his hospital room. The physicians and nurses noticed his curiosity and encouraged him, predicting that he would become a doctor one day.

The best thing about his appendicitis, Castro later recalled, is that it rescued him from the Mazorra family. When he returned to Dolores the next January, he did so as a boarding student. Recounting his exit from the Mazorras, he told journalist Carlos Franqui that "for the second time—third, fourth, fifth?—I made the determination to take action, to leave a situation which fate had confronted me with." Thereafter, he and he alone "decided all the problems of my life," he said, which is revealing not because it is true but because it was how he perceived things.[19] Former chums from Dolores recall a boy who seemed to shoulder a great sense of responsibility. At times, this inspired Castro to come to the defense of vulnerable individuals and groups; just as often, it led him to try to take on the world alone. Castro's glowing account of the teacher Emiliana Danger makes one wonder what influence a dedicated mentor might have had on a bright and energetic but solitary boy.

Friends, foes, and former teachers alike describe Castro in a cascade of contradictory adjectives. He was at once sober, reflective, happy, outgoing, modest, respectful, generous, brave, ambitious, restless, nervous, uneasy, audacious, tenacious, and ruthless, often at the same time. Like many kids his age, he was more interested in sports than schoolwork. "He wasn't much of a student," one classmate said, but he was a quick read and was an accomplished multitasker. Another remembered him fidgeting incessantly in class, playing with his pocket watch, his mind apparently on the loose. Then a teacher would ask him a question and he would engage, responding "as if it were nothing—as if he had twenty ears."[20]

Everyone who knew Castro as a schoolboy comments on his photographic memory. One classmate tells the story of a teacher who collected articles about the Second World War from the *Diario de la Marina*, the conservative daily favored by the Jesuits. One afternoon the man's paper went missing and Castro approached him to suggest that he be allowed to leave the school on a brief mission to get him another copy. Castro needed to visit the office of his father's friend and mentor, Fidel Pino Santos, and thought Pino Santos would be happy to part with his paper. As it happened, Castro was wrong, so he sat down and quickly read the articles, committing them to memory. Arriving back at school, Castro explained that he failed to acquire a paper, but had read and memorized the contents; if the teacher would provide him pen and paper he would re-create the articles for him. The teacher did so and Castro reproduced the articles verbatim. Later that day, a curious teacher went to the library to compare Castro's account with the originals. The articles matched word for word. The feat went up on the School's Wall of Honor. "It caused a sensation," a classmate remarked. "Do you know what it takes to re-create a newspaper article like this from memory?"[21]

This would not be the last mark Castro left on that wall. On November 6, 1940, Castro wrote a letter to U.S. president Franklin Delano Roosevelt, who had won election to a third term the previous day. "My good friend Roosevelt," Castro began. "I don't know very English, but I know as much as to write to you." Castro was a fan of Roosevelt's radio broadcasts. The president's latest triumph made him "very happy," he said, before continuing, "I am twelve years old. I am a boy but I think very much but I do not think that I am writing the President of the United States." (Actually, Castro was fourteen at the time, which raises the question of how he got this wrong. The most likely explanation is that he did not want his peers to know that he was behind in school for his age, both for what that might suggest about his intellectual acuity and because of the immense athletic advantage that that would have bestowed upon him.) Castro then asked Roosevelt to send him "a ten dollars bill green American." After all, he "had never seen" such a bill, and would simply "like to have one of them." He then gave Roosevelt his address and signed off, "Good by. Your friend. Fidel Castro." Oh, there was one more thing. Should the president "want iron" to build his "sheaps," the boy from Birán knew just where to find it, having grown up near "the biggest (minas) of iron of the land."[22] Much to everyone's surprise, someone in Roosevelt's office wrote back. When a letter from the president of the United States arrived at school, the administration promptly attached it to the Wall of Honor, making Castro, relatively unknown up to now, a minor celebrity.[23]

In standing up for himself over the course of his years in Santiago, Castro also stood up for others, and for what he knew was right. At private religious schools like La Salle and Dolores, Church teachings often conflicted with the mission of education. Castro and his friends learned this firsthand in a course on "Anatomy, Physiology

and Hygiene" when the time came to take up the subject of sex education. The lecturer carried out his end of the bargain well enough;
trouble arose when exam time arrived and the students discovered
that the course head had removed the offending pages from the
textbook. "We must do something," Castro announced. With his
classmates trailing behind him, Castro approached the teacher ("as if
it were nothing, with tremendous tranquility," a classmate recalled).
He requested the missing pages. The teacher responded that there
were some things the students were too young to know. How then,
Castro demanded, were the students to answer exam questions
based on these pages? When the ensuing discussion did not resolve
the conflict, the students put their heads together, and came up with
another solution, acquiring the pages from a book in an outside
library.[24]

When Castro saw something wrong, he tried to fix it, so much
so that his classmates nicknamed him "Lio" (trouble), as he was always getting himself in hot water. "He never permitted abuse and
had a tremendous facility in fixing problems," a classmate remembers. Another classmate, "short, fat, and homely," by his own description, made an inviting target. One day, the boy got rolled by a bully,
prompting Castro to come to the defense of his friend. The bullying
stopped. Dolores was notorious in Santiago de Cuba for excluding
blacks. But there was at least one "colored kid" in the student body.
When one of the teachers referred to the boy as "the negrito" and
asked what he was doing in the class, Castro protested, bringing an
end to the "derogatory remarks."[25]

Among the three to four hundred privileged and pampered students
at Dolores, it was not easy to stand out. But the Jesuits liked sports
and the great outdoors. Castro excelled at activities demanding
physical prowess. He was particularly fond of basketball and soccer.
"He ran like an arrow because he was tall and thin, and of course
this helped on the athletic field," one classmate said. Castro's prowess

at and passion for baseball is exaggerated. Still, he stood out at Dolores as a pitcher. He also loved to swim and row, his classmates say. Above all, he liked to escape to the mountains. When the boys arrived at a destination, "Castro was gone at the opening of the school bus door." If there was a high peak nearby, he was off; a cliff to climb, gone; a river to ford. Ba! He had "an unusual predilection for nature, for knowing its secrets, he had a tremendous affection for our excursions perhaps because they allowed him such contact." Everything was a competition among this group of kids. Once in the mountains, the boys would divide into teams and hunt for one another. Whoever had Castro on his team was at a great advantage.[26]

A favorite destination was the rugged area around Contramaestre, at the northeast margin of the Sierra Maestre. There, teachers and students forded rivers, climbed mountains, fished, and hunted. On the way home, they would often stop for a meal at the home of a classmate named René Fernández, whose family would feed and entertain the students. These visits generated a lot of anecdotes. One classmate recalled the time when the group was watching René's father stabling his horse after a long ride. This horse was famous in the family for its recalcitrance; only the elder Fernández knew how to handle it. That was all Castro needed to hear. Eager to demonstrate his horsemanship, he asked his friend's father for permission to ride the horse. As the skeptical father looked on, Castro mounted the horse "as if it were nothing, as if the beast had been accustomed to him its whole life, but that's not all, he rode the rest of the afternoon, to the farthest paddocks and back as if to prove that he was capable of dominating that superb animal." The Jesuits praised Castro for his courage, the classmate said. "His fellow students took note."[27]

Castro did not just show off at the Fernández house. Those who have entertained a busload of young boys know how rewarding (and how rare) it is when one of the boys engages an elder host. Castro did so at her house, René's mother remembered. "None of the boys would have anything to do with me, except Fidel and one other boy, who were always the most dear." René's sister concurred. "Truly, he was very sweet to Mama. While the others were roughhousing, Fidel entertained Mama in the kitchen." A teacher at Dolores confirmed Castro's generosity to those at the margins. "At Dolores," math teacher José María Patac recalled, "he befriended all the workers, talking to them constantly."[28] Castro stuck out in other ways, René Fernández reported. With an eye for detail and ingenuity, he was mesmerized by the family's dining room table, for instance, which had been handmade by René's father. Comprised of two immense circular pieces of wood, one inlaid within the other table rotated like a Lazy Susan, thus enabling diners to serve themselves without bothering their fellow eaters. Attention to detail was "just another characteristic that he had."[29]

Though René Fernández never anticipated Castro rising to the presidency of Cuba, he was not surprised that Castro ended up in politics. In junior high school, Castro was a natural leader, winning over peers not by virtue of organization or planning or conscious effort, at this stage, but on account of his natural gifts, which included "his way of treating others." Castro never waited around for others to do something. He "always took the initiative," Fernández explains, "inventing or planning something, and then, logically, we would follow him."[30]

Like many willful, confident kids, Castro was often the subject of unwanted attention. His blessedly meticulous penmanship is one result of this. He credits teachers at La Salle and Dolores for the good form. At Dolores, students who acted out were made to write sentences during recess: *I will not talk or misbehave in class. I promise to respect my superiors*. Recess detention was also the secret to Castro's preternatural capability with sums, or so he said. Long division problems were the favored sanction of a teacher named Salgueiro, who gave the boys "numbers to divide, with six figures in the dividend and three in the divisor, generally with twenty problems per punishment."

Salgueiro was a special case. Years later, Castro could still conjure his booming voice, "carrying out his ruthless punishment on the boys." Short and ill-tempered, Salgueiro strutted about the school like a peacock, proud of the terror he inspired. Naturally, the boys reciprocated by tormenting him. One semester, the Castro brothers returned to school from Birán with a parrot, a gift for another prefect who loved animals. By chance, the prefect placed the parrot in a cage in a little garden next to the classroom where "Salgueiro the terrible" ruled. Castro taught the parrot how to talk, not just idle nonsense, but to mimic Salgueiro himself: "Salgueiro, twenty times! Salgueiro, twenty times!" the parrot cried to the boys' delight. Faced with the choice of losing Salgueiro or the parrot, Dolores authorities "granted the bird asylum," relocating it to a convent in San José, where it dutifully learned to recite the Lord's Prayer.[31]

The Jesuits' discipline and attention to details fostered a stable environment in which Castro could settle down. Kids who aspired to a bachelor's degree took an exam in seventh grade known as *Ingreso* (Entry), sometimes *Preparatorio* (Preparation). The thirteen-year-old Castro passed his entrance exam uneventfully in June 1940. Entering the baccalaureate raised the stakes of a boy's education, with the expectation that from there he would go on to the university and ultimately to a position of national leadership. The bachelor's degree consists of five years of coursework. In his first year, eighth grade, Castro performed satisfactorily. He struggled in Math, uncharacteristically, while doing fine in Geography, History of the Americas, Spanish, English, and Physical Education. The next year, his last at Dolores, he began to stand out, particularly in Geography and Modern and Contemporary History, subjects which would remain dear to him throughout his life. He did well in Math this time, as well as in Spanish, English, and Anatomy, Physiology, and Hygiene, the course for which he had to scour Cuban libraries to find the missing pages of the anatomy text.[32]

To his immense satisfaction, Castro spent the summers between these academic years at home in Birán. He was the first person from either side of the family to qualify for the baccalaureate, an accomplishment that bestowed a certain honor at Finca Manacas. Though he was still expected to help out in the office, he was granted considerable latitude, and it was during these summers that he came to appreciate the solitude and serenity of the high country above Mayarí. But Castro's time on horseback was not totally self-indulgent. In 1940, his half-brother Pedro Emilio, to whom he would remain very close, ran for local political office as a representative of the new Opposition Front. Nineteen forty was a significant year in Cuban politics. The U.S.-led overthrow of the Grau-Guiteras government in January 1934 ushered in six years of political instability, in which six different presidents struggled unsuccessfully to address rising social discontent, often turning to Batista's army to impose the order that they could not achieve.[33]

By the end of the decade, Cubans, who saw eye to eye about virtually nothing, agreed to call a constitutional convention. In February 1940, a Constitutional Assembly opened in the capital, with representatives from across the political spectrum. Few expected the assembly to overcome the widespread divisions. The resulting 1940 Constitution was a pleasant surprise. It granted universal suffrage and curbed executive authority. It codified civil liberties, elevated the power of the judiciary, and made judges the final arbiter of electoral disputes. It provided a framework for free and fair elections. Though the new constitution was far from perfect (it lacked enabling mechanisms, making it more aspirational than practicable in the end), it was nevertheless regarded as a model in Latin America and around the world, reflecting the vision of a citizenry committed to the rule of law, open to compromise, tolerant of differences, and dedicated to the common good. Hypocrisy, someone said, is a sign of strength not weakness; only a people concerned about what is right can be criticized for falling short. Individuals and individual governments might fail, but for the first time in its history, Cuba had a self-made constitution to steer by.

In July 1940, Cubans went to the polls to elect the first president and Congress under their new constitution. One of the candidates in the presidential election was the man behind the preceding years of civil authoritarianism, Colonel Fulgencio Batista. Though this election is said to have been cleaner than previous contests, it was not untainted, as the experience of Castro's half-brother Pedro Emilio suggests. A political novice, Pedro Emilio lacked the support network that elevated his father's friend Fidel Pino Santos into office. As a result, Pedro Emilio had to turn for help wherever he could find it, including his young half-brother. When Castro returned to Birán for vacation in summer 1940, Pedro Emilio furnished him with a stout horse and a stern command to visit all the households on the plantation and emphasize the importance of the upcoming election. This included teaching the peasants how to vote, literally how to cast a ballot for their choice instead of the opposition candidate.[34]

The peasants were sparsely scattered, the weather scorching hot. Castro recalled long, tedious days on horseback. "I visited hundreds of campesinos," he said, most if not all of them ready to vote for a son of Don Ángel. If only they had been allowed. At the three polling places on or adjacent to the Castro farm, Batista's soldiers turned up on election day to garner votes, in some cases preventing citizens from casting votes at all. Castro's half-brother lost his election by eighty-two votes; between five and six hundred locals were said to have been prevented from voting.[35]

Castro went home for the summer between ninth and tenth grade and did not return to Dolores. Instead, he moved on to Havana to attend the country's most prestigious school, Colegio de Belén. Characteristically, looking back on the switch years later, Castro told an interviewer that the choice was entirely his; he had long heard of Belén, was intrigued by its reputation, and informed his parents of his decision. They were duly "enchanted," he said, and the rest is history. The world according to Castro. *I decided and my word was done.*[36]

Is there another explanation? Critics credit a lost fight with pushing Castro out the door at Dolores. But that seems to contradict everything his schoolmates suggest about the boy before and after. Castro's record as a quitter is thin. More likely, a conversation between his parents and Fidel Pino Santos altered his fate. Had his parents dreamed of sending their kids to school in Havana? Had Pino Santos twisted Ángel's arm? The historical record does not say and we will probably never know.[37]

Havana's size and human density astounded the easterner. Castro was met by his namesake and "pseudo godfather," as he put it, Fidel Pino Santos, now a representative in Congress. Pino Santos had promised Ángel and Lina that he would look after their son. Castro could not wait to escape his clutches. First, they toured the city, cruising by the new Capitolio and Presidential Palace, both a product of Machado's public works largess, both sparkling after a late-summer monsoon. Down the Prado they continued, out onto the Malecón, the magnificent seawall built by the North Americans at the beginning of the century. Santiago de Cuba sits well up its eponymous bay, and it has nothing to rival the tempest-tossed Malecón, seemingly all that saves Havana from being washed out to sea. After stopping for a quick drink at Pino Santos's Vedado home, Castro arrived at school with his heart in his throat. "I was a guajirito," he remembered, a peasant, "my new classmates savvy and world tested."[38]

Colegio de Belén, long since relocated to Miami, was situated in the eastern suburb of Marianao, a thirty-minute bus ride from downtown Havana. There, in 1925, the Society of Jesus opened what Cubans would come to know as the Palace of Education, a $1.5 million improvement on the original school founded in 1854 in the heart of the Old City. One can only imagine Castro's amazement as Pino Santos turned left off 41st Avenue onto 66th Street, the school's ornate pedestrian bridge and four-story columned facade looming over him. From the front the school appears more grand than elegant, its outside walls a reflection of the contemporary monumental state-building style. Walking through the school's magnificent bronze doors, decorated with paintings of the Last Supper,

Spanish conquest, and other Jesuit iconography, Castro would have discovered that the building's virtues lie within, its monumentality yielding to a combination of medieval fancy and youthful folly. Floor after floor of magnificently tiled cloisters rise from manicured courtyards dedicated to meditation, basketball, and play. Belén comprised both primary and secondary schools. Its simple, gridlike layout (four large cloisters attached in the middle) allowed for segregation by grade when necessary, while making school-wide convocations easy.

Now the Instituto Técnico Militar, the building's public spaces are especially impressive. School officials looking to convene the one-thousand-plus student body might choose from a handsome dining room, a plush theater, any one of the four courtyards, or the school chapel, such is the building's embarrassment of riches. Chapel seems too humble a name for the school's place of worship. The large nave is flanked by fluted Ionic columns, between which hang Arts-and-Crafts-style chandeliers, curiously at home amid the classical motif. The central and radiating aisles are ornately tiled. A generous second floor gallery accommodates overflow students, who might peek out from rows of square-shaped Corinthian columns. A large apse envelops an altar separated from the nave by an intricately carved marble rail. Over the apse looms a vast fresco that includes the Virgin and Child, Spanish conquerors, humble priests, and an African slave being hoisted to his feet by an earnest abolitionist. There are no Indians in sight. Alabaster bowls, parquet floors—truly the chapel has it all. The coffered ceiling is surely the highlight. Gold-plated flowers burst from a turquoise background surrounded by meticulously carved woodwork.

And that is only the chapel. Never mind for now the indoor swimming pool, billiard hall, and observatory. In erecting their new home, the Jesuits intended to make a statement. A statement they made. More than lucky, students at Belén were spoiled rotten at a time when only one in twenty Cuban children got as far as secondary school. Belén was a launch pad, built by insiders for insiders dedicated to nothing so much as to ensure that the boys retained their place in the social hierarchy. How then would a newcomer, an outsider, do?

By age sixteen, Castro had come to cut quite some figure. If you have to resettle at this age, it helps to be tall, handsome, athletic, smart, independent, and resilient. Castro was all of these things and more. Entering Belén, he had lost the roundness in his face that distinguished him at Dolores (and which he would later recover). He had a strong jawline, full lips, wide nose, heavy brow, and a dimple in the middle of his chin. He had brown hair that tended toward dirty blond at the end of a long summer in the sunshine. The boy that arrived for tenth grade was still rail thin. By twelfth grade he had become a veritable stallion. "We called him 'the horse,'" a Belén classmate remembered, such was his physical and athletic stature.[39]

The only thing worse than being dropped off at a new school is parents or guardians who overstay their welcome. "I was delighted to be free of my pseudo godfather," Castro remarked. The first night on the dorm made clear that he still lacked a few necessities. So the following day he hopped on a streetcar and headed into the center of the city, alighting at Parque Central, just off the Prado and across from the Capitolio. Castro walked from shop to shop, taking in the sights and picking up a belt, the school uniform, and a guayabera. During the chaos of opening days, the cultural chasm that distinguished the kid from rural Oriente from his cosmopolitan peers was impossible to miss. Castro wore his differences like the zoot suit he picked up in Santiago before departing for the capital, and it was not long before his classmates called him on it. "And what is *this*," they laughed, "a peasant?" Those boys were "members of the aristocracy," Castro explained years later, "the bourgeoisie, the oligarchy, proud of their customs and fashion. They had a good laugh at my expense."[40]

José Ignacio Rasco vividly remembered Castro's arrival at Belén in autumn 1942. Two years Castro's senior, Rasco grew up in Marianao, not far from the school, which he attended from first through twelfth grade. Rasco's father sold life insurance for a North American firm with offices in the capital. After graduation Rasco continued on to the University of Havana, where Castro joined him two years later. At the university, Rasco studied law, eventually opening his own firm, before ultimately returning to Belén as a schoolteacher. Rasco was a true believer—in Christianity, in private religious education, in the benefit of U.S. influence in Cuba, in class distinctions, in the status quo. As adults, Rasco and Castro could not have been more different. Rasco spent the Revolution on the sidelines, departing for the United States in 1960.[41]

The two boys had many classes together. They shared an interest in sports and politics and the fate of Latin America. Like the kids at Dolores, Castro's new classmates were impressed by his memory. "He had the most prodigious memory I've ever seen in my life," Rasco remarked. "We'd ask him, Fidel, what does such and such a book say on such and such a page, and he'd answer exactly." In Belén, students took two parallel exams in each subject, one corresponding to what they had actually covered in the classroom, the other a standardized exam mandated by the Department of Education. Castro's memory helped him significantly on standardized exams, especially, Rasco said; Castro often passed such tests "with perfect scores."[42]

Socially, Castro was at once "extremely shy" and charismatic. Students threw themselves at him. Castro was ecumenical in his friendships, did not play favorites, and was "a sensitive reader" of people and social situations. He possessed "a psychological radar to know what people were thinking," to read their minds, "to penetrate people," Rasco said. Castro's memory played a role here. Rasco recalled an incident just after the Revolution when, on a trip to Uruguay, Castro ran into somebody at the airport that he hadn't seen in years. He remembered everything about the guy. At the same time, Castro seemed a little reticent upon first arriving at Belén, something Rasco found "very curious." When other kids would argue about sports or politics, Castro held back, never really mixing it up with classmates until his senior year, by which time Rasco had moved on to the university.[43]

Like kids his age, Castro was more interested in what went on outside of class than in. Having entered Belén little interested in books and literature, he left the school a "fanatic reader." With women, Castro betrayed "panic-like fear." Infatuated by a girl from the local neighborhood in Marianao, Castro asked his friend for advice about how to talk to her. Tell her you like her and want to go out with her, Rasco advised. Castro did so and was summarily rejected. Rasco confirms the Dolores boys' accounts of Castro as a hard worker on causes that compelled him, recalling an audition for an "oratory academy" taught by a Jesuit father named Rubinos. To be admitted to Rubinos's class, each student was required to make a ten-minute speech, without notes. Rasco remembered Castro almost wetting his pants. "He was nervous, his legs were shaking. He was tremendously shy." Castro won admission to the class.[44]

Rasco reported that Castro expected to be the best at everything he tried his hand at. "He wanted to be champion in pingpong! But I was. The one thing he couldn't succeed in was pole vault; he was too big. I was champion pole-vaulter because I was very thin. I used to tease him, saying 'you know why you can't polevault? Because it's the only sport women have never done.' It used to drive him crazy." Rasco, whose egotism seems to have rivaled Castro's, remembers an incident on the baseball field that speaks to Castro's perseverance. "He wanted to be a champion pitcher, like me, but he had a problem throwing. So he would practice from dawn until dusk on one of the school's diamonds. When the catcher got tired and left, FC would throw the ball against a wall and continue practicing all alone."[45]

———

The Belén curriculum was a mixed bag, which Castro later criticized with increasing vehemence. In 1985, he described Belén as "a wonderful school," some of whose teachers "were highly trained scientists . . . very knowledgeable in physics, chemistry, mathematics, and literature." Convention has it that Castro never paid much attention in class, completing his coursework on his own on the eve of his exams. Photographs from Belén contradict this. In one image, a group of juniors are scattered around a bench in a physics laboratory, examining the conductivity of liquid. Some of the boys appear a little distracted; Castro focuses laserlike on the task at hand, as if relieved to be free from the rote learning that characterized Belén's history, religion, and language classes. The image confirms the good fortune of the Belén boys, the lab as beautiful as it is well-equipped, with elegant wood paneling and handsome shelves stocked with beakers, scales, mirrors, and stoves. (See Insert 1, Photo 13.)

Belén was not entirely to blame for clinging to recitation and memorization in its language and liberal-arts curriculum. The Commission on Cuban Affairs blamed U.S. educational orthodoxy introduced at the turn of the century for inhibiting experienced-based learning. By the time Castro showed up in autumn 1942, elite private schools like Belén were hamstrung by reforms written into the 1940 Constitution, which mandated that they comply with the niggling national teaching standards (even deploying public school proctors to oversee baccalaureate and other qualifying exams). Standardized tests put a brake on innovation in Belén's classrooms, forcing teachers to emphasize content over analysis and quantity over quality, turning students into receptacles. Still, the experience at Belén was not entirely oppressive, and Castro emerged from its gilded halls a forceful and confident debater.

It is often noted that the Castro home in Birán had everything—post office, telegraph office, bar, inn, company store, primary school, cockfighting ring, dairy, apiary, and bakery, but notably not a church. Absent a local church, and despite his mother's deep faith, Castro never came to appreciate the tranquillity and repetition of simple religious practice. He bridled at what he deemed to be the contrivance and even coerciveness of religious education. "Every day, we had the same ritual," he complained; "it was quite mechanical . . . repeating the same prayers over and over, saying the Hail Mary and Our Father mechanically, had no positive effect." The inability of a person so intuitive to recognize the role of ritual in promoting solidarity is striking. The sights, sounds, smells, tastes, and texture of church—the soft light, musty cushions, burning candles, prayerful murmurs, exotic verses, enchanting music, sour wine— left a budding revolutionary cold.[46]

Despite their differences, Castro and the Jesuits agreed that a healthy body was a key ingredient to a sound mind. Castro distinguished himself on Belén's athletic fields, as Rasco attests. But he was nowhere more contented than in the mountains. Compared to the Sierra Maestra or his native Sierra Cristal, the mountains of Pinar del Río, in western Cuba, and in Matanzas, to the east, seem small and insignificant. But one can lose one's way, get sucked down a river, or break a leg. Castro, as we have seen, claims never to have benefited from the give-and-take of a mentor. After Emiliana Danger, Amando Llorente, a pre-ordained priest at Belén, was the next closest miss. At Belén, he and Castro came to know each other well thanks to their shared passion for the woods.

Settling in at Belén, Castro found himself drawn to Llorente, a priest in training not so much older than his charges who was able to let his guard down with the boys. Castro could read a river, follow a trail, navigate a range of mountains, and Llorente and his fellow teachers soon put their trust in him. The teachers made him "Explorer General," a position roughly equivalent to an Eagle Scout. Photographs from these trips reveal a supremely confident Castro clad in khaki pants and shirt, boots with chaps, pith helmet atop his head. (See Insert 1, Photo 16.) Eventually, his teachers allowed him to lead excursions into the western mountains. Some of these trips lasted longer than expected, causing consternation among school authorities. Some required quick thinking and nimble footwork to avoid cresting rivers and flash floods. In a few cases, Castro is said to have gotten his teachers out of trouble, fording flooded rivers to lead a group to safety. The Jesuits admired Castro's competence and audacity. His classmates, scions of the Cuban elite, accustomed to the streets of the capital, noticed their teachers' noticing. Castro's prowess in the mountains won him recognition from Llorente and his colleagues in the school yearbook his senior year.[47]

Three years at Belén transformed Castro from a reticent peasant into a confident, self-assured young man. He left the school just before his nineteenth birthday, and photographs from his senior year suggest he had become comfortable there. One image reveals ten young men, all seniors, posing on a terrace in one of the school's courtyards. Seven of this fortunate cast sprawl casually on two benches. Three others stand behind, arms draped naturally over their friends' shoulders. The school day is over. The jackets have come off. Some of the boys have stripped down to T-shirts. The gabardine pants and cap-toe oxfords are the give-away. Privilege, thy name is Belén. The boys are well cropped, closely shaved, and simply beautiful. Castro is one of the standers. He appears a little darker than the others, his clothes perhaps a little less expensive. But he is no less at home in the photograph than they, no less confident, defying claims he did not belong. (See Insert 1, Photo 14.)

There are other photographs—from the football pitch, from the classroom, from a reception for a Putumayo Indian visiting from Colombia—confirming Castro's social status. In these photos, Castro is impossible to miss, tall, thin, chiseled, at once serious and at ease. Where it matters, he is central, now occupying the focal point, now seated at the side of a teacher, in team photos among the tallest, and always closest to the front.

One of the most anticipated events of the Belén school year was the awarding of prizes to students in each of the four classes pursuing the bachelor's degree. In 1945, the year Castro graduated, prize night was organized as a "parliamentary debate" featuring six distinguished seniors (*preuniversitarios*), charged with defending private religious education from state meddling. In late March of that year, as the event took place, the Cuban Congress debated legislation to compel private schools to bring their curriculum in line with national sentiment rejecting falangism, fascism, and Nazism. Like Jesuit schools throughout the world, Belén sided with Franco in the Spanish Civil War, seeing communism, not fascism, as the existential threat—and regarding the law before the Cuban Congress as leftist. That year, Belén officials thought to exploit prize night, always covered by the press, as an opportunity to advance their ideological agenda.

Castro was one of several seniors selected to address an auditorium packed with the archbishop of Havana, members of Congress, government officials, and numerous other dignitaries and well-wishers. The task of defending the school from predatory lawmakers was divided among the speakers. Castro was given the job of comparing state intervention in private education from country to country, including Europe and Latin America. His contribution was more descriptive than prescriptive, but he won praise for responding with composure to the intervention of at least one powerful politician, Congressman Dorta Duque. Still, Castro's remarks were not universally admired. A journalist for the communist newspaper *Hoy* (uncertain if the speaker's name was "Fidel Casto or Casto Fidel?") castigated "the aspiring starlet" for swallowing hook, line, and sinker the propaganda of "the Totalitarians of Havana!"—a delightful taunt given the way history turned out. Perhaps the students could be forgiven, the writer allowed, for falling into their teachers' trap.[48]

Being selected as a prize night speaker was only one of several honors bestowed on Castro his senior year. When his mother, Lina Ruz, showed up at graduation to celebrate the first person on either side of the family to be awarded a bachelor's degree, she swelled with pride as her son was awarded valedictorian and athlete of the year. In the words of the school yearbook, Castro distinguished himself "by his love of the school and the enthusiasm with which he has defended its name in almost all the official sports of the school." At once "excellent and collegial," he had earned "the admiration and affection of all." Noting that he had opted to pursue a career in the law, school officials predicted that "he would fill the book of life with brilliant pages."[49]

───────────

Looking back on Castro's education from those heady days at the end of senior year, it is hard but to conclude that a country boy had come a long way since first being shunted off to Santiago in autumn 1934. Castro's ragged path through school suggests that love is not the only thing that money can't buy. It can't buy sage parenting, either. Though able to appreciate the value of a good education, and able to pay for it, Ángel and Lina Castro seemed to have no idea about the kind of support required for a first-generation student to compete with the children of Cuba's elite. At times the couple seemed naive, not questioning the motivation for their son's obstreperous behavior at La Salle, for instance; at times they seemed willfully blind, surrendering Castro and his sister Angela to the Feliús with not the least idea about what they were in for.

Much of this is understandable, given Ángel's and Lina's own upbringing. But that does not make things easier on a young boy. Castro insists that he felt no ill-will toward his parents or his various hosts. His impetuousness and his willingness to deceive his elders suggests otherwise. This, too, is understandable, perhaps. The point is that this period left a mark. The young man who emerged from Belén in the spring of 1945 was both accustomed to going it alone and yet eager to be accepted. Years later, he would appear solipsistic, overconfident, and stubborn at times, conciliatory and apologetic at others. Looking on the bright side, his school days also left him confident, motivated, intellectually curious, and, above all, resilient.

A young man from his family background with his upbringing and education was bound to make mistakes and unlikely to forge a conventional path through life. But he would be hard to keep down and was developing the skills and strength to right and defend himself.

chapter four

QUIXOTIC
(IN THE FINEST SENSE)

A t *Belén they called him* "King of the Curve," his loop-
ing breaking ball notorious for making fools of right-
handed batters. But on a seasonable Saturday afternoon
in late November 1946, Castro's control eluded him, and Los
Comerciales bounded to a four-run lead over El Derecho halfway
through the second inning. Officially, there was not much at stake
besides bragging rights in this tilt between the law and the business school students at manicured University Stadium. But in the
hard-charging world of the University of Havana, bragging rights
mattered, and the would-be lawyers liked to think of themselves
as kings of the Hill. Castro did not contribute much at the plate
that day, going 0–4. He recovered his stuff in the middle innings,
but it was too little too late, and Los Comerciales advanced to the
Intramural Championship, 5–4. In all, this was a day to forget for a
losing pitcher: four strikeouts, seven walks, one put-out, two assists,

an error, hitless at bat. It was enough to make an aspiring athlete go into politics.[1]

In fact, politics may have had something to do with Castro's performance at University Stadium that day. Baseball was never Castro's first love. That was soccer and basketball. Arriving at the university in autumn 1945, Castro expected to pick up where he had left off at Belén, excelling at virtually everything he tried his hand at. When stiff competition prevented him from succeeding to his accustomed standard, he committed himself to student government. Even here he did not meet with unqualified success, never winning election to the presidency of the Law School, despite later assertions to the contrary. Still, the very week he got shelled by Los Comerciales, Castro was selected by his peers to speak at ceremonies commemorating eight medical students executed by Spanish authorities on November 27, 1871, during the Ten Years War of Independence. This was to be his national debut, and Castro determined to make the most of it.

Entering the University of Havana the previous autumn, Castro found himself in yet another large and unfamiliar environment. In middle and high school, the kids who generally stood out were athletes, a realm to which Castro was fitted by nature and age to succeed. At the university, student politics was the path to distinction. Student leaders commanded considerable attention and wielded real political power, a legacy of both the autonomy written into the university's charter and its monopoly on educating the country's future leaders. With much at stake, university politics did not lend itself to Castro's act-now, ask-questions-later manner of being in the world, and this nearly got him killed. Over time, he learned to navigate the complex network of allegiances atop University Hill, never shying away from conflict, exactly, but tempering his impulsiveness with growing political sensibility. And, above all, cultivating the right allies.

The purpose of the upcoming commemoration of the murdered medical students was to call attention to government corruption and persuade Cuban citizens to rededicate themselves to the dream of Cuba Libre—a Cuba free and independent of foreign rule. In July 1944, Ramón Grau, the former leader of the 1933 revolutionary government now turned mainstream politician, defeated the handpicked successor of outgoing President Fulgencio Batista in the presidential election. In the run-up to the election, Grau promised to curb the military's role in Cuban life and raise the standard of living throughout the country. His candidacy succeeded thanks in part to the work of former friends and associates from the anti-Machado coalition of the early 1930s, who seemed to take Grau's promises at face value.

The Grau who came into office in November 1944 retained few of the good and most of the debilitating traits of the revolutionary figurehead of a decade earlier. Grau had never had much of an appetite for conflict (his reluctance to confront Batista's treachery in October 1933 changed the course of Cuban history). Elevated to power a second time, Grau proved at once self-interested and aloof, doling out important ministries to the men who had helped him get elected, while turning a blind eye to their mendacity. Showcase in point was Minister of Education José Manuel Alemán, who—with Batista ensconced in Daytona Beach, Florida, and the army looking out for its own good—exercised power throughout the country via the so-called "action groups" spawned by the anti-Machado struggle, now become outright criminal gangs. Batista's rise and decade-plus monopoly on the use of force had driven these groups underground. With Grau's blessing, the action groups reemerged in Cuban society like Uzi-bearing rats, littering the capital with mutilated corpses, while raiding the treasury of every penny they could get their hands on. In 1947 alone, this uncivil war claimed the lives of sixty-four people, injuring dozens more.[2]

"Gangsters exist for political reasons," Congressman Rolando Masferrer told his colleagues that year. "Almost all political bosses

arm their groups and use them for electoral purposes." It was simply unrealistic, Masferrer observed, "to ask favors of them one day
and persecute them the next."[3] The congressman knew whereof
he spoke. Founder of one of the most notorious gangs, the Movimiento Socialista Revolucionario (MSR), Masferrer benefited from
the quid pro quo as much as anybody. He was not about to let idealistic university students spoil the feeding frenzy.

By 1945, intimidation and the threat of violence hung like a pall
over the Escalinata, the grand staircase leading up to the University
of Havana and the epicenter of student activism. For over two centuries the nation's only institute of higher learning, the university
exerted outsized influence in Cuban politics and culture. Anybody
who aspired to leadership in Cuba went there. Since Julio Antonio
Mella and friends first formed the Federación Estudiantil Universitaria (FEU) back in 1922, university students had made life difficult
for Cuban governments from a favorable perch atop University Hill.
It was university students who galvanized the opposition to Machado and propelled the 1933 Revolution. Student divisiveness was
partly to blame for the Revolution's demise.[4]

In down times, the university presented great opportunity for
those with an entrepreneurial bent, as the action groups competed
with one another to manipulate and control not only course grades
and degrees, but also faculty and administrative appointments, including the campus police. The year 1940 closed with assassinations
mounting, with several professors gunned down simply for trying
to carry out their jobs. The faculty council, still nominally in charge
on the Hill, expelled the alleged perpetrators and disbanded the offending organizations. The violence did not abate. By 1945, the year
Castro arrived, the old factions had consolidated into new organizations, including Masferrer's MSR, which made its predecessors look
like weaklings.[5]

The only thing worse than a police force in the command of
a criminal gang is one split between warring factions. As befits a
country coming apart at the seams, the second highest-ranking

police office in Cuba (the National Police Academy) belonged to a member of MSR's bitter rival, the Unión Insurreccional Revolucionaria (UIR), which was committed to MSR's destruction. UIR was founded by Emilio Tro, a veteran of both the Spanish Civil War and World War II (when he fought with the Americans and was awarded a Purple Heart). Like Alemán, Tro was a friend of President Grau. Grau awarded Tro leadership over the Police Academy, his office just down the hall from his nemesis, Mario Salabarría, chief of the Bureau of Police Investigations.

If this alphabet soup of gangs, leaders, and assignments seems confusing, it should. Not much but name differentiated these gangs from one another ideologically (MSR leaned slightly to the left, UIR slightly to the right). They shared common characteristics (entitlement, ruthlessness) and common goals (money, influence). With little to distinguish them, much was at stake. The only thing an aspiring student could not do was go without protection from one or the other. "In those days," recalled Enrique Ovares, who arrived on the scene a year after Castro, and who led the FEU for three years (1947–49), "everybody went around armed. You carried a pistol not to hurt anybody but to ensure that you yourself were not hurt. I had one, everybody had one. That's the truth."[6]

————————————

Castro spent the summer between high school and college playing basketball on an elite team based at the Havana Yacht Club. It was there he met Enrique Ovares. The two hung out together, talking sports and movies. At this stage in their lives, Ovares recalled, neither paid much attention to politics. As an athlete, Castro stood out for "his constancy, tenacity, and dedication." He never missed a practice, Ovares said. "If told to shoot fifty shots, he shot a hundred."[7] Concentrating on sports, Castro was able to maintain some distance from MSR and company his freshman year.

Alfredo Guevara, a classmate and lifelong friend of Castro's, remembered running into him for the first time on Plaza Cadenas, a shady oasis just outside the entrance to the Law School, in autumn 1945. Guevara and Castro came from very different backgrounds. Born and raised in Havana, Guevara attended city schools, eventually rising to a leadership in the Instituto Segundo Enseñanza, a network of public secondary schools across the country. A self-described anarcho-syndicalist at the time, Guevara looked disdainfully on the spoiled rich kids from Belén and other private institutions. Learning of Castro's private school background, Guevara expected the worst. Castro took Guevara by surprise. He was hard to pin down, Guevara said, and seemed to be motivated less by ideology than by a sense of historical inheritance. "Castro drank deeply in the sources of the War of Independence," which is another way of saying that he knew his history.[8]

In college, Castro continued to pay more attention to extracurricular activities than to classwork. At the university, students were evaluated not by class participation or fulfillment of regular assignments, but by their performance on final exams. Class was "a waste of time," Castro told an interviewer. "In that period, I studied very little, by myself with books and notes." He showed more interest in electives (Cuban and world history, political science, and English and French literature) than in required courses (civil, criminal, administrative, constitutional, and property law, for example). He was famous for pulling off acceptable (occasionally outstanding) grades simply by sitting down with the assigned texts the night before his final exams. This proved effective practically speaking but did not prepare him for the give-and-take of politics. At a time when many young men and women learned to engage the opinions of peers and professors they did not agree with, Castro remained aloof from class discussions. "In those days, I came and went."[9]

In March of his freshman year, Castro ran for political office as a class delegate from Legal Anthropology. Candidates were not above campaigning, and a copy survives of Castro's first political solicitation. At the time, Castro lived at the Hotel Vedado, on the corner of 19th and M Streets, not far from the university. In meticulous penmanship on hotel stationery, he reached out to his fellow students with a few simple lines: "Esteemed friend," he wrote a classmate, "the Law School elections will be held on the morning of the 18th. I hope you will come out this day to help in the triumph of our slate, for which I would be very grateful. Affectionately, Fidel Castro."[10]

Ovares remembered Castro running a disciplined campaign. He was a natural politician, Ovares reported, with "dedication, size, popularity, political ideals; he was eloquent, and he had followers." Castro won that first election handily, a victory that immediately embroiled him in the MSR–UIR turf war that passed for student politics at the time. As competitive as he was politically ambitious, Castro was simultaneously attracted to and repelled by FEU president Manolo Castro, a member of MSR. On the one hand, Carlos Franqui recalled, Castro aspired to political leadership himself, hence envied Manolo Castro's success and popularity. On the other hand, Castro was allergic to arbitrary power, refusing to yield to anybody simply for the sake of it. This inevitably brought him into conflict with Manolo Castro, Masferrer, Salabarría, and other MSR enforcers. Castro remembered feeling exposed. "I was totally alone in the university," he later remarked, "absolutely alone, when, suddenly, in that electoral process, I confronted the mafia that dominated the university."[11]

———————

There is no record of how Castro was selected to represent the university at the commemoration of the murdered medical students. But it is hard to imagine that he could have been granted the honor without a nod from Manolo Castro. The last time he delivered a public address was at the Belén award ceremony the previous year, where he parroted his teachers' words about the inalienable right of private religious schools to adopt whatever curriculum they saw fit. If Manolo Castro expected Castro to hew to a party line this time, he was in for a surprise, as Castro delivered a blistering attack on the political patronage that allowed the likes of Manolo Castro to establish a virtual dictatorship over the university.

The commemoration of the student martyrs began at Colón Cemetery at nine o'clock on the morning of Wednesday, November 27, 1946. It ended twelve hours later in the magnificent Aula Magna (Great Hall) on University Hill. Castro was the last of three speakers to address the crowd at the Colón Cemetery. By the time he mounted the rostrum, he had overcome much of the shyness described by José Ignacio Rasco back at Belén. Still, public speaking did not come naturally to him, and Rasco remembers Castro camped out at the Rasco home in Marianao the week before the speech, writing draft after draft of his remarks and committing them to memory. Called on to pitch against Los Comerciales in the middle of this preparation, Castro consented, but he could be excused if his head was not one hundred percent in it.[12]

Castro began his national political debut by invoking the patron saint of Cuban independence, José Martí, a poet and critic of such intellectual breadth and amplitude that Cubans left, right, and center continue to claim him as their own. Invoking Martí, Castro established the ideological foundation of his work through the triumph of the Cuban Revolution: the people's duty to hold one another and their government accountable to a sovereign and independent Cuba committed to the well-being not just of its own people, but of Latin Americans in general. Over time, Castro would build on this foundation, moving from an emphasis on civil and political liberties to an emphasis on social rights (security, health care, education), but he never abandoned it. History mattered to him not as curiosity but as inspiration for contemporary political engagement. The point of "flying on the wings of memory to events that have galvanized students across generations," he told the Colón Cemetery crowd, was to wake the people from their slumber.[13]

The martyred medical students mattered on this day, Castro said, not simply because they had stood up to colonial oppression, but because they defended the people's right to education, which was

essential to "moral improvement." That right was in deep jeopardy
in contemporary Cuba thanks to President Grau turning over the
Education Department to a notorious crook (Alemán), who was
committed only to lining his own pockets. Just days earlier, Alemán
unleashed his private police force on the protesting staff of a rural
normal school who asked for nothing more than resources sufficient
to carry out their job ("helping peasants improve their standard of
living"). Where was the outrage? Castro demanded. Where were the
patriots ready to stand up and make things right?

These were strong words coming from a young student with
little or no political backing. Alemán had friends throughout the
university, and one can imagine Castro's audience shifting uneasily
in their seats. But Castro was just warming up. Bad as the violence
of Presidents Machado and Batista had been, that was nothing compared to the "cynicism" engendered by Grau administration de-
pravity. "Batista and Machado had murdered many Cubans," Castro
remarked; Grau was "killing hope itself." The president had campaigned on a platform that promised a merchant marine, a court of
auditors, a new national bank, administrative transparency, and agricultural and industrial development. Halfway through his term, not
a single one of those promises had come to pass, and yet Cubans did
not seem to notice. Castro challenged elected officials who retained
a sense of honor to join with the students to root out corruption,
or—like the martyred medical students celebrated that day—to die
trying. If the politicians failed to step forward, the students were
ready to go it alone, once again demonstrating that "the pure blood
of vital youth has been and will remain fertile."

Rasco said that Castro struck a chord with his audience that
day. Journalist José Pardo Llada characterized the speech as "more
Martían than the Apostle himself" (the Apostle was Martí's nickname). Castro himself was "very pleased" by how his speech came
off.[14] Others were less than pleased. Two weeks later, Castro was
involved in a shooting incident on the outskirts of the university—
the only episode in which critics and defenders agreed that he

participated. Curiously, this was also the only one for which he was not dragged before the police. Castro never spoke openly about his role in the violence. Government historians gloss over it. Castro's enemies exaggerate it, ignoring the context in which such violence occurred. To complicate things further, sources changed their accounts about such incidents depending on their perception of what the interviewer wanted to hear.

All of which is to say that we may never know for sure what happened on December 10, 1946, when a group of MSR members, including Castro, concealed on the grounds of the Medical School, shot fellow student Leonel Gómez in the back as he exited nearby University Stadium. Before enrolling in the university, Gómez had been president of the Secondary School Association, second in influence among aspiring student leaders only to the FEU itself. Gómez was a member of UIR and a rival of Manolo Castro. Manolo Castro believed that Gómez was getting ahead of himself and needed to be brought in line. Fidel Castro had some lessons of his own to learn. His Colón Cemetery speech received widespread press coverage, with a few papers carrying his remarks in their entirety. Neither MSR nor UIR could have been happy with it, and it is likely that Manolo Castro's people reminded Fidel Castro that if he was not with them he was against them. Castro promptly signed on with MSR.

Simply signing on with a gang did not guarantee its protection. Protection had to be earned and loyalty demonstrated by participating in the dirty work. Gómez was shot in the back of the shoulder. Another bystander was shot in the leg. Still others may have been injured. Nobody was killed, nobody arrested. With MSR pulling the trigger, the police investigative unit was never summoned, and it is not clear how many bullets were fired and who exactly did the shooting. Rafael Díaz-Balart, a friend and fellow law student at the time, said that Castro burst into his home that afternoon saying, "I just shot Leonel." Who else may have been involved, Diaz-Balart did not say.[15]

In retrospect, critics point to this episode as evidence that one of the world's most famous guerrillas could not shoot straight. That seems implausible given Castro's early introduction to firearms in Birán and raises the question of whether Castro, if it was indeed he who pulled the trigger, had purposely shot to injure rather than kill. Regardless, he soon recognized MSR for the trap that it was, eventually soliciting Emilio Tro for membership in UIR.[16] There he joined his friend and future nemesis Rafael Díaz-Balart (brother of Mirta, his wife to be), who also knew firsthand the difficult choices confronting university students in mid-century Cuba. Determined to escape "the spiral of violence," Díaz-Balart abandoned Cuba for Princeton University in summer 1947. "It was not so much that one would get murdered," he explained, "but that one had to kill in an organized way."[17]

It was not long before Castro's outspokenness attracted the attention of Grau's henchmen. In early January 1947, Castro and Díaz-Balart reconstituted the old Student Directory founded in 1927 after President Machado disbanded the FEU, and now meant to serve as an alternative to that discredited institution. A few weeks later, the new Directory launched its first broadside, with Castro's name emblazoned atop a manifesto signed by delegates from the thirteen university faculties. The manifesto recapitulated the form and content of Castro's Colón Cemetery address, balancing historical references with an urgent call to action. This time the target was not only President Grau's decision to seek a second term (an "astonishing travesty"), but the student-on-student violence that Castro himself had so recently been a part of. Benefiting from his relationship to Grau, Masferrer, and Salabarría, Manolo Castro may have been content to stand idly by as one university student after another fell victim to the mayhem, the manifesto remarked; the rest of the student body had had enough. A new generation of students stood ready to defend "the glorious flag" for which previous student martyrs had died. It was "better to die on one's feet than to live on one's knees."[18]

Manolo Castro's election as president of FEU in 1945 terminated a period of relative tranquillity in university politics that had held since 1942, when student protest helped unseat a discredited prime minister. Manolo Castro was reelected FEU president in 1946, despite the growing perception that he was indifferent to student interests. Poised for defeat the following year, he resigned his presidency to accept the cushy position of directorship general of sports in the Grau government. His resignation left Humberto Ruiz Leiro, a UIR loyalist, atop the FEU hierarchy, thereby ensuring a contentious 1947 election.[19]

In March 1947, Castro was elected class delegate a second time and was later selected vice president of the Law School. The next month, the Law School Executive Committee, of which Castro was a member, withdrew its support for newly elected Law School president Federico Marín, who, the Committee charged, had failed to carry out his mandate. Marín was a member of MSR. All but one of the students calling for his removal belonged to UIR. There could be no doubt, one newspaper put it, that Marín's "defenestration" was the result of gang rivalries. Whatever the cause, Marín's ouster meant that Castro, then vice president, became acting president of the Law School for the first and only time in his career.[20] Castro did not last long in office. With a UIR member atop the Law School masthead, UIR now held the deciding vote in the upcoming general election. Enter MSR heavy Mario Salabarría. A day into Castro's term in office, he and a few friends in the FEU hierarchy were picked up by the police, charged with carrying unlicensed weapons, and held in isolation as warrantless searches were carried out on their homes (Salabarría himself was among the arresting officers). Leiro was severely beaten. With no weapons on them, most of the group was released within hours. Castro was held for nearly three days, before vociferous protests by fellow students induced President Grau to secure him a hearing before the Urgency Court, which promptly exonerated him.

The episode began a long series of politicized run-ins between

Castro and the National Police all of which were resolved in Castro's favor. Critics point to these arrests as evidence of Castro's involvement in the gang violence that marked this era.This was hardly unique to him, as Ovares and Díaz-Balart attest. Moreover, these arrests by a corrupt regime's brazen partisans constitute proof of nothing. In the most recent case, city newspapers easily discerned the motivation behind the arrests.At the time Salabarría's men went into action, Leiro was leading his MSR rival in the balloting for FEU president ten votes to three.

Castro responded to Salabarría's ham-handed intervention in university affairs like a seasoned professional, exploiting favorable attention in the press. At the end of April, presidents of the thirteen faculties of the University of Havana issued another manifesto which appears to have come from Castro's pen.The arrests of the student leaders, the beating of Leiro, the warrantless searches all called to mind the lawless days of the Machado presidency, the manifesto stated.The "intervention of foreign agents" into student affairs created "a climate of insecurity, coercion, and violence" incompatible with the university's educational mission.With the integrity of the university at stake, the students vowed to press on with their criticism "until they had established in the FEU an empire of decency and propriety, as the majority of students desired." Castro signed the document as president of the Law School.[21]

This was his last act in that role.That same day, the University Council, comprised of senior faculty under the influence of MSR, reinstated the deposed Law School president, thus bringing Castro's brief presidency to an end.To the surprise of many, this action did not kill the impetus for reform.With the MSR and UIR presidential candidates deadlocked in the most recent poll, a new contender came to the fore, Castro's old friend, Enrique Ovares, who shared much of UIR's vision for the student government while lacking the stain of gang affiliation. In fact, *Prensa Libre* reported, Castro proved instrumental in elevating Ovares and arriving at a peaceful resolution. How long the comity would last, no one could say, but for a moment, anyway, the good of the university appeared to have taken precedence over established political interests. As if to ratify the current peace, FEU leaders agreed to convoke a Constitutional Assembly later that year to make the selection of its officers more democratic. Despite losing their respective presidencies, Castro and his friend Leiro proclaimed victory and celebrated these events like statesmen.[22]

In summer 1947, just as the gang violence reached its peak in Havana, idealistic young men across Cuba flocked to the eastern city of Holguín to enlist in an expeditionary force targeting Dominican dictator Rafael Trujillo. There they joined a group of Dominican exiles calling itself the Dominican Revolutionary Party, which was founded in Havana six years before by the writer Juan Bosch, among others. The outbreak of war in Europe forced the Dominicans to postpone their plans for a marine and aerial invasion. The Allied victory in World War II stoked the hopes of democratic reformers throughout the Western Hemisphere at a time when local governments were flush with cash (from inflated sugar prices) and arms (thanks to the U.S. wartime policy Lend-Lease, which distributed weapons to friendly countries in exchange for access to military bases). In short, the immediate postwar period was a good time to be looking for men, money, and munitions, and by summer 1947, Cuba was awash in soldiers of fortune and the contraband of war.

In theory, the operation known to posterity as Cayo Confites (after the bite-sized cay where things came to a dispiriting end) was privately orchestrated and privately funded. Cuba had ratified the Havana Convention (1928) and was poised to sign the Rio Pact, both of which committed signatories to respect the sovereignty of fellow nations. In fact, members of the Cuban government exercised an enormous role in funding and planning the expedition, even as a hapless President Grau buried his head in the sand. Education Secretary Alemán, for one, provided much of the expedition's funding with money leached from the education budget. MSR leaders Rolando Masferrer and Manolo Castro purchased airplanes, landing craft, and ammunition, and recruited foot soldiers. Bosch and his fellow Dominicans did the lion's share of the early work. But the mission was delayed, and the Dominicans' purses ran dry, leaving Alemán, Masferrer, and Manolo Castro to assume an ever-expanding role, so that by the end Bosch was said to have felt like their prisoner.

The role of Alemán, Masferrer, and Manolo Castro in a mission to establish constitutional democracy in the Dominican Republic seems curious at first glance. What interest did these sowers of mayhem have in promoting democracy? Well, Masferrer, for one, had started out as a leftist proponent of the people's will and actively opposed the Machado dictatorship. His and Manolo Castro's antipathy toward Trujillo was sincere and long lasting. But so, too, was their thirst for power. A U.S. intelligence report looking back on the debacle in October 1947 confirms their motivation. Their participation "can only finally be explained in terms of gross self-seeking," U.S. ambassador Henry Norweb wrote Secretary of State George Marshall. The Cuban ministers "were to be given properties" in the Dominican Republic, "another was to be a collector of customs, another was to be Minister of Finance." A joke circulated among U.S. consular officers that at one point there were no fewer than twelve people on Cayo Confites "who expected to be the next President of the Dominican Republic," by no means all of them Dominican.[23]

Fidel Castro joined the expedition at its training ground at Instituto Politécnico in Holguín that July. Instinctively, he leaned toward the Dominicans who answered to Bosch, thus gaining his protection. Among the Dominicans Castro befriended was a daring and charismatic ship's captain named Ramón Mejías del Castillo, known by the nickname Pichirilo, whose experience would later come in handy.[24] Castro's participation in the expedition fit right in with his dreams for Cuba and veneration of Martí. From the outset of his political activism, Castro saw the fight for self-determination and social justice in Cuba as part of a hemispheric movement. In November 1946, ten days before his Colón Cemetery debut, the newspaper *Juventud Rebelde* noted the intervention of an apparently unknown law student named Fidel Castro at a ceremony in support of the student-led Czech resistance. Castro shared the floor at this event with the current Law School president and a delegate to the First Global Congress of Students to be held in Prague. The following year, Castro presided over the establishment of the student-led Cuban Committee for the Liberation of the Dominican Republic.[25] In short, Cayo Confites was not a one-time-only event for him. To the surprise of some (and consternation of many), he always tied his work in Cuba to liberation projects elsewhere.[26]

Castro's sister Juanita recalls the day her parents learned that their son had enlisted in Cayo Confites. Ángel, who had been talking to a friend in his office, entered the kitchen stricken. "I have just learned that Fidel has joined an expedition of Dominicans and Cubans intending to overthrow the dictator Rafael Leónidas Trujillo," he announced. Sure that this would be the end of Fidel, he asked Lina to visit the training camp and talk some sense into him. Lina, typically guarded, broke down in the company of her daughters. "She was dying of sadness," Juanita reports. By supper that night, Lina had recovered her resolve. "There's nothing to do but go to Cayo Confites," she declared, departing for the camp early the next day.[27]

Accompanied by Juanita and Enma, Lina made for Preston, the United Fruit port on the Bay of Nipe, where they boarded a steamer for the 150-mile trip up the coast. Arriving at Cayo Confites, Lina met a motley collection of men from across the Caribbean and Cuba, including well-heeled members of MSR. Lina went off to find Fidel. Once found, he was not easy to persuade. "I can't pull out," he told his mother. "To overthrow Trujillo is a democratic mission, and if the price is life, then all of us here are ready to pay it." Resisting further entreaties, Castro escorted his family off the cay, pleading with his mother not to cry. "Have faith," he urged; "everything will end well and nothing bad will happen."[28]

The expedition was a poorly kept secret. As early as January 1947, U.S. intelligence officials picked up noise of an impending anti-Trujillo conspiracy to be launched from Cuba. In February, the FBI trailed cash-laden Dominicans hunting for weapons in New York City. By July, U.S. officials knew that an international brigade of soldiers of fortune was assembling outside Holguín. At the end of that month, they learned of a fleet of six airplanes bound for Cuba from the United States. U.S. ambassador Norweb made repeated inquiries of Cuba's foreign minister as to what was going on. His counterpart replied just as repeatedly that nothing was going on at all. At the end of July, two Puerto Rican recruits "escaped" from the expedition and took their story to *The Miami Herald*. The *Herald's* subsequent article on the impending invasion exposed the Cuban denials as bald-faced lies. Meanwhile, the Trujillo government had been condemning the forces amassing in Cuba for weeks, pressuring the U.S. government to bring the "communist" machinations to a halt.[29]

Trujillo was not the only one becoming increasingly alarmed. The existence on Cuban soil of a heavily armed and well-trained invasion force, some 1,500 strong, did not sit well with Cuban Army Chief of Staff Genovevo Pérez Dámera. Though ostensibly bound for the Dominican Republic, such a force could readily be deployed against the Cuban government itself. Pressured on all sides, and with Trujillo threatening to invade the country, Grau gave the expeditionaries until the end of July to move out. On July 29, the force departed Holguín for the port of Antilla, located along the northern shore of the Bay of Nipe. On August 11, the force abandoned the mainland for Cayo Confites, an oversized sandbar 150 miles up the coast. For forty-nine torturous days, the expeditionaries languished on the mosquito-infested cay, in blistering sun, with little to eat, nowhere suitable to sleep, and no firm date of departure.

Through August and into September Grau remained at loggerheads with his conscience about the wisdom of the venture. His choice of whether to pull the plug or sign off on the expedition was made more difficult by an escalation of gang warfare in the capital. As if MSR was not busy enough trying to launch an amphibious assault on a foreign country, its agents tried to assassinate Emilio Tro in early September. In response, Tro's agents assassinated Rafael Ávila, chief of the Health Ministry Police and an MSR loyalist. In the ensuing tit for tat, Salabarría ordered Tro's arrest. But rather than arresting Tro, the police attacked the UIR chief and a fellow member, Antonio Morín Dopico, at Dopico's house in the Havana suburb of Marianao. As Tro and Dopico enjoyed a sumptuous lunch surrounded by their families, three police cars pulled up and unloaded on the house. A three-hour gunfight ensued in which Tro and five others, including Dopico's wife, were killed. The couple's infant child was shot and rushed to the hospital.

The astonishing spectacle was broadcast live on Cuban radio. It came to an end only after a diffident Grau dispatched the army. At the time of the incident, Army Chief of Staff Genovevo was in Washington, D.C., where U.S. officials lectured him about the sovereignty of other nations. Upon hearing news of what became known as the Orfila Massacre (after the neighborhood in Marianao), Genovevo returned to Havana, ordered Salabarría's arrest, and confiscated more than a dozen trucks laden with guns, ammunition, and other contraband from a farm belonging to Education Minister Alemán. Still unwilling to acknowledge what was happening just off the coast, Grau claimed that the seized weapons were part of a foiled coup.

By the end of September, with its disinformation campaign finally discredited, the Grau administration pulled its support for the Dominican invasion. U.S. pilots, poised to play a supporting role in the expedition, returned home. On Cayo Confites, the Cuban leaders of the expedition resolved to take things into their own hands. They loaded two transports, *Fantasma* and *Maceo*, and prepared to depart for the Dominican Republic. Curiously, *Fantasma*, with Masferrer aboard, headed west toward Havana rather than east in the direction of the intended target. Meawnhile, *Maceo* took off in the other direction after leaving behind some men who wanted out. With the force split and its numbers radically reduced, *Maceo* came to a halt off Nipe Bay, where the Dominicans on board considered their options. Castro and Pichirilo urged Maderne and Bosch to press on. Maderne and Bosch recognized that their reduced force had no chance of a success without air support.

Intercepted by the Cuban Navy on the afternoon of September 21, *Maceo* and *Fantasma* were escorted to the port of Antilla before being taken to Havana the next day. Castro anticipated that the expedition's demise would end the uneasy truce that prevailed among its members. A consistent critic of the Grau government, he was not looking forward to falling into its clutches when the boats arrived in Havana. As *Maceo*, escorted by the Cuban Navy, made its way through the channel at Antilla, it became obscured from its naval escort by a small island. At this point, Pichirilo, aware of Castro's desire to get away, lowered a dinghy into the water with Castro and three others aboard. Spotted by a navy patrol boat, the dinghy made frantically for the Cuban coast. The helmsman warned the passengers that they were about to be intercepted, prompting Castro to plunge into the water some 250 meters from shore. He was joined by two men from the dinghy, all of them fully dressed and laden with arms. "I hit the water and began to sink," Castro said. He did better after releasing one of two Thompson machine guns he was carrying. Worried about shots from above them and sharks below, the three men swam ashore at Cayo Saité, then spent the next several hours dodging government soldiers, before finally splitting up. Castro, familiar with the general area, recovered his bearings and struck out on foot for Birán, eventually hitching a ride in a passing car and arriving home just as the cock began to crow.[30]

The U.S. response to the failed operation makes for interesting reading in light of the nation's history of intervention in Cuba and elsewhere. U.S. intelligence officials had long cast a dark eye on countries intervening in one another's affairs—so long as the offending party was not the United States itself. From first getting word of Dominican exiles amassing in Holguín, the U.S. State Department dismissed the plan as "quixotic." U.S. diplomatic cables were full of self-serving comparisons between the "American and Latin-American mind," with the former described as practical, orderly, and sensible, and the latter impulsive, unpredictable, and irrational. Ignoring the U.S. government's notorious coddling of dictators, U.S. officials attributed the region's political volatility to "an ingrained fetish of revolution."[31]

Castro drew two critical lessons from the aborted mission: first, that secrecy was paramount in such operations; second, that for expeditions such as this you had to choose your own people. The mission to overthrow Trujillo was one of the worst-kept secrets in history, he said. Masferrer's recruiters strode through Havana plucking people off the streets who had no military experience, no knowledge of camp life, no ideological commitment to the cause. As a result, when things dragged on in August and September—amid scarce food, incessant rain, and pestilential insects—the recruits had no resources to draw on, becoming, alternately, morose, recalcitrant, and volatile. Never had such a mission been constructed of men "less apt." Years later, recruiting men and women for his own campaigns, Castro kept the lesson of Cayo Confites close at hand, personally overseeing (when not, indeed, conducting) the recruiting, and keeping his cards so close to his chest that his forces often did not know where they were headed until arriving at their destination.[32]

Participation in Cayo Confites precluded Castro from taking exams and fulfilling end-of-year requirements. It also prevented him from matriculating at the university in academic year 1947–48. Students could still enlist in courses and take exams without attending classes (as "free" rather than "regular" students), but they could not be elected to student government. And so Castro's career in university politics came to an end, just as his influence as a student leader mounted. In the days ahead, Castro exerted himself as a leader of a new generation of student and youth activists ready to take on corruption, colonialism, and dictatorship—not only in Cuba but throughout Latin America. He had not completely extricated himself from the thuggery that continued to dominate student life and Cuban politics through the triumph of the Cuban Revolution, but as his political reputation grew, he began to look for a way out of the gang warfare.[33]

Castro returned to the capital in early October 1947, just as a new controversy was brewing. In the aftermath of Cayo Confites and the Orfila Massacre, the Grau administration looked to burnish its tarnished reputation. October 10, Veterans' Day, was fast approaching and Interior Minister Alejo Cossío del Pino had the inspired idea of appropriating the Bell of Demajagua and transporting it from its home in Manzanillo to Havana for memorial services. Struck by Carlos Manuel de Céspedes on October 10, 1868, at the start of the Ten Years War, the bell became a symbol of independence and abolition as Céspedes recognized that there could be no overthrowing colonialism without eliminating the slavery that went with it. Céspedes's slaves won their liberty that day and helped launch the War of Independence.

Cossío del Pino asked the Manzanillo City Council if he could borrow the hallowed relic. The council was on the verge of granting permission when one of its members interrupted. Wait a minute, César Montejo demanded, whatever happened to the money recently allocated for schools and public works in Manzanillo? Had it not been pilfered by the very government now trying to conceal its corruption beneath the mantle of patriotism. Montejo rallied local citizens and veterans groups in protest. "Robbers," the people shouted, "never this bell!" With city papers trumpeting the dignity and valor of the protesters, the interior minister returned to Havana empty-handed, mumbling about a lack of "civility."[34]

Cossío del Pino was not the only one who appreciated the symbolic power of the Bell of Demajagua. Reading newspaper accounts of the affair, Castro believed that if anyone in midcentury Cuba could claim to be heirs to Céspedes and the fathers of Cuban independence it was students like himself. And so, he conferred with the FEU hierarchy and a couple of senators about borrowing the bell and bringing it to the university to serve as backdrop for a series of rallies meant to reawaken Cubans to the ideals for which the Republic once stood. The plan required money for transportation to Manzanillo and the return to Havana by train. The senators and student leaders liked the idea and offered financial support. Castro then reached out to Manzanillo veterans and the City Council. The parties invited Castro to a meeting, and in early November Castro and his friend Lionel Soto traveled to Manzanillo to make their case in person. After meeting Castro and assessing his character, the veterans and city leaders signed on, dispatching two of their number to help escort the precious cargo, all four hundred pounds of it, to the capital.

Meanwhile, the FEU had not been idle. Cuban students were good at ginning up publicity, and the bell-bearers were greeted at the rail station by a raucous crowd. The Grau administration also saw this coming, regarding the demonstration as an affront to Minister Cossío and a threat to government authority. Castro anticipated this. Before heading off to Manzanillo, he advised his friend Alfredo Guevara, FEU treasurer at the time, to collect weapons and foot soldiers sufficient to safeguard the bell's passage from the train station to University Hill. The bell arrived in Havana on the afternoon of November 3. Its presence united a divided city, as left and right, young and old, students and professionals, workers and public officials joined a long procession snaking its way past the Capitolio, through the Parque Central, before moving on to the university.

Castro warned Guevara that once in place, the bell needed to be guarded around the clock. "Castro was the only one of us to understand the threat clearly," Guevara remembered. For most of that night and into the wee hours of the following day, the students and their paid police maintained their vigil. At four in the morning, confident the threat had expired, the last tired sentinels staggered off to bed, to return in a few hours. When they did so, the bell had vanished. "We failed," Guevara admitted, before praising Castro's uncanny "intuition" to sense danger when no one else could feel it.

Arriving at the university the next morning, Castro was unhappy to learn that his warning had not been heeded and that the bell had been stolen. After chewing out his peers, he, Soto, and Guevara began to scour the city for the bell. They started at the home of FEU president Enrique Ovares, whom many considered an opportunist and a person of dubious loyalty. Departing Ovares's house, the students ran into Eufemio Fernández, chief of the Secret Police, member of MSR, and intimate of President Grau. Fernández was obviously trailing the students to gauge their response. Castro confronted Fernández and asked what he and his cronies had done with the bell. Naturally, Fernández did not say.

The fate of the bell became the talk of the town, with journalists, broadcasters, and citizens alike all weighing in on its location. Some expected the bell to show up at the Presidential Palace. Many attributed the professionalism of the heist to complicity between the National Police, the university police, and MSR agents within the FEU. On November 5, Castro and his fellow students announced that there would be a rally at the university the next day. The size of the crowd exceeded expectations, with an estimated thirty thousand people mounting the Escalinata and spilling into Plaza Cadenas and adjacent squares. As the principal organizers of the bell's pilgrimage, Castro, Guevara, and Soto each addressed the throng. Castro picked up where he had left off in his Colón Cemetery speech, accusing President Grau, Alemán, Masferrer, Fernández, Manolo Castro, and company of selling out their patriotism to naked self-interest. The government assumed immunity born of public cynicism, Castro said. Well, this audience had news for them: the "spirit of the university" was not dead, "the conscience of the nation" not yet extinguished. The kidnapping of the bell had awakened a sleeping giant. The Cuban people were fed up; the nation's youth would never surrender. The crowd rose up, as if on cue, chanting "Out with Grau!

Out with Grau!" Over the course of the following week, pressure mounted on the administration, which quietly returned the bell to Manzanillo.

It is hard to imagine a better outcome to the Demajagua affair from Castro's perspective. He had set out to expose government bullying and duplicity. The government responded with bullying and duplicity. The press was starstruck. Castro's image was emblazoned on newspaper front pages across the country. Initiating behavior that would become a hallmark, Castro dressed to impress throughout the affair, donning the charcoal gray pinstripe suit that would become his signature, complete with starched white shirt, pocket handkerchief, and a geometrically patterned tie. In the week between the disappearance of the bell and its return to Manzanillo, Castro made speech after speech and was granted airtime on the influential radio station CMQ. Exploiting his growing celebrity, he moved from one venue to another, criticizing government officials, confronting the police, educating the public. This was his first real experience in political mobilization, and by any measure it had been a smashing success.

People noticed. In the nearby town of Artemisa, for example, Juan Miguel Carvajal Moriyón, president of the Association of Secondary School Students, was looking for a speaker to address an upcoming rally. Carvajal regarded Castro's leadership of the Demajagua affair as "an act of extraordinary political transcendence." He tracked down the young maverick and asked him to come to Artemisa. Carvajal remembered Castro looking at him intensely, as if to gauge his sincerity. "I have many obligations in these days," Castro finally responded. "But if I can attend you can be sure that I will be with you." That was enough for Carvajal, who walked away "happy." Castro was "very deliberate, very precise," he said.[35]

Castro's obligations continued to mount through the winter of 1947–48. In late March 1948, representatives of twenty-one nations convened in Bogotá, Colombia, for the Ninth International

Conference of American States. The United States set the conference agenda: the rising tide of communism in the hemisphere. The
conference took place against the backdrop of mounting Cold War
tensions in Eastern and Central Europe, and on the Korean Peninsula. The Soviet Union was flexing its muscle in Germany. Czecho-
slovakia has just fallen to the communists. It was only a matter of
time, U.S. intelligence officials insisted, before Russia would try to
establish a beachhead in Latin America. Some regarded the leftist governments of Argentina's Juan Perón and Venezuela's Rómulo
Betancourt as evidence of beachheads already in place. That same
March, the countries of Western Europe signed the Brussels Pact,
the signatories pledging to help keep communism at bay. The
United States wanted a Brussels Pact for the Americas, and U.S.
diplomats arrived in Bogotá with hemispheric security topmost on
their minds.[36]

Other countries saw the hemisphere's principal challenge differently, as if one man's communism is another man's social democracy. The Allied victory in World War II sparked renewed debate
about the nature of democracy itself. More concerned about national sovereignty and social equality than free markets, the citizens
of Argentina and Venezuela elected leftist governments pledged to
universal suffrage, access to health care and education, land distribution, and rural development. Argentina's Perón and Venezuela's
new president, Rómulo Gallegos, headed for Bogotá no less interested than U.S. officials in hemispheric harmony, but their vision
of harmony excluded dictators like Rafael Trujillo and Nicaragua's
Anastasio Somoza, both of whom had cozy relationships with the
United States, while casting a jaundiced eye on the North Americans' talk about the inviolability of national borders.

In the months leading up to the meeting in Bogotá, Perón
reached out to sympathetic governments and civil society organizations across the hemisphere in order to counter what he interpreted as the U.S. desire to consolidate its economic dominance
over the Western Hemisphere. His delegation to Cuba included the

student representative César Tronconi, as well as Senator Diego Luis Molinari, both of whom were given a warm reception by Cuban students. In spring 1948, the University of Havana continued to reverberate with accusations that the Cuban government had betrayed the cause of democracy in the Dominican Republic. Castro played a major role in the agitation, presiding over not just the pro-Dominican Democracy Committee, but also over the Committee for Puerto Rican Independence. Indeed, there was scarcely a cause in Latin America's campaign for national sovereignty and economic independence that escaped Castro and his peers: the battle against the dictators Trujillo and Somoza, Puerto Rican independence, the fate of the Panama Canal Zone, the devolution of the Malvinas (Falkland Islands) to Argentina, the U.S. occupation of Guantánamo Bay, the Guatemalan revolution, just to name a few.

At the urging of the Argentines, the Cuban students agreed to help establish a new Latin American Student Association. The upcoming Ninth Congress provided the perfect context in which to unite students from across Latin America to promote democracy and national sovereignty. Though not enrolled in the university at the time (hence not involved in the FEU), Castro made plans to travel to Bogotá by way of Panama and Venezuela.[37]

In fact, he chose a good time to leave the country. On February 22, 1948, Manolo Castro was gunned down in central Havana. The perpetrator, Gustavo Ortiz Fáez, was picked up a few blocks away, his gun still smoking. Rolando Masferrer and his confederate Mario Salabarría thought to pin responsibility on Castro. A few days later, Castro was arrested and charged with the murder. Taken to police headquarters, he was given a paraffin test, which proved negative, and released. Former friends Frank Díaz-Balart and Enrique Ovares vouched for Castro's innocence. "Castro had absolutely nothing to do with the murder of Manolo Castro," Ovares insisted, "no connection to the cell from which the murderer came."[38]

Castro did not waste the opportunity to accuse his accusers of willful misdirection. He charged Masferrer of wanting "to take over the leadership of the university to make it serve his personal interests." When the students resisted Masferrer's overtures, he dispatched his bullies to intimidate the students. Now Masferrer sought to blame innocent people to disguise his own complicity in the murder. In short, Castro said, Masferrer hoped to "profit from the death of a friend." Curiously, since participating in Cayo Confites, Castro had developed grudging respect for Manolo Castro's intelligence and idealism. At the time the former FEU president was gunned down, Castro had ceased to consider Manolo Castro the students' most salient problem. Looking back on these events years later, Castro noted that Manolo Castro was not involved in university politics at the time of his death, and there was no reason for him to have been assassinated. Far from encouraging the crime, Castro said, had he known it was going to happen he would have tried to prevent it.[39]

Castro set out for Bogotá on Monday, March 22, 1948, in the company of fellow student Rafael del Pino. On the eve of his departure, a journalist from *Bohemia* magazine caught up with the rising young leader to discuss his hopes for the trip. The aim was very simple, Castro explained, to unite "university students in the anti-imperialist struggle." This put the students on a collision course with the U.S. delegation, which intended to consolidate its control over the nations of the south.[40]

This was Castro's first trip outside Cuba. In a letter to his father, Castro provided a detailed account of his itinerary. The trip had begun with four days in Caracas. Castro was spellbound by Venezuela's landscape and impressed by the riches generated by "its massive petroleum production." Venezuela had just experienced a smooth democratic transition, Castro reported, with provisional president Rómulo Betancourt peacefully surrendering the reins of power to his successor. Venezuela's government contrasted favorably to Cuba's own. "Politically speaking," Castro observed, "the country moves along admirably," with Betancourt leaving office without having enriched himself. In short, the country's public administration was "honorable," its people "satisfied" with an administration "under-taking measures to benefit the country as a whole."[41]

From Venezuela, Castro and del Pino moved on to Panama. Impressed by what they saw in the young Cuban leader, the Panamanian students invited him to address a public audience on March 30. This was an honor he would never forget, he told his fellow students, "one I surely do not deserve." He said he spoke for all Cuban youth in sympathizing with the Panamanians' fight against colonialism. "Brothers at the beginning of history"—i.e., in the struggle against Spanish colonialism—Cubans and Panamanians would be "brothers to the end," he said, "brothers in culture, brothers in roots, members of the great family of Latin American nations." Latin Americans would need to draw on that common history, those common ends, to succeed in the ongoing "struggle for the defense of the rights of our America."[42]

In the uproar over the Demajagua affair, Castro demonstrated a precocious awareness of the power of symbols to mobilize public sentiment. He had not left that awareness at home. In Panama, he visited a hospital where a student named Sebastián Tapia lay paralyzed after clashing with government soldiers during a rally against U.S. occupation of the Canal Zone. Years later, witnesses credited Castro with the ability to make the humblest interlocutor feel like the most important person in the world. Castro's visit to Tapia's bedside left a deep impression on the Panamanians, which he reinforced by laying a wreath at the foot of a bust honoring Amador Guerrero, Panama's first president, after whom the hospital was named. Castro was clever. Such visits had a strategic dimension to them. But no one doubted his sincerity.[43]

Castro departed Panama on March 31. His plane flew along the Pacific coast toward Medellín, "one of the richest, most industrialized" cities in Colombia, he told his father. From Medellín, he continued on to Bogotá. Far below, "the Magdalena and Cauca rivers overflowed their banks, shimmering like white rays on the surface of the earth." Castro was impressed by Bogotá. "Modern and almost as big as Havana," the city "swarmed with people in the streets like nothing I've ever seen before." He found Bogotá to be "a very cultivated, civilized city," with many of its residents "of Indian blood and characterized by tranquility." Like Venezuela, Colombia compared favorably to Cuba. Colombia had a cash crop of its own, in this case coffee. But unlike Cuba, "whose only source of wealth is sugar, thereby exposing it to disastrous undulations in the global market," Colombia possessed "rich silver and gold mines, raised its own cattle, and produced all the food it consumes." Colombia's standard of living was high, the cost of living cheap. He and his friend had found "cheap rooms in a good hotel (the Claridge) with magnificent food."[44]

Castro promised his father that he would not ramble on, lest he have nothing to say later. But he could not help himself. So far, the trip had been a "total success," he said. In Panama, he had spoken for "a half hour on the country's most popular radio stations." In Venezuela, former President Betancourt himself had met with the students ("We were in the actual home of the Venezuelan president and the family treated us very kindly," Castro said). Meanwhile, in Bogotá, he expected to interview the chief diplomats from many of the participating nations. All of which got him thinking about Cuba's lack of political accountability. How different this all seemed from "Cuban democracy, where the doors of the houses of government are closed to citizens."[45]

The Ninth Conference of the Americas opened with great fanfare on April 1, 1948. U.S. secretary of state George Marshall provided the introductory remarks. The conference was expected to result in a new Organization of American States, a collaborative endeavor meant to serve the popular aspiration for peace and plenty. Just days after inaugurating this meeting, the United States would announce the Marshall Plan, a commitment of $13 billion (roughly $30 billion today) to rebuild war-torn Europe. Some Latin American leaders anticipated a similar plan to spur industrialization and economic development on this side of the Atlantic. They would be disappointed, with the U.S. delegation offering nothing so much as stern warnings that there could be no neutrality in the unfolding contest between democracy and communism.[46]

On April 4, FEU officers Enrique Ovares and Alfredo Guevara arrived in Bogotá. Their sudden entry into the mix created awkwardness among the student assembly. Just who was in charge of the Cuban delegation, anyway? As elected representatives of the FEU, Ovares and Guevara had every right to assert themselves. And yet Castro was personally known now to student delegates from Argentina, Venezuela, Panama, and Colombia. Many had praised him to their peers from countries he had not yet visited. His youthful shyness gone, Castro rose to address the issue, acknowledging his compatriots' role while reminding the assembled crowd of his leadership in making the congress a reality. Years later, Ovares insisted he retained control of the Cuban delegation; Guevara reported that the congress embraced Castro's leadership of both the Cuban delegation and the Student Congress itself.[47]

The clash between Castro and Ovares was never really a contest, Guevara explained. Ovares attained his position in the polarized world of the University of Havana by being studiously noncommittal. Castro achieved his position of influence by virtue of his idealism and charisma. Guevara described Castro at this stage of his career as "a spontaneous leader who simply dominated an assembly within minutes of appearing, even when others had exerted much time and effort organizing." Ovares could not compete with Castro's "enthusiasm, stature, oratorical ability, or the passion he transmits in everything he does." Castro did not want to distract from the task at hand, and he and Ovares reached a "modus vivendi." Still, everyone knew where the real power and influence lay, according to Guevara. It had been Castro who welcomed Perón's representatives to Havana, he who had done the advance work in Venezuela and Panama, he (second only to the Argentines) who had imagined the Student Congress in the first place.[48]

Arriving on March 31, Castro spent several days getting oriented before the Student Congress officially opened on Monday, April 5. Castro and Rafael del Pino almost did not make it to the first meeting. The previous Saturday, delegates to the Ninth Conference attended a reception at the Teatro Colón, on 10th Street, just down from Plaza Bolívar, in the heart of the Colombian capital. Having slipped into the theater unannounced, Castro and Pino engaged in a bit of mischief, ascending the balcony and showering the guests with a manifesto listing the student demands—an end to Trujillo's dictatorship, along with U.S. and British colonialism in Puerto Rico, Panama, and the Malvinas. Years later, Castro conceded that there was nothing original or revolutionary about this wish list. The point was simply to make the delegates aware of students' presence in the city. Returning to their rooms at the Claridge Hotel, the two were met by Colombian police. They were taken away, fingerprinted, interrogated, and eventually released, their naïveté more apparent than their threat. The Student Congress proceeded uneventfully, with the students hammering out responses to the various parts of their agenda.

On Friday, April 9, the Cuban students were scheduled to meet with Colombia's liberal opposition leader, Jorge Eliécer Gaitán, whom Castro had briefly encountered a few days before. Popular among Colombian students and dissidents, Gaitán embraced the idea of the Student Congress and agreed to help wrap up the event. On their way to Gaitán's office that afternoon, the Cuban delegation encountered a frantic crowd fanning out from Bolívar Square in the heart of the old city. "They killed Gaitán! They killed Gaitán!" the people shouted. As if on cue, the city erupted in violence that left hundreds of people dead (many more hurt) and millions of dollars of property destroyed. By now, readers may anticipate Castro's response. Rather than retreat to his hotel room, as Guevara and Ovares had done, he joined the melee, as if to support, even steer a revolution dedicated to . . . well, nobody knew quite what.

Looking back on the so-called Bogotazo years later, Castro portrayed his participation in the ensuing chaos as the work of a budding revolutionary. He tells a detailed if somewhat tedious story of his every move, as if his later success earned a reckless rabble-rouser the right to be taken seriously. "I smashed a typewriter . . . I joined the multitude . . . I grabbed a tear gas gun . . . I put on a uniform . . . I restored order . . . I harangued a crowd . . . I climbed into a jeep . . . I advised the garrison chief what to do . . . I fired some shots"—all evidence of his "Quixotic streak," he explained, "in the finest sense of the word."[49]

In fact, Castro had run around the disabled city like a chicken with its head cut off. Desperate for a scapegoat, the Colombian government accused the two young Cubans they had picked up at the Teatro Colón the previous week of plotting with communists to overthrow the government, thus grossly exaggerating Castro's influence and organizational ability. The disorder lasted several days, by which time an all-points bulletin circulated through police and military circles with Castro and del Pino in the crosshairs. On the afternoon of August 11, with a 6 p.m. curfew closing in on them, the two were picked up off the street by some sympathetic Argentine officials who delivered them safely into the hands of the Cuban embassy, where they were joined by Ovares and Guevara. Within hours, the students were on their way home to Havana aboard a Cuban government airplane dispatched to Bogotá by one of Grau's ministers to pick up some champion fighting bulls.

It had been a remarkable three years. Castro arrived at the University of Havana in autumn 1945 as a nineteen-year-old youth little known beyond the athletic fields of Colegio de Belén. Returning to Havana from Bogotá nearly three years later, he had developed a reputation among his peers as a bold and persuasive student leader, committed to the economic and political well-being not just of Cuba, but of Latin America besides. His trajectory from one to the other was anything but smooth. Eager to fit in on University Hill, he tried his hand first at sports then at gang warfare before finally committing himself to politics. The things that made him good at the first and susceptible to the second (his athleticism and love of action) accompanied his progress, lending his political activism a cartoonlike quality at times, as his behavior during the Bogotazo attests. Along the way, the characteristics that would come to distinguish Castro as a leader were becoming set in stone, conspicuous among them uncompromising idealism, a self-confidence easily mistaken for arrogance, and an audacity bordering on recklessness. Alfredo Guevara's response upon first encountering Castro in the Plaza Cadenas on the first day of law school captures the ambiguity of his emerging personality and provides a fitting epitaph to this stage of his life: "I hope this guy is for good," Guevara thought to himself, "because if he is for ill he will be impossible to resist."[50]

chapter five

SALAD DAYS

"The speaker should shut his mouth!" a voice rang out.
"He speaks for the last time." It was hard to tell where the
voice came from, so thick was the crowd in Plaza Cadenas
one sultry afternoon in early summer 1949. But there could be
no doubting the sincerity of the threat. More than five hundred
students, including presidents of the thirteen university faculties,
crowded into the plaza to hear leaders of the new "30 September
Committee," named for the day in 1933 when Rafael Trejo was
gunned down by police, launch a campaign to end the *gangsterismo*
that had plagued the university for the better part of two decades.
With roots in the anti-Machado revolution, the gangs benefited
from the malign neglect of former friends in the Auténtico Party
(officially Partido Revolucionario Cubano), founded in February
1934 after the collapse of the 1933 Revolution. President Grau,
an Auténtico founder, had encouraged the gangs by his passivity.

Newly elected Auténtico president Carlos Prío Socarrás formalized the unsavory relationship, exchanging government sinecures for a pledge from gang leaders to cease and desist. The success of the Pacto de las Pandillas (Pact of the Gangs), as the agreement became known, depended on keeping it secret. This required, among other things, suppressing dissident voices at the university, which was like trying to keep the lid on a boiling pot. Trouble was inevitable.

Just the previous April, the university government itself fell victim to violence when gunmen associated with MSR founder Rolando Masferrer (now a senator with legislative immunity) assassinated FEU vice president Justo Fuentes. Later that month, the same group cut down another student, Luis Felipe (Wichy) Salazar. The rally in Plaza Cadenas that day amounted to a declaration of war by the students against the government-gangster nexus, only this was to be a battle of moral suasion in which weapons were strictly prohibited.

Despite the heat, a note of menace shivered through the crowd. The last thing that the organizers needed was for a peace rally to erupt in gunfire. Max Lesnik, one of the founders of 30 September, looked up at the speaker to gauge his response. There stood Fidel Castro, unflappable, baiting the gangsters to expose themselves. Castro "has always been very clever when it comes to finding out what lies behind appearances," Lesnik said. In the days leading up to the rally, Castro collected the names of all those implicated in the pact, along with the offices they ostensibly occupied. The gangsters were never very far from the university. On this day, they arrived on the scene just as Castro gained steam. "It was a courageous and audacious act," Lesnik recalled, complete with "names and documents proving his assertions." The gangsters "were furious and informed the committee that we would pay with our lives. Fidel was informed even as he spoke."[1]

On the face of it, Castro made an unlikely medium for an antiviolence message. Since becoming politically active in the spring of 1946, Castro sought protection first from MSR, then from UIR, while articulating an anticorruption platform that made neither the gangs nor the government happy. After returning from Bogotá, he began to spend less time with thugs and more time with genuine political leaders like Lesnik. Lesnik was an acolyte of Eduardo Chibás, who founded the Ortodoxo Party (formally Partido del Pueblo Cubano) in May 1947. The party had its origins in discontent with the administration of Ramón Grau, once a fellow revolutionary and political ally, lately a hapless and corrupt Cuban president. The name *Ortodoxo* signaled a return to the original principles that had once animated Grau's Auténticos: national sovereignty, constitutionalism, clean government, and social welfare, among others, now all irredeemably compromised by an administration dependent on U.S. loans and committed to its own enrichment. Chibás was the force behind the Ortodoxos, a controversial muckraker whose Sunday talk show on radio CMQ was so popular that it competed for listeners with Cuba's beloved *radionovelas*. In June 1947, nearly half of all Cubans were said to have tuned in to hear him denounce the latest evidence of Grau administration malfeasance.

Despite a late start getting mobilized, Chibás competed in the 1948 presidential election, losing out to his old Auténtico Party ally, Carlos Prío. The Ortodoxo Party won two seats in the House that year, and nine in the ensuing midterm election. Its slogan was "Honor Against Money" (and, more prosaically, "We Promise Not to Steal!"). In October 1948, Chibás accused former education minister Alemán of stealing $20 million from the education budget. Early the next year, he accused minsters of the new Prío administration of embezzling close to ten times that much. Better at launching accusations than at backing them up, he eventually found himself in trouble. In short, Chibás emerged as the conscience of the nation at a time when many Cubans seemed to have forgotten what a conscience even was. Lesnik noticed and immediately signed on, becoming the head of the Ortodoxo Youth. Castro noticed, too, eventually recognizing affiliation with the Ortodoxos as a way to escape the gangs.[2]

Lesnik and Castro first crossed paths in the Plaza Cadenas in autumn 1948, at the start of Lesnik's freshman year. In the wake of Cayo Confites, Demajagua, and the Bogotazo, Castro had "a reputation among the students of the highest magnitude," Lesnik said, and was "known on a different level among the national press." Journalists regarded Castro as "a leader among his peers and a person capable of staging a demonstration, confronting the police, or throwing a pistol in his belt to exchange fire with a rival group." Politically ambitious himself, Lesnik was eager to make the acquaintance of those who had "taken a political position against the corruption and gangsterism of the time." Castro was "young, rebellious and politicized." From their first meeting, Castro struck Lesnik as "someone bound to be the leader of a very different Cuba . . . or become a martyr."[3]

Lesnik had reservations about Castro. Still only twenty-two at the time, Castro possessed what Lesnik called "an exaggerated propensity to violence." He was idealistic but undisciplined, committed but impetuous. He had "no appreciation for the ideological fundamentals of the revolutionary process." Nonetheless, Lesnik recognized in him what others had seen: "a figure who had the makings of an exceptional leader—a good speaker, great agitator, valiant, audacious." By the time the two met, Castro was already sensing the limitations of "the sterile struggle of violence for violence sake." While retaining his idealism, sense of duty, and fearlessness, Castro had begun to take his role as a student leader more seriously, seeking a place at the table with Lesnik and even Chibás himself. Lesnik and Chibás were happy to have Castro on their side, but only if he truly and unequivocally quit the gangs. The initial evidence was equivocal, Lesnik recalled, describing Castro as a "kaleidoscope," always adapting to the circumstances, now violent, now thoughtful. But there was more to Castro than met the eye. "It is often said," Lesnik remarked, "that Fidel talks a lot. What is less known is that he listens more than he speaks. He is a very patient person. Before making a decision, he spends a great deal of time in reflection."[4]

Castro told Lesnik he wanted to join the 30 September

Committee. Lesnik and Guevara sat down with Castro to establish a few conditions. First, there could be no guns in the committee. Very well, Castro replied, but didn't Lesnik himself have a gun? Yes, Lesnik conceded, but he no longer carried it. Second, the group had written a manifesto denouncing the public sinecures; all committee members had to sign it. Castro, who never met a manifesto he didn't like, readily agreed. At that point, Guevara asked Castro who he thought would be the best person to inform the FEU about the new 30 September Committee. That would be me, Castro replied, thus setting the stage for the speech that begins this chapter.

Cubans reserve the adjective "transcendental" to distinguish events that achieve a place in the timeless struggle for Cuba Libre from everyday events. In Lesnik's opinion, Castro's performance that day belonged in the pantheon. Castro raised the hair on the back of necks across the city that day, "denouncing the gangsters, confessing his role, and naming names." *Basta ya!*—Castro declared—enough with the self-immolation. It was time for students to stop killing one another and turn their attention to the power behind the violence.

With his speech coming to a close, Castro's life was in danger. Lesnik did some quick thinking. The original plan was to escort Castro off University Hill on foot. That was now plainly inadequate. It was 7 p.m., still light out, and Lesnik thought to exploit the daylight to save his maverick friend. He told Castro to get in his car, a convertible, located in a nearby parking lot. "We'll take my car, you'll sit next to me, and we're going with the top down." Lesnik's close ties to Eduardo Chibás gave him a degree of immunity from the gangs. "It would have been a scandal for the gang leaders to gun me down in the open," he said; "it simply wasn't possible." Lesnik took Castro to his house, where he remained for two weeks. With Castro's enemies more determined than ever to kill him, Lesnik advised Castro to leave the city. He eventually did so, taking off for the tranquillity of Oriente Province.[5]

———————————

This was Castro's second extended stay in Birán in just over a year. The previous summer, back from Bogotá and confronting one accusation after another, he sought the calm of the countryside. There, according to his sister Juanita, a conversation with his parents temporarily altered the direction of his young life. The conversation went something like this: "Fidel, it's time to think hard about your future. . . . All we want for you is to have a career. Forget about all this stuff you've been involved in and carry on with your studies! Where would you like to go to school besides Cuba? Choose any university you'd like in the United States." These were the words of Ángel, the self-made man, urging his son to avail himself of the opportunity he himself had never had. Castro would not hear of it. "Papa," the son replied, "to study in the United States is very expensive. Let things calm down a bit here and you will see that I will finish my degree." The father persisted. When it came to education, the parents would hold nothing back. "You always wanted to go to Harvard," Ángel continued, "that's what you should do. This old man will not have lived in vain and has not forgotten what he promised you—to provide the time you need to finish your degree."[6]

Castro rose and embraced his father. This rare moment of intimacy inspired Lina to speak up. Fidel could finish his degree wherever he wanted, she said. Meanwhile, there were more pressing matters, namely, his relationship with Mirta Díaz-Balart, which a mother did not want to see squandered. The couple were obviously mutually enamored, Lina said. Why not start a family? "Why not get married and go together to the United States?"[7] Castro's friendship with Rafael and Frank Díaz-Balart, and his eventual betrothal to their sister, discredits retrospective accounts of José Ignacio Rasco and other critics that Castro remained an uncultured knave who never fit in at La Salle, Dolores, Belén, or Havana University. The Díaz-Balarts were members of the elite. Collectively, they would never have befriended, socialized with, and consented to their daughter's marriage to the stick figure caricatured in such accounts.

The Díaz-Balarts hailed from Banes, the United Fruit company

town near Nipe Bay. Their father, Rafael José Díaz-Balart, was a lawyer at United Fruit and had once been the town's mayor. In 1933,
Rafael José was elected representative from Oriente and developed
an intimate working relationship with Fulgencio Batista, who himself grew up in Banes. Rafael and his namesake both served in the
second Batista government. In Banes, as in other U.S.-owned and
dominated company towns in Cuba, cultivated, educated families
like the Díaz-Balarts enjoyed life on a par with the North Americans who managed the place. Banes was divided into clearly segre-
gated neighborhoods, with the U.S., Cuban, and other expat elite
living on one side of the tracks (in this case, river), and the Cuban
and other seasonal laborers living on the other.

Jack Skelly, the son of a United Fruit executive who grew up
with the Díaz-Balart kids, described management's side of town
as having a "semi-millionaire, country-club style." A country club
there was—known locally as "the American Club"—complete
with clubhouse, golf course, tennis courts, and polo field. Banes also
boasted a library, elegant parks, and a magnificent church. Adjacent
to the polo field were the large, airy homes and elegant front lawns
of the Skellys, Díaz-Balarts, and other United Fruit Company administrators. Castro said that despite his parents' phenomenal success
they never mixed socially with neighboring company-town aristo-
crats. He certainly did. He was a frequent guest at the Díaz-Balarts,
often accompanying Rafael, Frank, and Mirta to their beach house,
just outside town.[8]

Castro accepted his mother's suggestion that he and Mirta tie
the knot. And with good reason, evidently, as Skelly describes the
young Mirta as one of the most eligible "young muchachas" in the
east. A wedding date was set for early October 1948. Banes made a
spectacular backdrop for a wedding. By all accounts it was a fabulous event. The festivities kicked off on the evening of October 10,
with a shower for Mirta at the American Club. A surviving photo
reveals a slight, beaming Mirta in a sleeveless, full-length, flower
print dress, surrounded by girlfriends. If she or her well-heeled

friends harbored any doubt about her husband to be, it is not visible here. Mirta looks equal parts innocent and ecstatic, her gaggle of girlfriends enthusiastic.

The couple were married the following Tuesday, October 12, 1948, at 10 a.m. in The Church of Our Lady of Charity in Banes.[9] Castro's mother, Lina, led the Birán delegation, which included his older siblings, Angela and Ramón, and their spouses and children, as well as his younger brother, Raúl. To their eternal disappointment, Enma and Juanita were off at school and unable to attend. "The wedding was elegant," Lina wrote her daughters. "Mirta looked gorgeous and happy, Fidel, too, it goes without saying; they made a handsome couple, indeed." The town's who's who turned out for the occasion, and "there was a spectacular reception at the American Club." Lina remembered feeling overcome with contentment. "For the first time in a long while, I saw Fidel at peace," she said, "totally enamored—which is all we wanted for all of you, to be happy." The couple was showered with gifts, the most conspicuous a pair of alabaster lamps from Fulgencio and Marta Batista. The lamps made "a big impression," Lina reported, despite being "not all that pretty."[10]

Before bidding the newlyweds farewell, Lina took them aside and presented them with a gift of 10,000 pesos ($100,000 in today's money). Castro was flabbergasted. "Ten thousand dollars?" he said. "No, mama, the old man has lost his mind, that's more than we can accept." Never mind, his mother rejoined. Amid further protests and fervent thanks, the couple were off, first to Miami, then on to New York City. This looked to be an auspicious start, with the family hoping that the wedding marked the first stage in Castro's domestication, with children, a law degree, and—who knows!—his return to Birán to run the family business all to follow. "Everybody regarded that marriage as the way to save me," Castro remarked years later, "to tranquilize me with bourgeois concepts. After that marriage, they were prodigal with me."[11]

A little prodigality goes a long way. The couple arrived in

Miami in mid-October ("There were few tourists," Castro observed, "so prices were low"). This was his first trip to the United States. Fond of food, he was struck by the number of options available, waxing rhapsodical about the "T-bone steak" and "smoked salmon." The newlyweds went to the beach and took in the sights. Miami did not feel all that different from Cuba, however, and they soon left for New York City. Arriving in New York, Castro described a sensation akin to that of encountering Havana for the first time, awed by its grandeur and energy, while appreciating the potential for loneliness in a city of millions of people "struggling to make a living."

The couple rented the basement apartment of an elegant brownstone at 156 West 82nd Street, on Manhattan's Upper West Side. "That was my first experience of a harsh winter," Castro recalled. "The only thing we had was a very old heater." Castro used outings to the local delicatessen to practice his English. The city's delis fascinated him, with their combination of food, staples, medicine, and hardware. This seemed "very strange," he said, "as in Cuba the pharmacy is the pharmacy, the bodega the bodega, and never the twain shall meet." The newlyweds lived a simple, domestic life, with trips to the countryside and occasionally to New England to keep them busy. "We'd buy food in the delicatessen and take it home to cook, as I always loved to do that."

On weekends, they were often joined by Mirta's brother Rafael, who was studying in Princeton, and his new wife. Familiar with the area, Rafael functioned as a tour guide. Together the two couples took in the sights—the Museum of Natural History, the Statue of Liberty, and the Empire State Building. They went to Broadway plays and ate in local restaurants. This high living was not cheap, especially when they hosted their inlaws. Despite the Díaz-Balarts' own wealth, Castro remembers often picking up the tab. Castro also frequented the bookstores that dotted Columbus Avenue and Avenue of the Americas. He bought an English-language copy of Marx's *Capital* in a local bookstore, regarding the nation's willingness to allow the sale of Marxist literature as a contradiction.[12]

Through all the sightseeing, Castro remained fixated on the idea of studying "political economy" at Harvard, Columbia, or Princeton. He and Mirta bought a used car, drove to Cambridge, Massachusetts, and apparently checked out Harvard in person. In truth, Castro would not have been qualified for graduate school in the United States even had he already possessed a law degree, which he did not. "The title of Bachelor and certain degrees are granted in Cuba after very abbreviated schooling," the Cuba Commission noted back in 1935: "Cuban students who go to institutions of higher education in Europe and North America for advanced work find themselves in an embarrassing and disappointing situation." Someone with a doctorate from the University of Havana might be classified as a freshman.[13] Castro seemed to recognize this. Despite visiting the Ivy League schools, he called the idea of his studying political economy in the United States "an illusion." Even had he been qualified to attend a U.S. university, the demands of graduate work in the States did not jibe with his solipsism. In U.S. graduate programs, students were expected to attend class and participate in intensive class discussions, which Castro never liked to do.

Castro was constantly surprised by the cultural differences he encountered in the United States. One day, he and Mirta visited the Díaz-Balarts at Princeton. Castro remembers strolling the opulent grounds on the day of the Harvard-Princeton football game. Amid the merriment and colorful tents, one thing especially caught his attention: lawns "overflowing with young men and women, who interacted with extraordinary freedom, kissing and caressing one another, in front of everybody." He was not opposed to "natural relations between the sexes," he insisted, but this struck him as "true debauchery." The couple's time in the United States overlapped with the 1948 presidential election, in which Harry Truman defeated Thomas Dewey, to everyone's astonishment. Out on the streets one afternoon in New York, the president-elect's caravan whizzed by the

Castros with great fanfare. Castro conceded to not knowing much about Truman at the time. But he admired the way an underdog had thrown "himself into battle and won a great victory."[14]

To his family's surprise, the newlyweds returned from the States just before Christmas. Arriving in Miami on the way home, Castro used what was left of the wedding money to buy a Lincoln Continental. Once back in Havana, he realized he needed money more than a flashy car, and he quickly sold the Lincoln, using the returns to move into a new apartment in Vedado. As if humbled by his brush with higher education in the United States, he resolved to finish his law degree as quickly as possible. Taking stock of the many exams between him and a degree, he calculated that it would take him a year and a half of preparation and test taking. Friends and family remember him throwing himself into his studies with customary abandon. In boarding school at the time, Juanita often visited the newlyweds on weekends in the company of her sister Enma. Castro "rose at exactly seven in the morning," Juanita recalls, "studying until sunset with complete dedication." By the following June, when Castro renounced the Pacto de las Pandillas with Lesnik looking on, he and Mirta were expecting their first child. At Lesnik's suggestion, he retreated to Oriente once more. It would be both cooler and calmer there than in the capital, and Mirta and baby would have the support of her family in Banes.[15]

Castro did not let his studying that summer get in the way of occasional fun. Skelly remembers meeting Castro at a United Fruit Company beach party, where he showed up in the company of his in-laws. The young men passed many hours at the fireside "arguing the merits" of capitalism. Barbara Gordon, like Skelly, the child of an ex-pat U.S. administrator atop the United Fruit hierarchy, reports that Castro had been coming to those picnics since befriending Rafael at the university. Gordon was friends with Mirta, and remembers her and Castro's courtship as "normal, natural, and unremarkable." Such picnics included a mix of U.S. and Cuban administrators, as well as friends from neighboring plantations, officers of company ships, and sometimes personnel from the U.S. naval base at Guantánamo Bay, a few hours to the south. Dinners were at once low-key and elaborate, and might include goat stew or roast pig, along with rice, beans, and plantains. A local band entertained the crowd in the evenings, and naturally there was plenty to drink. Skelly recalls sitting at a picnic table with a group of young friends when Castro showed up on Mirta's elbow, a cigar neatly tucked away in his chest pocket. According to Skelly and Gordon, social interactions in the east were more relaxed than in the capital. There was never any question of Castro fitting in or being unwelcome at these United Fruit Company affairs.[16]

Often Castro would remain at the beach for a few days as Mirta and the new baby retreated to her parents' home. "Night after night," Skelly recalls, the boys would talk politics over games of canasta. By this time, Carlos Prío had replaced Ramón Grau as president. In office for nearly a year, Prío had done nothing to curb the rampant corruption. Skelly remembers Castro and Rafael Díaz-Balart being "on fire" at the very mention of Prío's regime. In those days Rafael, not yet a Batista man, "saw eye to eye on everything with Fidel," Skelly says. Díaz-Balart was better read, but Castro stood out for his "eloquence." His "line of reasoning was sharper." Skelly notes that Castro passed many a night whiling away the hours in conversation with local fishermen, explaining his plans for Cuba.

Puerto Rico Beach provided a break from violence but not from guns. "Fidel loved guns and rifles in those days," Skelly notes, and often spent the time hunting. Skelly confirms Paquito Rodríguez's account of Castro's mischievousness. Once, while paddling contentedly around the swimming hole, Skelly heard the "crack, crack" of a gun and saw the water dancing up around him. Whipping around, he found Castro sitting on the "porch with a .22 in his hand, cigar in his mouth, laughing like hell, yelling, '*te la voy a pelar,*

Americano' (I'm going to scalp you, American)!" Castro was "very charming," Skelly concludes, just like Batista.[17]

Gordon remembers Mirta's stepmother being strict with the family's only daughter (Mirta's biological mother died in childbirth). The couple often "hid out" at Gordon's house just down the street from the Díaz-Balarts' to escape a mother's watchful eye. "We had a big property with a large porch and a beautiful, secluded garden in the rear," Gordon says. "The two were always very proper." Gordon recalls Castro attending at least one big U.S. Independence Day celebration at Puerto Rico Beach. United Fruit always provided food and drink and music and fireworks. Asked to describe the young man, Gordon describes Castro as "a typical kid, just like the rest of us, playful, energetic. And very fond of Mirta." Castro also struck Gordon as "open, friendly, warm, a talker, not a dancer. We were typical teenagers."

Gordon has a photograph from January 1949 of Castro and his blushing bride at the beach. Side by side, they hold hands against a brilliant blue sky, with only a vigilant stepmother in the background. They were just back from their honeymoon in the United States, though by the gleeful smile on Mirta's face the honeymoon was not yet over. Nestled in the crook of Castro's arm, she wears a white blouse, capped at the shoulder, and a green wool skirt. Castro wears flannel pants, a black belt, and a white long-sleeve shirt with flap pockets, neatly tucked in. (The last unsolved riddle of his life may be his ability to stay cool, despite seeming radically overdressed.) A pocket watch hangs from belt loops of striped, gray-flannel pants. She looks fourteen. He looks as young as he did before he became involved in university politics—closely shaved, baby-faced—though with one notable difference. Having given up sports by summer 1946, he is developing the paunch that will accompany his rise to power. And there is hint of the double chin that he will try to conceal beneath that parsimonious beard. The photograph reveals the couple as contented as they will ever be.

Besides providing tranquillity and recreation for the expecting couple, the extended sojourn in the east afforded Fidel and Raúl Castro an opportunity to get to know each other as young men. Fidel was four years older than Raúl. The two had not spent much time together since Fidel's summer vacations from Belén, when Raúl was just entering his teens. In 1949, having dropped out of school, Raúl was working in his parents' business, and seemed pleasantly surprised to learn that his brother had become a font of higher learning. "You know Juanita," Raúl spoke up one day, "the more I talk to Fidel the more I realize that we have a lot in common; he's well prepared and dominates any discussion." The brothers talked for hours that summer, Juanita notes, with the younger brother listening (too) attentively to his older brother's opinions. Nobody bothered to question what all the chitchat was about, focusing instead on its happy effect: Raúl's decision to accompany his brother to Havana in the fall to finish his baccalaureate. He, too, wanted a university education, and the family was thrilled, Ángel especially. Fidel could help Raúl prepare for the university entrance exams, and generally watch over him. Curiously, Castro turned out to be a natural, if conventional, teacher, surprising in an autodidact. "You can't imagine what a fine teacher he is," Raúl wrote his sister. "He's put me to work studying the dictionary and gives me lots of homework, for example, assigning me words from A to C one day, more words the next, and so on. He says that the dictionary teaches a lot and I totally agree!"[18]

With Fidel's help, Raúl was admitted to the Social Sciences Faculty at the University of Havana. There, Raúl's education continued, much of it of political rather than academic in nature, as was the norm in those days. Like his older brother, Raúl came into contact with socialists and members of the Cuban Communist Party (PSP). Unlike his brother, Raúl found the communists' arguments compelling, eventually joining the Union of Young Communists. This was all unbeknownst to the family back in Birán, of course. "Never in their wildest dreams could my parents have imagined that Raúl would fall for that," Juanita says. "Had my father known, he would have gone directly to Havana and put an end to it."[19]

———————————

Mirta gave birth to a son on September 1, 1949. Named Fidel Ángel Castro Díaz-Balart after his father and grandfather, "Fidelito," as he was known, kept Castro close to home through much of that fall and winter. Fidelito was not the first grandchild but all agree he was the most spoiled. Fidelito was a happy, exuberant child, his demeanor mirrored in the face of a beaming father. Nothing made Castro happier than his son. "Fidel has a son," Lina said to Ángel, "he's about to finish his degree, he's put aside university politics, and Raúl has returned to his studies thanks to brother's influence. What more could we possibly want?"[20]

Once back in the capital, the couple lived in an ample apartment in Vedado, accompanied by Mirta's brothers, Rafael and Frank. The excitement of a new child did not distract the single-minded Castro from preparing for an avalanche of exams that coming June. "If there's one thing I admire about Fidel," Enma wrote home that year, "it's his determination to study without end and finish his degree . . . he studies from morning 'til night, rising early, putting on a robe, that's all."[21] Castro would not have been able to pay the rent, dedicate himself to studying, and support his growing family without his parents' generosity. After graduating from high school, Juanita returned home to help run the family business. She remembers Ángel marching into the office one day and asking her to arrange for a monthly stipend of $500 (roughly $5,000 today) to be sent to Fidel. Lina, too, wanted to do her part. She opened up credit accounts in several stores in Havana where the couple could buy groceries and other necessities, promising to pay the bill. The parents treated the newlyweds like the college students they were, buying them furniture on visits to Havana, and taking them out to nice restaurants.[22]

At the University of Havana, students did not have to matriculate

to take final exams. Due to his political activity—and his participation in Cayo Confites and the Bogotazo—Castro had not taken
an exam since the end of his freshman year. He passed ten exams
in June 1946, passed seventeen more in December 1949, leaving
twenty-two to go by the following June. He did this work entirely
on his own, consulting nobody, attending no classes. He later remembered achieving "outstanding" marks in "the majority" of the
exams, which is not quite true, but he earned "outstandings" in
roughly half of them, including labor law, civil law, penal law, family law, property, administrative law, and legal anthropology, as well
as in political economy, juridical philosophy, and Cuban and Latin
American history.[23] Castro was not under any illusion about how
his professors regarded this. Years later, he told a friend that at least
one professor criticized his "disengagement" and reproached him
"for not dedicating myself more seriously to coursework." Castro
himself seemed a little ambivalent about his feat, remarking later,
"I never told him that for one of the subject tests (Family Law) I
only studied three days, and for the other (Labor Law), one day.
In truth, that did not constitute prowess; I was always an irregular
student. To pass these subject tests was easy if you possessed a good
memory."[24]

In June 1950, Castro became the first person on either side of
the family to graduate from university. Ángel Castro, now seventy-
four and generally rooted to the farm, made the trip to Havana.
"It is worth the pain as the boy has made my dreams come true,"
he said. For the occasion, and in the manner of proud parents back
in Spain, Ángel presented his son an eight-carat diamond solitaire,
large enough to build a church on. "No, Papa," the son responded.
"I can't accept that. Save it for Mama, she is the one who deserves
it for all the sacrifice she has endured." What the graduate really
needed was a loan, which he intended to use to rent office space.
Ángel complied, allowing Castro and two friends to open a law firm
at 57 Tejadilla Street in the Rosario Building in Old Havana, around
the corner from Plaza de la Catedral. In a neighborhood thick with

law offices, Aspiazo-Castro-Resende, as the firm was called (after Castro and his associates, Jorge Aspiazo and Rafael Resende), soon made a name for itself, taking up the cause of poor and indigent city dwellers.[25]

Castro's first cases evolved from practical necessity. The office needed furniture, so they consulted carpenters and purchased wood at a local lumberyard. In the season Castro arrived, many of the carpenters he met were indebted to the yard owner. Castro resolved the brewing conflict by helping the yard settle accounts with wealthy debtors while forgiving the smaller obligations to the individual artisans. The carpenters and their friends came to know and like him, calling on him when they were in trouble. He advised them about their rights and the workings of the law. His partner Aspiazo tells the story of him and Castro going to visit one of the carpenters in his home. The carpenter was delayed, and the two lawyers sat in his kitchen with his pregnant wife and their little girl amid humiliating squalor. The client never showed up, and the two got up to leave, Aspiazo recalled, but not before Castro asked Aspiazo for five pesos, which he slipped underneath a coffee cup on the way out of the kitchen. "Tell your husband not to worry about the debt," Castro told the woman as he walked out the door.[26]

In September 1951, Castro sued two powerful public officials, including the notorious police lieutenant Rafael Salas Cañizares, for the murder of an Ortodoxo Party activist named Carlos Rodríguez. He also defended squatters in a Havana slum called "La Pelusa," who were to be evicted to make way for an upscale development. Neither suit succeeded, but Castro's advocacy was sincere (and pro bono), and people noticed. Aspiazo-Castro-Resende did not limit their advocacy to Havana. They helped small farmers retain their land and defended students hauled into court for disturbing the peace. Much of this was run-of-the-mill stuff, Aspiazo conceded. Still, he remembered his newly minted partner being commended by a judge after a particularly elegant closing statement. To Aspiazo,

Castro was a tireless "crusader," an inveterate opponent of "price gouging among utilities and transportation companies," and of "abuse, embezzlement, and dishonesty" of all kinds.

Castro's legal acumen proved as useful in getting himself out of legal jeopardy as it did in representing clients. In autumn 1950, public secondary school students across the country protested a series of decrees issued by the new education minister, Aureliano Sánchez Arango, which restricted the rights of student organizations. To ensure compliance, Sánchez Arango posted a police officer at the door of all secondary schools. In early October, as school was set to begin, students in the city of Cienfuegos went out on strike, calling on peer institutions across the nation to join in. Others readily did so in strikes and public demonstrations. Alarmed by the unrest, Interior Minister Lomberto Díaz banned student associations entirely, while prohibiting public assemblies. In Cienfuegos, the president of the student association was expelled from school for six months. What were concerned students to do?[27]

Contact the FEU, someone in Cienfuegos suggested. At the university, the FEU had created an ad hoc "Fighting Committee" to support peers across the country, even declaring its own seventy-two-hour strike in an act of solidarity. With the Cienfuegos strike entering its sixth week, the students scheduled a public demonstration for the afternoon of November 12. They notified the FEU, which dispatched Fidel Castro and Enrique Benavides Santos to Cienfuegos. The two arrived at the association's headquarters on the evening of November 11, just as student leaders were involved in a heated discussion. Local army and police officials had ordered them not to hold a public rally. They had a constitutional right to meet and speak as they saw fit, Castro informed the group. Off they marched to army headquarters, where Castro repeated what he had told the students to the captain of the local police, a man named Faustino Pérez Leiva. Pérez Leiva was not impressed. "I don't know the laws," he said. "I don't know the students' grievances. I don't discuss orders. I enforce them. The meeting is over."[28]

The students faced a difficult choice: they could cancel the rally, as the government ordered, thereby forsaking their principles and forfeiting their rights; or, they could assert their rights and confront the government, knowing full well that they would be brutally suppressed. They voted to proceed, vowing to occupy City Hall that evening and put their case to the people of Cienfuegos. That afternoon, calls went out across the province for people to support the students and vindicate the Constitution. As the organizers made their way toward City Hall, Castro and Benavides were arrested and charged with creating a civil disturbance. With Castro out of their way, police and army officers descended on the crowd with clubs, bullwhips, and machetes. Scores of people were injured.[29]

By autumn 1950, Castro was known to police and army officials throughout the country. That night a question arose about what to do with two outsiders who could not mind their own business. Since the Machado days, one favored solution was to release captives at gunpoint and order them to flee, then cut them down on the run—the *Ley de Fugas*—thereby absolving police and army officers of culpability.

Early in the morning of November 13, Castro and Benavides were removed from their cell by rural guards, herded into a waiting car, and driven into the countryside. A second car followed also full of police officers. Aware of their captors' plans, the two tried in vain to kick their way out of captivity. After a long drive, the cars stopped and the doors opened when, suddenly, a third car pulled up alongside the others. A man leapt from the car and cried out: "What's going on with these boys? Answer me!" It was the president of the Cienfuegos city government, who was suspicious about what the officers had in store for the captives. The men were returned to the city jail, where yet another protest erupted at dawn on their behalf. By this time, Ortodoxo leaders back in Havana had been informed of these developments. Thanks to the intervention of Eduardo Chibás the two were freed on bail.[30]

Castro did not wait for the trial to defend his presence at Cienfuegos. On November 15, he published a broadside in the local newspaper addressed "To the People of Cienfuegos." For months, he explained, students in Cienfuegos and throughout the province of Santa Clara had been campaigning for the delivery of much needed classroom material. Rather than engaging the students constructively, the secretary of education launched a costly and cynical publicity campaign meant to discredit and ultimately silence the students. Lacking resources to refute the government's disinformation, the students responded by the only means available to them. They took their grievance to the street. In doing so, they were hardly imperiling the public welfare or acting irresponsibly. On the contrary, Castro wrote, by defying attempts to stifle them, they were vindicating "the glorious history and elevated principles of the nation." Judging by their overwhelming response, the people of Cienfuegos thought so, too.[31]

"To the People of Cienfuegos" constituted the earliest (and one of the fullest) defenses of civil rights and liberties that Castro ever made. Governments restricted the rights of speech and association at their peril, he said. Once civil liberties are suppressed, aggrieved citizens have little recourse besides violence. Moreover, it was imprudent to leave the fate of "fundamental rights" in the hands of "capricious ministers." Suppose a minister "lacked morals and scruples, or was the bastard son of the current situation?" Customary rights and constitutions elevated liberty behind the reach of individual whim. Wasn't it always the same with tyrants? They claim with perfect equanimity that they are all that stands between public order and chaos. The people know the truth, Castro said. It was ministers like Alemán and Sánchez Arango, "who disturb the public and private peace, who do not respect public norms and sentiments, who violate the Constitution and mock the rights of citizens, who upset the apple cart of natural order, peace, and justice."[32]

In this, as in so many of Castro's public remarks, the constitutional lawyer vied with the street fighter to combat the bullying
perpetrated on the Cuban people by Sánchez Arango, Alemán, Salabarría, and the rest. Where were the public officials who looked on
their office as more than an opportunity for self-aggrandizement?
he asked. Castro cited chapter and verse of the 1940 Constitution
to vindicate the student protest and his role in supporting it. *Cubans may enter and remain in any part of the national territory, come and
go as and wherever they please without needing permission from anybody*,
the Constitution declared. The interior minister had treated Castro and Benavides as "strangers." In Cuba, "there is no such thing
as strangers, no such thing as instigators among invited guests."
Neither Castro nor the students would be intimidated. He looked
forward to confronting the government's "lies and bad intentions"
at trial.[33]

The trial took place on December 14, 1950. Castro and Benavides traveled to Cienfuegos on the overnight train. The FEU
assigned a local lawyer from Cienfuegos named Benito Besada to
defend the accused. Years later, Besada remembers the travelers falling into bed at his home that morning as he went off to consult the
prosecutor. When he returned, he found Castro sound asleep with
Emile Zola's book *J'Accuse!* lying on his chest. Besada shook Castro awake and warned him that proceedings in so-called Urgency
Courts like this one were always a little unpredictable. There was
no formal indictment and no way to anticipate the judges' states
of mind. No problem, Castro replied, informing his colleagues that
he intended to act as his own defense attorney at the trial. The case
was bigger than the two individuals, he said. The Constitution itself
was on trial here, and he intended to vindicate it in his testimony
and in cross-examination of witnesses. Besada and Benavides worried that Castro would only complicate an otherwise straightfor-
ward legal process. Castro cut off their protests by returning to Zola.
After lunch, the three men headed for the courthouse, where Castro
asked Besada to procure him a gown to wear in court.[34]

The trial began with testimony of the local police captain, Manuel Pérez Borroto. Pérez repeated the charge that the accused had come to Cienfuegos only to disturb the peace and claimed to have evidence to support his accusation. The courtroom was packed with students, dissidents, and the general public, some won over by Castro's recent newspaper article. One by one, prosecution witnesses took the stand. None of them could confirm the police captain's account. Finally, Castro's and Benavides's names were called. The two objected to the style of the court proceedings and announced that they would waive their right to testify. At this point the judge asked if they had representation. Castro informed the judge that he would defend himself. Castro then donned his black robe and took his place alongside Besada.

When his turn came to cross-examine witnesses, Castro called Pérez, whose case promptly disintegrated. As Castro lit into Pérez for debasing the public trust, the government prosecutor interrupted and asked the judge to dismiss the case. Castro then used the opportunity of his closing statement to launch a structural critique of corruption and injustice in Cuba. "Fidel spoke in the manner of Zola, with a no less valiant 'J'accuse!'" Benavides recalled. Such talk was unheard of in the Villa Clara Court. When the judges retreated to their chamber, Castro asked Benavides how he thought he had done. "Well, kid," Benavides replied, "I'm sure they are going to find you guilty." In fact, the judges ruled two to one in Castro's favor, and the charges were dropped. The room erupted in celebration as the chief magistrate ordered the courtroom cleared. Castro and Benavides were surrounded, the episode putting yet another feather in a young lawyer's cap.[35]

Castro's law degree also came in handy back in Birán. In 1951, Ángel asked his son to help settle accounts with his friend Fidel Pino Santos, slowly dying of hepatitis. In the heart of the Depression, Ángel had transferred the title of Finca Manacas to Pino Santos in return for credit needed to keep his business afloat. This enabled Ángel to avoid the usurious fees that caused many Cuban farmers to lose their businesses to U.S. banks. Ángel's debt did not amount to anything close to the value of his enterprise. By the early 1950s the debt was all but paid off, with neither Ángel nor Pino Santos paying much attention to the paperwork. With Pino Santos on his deathbed, Ángel asked Fidel to take on the sensitive task of approaching his godfather not-to-be to ask him to restore the title to Ángel's name. Castro agreed. "It was a delicate problem," he said. Pino Santos "was an age-old friend close to death." More than a business transaction, this "was fundamentally a mission of diplomacy."

Castro found Pino Santos physically feeble but mentally lucid. "I had no problem persuading him," Castro said. "He told me that he understood, that I was right, and from his hospital, he gave me instructions about how to resolve the issue, including transferring power of attorney to me." By midsummer 1951, the matter was settled, the papers filed in municipal court in Santiago de Cuba. Pleased by the outcome, Ángel rewarded his son $3,000 pesos for a job well done. Looking back on these events years later, Castro characterized the relationship between Pino Santos and his father as "just" and "logical," an intriguing statement coming from a critic of capitalism.[36]

———————

Despite a good start as an attorney, Castro and his partners recognized that he was more cut out for politics than for legal work, and he soon left the firm. In fact, he had dabbled in national politics even before he received his law degree. In 1948, he ran for the position of Ortodoxo Party delegate to the Oriente Provincial Assembly. Chibás's platform of honest government, economic independence from the United States, and agricultural and industrial development jibed with Castro's own budding political commitments. So did Chibás's fearlessness and unwillingness to compromise. Skeptical of Castro's *pistolero* past, Chibás came to know Castro through Lesnik and other friends at the university. There was plenty to like in the young firebrand, as Chibás himself learned at the party meeting that year. Ortodoxo cofounder Emilio Ochoa was running for governor of Oriente Province. The party's reach was limited, and Ochoa wanted to unite with other parties to form a political alliance. Could the Ortodoxos join such an alliance and still be worthy of the name? A meeting of party delegates was called in Havana, with Ochoa, Chibás, and Castro in attendance.

As Chibás listened attentively, Ochoa discussed his plan. It was agreed that the plan would not be adopted without unanimous support. Chibás polled the delegates, all but one of whom gave their consent. The holdout was Castro. There can be no coalitions with tainted parties, Castro insisted, in his best imitation of Chibás himself. A coalition would water down the party's ideology. The only beneficiaries would be the party's more established rivals. Ochoa's motion was defeated. Castro was vindicated at the next meeting of the Ortodoxo National Assembly, where a platform opposing political coalitions carried the day. Ochoa took revenge on Castro at the next meeting of Ortodoxo delegates by simply not inviting him to attend.[37]

In autumn 1951, Castro ran again for Ortodoxo Party delegate, this time from the Cayo Hueso neighborhood of Central Havana. Castro saw Cayo Hueso as a stepping-stone to winning a nomination to the Cuban House of Representatives, hoping to replace a popular local figure named Adolfo Torres. Torres remembered Castro approaching him to explain that he intended to take over Torres's seat. Castro then copied the names of every Ortodoxo member in the neighborhood and sent them personal notes. He later thanked voters for showing up. Castro's initiative inspired Torres to take action himself. "So great was his connection to the masses," Torres said, "that I had to quickly set my mind to address the situation."[38]

Castro's former law partner Jorge Aspiazo remembered the candidate making house calls among the shopkeepers and slum dwellers he had represented as an attorney. Castro had a ready-made constituency. "He visited every single Ortodoxo member in the neighborhood of Cayo Hueso. He would explain the objective of his visit, asking constituents to look him in the eye. He then described his plans for the country. If they trusted him, they should vote him, if they didn't trust him, they should vote for someone else." To everyone's astonishment, Castro won easily, gaining more than three hundred votes.[39]

Castro's fellow Ortodoxo candidates benefited from his energy and organization. The archives overflow with pamphlets he wrote on his own and others' behalf. The pamphlets are at once attractive, decorous, and forceful. A typical pamphlet alerts the audience to an upcoming radio show, timed to commemorate an important date in history when Cubans rose up to confront injustice. Besides mentioning speeches by fellow candidates, there is almost always a deferential nod to senior members of the party, usually Chibás, Ochoa, or Roberto Agramonte. Then comes a reminder of what is at stake in the local and national elections: "Against crime! Against theft! Against corruption! Against barbarity! Against the miserable exploitation of our people rises the valiant and accusatory voice of the Ortodoxo Party!" Be sure to turn up, the candidate urges, before signing off in peronalized calligraphy, "Fidel Castro."[40]

Once elected, he followed up with customized thank-you notes. "Dear Comrade," reads one, "by this means I express my sincere gratitude for your collaboration in the primary election for Ortodoxo Party delegate from the barrio of Cayo Hueso, which I won." Then comes an expression of satisfaction for the success of his fellow candidates, along with the assurance that the delegates-elect took nobody's support for granted. He finishes with a vow to "fight without rest until the final victory." Similar note cards went out in the new year, always accompanied by a thank-you, a quote from Martí, and a pledge to never to give up the fight.[41]

Flush from the Cayo Hueso victory, Castro put his name up for nomination to the Cuban House of Representatives in the upcoming 1952 election. Meanwhile, he looked for every opportunity to get his message out, eventually winning a half-hour slot on the local radio station in Havana, "La Voz del Aire" (On Air). Lesnik remembers being impressed by Castro's energy and ingenuity. "I was the head of the Young Ortodoxos," Lesnik explained, "and he had influence among all the youth of the party and among the workers and among the most fervent party activists. He made a fabulous campaign, sending out one hundred thousand envelopes, each with a hand written personal note." Nobody had ever seen anything like this, Lesnik said. "I used to send out thirty cards at Christmas time to members of my executive committee. He sent cards to everyone affiliated with the party in the province of Havana."[42]

In August 1951, the Ortodoxo Party suffered a grievous blow: after charging a Prío administration official with corruption that he could not substantiate, Chibás shot himself in the stomach at the close of his weekly radio broadcast. He died ten days later, instantly becoming a martyr and creating an opening among the ranks of Ortodoxo members, radical reformers, and opportunistic dissidents. Castro said and did all the right things in the days following Chibás's suicide. It is hard to find a picture from those days and not identify a solemn Castro gazing out from among the mourners. Castro's growing stature in the party is evident in newspaper accounts from the time. "This is the most extraordinary grief that has ever happened in the history of the country," Castro was quoted in *Alerta*. "It is enough by itself to banish in terror the spokesmen of the outrages of criminal and ruthless government that the Republic endures."[43]

Chibás died August 16, 1951. The following day, at a ceremony at Colón Cemetery, Ortodoxo leadership issued a declaration written by Castro vowing to carry on their leader's campaign, commitments, and ideals. Corrupt members of the Prío government were warned not to take comfort in Chibás's passing. His life and work would find new urgency in the thousands of Ortodoxo members more dedicated than ever to redeeming Cuba from passivity, decadence, and gluttony.[44] With Chibás gone, journalist José Pardo Llada became the most known Ortodoxo figure. Pardo Llada had a beige Chevy, recognized wherever he went. Castro bought an exact replica for his campaign for representative. "He went everywhere

in it," Lesnik says. "Everyone would run up to it, thinking Pardo
Llada had arrived! People would run up to Fidel and say, 'Hey, is this
Pardo Llada's car?' Fidel would reply, 'Yes, he lent it to me for the
campaign.' He wanted everyone to think that he had Pardo Llada's
support!"[45]

———————

Castro's growing political commitments complicated things on the
home front. By the first years of the new decade, the house husband
who liked to boast about his spaghetti Bolognese seldom made it
home for dinner. "Fidel almost never comes home," Mirta wrote
Ángel and Lina back in Birán. "He lives for Ortodoxo Party politics, and to tell the truth I feel abandoned; we don't talk much, as
he spends entire days away." Ángel and Lina's financial assistance,
Mirta confessed, was all that kept her "afloat."[46] In short, Mirta was
finding out the hard way that there would be no domesticating her
husband. The comforts of the hearth could never compete with the
excitement of the forum—and later the coliseum. One wonders
how Ángel and Lina responded to her cri de coeur. They, too, once
voiced the hope that their son would settle down. As lifelong fighters and dreamers, they must have recognized themselves in their
son's attraction to the strenuous life. Born with privilege and stability thanks to them, his and their life projects would be very different.
Comfort and ease were not for him by choice any more than they
had been for them by necessity.

It was around this time that Castro broke the news to Mirta that
they would not be moving to Paris, a dream that the newlyweds had
apparently hatched together and which Mirta continued to cling
to in the face of mounting evidence to the contrary. Enma Castro
remembers the scene as if it were yesterday. While visiting Mirta
one evening, she witnessed her brother return home from work in
a state of great agitation. "Mirta," he finally blurted out, "we're not
going to Paris. I got this wrong. I'm not going to study in the Sor-
bonne. I'm staying here in Cuba and announcing my candidacy for

representative from the Ortodoxo Party. I will fight in Congress, and one day I will seize power!" Mirta saw dreams of walks along the Seine and afternoons in the Jardin du Luxembourg dissolve before her eyes. "But Fidel," she cried out, "you promised! And not just me, your parents, too, that we would go to Paris and you'd get your master's degree. You can't do this. You just can't!"[47]

Unaccustomed to being challenged, Castro exploded, grabbing the closest object at hand—in this case one of the matching alabaster lamps presented the newlyweds by the Batistas—and smashing it on the floor. "Coño, Mirta!" he exclaimed. "Don't argue with me, we're not going! That's that!" Enma dropped to her knees in a vain attempt to corral the shattered pieces, and for all she knew a marriage. Mirta recoiled in shock, as if recognizing in this act of destruction a harbinger of things to come.[48]

chapter six

WE FINALLY
HAVE A LEADER

T he crack of gunfire prompts the mind to seek alternative explanations. "Listen to the drums!" journalist Marta Rojas exclaimed. "The marching bands must be coming! Or are those fireworks?" It was early, not yet sunrise, on the morning of July 26, 1953, Carnival in Santiago de Cuba. Carnival never sleeps, and the contest for best band between rivals Tivoli and Los Hoyos would not end until the pinning of medals later that morning. But it wasn't drums Rojas heard. And it wasn't fireworks. "Those are gunshots," her colleague Panchito Cano replied. "From up the hill. Our work is done. We're fucked."[1]

Marta Rojas was twenty-two and a recent graduate of the School of Journalism at Havana University. In summer 1953, she worked as an intern for a television station covering rugby and soc-cer, a job she won not because she was sports-minded, she recalls, "but because I had good diction and was very pretty." Every July, in or out of school, Rojas returned to Santiago from Havana, always making it home for Carnival. On the evening of July 25, she scooped up her boyfriend and headed out to celebrate with a group of other couples. Carnival invites flamboyance, masquerade, the exotic. That evening, Rojas went for something understated—a simple blouse and pleated skirt cinched at the waist with very deep pockets. A fateful choice.

Panchito Cano was a veteran photographer formerly on the staff of *Bohemia* magazine, now a stringer based in his native Santiago. That night Cano wandered the city capturing the exhilaration of Carnival for *Bohemia*, a prestigious assignment, which, short of a natural calamity or coup d'état, was sure to land him on the front cover. His and Rojas's families were neighbors in Santiago. He knew about her interest in journalism. Bumping into her amid the merrymaking, he suggested she come along to help carry his equipment and provide another set of eyes. Rojas readily agreed. Bidding goodbye to her friends, she strolled off with Cano, snapping the occasional photograph while collecting Cano's rolls of exposed film in the pockets of her skirt.

Cano did not need to know the exact nature of the gunfire to understand what it meant. Innocently, Rojas interpreted the gunshots as an opportunity. "Never mind the festivities," she told Cano. "Let's cover the shooting." People ran in all directions, including fellow journalists. Some took off downhill toward the offices of the city's leading newspaper, *Diario de Cuba*, in search of information. Cano and Rojas ran uphill, in the direction of the gunfire. Approaching the Moncada Barracks, Cano met a colleague who reported a mutiny in progress. As the group looked on from a distance, Rojas dashed home to assure her parents that she was okay and to request permission to return to Cano. "You're crazy, and way too young," they said. "This is what I went to school for," she replied, before rejoining Cano near "Coca-Cola Post" (Post 2), named for the U.S. factory across the street from the barracks, just as the gunfire died down.

By 7 a.m. or so, a group of journalists milled around Coca-Cola Post, speculating about what had just transpired there. They were joined by members of Santiago's civic associations as well as by curious onlookers. Military police held back the crowd, its chatter broken by an occasional pop, pop, pop. Coca-Cola Post sits at the highest point of the Moncada parade grounds, affording onlookers a decent view of the barracks. Rojas remembers seeing soldiers roughly corralling small groups of what looked like fellow soldiers. The rough treatment and occasional gunshots prompted a few journalists to try to force their way inside. Ernesto Ocaña, an eminent photographer, was struck hard by a guard. The blow sent Ocaña's camera skidding across the pavement, where it was crushed by a heavy boot and kicked aside. "Journalists will come in when the Colonel says you can come in," a lieutenant snapped.

"The Colonel" was Alberto del Río Chaviano, commander of Moncada, the second largest military barracks in the land. After several hours, the sporadic fire ceased and the journalists were escorted to a waiting room in the colonel's headquarters. As their wait stretched on interminably, it dawned on some that Chaviano himself was not yet on the scene, as if sleeping off a big night out. Most of the assembled journalists recognized one another. Few if any knew Rojas, only recently a student. Cano was known to colleagues and to Chaviano's staff as a veteran, if disheveled, professional (think "Columbo," Rojas said, "but with a camera in his holster"). While the journalists waited, Cano absentmindedly paced the hall outside Chaviano's office. But his antenna was out, and he caught sight of two women being fiercely interrogated in a nearby office. He urged Rojas to request permission to go to the rest room at the end of the hall to check out the scene for herself. Rojas did so, peering into the room on her way back, where she saw the women, one with her head turned, the other fixing Rojas intently with her gaze.

More time passed, until, finally, around mid-morning a soldier announced Chaviano's arrival. The journalists filed into his office, where he recounted the morning's events and promised a tour of the barracks. "At this point Chaviano said something strange," Rojas remembers, that the tour was "not quite ready," that his staff was still "preparing the theater of facts." This expression brought to mind the staging of a Western, and of something gone terribly awry. "I knew that when a crime is involved, you touch nothing before the forensic team arrives," Rojas said. "And yet here was Chaviano and company staging the grounds for us journalists." Chaviano read talking points passed on from Havana: the exchange of fire was not a conflict among soldiers, but between soldiers and a group of dissidents led by Fidel Castro on behalf of deposed president Carlos Prío. The attackers had been thoroughly routed. There were nineteen soldiers killed and twenty-seven wounded. There were sixty-one dead insurgents. Curiously, and despite what the journalists saw with their own eyes, there were no survivors among the attackers besides the two women that Cano saw being interrogated and those who had retreated early in the battle.

Sixty-one dead attackers and not a single wounded. The skewed figures along with earlier reports of captives increased the journalists' suspicion that things were not quite right. The ensuing tour magnified their disquiet. Bloody, mangled corpses littered the barracks' stairways and floors, but the uniforms of the dead appeared clean and free of bullet holes, and many of the bodies lay amid remarkably little blood. Similarly, the boots of the dead insurgents were unlaced, as if *the theater of facts* had been hurriedly (and inadequately) staged. As the group led by Chaviano snaked its way around the bodies, Cano took close-ups, more convinced with each step that he was collecting evidence of a massacre. When the tour ended, the journalists were herded onto the parade ground in front of the barracks and ordered to wait once more.

By this time it was mid-afternoon. Humidity and a blistering sun transformed the barracks into a furnace. There were no trees, no shade, nowhere to escape the heat, Rojas recalls. An hour or so later, Chaviano fielded another call from Havana, and Cano surmised correctly that the message included an order to confiscate the evidence. Thinking quickly, Cano sidled up to the bed of a nearby truck and deposited his film from *the theater of facts*. He then approached Rojas to ask if she still had the rolls of film from the night before. When she said yes, he told her to exchange them for those he had dropped on the truck bed. Rojas did as commanded, filling her pockets with the film from the barracks. Cano then scooped up Rojas's rolls just as one of Chaviano's men emerged with a tray and ordered the journalists to surrender their notebooks and film. The journalists grumbled but complied, including Cano, who loaded the tray with images of Carnival.

Marta Rojas was all but ignored. No one noticed the rolls of film concealed deep within the pleats of her skirt. "After a few more hours of waiting around, we were released," Rojas says. "We made our way down Aguilera Street to the darkroom of a friend." The time was now nearly 6 p.m. Within hours, Cano's sleight of hand was discovered and he immediately went into hiding. His handsome assistant was not suspected. At Cano's insistence, Rojas returned hurriedly to Havana, where she delivered the negatives to the editor of *Bohemia*. By the end of the day, a strict censorship descended over Cuba preventing publication of the Moncada photographs. It was not until four and half years later—in January 1959, after the triumph of the Revolution and the flight of Fulgencio Batista—that the photographs appeared in *Bohemia* for all, including skeptics, to see.

The Moncada attack was inspired by the coup d'état of Senator and former president Fulgencio Batista on March 10, 1952. That spring, Batista was the trailing candidate in the upcoming presidential election. Polls suggested that victory was badly out of reach, which meant that if Batista intended to attain the presidency of Cuba once more he would have to seize it for the second time in a generation. The previous summer, Batista had been approached by a cohort of young officers disgusted by the violence and corruption of the Prío administration and asked to do just that. Batista declined, hoping to forge a populist political coalition that would sweep him to electoral victory. By February, the coalition had not emerged. Approached by his fellow officers a second time, Batista consented. In the early morning of March 10, he seized Camp Columbia, Cuba's largest military base, located on the outskirts of Havana, while commandeering important military installations and civil institutions across the land.[2]

Few besides a handful of army officers saw the coup coming. In early 1952, Cuba was enduring yet another in a succession of corrupt, self-serving governments that delivered order, opportunity, and prosperity to those at the top of Cuban society, while largely neglecting the middle and lower ranks. The character of life in mid-century Cuba is captured by a 1950 World Bank study commissioned by the Cuban government and known as the Truslow Report, after its chairman, Francis Adams Truslow, president of what is now the New York Stock Exchange.[3] According to the report, not much had changed in Cuba since the visit of the Commission on Cuban Affairs in 1934.[4] Like its predecessor, World War II provided a timely stimulus to Cuba's sugar economy. As before, the sugar boom continued into the postwar years, so that by 1950 Cuba boasted the third highest income per capita in Latin America (highest among the nations of the tropics). Most of that wealth was concentrated at the top of Cuban society and in the cities, especially in Havana. Most of the profit went to outside investors. The little that remained in Cuba was channeled not into new infrastructure, industries, and markets but into the pockets of the politicians and labor leaders who greased the gears of the sugar monoculture. This was a legacy of the early years of the Cuban Republic, when a shortage of capital and affordable loans steered would-be entrepreneurs into politics, corrupting the political and legal system from top to bottom, ultimately transforming politics into profiteering.

Cuba's overreliance on sugar and end-of-nose decision making had adverse consequences for labor, education, and public health. In fact, the Truslow Report explained, Cuba's position among

Latin America's top economic performers was misleading. If more prosperous than its neighbors, per capita income in 1950 was only slightly higher than it had been in 1920, and the nation owed its prosperity to a sugar industry that had all but ceased to grow even as Cuba's population doubled. In the best of times, the sugar industry provided employment for between three and four months a year. In the face of an exploding population, the continued reliance on a static (if booming) sugar industry spelled trouble.

Trouble was not hard to find once you ventured off Havana's grand boulevards into the inner city or out into the countryside. By 1950, Cuba's vaunted public school system was teetering, thanks partly to population growth, and partly to patronage and corruption, as powerful unions ensured that teachers retained their posts irrespective of performance. In rural areas, schools were crowded, widely dispersed, and short of teachers and supplies. A visitor to a local school in Oriente Province, for example, estimated that 90 percent of the farmers in the municipality were illiterate, while only 150 of the two thousand school-aged children were enrolled in school at all. In the face of figures like these, the report predicted, "the new generation will be no better equipped educationally than the present one to cope with" the challenges of modern life. It was not that Cuban officials weren't trying, the report emphasized, simply that "no ordinary measures" could remedy the situation and make Cuban education "what it should be."[5]

Similar discrepancies afflicted public health. A wealthy Cuban or foreign tourist seeking a doctor in mid-century Havana could expect a level of care not so different from that in Sarasota, New York, or Boston. Moreover, years of assiduous work combating tropical disease had proved so successful, the report found, that tropical disease was simply "not a serious problem." Still, overall health remained poor due to the prevalence of parasites. Parasites abounded in urban and rural Cuba alike. "It is authoritatively estimated that between 80% and 90% of the children in rural areas are infested by intestinal parasites," the report observed. Inadequate education compounded the scourge, which local officials attributed to deficient sanitation and a contaminated water supply.[6]

Finally, there was the problem of malnutrition. One need not be an agronomist to recognize that Cuba is extremely fertile. The list of crops that flourish there is seemingly endless, with rich forests and grassland blanketing the island. And yet, the report noted, between 30 percent and 40 percent of Cuba's urban population suffered from poor nutrition, over 60 percent in rural areas. Meanwhile, the nation imported virtually all it consumed. This problem, too, could be traced back to distortions of the sugar economy. Cuba's abundant raw sugar production might have spawned all sorts of secondary industries, including "baked goods, cereal products, canned and frozen foods, preserved fruits, jams, jellies and candies." Those not consumed at home could be marketed abroad, providing income while stimulating local industries and markets. Of course, a productive economy required still "more agricultural crops, eggs and livestock," but surely Cuba could produce these on its own. Its inability to do so confounded the Truslow commissioners. Something was radically "amiss when one of the [world's] richest agricultural countries" could not feed itself.[7]

In sum, though mid-century Cuba had much to commend it—especially in contrast to its neighbors—the nation was plagued by problems that had afflicted it for decades: rampant corruption, lack of domestic industry and markets, insufficient purchasing power, unemployment, and substandard education, health care, and nutrition, particularly in rural areas. The situation demanded deep structural change and the stakes were hard to exaggerate. If the country continued on its current path, the report warned, "control may well pass into subversive but specious hands—as it has done in other countries whose leaders have ignored the trends of the times."[8]

———————

It was precisely to save Cuba from this scenario that Fulgencio Batista ousted President Carlos Prío. Or so he claimed. At 6 p.m. on the afternoon of March 10, Batista addressed the nation, explaining that his coup was not in fact a coup at all but a "Revolution" undertaken by "patriotic" officers acting on behalf of the Cuban people. Prío had been plotting a conspiracy of his own, Batista said, and intended to remain in power indefinitely. The sole aim of the "Revolution" was to restore the rule of law and promote economic and social prosperity. The 1940 Constitution was now suspended, the Revolution itself now the law of the land. According to its law, Batista was now chief of state and head of a Council of Ministers, with complete legislative and executive authority (the role of the judiciary supposedly remained unchanged). Batista vowed to remain in power long enough to fulfill the people's will and hold free and fair elections. Only his "love for the people" had compelled him to act, he said. "Shoulder to shoulder we must work for the spiritual harmony of the great Cuban family."[9]

It is hard to say how many Cubans accepted this explanation. Censorship and a fierce crackdown on labor and student dissidents accompanied the coup. The police and the military seized control of the airwaves and occupied the usual demonstration grounds. Batista was an unlikely harbinger of revolutionary change. His former term in office was known neither for its vision nor its transparency nor for promoting *spiritual harmony*. When he last left office in 1944 (bound for Daytona Beach, Florida, with sacks of cash), his handpicked successor was soundly defeated in that year's presidential election.

If unconvinced by Batista's justification for the coup, Cubans appeared largely resigned to it. The nation responded with "a mixture of confusion, resentment, and hope," *The New York Times* reported. And no little fawning. In the first few days of the new regime, Havana's elite flocked to the Presidential Palace to salute the new chief of state.[10] Meanwhile, labor and student leaders reacted with a combination of rage and incredulity. Labor quickly fell in line, exchanging a promise to halt all demonstrations for a government pledge to honor existing labor legislation. By contrast, students and young activists remained un-mollified. On University Hill, loudspeakers crackled with the defiant words of the FEU. "Once more, we are the standard bearers of the national conscience. We are defending the constitution, the people, and the democratic process."[11]

In the initial hours and days following the coup, young militants waited in vain for Prío's people to enlist them in armed resistance. For a solid week, journalist Carlos Franqui recalled, "we young people, students and revolutionaries, kept going from university to the unions, from the home of one opposition leader to another, from Ortodoxo headquarters on the Prado to the communists on Carlos III, asking them to take a stand, demanding action, strikes, protests, and demonstrations. Nothing."[12] When, by the end of a week, it became clear that neither Prío nor his party nor even the Ortodoxo leadership had anything to contribute besides hot air, young Cubans began to cast about for peers capable of exercising leadership. For nearly a year, the opposition remained as divided as Cubans themselves. But time did not diminish the revolutionary fervor. "The world changed on March 10," former activist Rosa Mier recalled. Batista had crossed a line, and young Cuba resolved to stop him in his tracks.[13]

Pro-Batista officers were not the only ones who had been plotting Prío's exit from office that winter. The question was how to accomplish this goal, by violence, or via the legal process laid out in the Cuban Constitution? Fidel Castro, for one, believed that a free press and the Cuban Constitution provided all necessary means for ousting a corrupt president. On March 3, 1952, just one week before the coup, Castro appeared before the Court of Auditors (*Tribunal de Cuentas*) to formally charge Prío with abusing the public trust. The Court of Auditors never reached a verdict. Batista's coup took care of that. By this time, Castro had bigger things to worry about. Late the previous year, Castro had filed yet another criminal complaint on behalf of the family of deceased transit worker Carlos Rodríguez, accusing police lieutenant Salas Cañizares of Rodríguez's murder.

This time, Salas Cañizares was found guilty, put on probation, and fined 500 pesos. In one of his first acts in power, Batista promoted Salas Cañizares to the post of chief of police, and Salas Cañizares was known to be out for revenge.

Castro spent the night of March 9–10 at his apartment in Vedado. News of the coup sent him scrambling, first to the home of his half-sister, Lidia, a dissident in her own right, then to the Andino Hotel, a former residence near the university. At Lidia's, he ran into fellow activist René Rodríguez, who would serve as his eyes and ears over the next several days.[14] With Rodríguez doing the legwork, Castro canvassed officials in the deposed Prío government to discover their plans for armed resistance. Though Castro loathed Prío, there was no question in his mind that Batista was the graver danger. It simply never occurred to him that Auténtico leaders would treat the coup as a fait accompli. At the university, students were approached not by the ousted president's people but by Rolando Masferrer, who warned them that they were being watched. Castro dispatched Rodríguez to the home of Ortodoxo leader and presidential candidate Roberto Agramonte, who laid out the party's plans for civil resistance. *Civil* resistance? Castro asked on Rodríguez's return. Batista knew but one language: brute force. With every passing second, his grip on the country tightened. Time was running out.

Castro abandoned the Andino Hotel the following day for the home of his friend Eva Jiménez in the Havana suburb of Marianao. In a cubicle off Jiménez's kitchen, he set to work drafting his response to the coup entitled, "Revolution, no! Usurpation," a ringing defense of constitutionalism over brute force, which he then delivered to *Alerta* editor Ramón Vasconcelas. Under pressure from Batista's censors and Ortodoxo officials alike, Vasconcelas declined the piece, but not before calling Castro "the last hope of the Cuban people."[15]

Within a few days, Salas Cañizares announced that Castro had nothing to fear from him, easing concern about Castro's safety.

Freed from hiding, he raced from place to place, consulting fellow militants about a joint response. With the opposition stymied, Castro took things into his own hands. At a rally at Colón Cemetery, Emilio Ochoa, civil resister in chief, outlined the Ortodoxo Party's official policy. In the middle of Ochoa's speech, Castro mounted a nearby tomb, decried the party's passivity, and called for armed resistance. "Who in the world is *that*?" murmured voices in the crowd. "Fidel Castro," others replied. The crowd began to show its support for Castro just as the police closed in. Their path was blocked by a phalanx of Ortodoxo women no less exasperated by the party's submission. Castro escaped and violence was averted. But partisans of armed resistance within Ortodoxo ranks had thrown down the gauntlet, and the influence of the old guard would never be the same.[16]

On March 24, Castro tried another tack, filing suit against Batista before Havana's Court of Appeals. He was not the only person to do so. Veteran politicians Eduardo Suárez Rivas and Pelayo Cuervo Navarro filed a suit of their own in the Supreme Court, only to see their case thrown out in early April. Castro challenged the magistrates to apply existing laws. By setting aside the Constitution and the rule of law, Batista exposed Cubans' lives and property "to the whims of bayonets," he said. All the safeguards that stood between liberty and tyranny went the way of the Constitution. Batista was now distributing administrative posts like party favors, replacing the popular will with "a juridical farce created in the barracks behind the back of popular opinion."

However distressing, these developments had been anticipated by the drafters of the 1940 Constitution. Castro cited six articles that condemned the perpetrator to at least a hundred years in prison. In his post-coup address to the nation, Batista had argued that his takeover was not a coup at all, but a revolution. In fact, Castro said, it was a "restoration . . . to barbarity and brute force." Anticipating a claim he would make years later, Castro insisted that revolutionary force was something altogether different, animated by the public will and fueled by popular participation. Batista mobilized no public, broached no arguments, advanced no revolutionary vision. The coup lacked what Castro called "revolution generating right"—a new conception of the nation "based in deeply rooted historical and philosophic principles."

Batista had also claimed that his coup would not affect the judicial branch. This suit would be a test case, Castro told the court. The judges faced a simple choice: they could defend the rule of law and acknowledge Batista as the mockery that he was, or hang up their robes and go home. Surely, they would not allow some bayonet-wielding corporal to defile "the august courtroom of the magistrates."[17]

This lawsuit, too, was thrown out, Castro's response to the coup largely ignored by a press fixated on the conciliatory gestures of leading political figures. In spring 1952, Castro was still relatively unknown outside student (and police) circles. Though an Ortodoxo delegate and candidate for representative, he lacked a platform within the party from which to make his opinions known. Still, he repeatedly stuck his neck out, continuing to draw attention to himself through gestures big and small.

Among those impressed by Castro that spring was Rosa Mier, a young woman whose politicization reveals the two or three degrees of separation linking dedicated militants in mid-century Cuba. Mier was twenty-four at the time of the coup, a town councilor from the village of Guanajay, some thirty miles southwest of the capital. She lived with her parents, members of the ruling Auténtico Party, whom she describes as "well off and apolitical." As a child, Mier went to private schools and attended the University of Havana. In Guanajay, as in Cuba generally, Batista's coup was greeted with a collective shrug. "People were passive," Mier explains. "There was little surprise and widespread acceptance." And why not? What did it matter if Cuba were ruled by this corrupt official versus that one? Batista had anticipated this response, and his future depended on it. What he had not considered, Mier says, is that in Cuba "there are always a few people ready to stand up for right."[18]

Introduced to Castro through fellow female activists, Mier came to know him well. In group settings, Mier reports, Castro was "overpowering, infatuating, irresistible, radiating authority and confidence." In person, he was warm, kindhearted, and authentic. He was also inveterately curious and could be very playful. Mier encountered the playful side of Castro through a stroke of serendipity. As a member of Guanajay's town council, she had access to the office of the local newspaper, *El Heraldo*, which she used to produce documents for what was coming to be known as the Movement, a dissident group centered on Castro and a few others, described below. One day Mier was scheduled to travel to Guanajay to pick up a run of pamphlets. At the last moment, her car broke down, prompting Castro to offer her a lift. He, too, had business in Guanajay, he said, and suggested they take his car.

Arriving in town, they went first to the printer, where Mier picked up her pamphlets. Thinking to stash them in the trunk of Castro's car, she discovered ten thousand copies of the radical newspaper *El Acusador* "just sitting there." If Castro were caught with these, she knew, that could be the end of him, and yet there he was, cool as a midnight swim, utterly imperturbable. Tickled to be in Castro's presence for the day, Mier insisted on introducing him to a few friends. First, they visited her uncle, owner of a local bakery. Needing to safeguard her documents, she then drove Castro to her home, which he examined in loving detail. "He was so interested, so impressed," she said, "and he asked me my birthday." July 5, 1927, she replied. "He started counting with those piano-player fingers of his, and I said to myself, what's he doing, this man with so much intelligence?" After a brief pause, Castro burst out, "I am eleven months your senior!" Castro was clearly enjoying himself and appeared to be in no hurry. Mier then took him to meet her family doctor and fellow town councilor, Alberto Nuevo. "I have met an extraordinary man," she told her friend. Within minutes Castro and Nuevo were referring to one another by their first names. Within the hour, the three had retreated to the doctor's office, where he opened a bottle of champagne.

The day passed in a blur. After more visits and more drinks (and, this being Cuba, no little coffee), it was time to return to Havana. The two had enjoyed themselves so much that they had forgotten to take time to eat. The alternating alcohol and coffee had left Castro exhausted. "Look," he said, "I'm too tired. Everywhere we go we get wine and coffee but no food. Now YOU will drive." Mier got into the driver's seat, more than a little nervous, she said, as "Cuban men never let women drive." On the way home, they stopped by a roadside stand for a quick sandwich. They had no money but for a few pesos a colleague had given Castro to pay for gas. Flushed by the day's events, Mier took a chance, asking Castro to dance. "I don't know how to dance," he replied, visibly upset. "So, we just ate," she said. "Fidel doesn't have a musical ear."

No, but he had an eye for injustice and continued to expand his circle by intervening when others simply looked the other way. Later that year, Castro attended a meeting of fellow conspirators in the city of Matanzas, forty miles east of Havana. While there, he learned about the plight of workers on a nearby farm uncompensated for months of labor. So he paid the farm a visit, introduced himself as a lawyer, and said he wanted to help. Several of the men remembered greeting Castro with skepticism. "Sure," the men responded, "like all lawyers." Castro insisted that he was not like most lawyers and asked to speak to their leader. After a few minutes, a young man approached, seemingly little more than a teenager but actually a local labor representative named Paulino Perdomo Ramos. Perdomo was no less suspicious of the interloper than his companions, but Castro convinced Perdomo to hear him out.[19]

An impromptu meeting was called at Perdomo's house. Castro introduced himself once more, promising on his word of honor to deliver the overdue wages within four days. But he could only do so, he explained, if the men signed off on his representation. "Listen, lawyer," Perdomo said, "this business of your word of honor has little currency with us. In truth, we don't know the meaning of the word; it's been beaten out of us." Not one to give up easily, Castro persisted and at last the men agreed. Castro drove away telling the men to expect an update within two days. One of the workers, Anisio Ruiz, remembered the men scratching their heads in astonishment. "'Who is this guy?' we asked one another. 'Where did he come from?'" The men had gone six months without hope. And then "this apparition appeared and charged us nothing."[20]

Two days later, a telegram arrived, prompting Perdomo to remark, "this guy may be for real." Two days after that, a car pulled up at the farm driven by Castro and missing one of its front doors. Castro leaped out, dressed in his signature pinstripe suit, a yellow envelope in hand. Not only had he recovered the men's wages, he told the workers, but he had resolved the dispute that precipitated the problem in the first place. The men insisted Castro accept payment for his services (a few pesos, some gas, a beer). Castro wouldn't hear of it. Looking back on the episode years later, one of the men, Dimas Carmona, remembered being amazed by a young lawyer's disinterest. "He did this for nothing," Carmona said. He alone received 500 pesos in back pay. The relief could not have come at a better time. "Castro saved my holiday."[21]

Meanwhile, Castro continued to conspire with fellow militants. On May 1, 1952, he attended a vigil commemorating the death of activist Carlos Rodríguez at the hands of Batista's police. There he met Jesús Montané and Abel Santamaría, young members of an Ortodoxo cell centered on Santamaría's home in Vedado. Montané was a manager at General Motors in Havana, Santamaría an accountant at Pontiac. The two were among the first to mobilize in the aftermath of the coup, combining with journalist Raúl Gómez García to produce an underground weekly, whose name, *They're All the Same (Son los mismos)*, spoke to the conviction of many dissidents that if Batista was worse than his predecessors, it was only by degree.

Castro envied Montané's and Santamaría's success at getting their message out in print. Montané remembers thinking that in Castro the opposition might just have found its leader. Castro was "the only one capable of really getting the movement going," Santamaría told a friend. Other activists described Santamaría in the exact same way ("just the person we've been looking for," said Melba Hernández). Castro and Santamaría complemented one another, with Santamaría's thoughtfulness a nice balance to Castro's charisma. At the same rally, Castro learned about a small ham radio in the possession of an Ortodoxo physician and inveterate tinkerer named Mario Muñoz, from the city of Colón. Castro quickly made arrangements to visit the doctor to see about borrowing his equipment. Ten days later, the transmitter was in place atop the roof of the School of Engineering, providing live coverage of yet another antigovernment demonstration. Its limited range did not moderate the enthusiasm of the crowd, which regarded the broadcast as a symbol that a true opposition was at long last taking shape.[22]

As summer yielded to fall, militant cells began to form in cities, villages, and towns across the country. The University of Havana remained a focal point. Carmen Castro, a young dissident, remembers the university becoming a "veritable beehive of patriotism," with some of the students engaged in strategizing, others immersed in weapons training. Castro approached the students in charge of the latter, Pedro Miret and Lester Rodríguez, to see about combining forces. Miret and Rodríguez agreed, and before long they were leading as many as twelve hundred dissidents in the fine points of assembling and disassembling M1 and Springfield rifles and operating mortars. From there, the dissidents graduated to live-fire exercises conducted at ranges throughout the city and surrounding countryside. Disguised as "upstanding members of the bourgeoisie," as Castro put it, the would-be combatants registered in hunting clubs and took up clay pigeon shooting. This was all perfectly legal,

Castro emphasized, and Batista's police had bigger fish to fry. "They knew we didn't have a cent."[23]

―――――――――

As his activities increased, Castro began to attract unwanted attention. In early February 1953, dissidents flocked to the Colón Cemetery to bury a young student named Rubén Batista, gravely injured by police the previous month. At the head of the demonstration marched the Frente Cívico de Mujeres Martianas (the Civic Front of Martían Women, known colloquially as the Mujeres Martianas), a coalition that included Castro's new friend Rosa Mier, as well as Pastorita Nuñez, Aida Pelayo, and Carmen Castro, all of whom would play significant roles in the ensuing revolution. The women carried an immense banner emblazoned with the words, "The Blood of the Good Shall Not Be Shed in Vain." Behind the banner came the slain boy's family and a large group of armed activists who expected to be confronted by police. They were not disappointed. When the funeral was over, the police moved in looking for Pelayo and Castro, who were thought to be behind the demonstration. Both escaped, disappearing into the protective crowd. The intervention by police turned up the tension, and the demonstrators headed back toward the university chanting "Down with tyranny! Death to Batista!"

Passing the opulent house of a Batista supporter, its fences festooned with images of the dictator, the crowd erupted, ripping down posters and overturning cars. The police dispersed the marchers by firing shots into the air. Desperate for a scapegoat, the authorities blamed the disturbance on "Ortodoxo militants led by the doctor Fidel Castro." In fact, thousands of witnesses placed Castro at the cemetery, blocks away from the riot.[24] A few days later, journalist José Pardo Llada attributed the government's accusation against Castro as an attempt to sow fear and confusion and thereby justify future aggressions against young activists. Castro was making waves.[25]

March 1953 was as quiet as January and February were raucous. For nearly a year, Castro had approached militants of various parties urging them to join him in a campaign to oust Batista by force. "We began to recruit and train men not in order to make a revolution," he told an interviewer years later, "but rather to engage in a struggle along with others."[26] With the anniversary of the coup fast approaching and Batista looking more entrenched than ever, Castro, Santamaría, and their circle resolved to go it alone. This necessitated a shift in strategy from simply raising hell to developing a feasible plan to overthrow the government. This, in turn, meant raising money, identifying and training combatants, and gathering arms, all the while maintaining secrecy in a community riddled by hacks and government infiltrators.

The new direction called for discretion rather than publicity, launching Castro on a new path for which he had little experience. A quiet Castro was grounds for suspicion, and Batista's agents might have devoted more attention to him during this stage but for rumors circulating in army headquarters of several other insurgencies brewing both inside and outside Cuba. In early March, Rafael García Bárcena, a popular philosophy professor at the Superior War College, apprised Castro that he planned to launch an assault on Camp Columbia, the nation's largest military barracks, just outside Havana. Right, Castro said, everybody who was anybody knew that, including rival action groups, Batista's police, and the U.S. embassy.[27] Bárcena shrugged off Castro's warning and carried on, eventually selecting Easter Sunday, April 5, 1953, as D-day. Castro, anticipating a fiasco, evacuated the capital, counseling other Movement leaders to lie low. Predictably, on Easter morning, Bárcena and his group were arrested and his conspiracy crushed. Bárcena was tried and sentenced to two years in prison. Years later, Castro said he might have welcomed the prospect of working with the renegade professor, had he reached out to no one else. Ecumenical and inclusive by nature, Bárcena insisted on consulting others; the result was "the most publicized action in Cuban history."[28]

Barcena's collapse was Castro's boon. Not only did it confirm Castro's instincts about the need for secrecy, but Castro picked up a core of disciplined activists still committed to overthrowing Batista. Castro gleaned another important lesson from Bárcena's foiled conspiracy. He had competition, and there was no time to waste. He stepped up his fundraising while infiltrating other dissident groups in an attempt to appropriate their arms.

Rumors abounded that spring and early summer of conspiracies hatching and exposed—and of weapons caches washing up along Cuba's coast. Some of the threats were undoubtedly hyped by the government to justify its crackdown on dissidents. Evidence of the government's genuine concern is discernible in the fact that it seems to have taken its eyes off Castro and company. The Movement's immediate need was money. One of its emerging ranks, an accountant named Raúl Martínez Ararás, was friends with Ortodoxo senator José Gutiérrez Planes, a militant with deep pockets. Martínez and Castro visited Gutiérrez at his home in Matanzas. Over the course of a long conversation, Castro convinced Gutiérrez of his capability and vision. The next week Gutiérrez sent Castro a check for 5,000 pesos, later providing access to other wealthy friends.[29]

It was not just the rich who contributed to the Movement. Castro's foot soldiers came up with everything they could. Jesús Montané contributed $4,000 of severance pay from his job at General Motors, which had recently closed up shop in Cuba. Ernesto Tizol mortgaged his chicken farm. Oscar Alcalde mortgaged his laboratory and liquidated his accounting business. Renato Guitart donated $1,000. Pedro Marrero sold his furniture and refrigerator. The list goes on.[30] Estimates of the amount raised by the rebels fall between $16,000 and $35,000. Critics say that Alcalde, among others, stole from his employer to fund the Moncada attack. Castro insisted that all the money was meant to be repaid.[31]

The Movement's fundraising was impressive, especially given the donor pool. Still, whether $16,000 or $35,000 (or somewhere in between), this was not a sum of which militant dreams are made. In the immediate aftermath of the Moncada attack, Colonel Chaviano described the insurgents' weapons as state-of-the-art instruments of war. In fact, their weapons could not have been more rudimentary. Castro later listed one (broken) machine gun, three Winchester rifles ("from the time of Buffalo Bill"), and a motley collection of low-caliber pistols, rifles, and shotguns. Two of the three Winchesters came from the Castro home in Birán.[32] Castro's evolving plans involved a group of combatants, posing as Cuban soldiers, staging a surprise attack on one or more military garrisons. This required uniforms, which Castro attained through an orderly at Camp Columbia, who raided the laundry and bought surplus outfits from soldiers looking to make some cash.[33]

After procuring weapons and uniforms, Castro's next task was to identify a feasible target. Even with the element of surprise and despite his military connections, Bárcena had stood little chance of commandeering the garrison at Camp Columbia, home to the nation's arsenal and seat of military power. With his meager budget and rudimentary weapons, Castro could not even fantasize about such a strike. He fixed his gaze on two isolated garrisons in Oriente, Santiago de Cuba's Moncada Barracks and army headquarters in Bayamo. The nation's second largest military installation, Moncada paled by comparison to Camp Columbia, and it looked to be an inviting target. The capture of Moncada would provide Castro the keys to the city and potentially the east, so long as the attackers could cut off access from the rest of Cuba. Which is where Bayamo fit in. The city is situated along the Río Cauto, one of the principal communication routes connecting Oriente Province to the rest of Cuba. With control of the Bayamo garrison, the rebels might sever communication, leaving the province in rebel hands. Oriente was also symbolically and culturally strategic. Virtually every rebellion ever launched in Cuba began there, its isolation, geography, and climate providing a safe harbor for individuals out of favor in the capital. In sum, Castro later remarked,

Oriente was "a logical place to strike"—"hot humid, and languid," hence "more likely to be caught off guard."[34]

———————

By early summer 1953, Cuban intelligence officials were monitoring chatter about an impending attack on Oriente, perhaps even on the Moncada Barracks. The rumors emanated not from Havana, but from Montreal, Canada, and the Ritz-Carlton Hotel, where former president Carlos Prío convened a meeting of displaced Auténtico and Ortodoxo party leaders, including Emilio Ochoa and José Pardo Llada. By the so-called Montreal Pact of June 2, 1953, the conferees pledged to oust Batista, establish a provisional government, and restore the 1940 Constitution. To young dissidents looking on from Havana, the significance of the pact lay not in its program, which was essentially meaningless without a method of toppling the dictator, but in its confirmation that little or nothing separated Auténtico from Ortodoxo party leadership. Santamaría and Montané had gotten it right: *son los mismos*—the politicians really were the same. But were they? The Montreal Pact signatories were no less committed than the other groups to the use of force. With Prío providing the financial backing, Ochoa and Pardo Llada reached out to army and navy officers thought to be wary of Batista and willing to lend their support for a violent overthrow.

And they were not the only ones. In June and early July, newspapers in Cuba and New York claimed to possess evidence of insurgents amassing in training camps across the Caribbean Basin. The Batista government took the rumors seriously. In June, guards at the Moncada Barracks were put through their paces, as the government scoured the coastline for more weapons dumps. News of an impending invasion led Castro to expedite his plans. In May, he had set a launch date of Sunday, July 26, 1953, which coincided with the celebration of Carnival in Santiago de Cuba, a favored distraction for insurgent forces across the centuries. With Cubans flocking to Santiago from all over the country, who would notice a few cars full of gun-toting guerrillas?

Castro's idea was to take the Moncada and Bayamo garrisons simultaneously by surprise, avoiding a firefight which the rebels would surely lose. In the event of a firefight, the rebels would be able to distinguish one another from the soldiers by their shoes—which were not "military-issue," Castro later noted, but "low-cut street shoes."[35] Castro assumed that if he and his men could disarm the Moncada Barracks, he could appeal to the soldiers to join the campaign against the dictator. The city and nation would then learn about the events via a radio broadcast that included Castro reciting Chibás's last speech. With both Moncada and Bayamo in rebel hands, he would put "the Cuban people immediately on a war footing."[36]

In Santiago, much of the logistics burden fell on the shoulders of Renato Guitart. Castro had met Guitart at Rubén Batista's bedside vigil the previous winter. The two hit it off immediately and spent much of the succeeding evening in conversation. Guitart returned to Santiago committed to Castro and his revolutionary vision. "I went to the hospital to see Rubén and there I met a guy who is a phenomenon, what a mentality!" Guitart told his father upon returning home. "How active! That man is a revolutionary, dad! He has a forceful personality, and lives very much in the future. A man like that is only born every 500 years!"[37] Castro was equally impressed by Guitart. At the time they met, Guitart was a member of Justo Carrillo Hernández's dissident group, Liberating Action. Castro asked Guitart to approach Carrillo about combining forces. Carrillo declined, but Guitart came on board. In planning the assault on Moncada, Guitart was the only person in Santiago whom Castro trusted with the details, assigning him to provide intelligence on the attack site and to carry out necessary arrangements.

In May, Castro dispatched Oscar Alcalde, treasurer of the Movement, to Santiago to gather evidence about the Moncada Barracks. Ingratiating himself with soldiers at the various guard posts, Alcalde derived a rudimentary sense of the lay of the land. A few days later, Castro traveled to Santiago with Raúl Martínez and Ernesto Tizol in search of a safe house in which to store guns and ammunition.

Born in a peasant family in rural Galicia, Ángel Castro was a first-generation landowner determined to ensure that his children never had to suffer the hardship he endured.

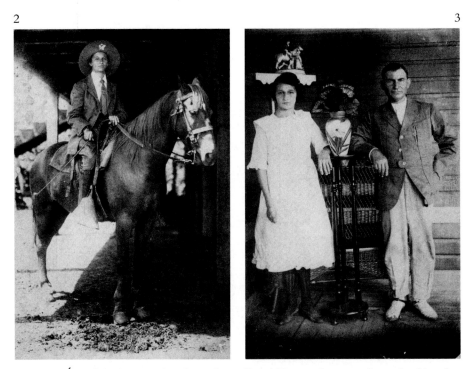

In 1920, Ángel (45) met Lina Ruz González (17, seen here on horseback), who entered his household as a servant but quickly became his soul mate. Despite their age difference, the couple forged an effective partnership, with Ángel taking care of the farm work while Lina balanced the books, ran the company store, and raised a family. The couple would have seven children in total, all of them born before they were married in 1943.

Fidel Castro, pictured here as a young boy, was born on August 13, 1926, on his parents' vast farm in Birán, in what was then Oriente Province. Castro credited growing up alongside the children of his father's Cuban and Haitian laborers with inoculating him against the snobbery and racism prevalent among many wealthy Cubans.

The Castro farmhouse. The area underneath provided shelter for animals and farm equipment, while the generous porch was the site of social gatherings, card games, and political wrangling.

The one-room school-house on the Castro property. Castro always appreciated the value of education but never had much patience for the give-and-take of the classroom.

At age seven, Castro was sent away for private tutoring to this home in Santiago de Cuba, where he passed six long months at the hands of an incompetent tutor. Starved for intellectual nourishment, as well as food, he regarded the experience as a form of banishment.

The next year, Castro, at left with brothers Raúl and Ramón, entered Colegio de La Salle, an elite private school in Santiago de Cuba, where he relished the contact with peers and recreational excursions around Santiago Bay.

On school holidays, Castro loved to ride and hunt in the countryside above Birán, much of it owned or leased by Ángel, sometimes in the company of friends and siblings, but often on his own. So much time spent alone in the wilderness instilled in him the virtue of self-reliance, which proved useful as he moved from boarding school to boarding school, from university to politics, and from politics to guerrilla warfare.

Castro, standing at left, surrounded (moving clockwise) by sister Angela, brother Ramón, sister Juanita, an aunt, and brother Raúl.

At the age of twelve, having worn out his welcome at La Salle, Castro, second from the left in the front row, moved up the hill to Colegio de Dolores, one of the most prestigious schools on the island. Peers and prefects alike were impressed by his curiosity and athleticism.

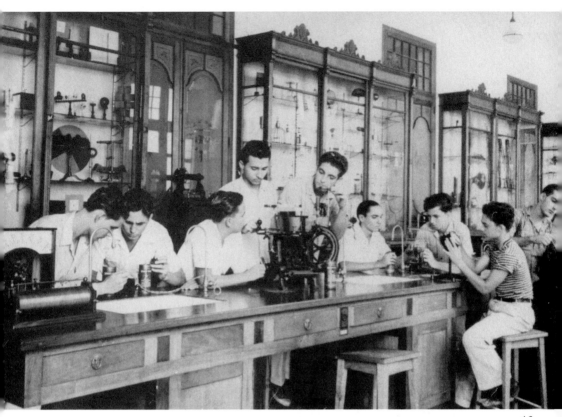

In autumn 1942 Castro departed Santiago de Cuba for the nation's capital and Colegio de Belén, a veritable factory of politicians and businessmen. Castro, second from the left in both photographs, quickly made a name for himself as a top athlete and student leader.

15

Though accomplished at soccer and basketball, Castro (second from left, above, and at left, below, in Pino del Río) also loved hiking and mountain climbing, sometimes helping his teachers get the boys out of dicey situations.

In his last year of high school, Castro was selected as one of several Belén seniors to defend private school education before an audience of alumni, family, and political luminaries. Castro, who would later dismantle Cuba's private education system, delivered a much lauded performance.

18

One of three valedictorians of the class of 1945, Castro's caption reads: "He stood out in all subjects related to letters. Excellent and dependable, he always defended the School flag with valor and pride. . . . He goes on to a career in the Law and we have no doubt that he will fill the book of his life with brilliant pages."

After scouring the region for several days, they came upon a farmhouse on the coast road east of Santiago near the town of Siboney. Tizol was a chicken farmer and the idea was to persuade the owner to rent the property, Casa Blanca, for his chicken enterprise. After much persuading, the owner agreed. In mid-June, Abel Santamaría moved out to the "chicken farm," setting to work on alterations designed to disguise its real use. This included erecting a wall between the road fronting the house and a parking lot and reinforcing a fifteen-foot well in which the militants would store guns and ammunition. Meanwhile, Guitart rented properties in Santiago and Bayamo to house guerrillas in transit and to store still more guns, ammunition, and uniforms, which began to arrive in the east via automobile, train, and bus. Guitart also outfitted these properties with refrigerators and collapsible beds.

Despite the accelerating pace of preparations, Castro checked in on his family whenever he could. His younger sister, Enma, attended the elite Colegio de las Ursulinas in Havana, and was due to graduate on June 12. A week or so before, Castro dropped in on Enma to offer his congratulations. "I graduate on the twelfth!" Enma remembers telling her brother. "Yes, I promise to come!" Castro assured her. Raúl Castro, just back from a student congress in Vienna and a tour of Eastern Bloc countries, attended the graduation. His brother did not make it. Immediately after graduating, Enma Castro returned to Birán. Her father asked if she had seen Fidel. Yes, she had seen him, and all was well. "Something tells me he's up to something," Ángel remarked. "Tell him to stop conspiring and start working! I'm not sending him any more money."[38]

Raúl Castro's trip abroad meant that he figured little in preparations for the attack. In fact, he nearly missed being able to participate at all thanks to some rough treatment meted out to him by Batista's police upon his return from the communist bloc. Stepping off the boat at the beginning of the month, he and two Guatemalans, both students, were detained by Cuban intelligence officials, interrogated, and thoroughly searched. Afterward they were taken to the city jail,

Castillo del Príncipe, where they were brutally beaten by a group of prisoners egged on by the police. The incident sparked a vehement protest at Havana University, where Raúl Castro was enrolled in the Law School.[39]

By mid-July, people, arms, ammunition, and supplies were heading east. On the 22nd, Haydée Santamaría, Abel's sister, left Havana by train bound for Santiago de Cuba with two suitcases bursting with guns and uniforms. Two days later, Melba Hernández followed suit, her own baggage loaded with contraband. In Santiago, Guitart, who knew the city best, dashed about purchasing food, fuel, and other necessities required to feed the commandos, finish their uniforms, and send them on their way. Castro himself remained in Havana until the day before the attack. Crisscrossing the city and province, he chased down cell leaders, ordering them to collect their men and deliver them to established checkpoints. He then sent the men on to Santiago, one group at a time. The government-imposed state of alert made the process of gathering and dispatching the cells tricky to say the least. In the furious days leading up to the attack, not a single one of the recruits was picked up on charges of suspicious activity, though Gildo Fleitas and Melba Hernández were arrested and held for three days on weapons charges after getting in a car accident.[40]

Cuban intelligence had an inkling that something was up. On or around July 22, the Servicio Inteligencia Militar (SIM) received news of a cache of weapons accumulating in a town east of Santiago. The next day, the queries of SIM Lieutenant Armando Acosta Sánchez were brushed off by Colonel Chaviano, chief of the Moncada garrison. "I am in charge here and I know everything that happens," Chaviano told Acosta. "There is nothing unusual going on." Chaviano's arrogance did not end the rumors, some of which had camouflaged insurgents launching an attack on the garrison. Taking its lead from Chaviano, government authorities more or less shrugged off the threat, only slightly increasing the guard at Moncada.

Thanks to the strict discipline maintained in the cell system, most of the men sent to Oriente did not know where they were headed or what they would be asked to do. Juan Almeida, for instance, thought he was bound for Carnival for some well-earned rest and relaxation. Telegraph operator Manuel Lorenzo was simply asked to come along for an important job in the east. In the week after the attack, Raúl Castro told his sister Juanita that the insurgents committed "to fight the dictator, but without knowing the objective each would have." The point was that no one should possess any more information than was essential to their specific task.[41] Friends and neighbors were not to be trusted. "Batista's people were everywhere and the smallest error could sink the entire operation." One of the last stops Castro made was at the home of his friend and contributor Naty Revuelta, whom he had charged with producing a stencil copy of the Moncada Manifesto to be distributed to newspapers and radio stations as the attack was taking place.[42]

Manifesto in hand, Castro began a helter-skelter drive to Bayamo and Santiago, via Matanzas, Colón, Santa Clara, Placetas, Cabaiguán, Sancti Spíritus, Ciego de Ávila, Florida, and Camagüey, taking care of last-minute details, making sure that men and materials were on their way. He arrived in Bayamo at sunset on Saturday, where he checked in on an assault group at the Gran Casino hotel. On the way to Santiago, he and his driver, Teodulio Mitchell, were detained at an army checkpoint near the town of Palma Soriano. Mitchell recognized the soldier who pulled them over. This was Castro's lucky day: a friendly salute, a fraternal wave, and the two were on their way. Past midnight and with less than five hours to go before the attack, the two descended the hilly highway into Santiago de Cuba.

By shortly after midnight, Carnival is on full boil. Leaving their car, Castro and Mitchell disappeared into the crowd, grateful for the anonymity. Within minutes, the two were greeted by a conga line in which waddled the portly and affable Gildo Fleitas, who had missed a rendezvous earlier that day, and whose well-being had become a source of consternation. Just a mechanical problem, Fleitas assured a relieved Castro. Castro was quickly surrounded by a group of revelers only recently arrived in the east and who had no knowledge of the mission that awaited them. Among the merrymakers was Dr. Muñoz, the ham radio operator and mechanical tinkerer first drawn to Castro's attention the previous May. Catching word of an adventure whose details he could not fathom, Muñoz signed on that very day, journeying the six hundred kilometers from his home in Colón to the eastern capital. "Has zero hour arrived?" Muñoz wanted to know. "Yes, doctor," Castro replied. "It's zero hour." "Congratulations!" Muñoz exclaimed. "What a day you've picked! I'm forty-one years old today, and I'm placing those years in the hands of a 26-year-old!"

On Saturday night, July 25, 1953, the rebels pulled out of Santiago at around 10 p.m., bound for Siboney and Villa Blanca. Most of the men still did not know the nature of their mission. Castro arrived in Siboney around 10:30 p.m. Weapons were withdrawn from the dry well outside the farmhouse and laid out on a bedroom floor. Uniforms were dropped down from a trapdoor in the attic, with last-minute adjustments made and ironing done by Haydée Santamaría and Melba Hernández, the only women in the group. The rebels' cache consisted of forty shotguns, thirty-five .22-caliber rifles, sixty handguns, twenty-four assorted-caliber rifles (twelve of them dating from the turn of the century), one .30-caliber M1 Garand rifle, and an unusable .45-caliber machine gun.[43]

Castro ordered the men to bed and headed back to Santiago. He returned to Siboney and Villa Blanca two hours later to begin final preparations for the assault. Uniforms were distributed amid much fuss about sizing and military insignia. Fed up by the bickering, Castro ordered everyone to turn in the uniforms, at which point they were redistributed by those with some knowledge of sizing. The distribution of weapons created excitement for some, consternation for others. Those who knew a weapon of war from a curio found the group's arsenal laughable. Ammunition was scarce, many of the guns antique, and some of the "commandos" had never fired a shot.

The time had come for Castro to reveal his plan. "We're going to attack the Moncada Barracks," he began. "It will be a surprise attack. It shouldn't take more than ten minutes."[44] As Castro spoke, a rough outline of the barracks was pinned to the wall. Arriving in Santiago from the east, the rebel caravan would depart the Siboney road at a traffic circle at the intersection of Avenida de Americas and Avenida Victoriano Garzón. Taking the fourth (*not the third!*) exit in the traffic circle, the cars would emerge on Avenida Victoriano Garzón, proceeding less than a mile to a right turn on Avenida Moncada. Leaving the military hospital on the left and the officers' quarters on the right, the cars would proceed five hundred meters to Post No. 3, where, if all went according to plan, the rebels' uniforms would confuse the guards long enough to allow them to disarm two sentries, storm the barracks, seize the weapons, and capture the somnambulant soldiers.

Meanwhile a second group would occupy the Saturnino Lora Civil Hospital, whose roof and windows commanded the rear entrances to the barracks, thus allowing the rebels to cut off any escape. A third group would do the same at the nearby Palace of Justice, whose commanding position in the neighborhood afforded occupants a favorable vantage on the surroundings. With the barracks and its three thousand modern weapons in rebel control, the attackers would then commandeer the communications center and proclaim yet another "Sergeants' Revolt," this one committed to the good of Cuba. The news would sow chaos in military ranks throughout the country, buying time for the rebels to consolidate their position. "Our plan was to immediately get the weapons out of Moncada," Castro later explained, "and distribute them to various buildings across the city." With the railway lines cut, the only plausible source of military support was from the air or via the

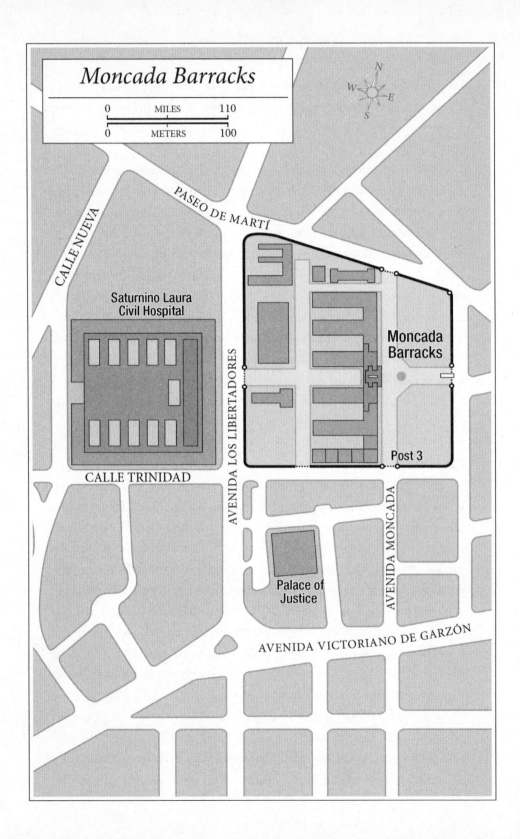

Moncada Barracks

0 MILES 110

0 METERS 100

PASEO DE MARTÍ

CALLE NUEVA

Saturnino Laura
Civil Hospital

AVENIDA LOS LIBERTADORES

Moncada
Barracks

Post 3

CALLE TRINIDAD

Palace of
Justice

AVENIDA MONCADA

AVENIDA VICTORIANO DE GARZÓN

Central Highway, which the Bayamo garrison attackers had been assigned to cut. After securing Santiago de Cuba, the rebels would reveal their true identity and motivation to the city and the nation, broadcasting a recording of Chibás's last words, along with the Cuban national anthem and a bracing hit parade. The nation would rise up in support of the Revolution and its premise, namely, that there was indeed "such a thing as sovereignty on this planet," and that sovereignty was "a real, respected right after the two Wars of Independence in our nation."[45]

The plan did not meet with universal approbation. Victor Escalona, leader of the Almendares cell, shuffled forward. "We don't want to take part," Escalona announced. "We?" Castro replied. "My group and I," he said. Why, Castro demanded. Because the "arms are inadequate," Escalona replied. Then come with me, Castro said, leading the opt-outers to the kitchen, where he posted an armed guard. The Almendares men were not the only naysayers. Returning to the main room, Castro met Abel Santamaría, who informed him that another group was passing. "Which one?" Castro demanded. "The student group," Santamaría replied. "They said they wouldn't fight with those arms." The students were put in a different room with yet another guard.[46]

Amid mounting tension, another person stepped forward, the telegraph operator whose job it would be to announce the good news to city and the country. What was his objection? Castro asked. "I don't want to do anything illegal," the man replied, before being hauled off to join the students. Castro's voice rose. "Is there anyone else who wants to pull out?" he bellowed. When no one else stepped forward, he repeated his command to "be humane with the enemy." The group then boarded the sixteen cars bound for Santiago, Castro in the lead.[47]

Just after 5 a.m. on the morning of July 26, 1953, the caravan entered Santiago de Cuba along the Siboney road, approaching the traffic circle at Parque Ferreiro. Instructions were to take the fourth exit out of the circle onto Avenida Victoriano Garzón. Most of the cars did so. The car driven by Ernesto Tizol, the chicken farmer, did not. Instead, it veered off onto Avenida de las Americas, eventually ending up on Quintero Heights, overlooking the city. Some of the cars behind Tizol followed him, depriving Castro of between 20 to 30 percent of the combatants. Tizol later claimed that his diversion had been a mistake. His brother-in-law, Raúl Martínez, reported that Tizol had diverted from the course intentionally, believing the plan to be unworkable. Tizol was one of the few attackers who knew the route intimately, having traveled repeatedly to Santiago to arrange the rental of Villa Blanca. The idea that his diversion was a mistake seems unlikely, though it is not clear that his and the others' presence would have made much difference in the end. Tizol was not the only person in the caravan with misgivings. According to some reports, Dr. Muñoz's elation scarcely outlasted the conga line. Hearing what seemed to him a suicidal plan, Muñoz withdrew his support, telling Hector de Armas that this was not what he had signed on for.[48]

The Moncada Barracks is shaped like a comb, its terraced front facing a parade ground, with six radiating wings reaching back toward a shooting range, located to the rear. Each wing is accessed by staircases descending from the front terrace. The first wing (or east end) of the barracks housed the arsenal and administrative offices. The remaining five wings consisted of sleeping quarters. The main entrance to the fortress is a grand staircase that marks the midpoint of the terrace and parade ground. Reconnaissance suggested that this entrance was covered by fixed weaponry from at least two guard posts. Castro planned to access the barracks from the south, along Avenida Moncada, which continued down the front of the terrace, impeded only by a chain at Guard Post No. 3. Masquerading as a caravan of high military officials (in beat-up cars—don't ask), the men would then silently disarm the guards, lower the chain, and proceed to the barracks proper. In the event that some unexpected glitch spoiled the element of surprise, the attackers would be ready. Abel Santamaría's group would cover the attackers from atop the Civil Hospital. Meanwhile, to one side and slightly behind the barracks stood the Palace of Justice, the city's main courthouse. Raúl Castro and a few others would occupy the courthouse, head to the roof, and act as snipers, neutralizing the barracks' mounted guns.

Things went immediately awry. Just before turning off Avenida Victoriano Garzón onto Avenida Moncada, Castro allowed the car driven by Pedro Marrero to pass him. Marrero's mission was to surprise the guards and lower the chain that barred access to the terrace stairways. As Marrero advanced down Avenida Moncada, his car was surprised by two soldiers out on foot patrol, armed with Thompson machine guns. The patrol ordered Marrero to halt. "Open the way, here comes the general!" shouted Renato Guitart, as Marrero continued on. Seeing the attackers' uniforms, the patrol did not immediately open fire, allowing Marrero to proceed to Post 3, disarm the sentries, and lower the chain. So far so good.

At this point, the plan called for Marrero to proceed into the parade ground (or move his car out of the way), thus allowing the following five cars to clear the guard post. But in the excitement of disarming the sentries, Marrero and his men simply charged up the stairs and into the administration building, leaving their car sprawled across the entrance, thereby stranding their comrades in the cars behind. Meanwhile, the two machine-gun-wielding foot soldiers were not fooled for long. They took off after Marrero's car, before, sensing danger from behind, wheeling to confront Castro's car as it approached the guard post. The soldiers raised their weapons. Castro hit the gas, his car lurching forward with some of his men half in and half out. The sound of gunfire rang out as Castro swerved sharply up onto the curb, where his car stalled. Amid whizzing bullets and the wail of sirens, he and the passengers of the other cars tumbled out and ran for cover in nearby officers' quarters, adjacent buildings, and military hospital.

Only five of the ninety or so insurgents who departed Villa Blanca ever penetrated the barracks gate—Marrero, José Luis

Tasende, Carmelo Noa, Flores Betancourt, and Rigoberto Corcho. Rather than joining them in the building, according to plan, Castro was forced to waste his time extricating his men from the military hospital. With most of the men back on Avenida Moncada, he urged them toward Post 3. Finally, he commandeered one of the other cars and headed toward the barracks. At this point, everything that could have gone wrong did. Castro's car was smashed into by another rebel car speeding in reverse as its occupants tried to escape what had become a shooting gallery. Now out of the car and back on the street, Castro was fully exposed. He paused for a moment, as if weighing his options.

"I did not see Fidel shooting," said Gerardo Granado, "but I assume he did. Fidel stayed in the street the whole time, giving instructions to someone, but I did not see who it was." Carlos Bustillo remembered Castro advancing as far as Post 3. "Fidel was behind the left sentry box and Héctor de Armas and I were in back of the opposite one." There, the three men's progress was stalled by machine gun fire pouring from the building. "The only thing we could do was stick close to the wall," Armas reported, "until Fidel ordered the retreat."[49]

Predictably, the two other groups had better luck against civilian targets. As Castro and company turned onto Avenida Moncada, the others continued down Avenida Victoriano Garzón to Avenida Los Libertadores, where Raúl Castro's group turned right into the Palace of Justice, which sat on the corner, entered the building, disarmed the guards, and mounted the stairs onto the roof, before opening fire on the fortress. Santamaría's group drove past the courthouse and turned left onto Calle Trinidad, where they abandoned their vehicles, entered the Civil Hospital, and disarmed the guard. They then took up positions at the rear of the building overlooking the back of the barracks, their effectiveness marred by an imposing wall. Santamaría and his men were later joined by his sister, Haydée, Melba Hernández, Dr. Mario Muñoz, and Raúl Gómez García, delayed by Tizol's detour onto Avenida de las Americas.

Once in place, there was not much for Raúl Castro's and Santamaría's groups to do. The hospital roof proved less useful than supposed, and the men on the courthouse roof were thoroughly outgunned. The attack was over before it really started. Witnesses differ about how long the shooting lasted. Some said two hours, some said a matter of minutes. It was likely closer to the latter. In the brief exchange, fifteen soldiers and three policemen died, twenty-three soldiers and five policemen were injured. The rebels suffered nine deaths and eleven wounded. Sporadic gunfire continued to echo through the neighborhood long after Castro retreated and the attackers were disarmed. By this time the shooting was one-sided, the work of professional soldiers executing captives at point-blank— eighteen that morning, thirty-four more over the ensuing three days.

Critics accuse Castro of abandoning his comrades as he retreated. In truth, he confronted the unpalatable decision familiar to any commander in chief in the face of insurmountable odds: withdraw immediately, thus saving many lives, or hold tight in an effort to rescue captured and fallen comrades. The first exchange of gunfire brought the barracks immediately to life, with the situation becoming riskier by the minute. That said, Castro's decision to pull out looks callous given the fate of the captives swept up in his wake.

The retreat left four groups behind: a few attackers holed up in the officers' housing on Avenida Moncada; the five occupants of the first car who breached the administrative wing of the barracks; the six men (including Raúl Castro) who occupied the Palace of Justice; and the twenty men and two women who commandeered the Civil Hospital. Each group had to decide on its own whether to surrender or flee. A few of the men in the military housing gave themselves up. Others were discovered hiding under beds, some changed into stolen civilian clothes. Approaching the soldiers, hands in the air, one of this group, Pedro Miret, was kicked in the groin and brutally beaten by apparently leaderless soldiers. Others received similar treatment before being rescued by a few doctors from the military hospital.

The five rebels who penetrated the barracks had to fend for themselves. Pedro Marrero tried to surrender. He was dragged onto the terrace and beaten to death with the butt of a gun. Two of the others met the same fate. One witness recalled soldiers pummeling the captives with rifle butts while an officer ordered them (futilely) to stop. José Luis Tasende tried to escape this fate by leaping out of a window onto an adjacent street. He hurt his leg in the process and was taken to a local emergency room before being discovered by a policemen and turned over to regimental intelligence. An iconic photograph shows Tasende cowering in a prison cell with bound wrists, bare feet, and a desolate expression on his face. Sometime later, he was removed from the cell, taken to the shooting range, and executed. One witness confessed to being "bothered" by Tasende's execution on account of his leg wound. He "did not care about the fate of the other prisoners," he said.[50]

Meanwhile, with their exit cut off, the rebels occupying the Civil Hospital tried to disguise themselves as nurses and patients. Nineteen of the twenty-two (not including Haydée Santamaría and Melba Hernández) were apprehended and led to the back of the hospital. On the way, the physician Dr. Muñoz was shot in the side at close range before being finished off in the temple, a harbinger of things to come. The captives were placed in a holding cell around 8:30 a.m., before being taken to regimental headquarters, interrogated by the Regimental Intelligence Service, and tested for paraffin. A few of the rebels, Abel Santamaría and Boris Luis Santa Coloma, among them, were placed in a prison cell. The rest were led straightaway to the shooting range where they were executed.

Raúl Castro's group at the Palace of Justice had better luck, with all six of the men escaping initially to the countryside. Initial success at disappearing into the city or escaping into the countryside was no guarantee of making it out alive. By the end of the fourth day after the attack, sixty-one rebels suffered the fate of Mario Muñoz. Most were dispatched at the shooting range behind the barracks, now converted into a killing field. Santamaría, among others, was shot at Villa Blanca, after the citizens of Santiago wearied of the sound of rebels being executed without trial. Others were felled where they were found, on hillsides outside Santiago, on farms near Bayamo, in the woods of Damajayabo, and elsewhere, as a lethal dragnet tightened across Oriente.

By mid-morning government forces were closing in on dissidents all over Cuba, not just in Oriente Province. In Havana, Ortodoxo leadership was swept up, Auténtico, too, presumably for being associated with the alleged mastermind of the attack—not Fidel Castro, but former president Carlos Prío and, still more incoherently, the communists. Closer to the scene of the attack, rebels discovered in flight were brought to Moncada, where they received the same treatment of those apprehended in the Civil Hospital. By mid-afternoon, thirty-three executed rebels lay in underclothes in the shooting range at the back of the barracks, their military uniforms stripped from them by vengeful soldiers. When Colonel Chaviano came upon the scene, he ordered the rebel cadavers to be distributed around the grounds, where Marta Rojas and Panchito Cano and their fellow journalists encountered them. The dead had to be dressed before being dropped, which accounts for the over-hasty staging Rojas described, including unlaced boots, suspiciously clean uniforms, and gunshot-riddled bodies with no entry marks on their clothes.[51]

Leaving the Palace of Justice, Raúl Castro headed out of the city along the railroad tracks toward the village of Dos Caminos, fifteen miles north of Santiago, where the tracks turn sharply east. He hoped to find shelter in Birán. The following morning, he was spotted walking the rails in the direction of the town of San Luis and picked up by three policemen. In San Luis, he was interrogated and his alibi quickly exposed. But he passed a paraffin test (suggesting he had not fired a shot at the Palace of Justice), which likely accounts for his survival. The next day, Tuesday, July 28, he was transferred to the town of Palma Soriano, held for three days, then transferred again, this time to Santiago city jail on Thursday afternoon, July 30. By that time, the slaughter of rebels and innocents had halted thanks to the intervention of two like-minded civic groups from Santiago de Cuba, one appealing through the Masonic grand master, Carlos Piñeiro del Cueto, resident of Havana, directly to Batista, the other through the archbishop of Santiago, Enrique Pérez Serantes, to Colonel Chaviano.

As Raúl Castro and his group of commandos departed the Palace of Justice, his brother was on his way to Siboney in a Buick Studebaker overloaded with nine men. They arrived at Villa Blanca around 6:30 a.m. There they joined a group numbering between forty-five and fifty men in total, all confronting the question of what to do. Should they disperse into the hills? Regroup for an attack on a smaller garrison, say, at El Caney? Return to Santiago? Amid the chaos and recrimination, the group split up into smaller cells and walked into the hills. Within a half hour, Castro and eighteen others crossed the Siboney road and headed north into the Gran Piedra Mountains. For two days, the eighteen men stayed together, relying for sustenance on the generosity of local peasants with little to share. Around midday Monday, July, 27, Castro received the first inkling of the developments at the Moncada barracks in the wake of his retreat. A local peasant had a shortwave radio, allowing the fugitives to hear Fulgencio Batista giving his version of the previous day's attack. The government's report listed thirty-three dead insurgents. The fugitives could think of only nine casualties at the time they withdrew. Moreover, one of the people counted among the dead was Emilio Hernández, who had not even made the trip to Moncada, having pulled out of the attack back at Villa Blanca.[52] There was no word on whether Raúl Castro was alive.

Avoiding capture while scavenging for food amid a destitute population in a steep, wet, and unforgiving climate is like trying to rob a house with a football team which has had too much to drink.

On Tuesday morning, July 28, Castro ordered the group to break up, before continuing on with Juan Almeida, Oscar Alcalde, José "Pepe" Suárez, Mario Chanes, Pancho Gonzáles, Armando Maestre, and Eduardo Montano. Over the course of the next several days, Castro's band advanced little, moving in circles, which seems surprising given their leader's experience in the mountains. The group spent three nights in caves and cow pastures before arriving at the farm of Luis Piña, a few miles up the road from Villa Blanca, on the evening of Friday, July 31. Frustrated by their lack of progress and doubtful the group could elude capture much longer, Castro convinced Almeida, Chanes, Gonzáles, Maestre, and Montano to surrender the next day. At 7 a.m. the next morning, the five departed for the Siboney road and a rendezvous with Archbishop Serantes, who had stepped in to prevent further massacre.

As the archbishop made his way to the rendezvous point, Lieutenant Pedro Sarría Tartabull led a party of fifteen soldiers into the hills above the hamlet of Sevilla, where a local peasant steered them in the direction of Luis Piña's home. After their fellow fugitives departed, Castro, Alcalde, and Suárez dozed off in a lean-to. They awoke with the gun barrels of Sarría's men in their ribs, a few of the soldiers bent on avenging fallen comrades. A bit of indirection on Castro's part saved his and the other two men's lives. Asked for his name, Castro replied, "My name is Francisco González Calderín," while simultaneously communicating to Sarría his real identity. Thanks to Sarría's professionalism, the three were delivered not to the Moncada Barracks, which would have been the end of them, but to the city jail, where the press and the archbishop were waiting, thus ensuring that Castro lived to fight another day.[53]

The scale of the massacre is not debated by serious historians. But the nature and degree of atrocity has remained a bone of contention since both the rebels and the government first attempted to spin events in their favor nearly seventy years ago. Castro and his companions accused the government of torturing captives before executing them. Abel Santamaría is said to have had his eyes gouged out before he was executed, Boris Luis said to have been castrated. Santamaría's case testifies to the difficulty of resolving the dispute. The supposed eyewitness accounts of his sister Haydée and Melba Hernández evolved over time, both admitting years later to exaggerating their story.[54] In testimony provided in Miami, the funeral director who recovered the dead, Manuel Bartolomé, reported seeing no sign of mutilation on Santamaría's corpse. Meanwhile, the very fact of Bartolomé having gone into exile disqualifies him in the eyes of Castro defenders.

Lieutenant Jesús Yánez Pelletier, who later saved Castro's life in prison and became his bodyguard upon the triumph of the Revolution (before being dismissed and going into exile himself), reported seeing Santamaría alive on his way to execution at Villa Blanca. Yánez Pelletier, too, reports that Santamaría's face was not disfigured. Moreover, photographs of the Siboney dead, purportedly suppressed by the Cuban government, are said to show no evidence of disfigurement, according to those who have seen them. All of which suggests that people will believe what they want (and need) to believe.

Castro accused Batista of authorizing the summary executions. According to received opinion in Cuba, Batista dispatched Inspector General Martín Díaz Tamayo to Santiago that afternoon with orders to "kill ten rebels for every fallen soldier." Former Oriente governor Waldo Pérez Almaguer refutes this account, blaming the massacre on a rogue officer, Colonel Chaviano. Likewise, Adolfo Nieto Piñeiro-Osorio, one of the judges who would preside over Castro's trial, insisted that the "savagery could not be blamed on Batista." Not directly, that is. Nieto attributed the violence to vengeance on the part of soldiers who lost friends and family. But that raises the question of why soldiers from the lowliest private to the barracks commander himself believed they could get away with it.

In the aftermath of Batista's March 1952 coup d'état, even a skeptical Castro was surprised by the passivity of Cuba's leading politicians and opposition groups. Surely, in the face of so grave a threat to the country's political institutions, its leading lights would forget their self-interest for a moment and step up. Then nothing. In the wake of their paralysis, Castro and many of his young peers decided a response was up to them. But Castro did not immediately choose violence as the way to oppose a dictator. He first appealed to Cuba's highest court to uphold the Constitution of 1940, which laid out explicit directions in confronting a criminal who would try to set aside the Constitution. Castro's suit was thrown out. Left with no civil remedy, Castro decided to take up arms. This remedy to Batista required, at once, reaching out to like-minded men and women he could trust, articulating his revolutionary vision, consolidating an action group, and raising money to buy weapons and other supplies. All the while he continued to defend the cause of justice, which only deepened the commitment to him of an increasingly tight circle of activists.

Cuba has a long history of patriots and martyrs undertaking what seem to an outsider like harebrained schemes to overthrow illegitimate authority. Succeed or fail, Castro's aim in attacking Moncada was to set an example of duty and self-sacrifice worthy of the heroes of Cuban Independence and thereby awaken a slumbering public. Even by this modest standard, the attack was not terribly successful, as the mainstream political resistance still clung to the idea that Batista could be deposed by means of a civil opposition.

Still, the younger generation noticed, Rosa Mier says. She remembers feeling "very strange" upon first learning of the attack. Fidel Castro just had to be behind it, she thought. "And yet how did he do it without our knowing?" Three days after the attack, from his hideout above the village of Sevilla, Castro contacted Mier's friend Carmen Castro via shortwave radio. After briefly describing his predicament, he asked her to get money to Santiago de Cuba to provide for the young men already imprisoned there. Impressed by Castro's daring and by his concern for the well-being of his men while his own life remained in mortal jeopardy, Carmen Castro promised to do what he asked and hung up. She then looked solemnly up at her friend Mier and said, "I think we finally have a leader."[55]

chapter seven

GOD AND THE DEVIL

S undays at Finca Manacas provided a welcome break from the relentless toil of farm work. On July 26, 1953, "a precious summer Sunday," in Juanita Castro's words, Ángel and Lina gathered around the dinner table with their daughters, Juanita, Enma, and Augustina, and their granddaughter Tania, daughter of their eldest son, Ramón. While the women chatted amiably, Ángel quit the room to tune into the latest newscast. A special bulletin brought the nearby conversation to a halt. "We interrupt this broadcast to inform you that a group of rebels assaulted the Moncada Barracks today. . . . There is talk of many dead and injured. We will keep you informed."[1]

The news sucked the air out of the room. "I don't know why," Ángel broke in, "but something tells me Fidel is mixed up in this." Oh nonsense, Enma chided. "How ridiculous to think that Fidel has anything to do with that. Get that out of your head." Just shy of convinced, the family struggled to distract itself, as members of the rural guard, posted at the farm, retreated to the nearby army barracks at Central Marcané. Hours later, a clerk from the company store burst through the door shouting, "Doña Lina, Doña Lina, I just heard over the radio that the leader of the Moncada assault is Fidel!" Juanita thought first of Raúl, her nearest and dearest sibling. His devotion to his older brother surely pulled him into this, she thought. Eyes brimming with tears, Lina collapsed in a chair, murmuring, "My God, My God."

Moments later, another radio bulletin: "We interrupt again to confirm that the leader of the Moncada attack is Fidel Castro Ruz. His brother Raúl was also in the group. More to follow." Ángel, notoriously reserved, broke down in tears. Lina fingered her rosary. Juanita remembers her father cursing Fidel. "I entrusted Fidel with Raúl, my youngest son, expecting him to make Raúl into a good man, and look what he's done! He's made him a murderer!" Years later, Castro confirmed feeling guilty for having included Raúl, barely twenty-one at the time, "in that rash and daring action."[2]

By nightfall, the Castro home was doubly encircled, first by friends and workers concerned about the boys, then by a larger ring of soldiers stationed to keep a lookout for the fugitives. The soldiers' presence buoyed Ángel. "Fidel and Raúl must surely be alive," he told the others. Why else would the government deploy soldiers there but to cut off their escape? Ángel's logic proved a tonic to the others, with Enma remarking that Fidel would never fall into so obvious a trap. Still, no one slept that night. "Ay Viejo," Lina sighed, "more victims, more families torn apart by suffering fathers, brothers, sons in mourning. Will there ever be peace in Cuban homes?"[3]

News of the massacre of captured assailants sent Lina and Juanita speeding to Santiago the next morning in an attempt to mobilize influential friends to save as many lives as possible, including, of course, Fidel's and Raúl's. They stopped first at the office of Archbishop Enrique Pérez Serantes, a frequent guest at the Castro home. In the immediate aftermath of the attack, Santiago buzzed with soldiers, onlookers, and worried families. "At first, they told us that Fidel was dead," Juanita recalls. "Then that both Fidel and Raúl were dead." Finally, the authorities confirmed that the brothers were alive . . . and on the run. Meanwhile, mother and daughter joined forces with Castro's wife, Mirta Díaz-Balart, whose own father and brother worked for Batista, and who possessed a written order that her husband must be captured alive. What about Raúl? Lina demanded. The same, Mirta replied. "The order is to bring them in alive."[4]

The family received confirmation of Raúl's safety on Monday when police in the town of San Luis telephoned the Marcané barracks to verify his identity. The officer in charge at Marcané was a family friend, who notified Ángel and Lina of Raúl's whereabouts before heading off to San Luis to identify Raúl in person. On Tuesday, at the insistence of this same officer, Raúl was transferred to Palma Soriano, where he remained for three days until being taken to the Santiago Vivac (city jail) on Thursday afternoon. The intervention of this officer and Raúl's protracted transfer undoubtedly saved his life, as rebels turned over to Chaviano's men before noon on Wednesday, July 29, did not make it to the jail alive. Meanwhile, skeptical of government pledges, Lina and Juanita hurried to Palma Soriano, where they saw Raúl with their own eyes. They were finally able to speak to him that Friday at the jail, where, asked if he knew his brother's whereabouts, Raúl could only shake his head.[5]

Lina and her daughters returned to the jail the following day, Saturday, August 1, laden with food for the prisoners. Approaching the entrance, they were greeted by police barricades, swarms of military vehicles, and an excited crowd. This could only mean one thing, Lina concluded. "They're both alive!" she exclaimed. "And they are together! They are together!" Lina was right: Fidel and Raúl were alive, safe, and together. At least, for now.[6]

———

Brought to the Santiago Vivac that morning, Castro was plopped down on a bench at the end of a long hall. The commotion attending his arrival confirmed rumors circulating among his fellow captives that Castro had survived. With Lina and her daughters already at the jail to see Raúl, Castro was permitted a brief visit with his family before being led to the warden's office and a private interview with Chaviano.

The interview lasted several hours, after which the press was granted access to the new celebrity. Carlos Selva Yero, a reporter with Radio CMKR, recalled wading through a crush of spectators outside the jail eager to catch a glimpse of the rebel leader. Selva found Castro standing in the middle of a room, as if awaiting a public audience. He was dressed in a light-colored short-sleeved shirt and denim pants, worn at the knees. His chin was covered in stubble and his face was sunburned. Selva remembered Castro appearing preter-naturally serene. He said that he and he alone—not Carlos Prío, not the Ortodoxo Party, not the Communists—was responsible for the attack, whose aim had not been to harm innocent soldiers but to re-turn sovereignty to Cuba and improve the lives of rural citizens. He then went on to list a number of reforms to be enacted should his "revolution" have been successful, including land reform, improved access to health care and education, and an end to political corrup-tion. In short, he said, the rebels wanted to "regenerate Cuba."[7]

Castro's comments caught Colonel Chaviano off guard. Alarmed by the direction the interview was taking, Chaviano cut Castro off and seized Selva's tapes, which he sent off to SIM for cleansing. In the end, twenty minutes of tape were cut to eight. The tape was broadcast that afternoon, with Castro's avowal of personal respon-sibility printed in newspapers across the land. Later that same day, the prisoners were moved to Boniato Prison, located in the foot-hills of the Sierra Maestra, just outside Santiago. Castro's forthright demeanor won him many admirers. But not everyone was happy with what they heard from the young rebel, including Lieutenant Ángel Machado, who was so incensed by Castro's remarks that he ordered Castro's jailer, Lieutenant Yánez Pelletier, to poison Castro. Yánez Pelletier refused and was later relieved of duty.[8]

Castro's treatment at Boniato in the two and a half months between the day of his arrest (August 1) and the day he went on trial (October 16) is the subject of debate. Castro insisted he was kept in isolation and denied visitors as well as the right to review the charges against him ("I spent seventy-five days in an isolation cell," he said. "No one was allowed to speak to me"). Others claimed that he had many visitors, including defense attorney Baudilio Castellanos, who was assigned to the case.[9] Nobody denies that Castro was isolated from the general prison population in a wing of the infirmary. Still, thanks to friendships forged with members of the prison staff, he succeeded in communicating with his fellow insurgents, even orchestrating a hunger strike that culminated in more privileges. The success of the hunger strike suggests that Castro retained the loyalty of his men despite the abject failure of the attack. At least one witness testifies that Castro remained engaged and upbeat through this stage of his incarceration. "While I shaved," recalled Luis Casero Guillén, an Auténtico Party leader swept up in the government dragnet, "a shirtless Fidel would hang his arms out the cell bars and ask me questions about the merchant marine." Casero was impressed by Castro's curiosity and intuition. Far from the nihilist thug described in government propaganda, the man Casero came to know was an "idealist and intellectual."[10]

Castro liked to boast that between the time of Batista's coup in March 1952 and the date of the Moncada attack sixteen months later, he put thirty thousand miles on his 1950 Chevrolet.[11] Gas station receipts bear him out. Since first arriving at the University of Havana in autumn 1946, he had been a veritable whirlwind of political activism, somehow managing to extricate himself from the countless controversies that embroiled him. Still, all the activity and engagement did not a political platform make, and prison provided an opportunity to elaborate and sharpen his political program. "Prison will be tougher for me than it has ever been for anyone else," he wrote a friend, before admitting to his brother Ramón that, but for the fact of it being forced on him, prison constituted a rare opportunity for "a good rest. I know how to use my time," he said. "I read and study."[12]

⸻

He also wrote letters, mostly to family at first, later to an expanding range of friends and fellow dissidents. His letters were censored, and though his candor and charisma eventually endeared him to prison officials, his early correspondence was nonpolitical and businesslike. Even to his wife, Mirta.

Castro had not set eyes on Mirta since departing Havana on the eve of the attack (which she had known nothing about). Mirta traveled to Santiago de Cuba the day Castro was brought to the Santiago Vivac, and she had later dropped off clothes for him at Boniato. But that was that, and a frustrated husband reached out on August 18, noting that he had received little news of her and still less of their son, Fidelito. Fidelito, now four, was set to begin kindergarten, and Castro wanted to know where Mirta had enrolled him. He himself was holding up just fine, in case she wondered ("prison bars dent neither my spirit nor my mind nor my conscience"). He then asked her to send along some books, including the complete Shakespeare and Julian Marías's magisterial *Philosophy*, along with any novels she thought might suit him. Finally, with his trial date looming, Castro was, as always, concerned about his physical appearance. He asked her to drop off a freshly dry-cleaned suit, along with "a collared shirt and a tie by the start of the trial."[13]

Known officially as Causa 37, the Moncada trial opened on Monday, September 21, 1953, in the packed plenary room of the Palace of Justice, just a few hundred yards from the barracks. Presiding over the tribunal were three judges, Adolfo Nieto Piñeiro-Osorio, Ricardo Díaz Olivera, and Juan Francisco Mejías Valdivieso, who shared the cramped space with the prosecutor, Francisco Mendieta Hechavarría, along with fifty-six defendants (many of them innocent opposition figures picked up by the police), twenty-seven defense attorneys, some two hundred soldiers, and a public throng estimated at between three and four hundred, including friends and families of the victims and the accused. There were no juries in Cuban criminal trials. Journalist Marta Rojas remembers that first day as the hottest in a scorching summer, with the heat and humidity ratcheting up the tension in an already explosive courtroom.[14]

After what seemed like an interminable wait, the din of an impatient crowd was silenced by the jangle of metal chains, as fifty-six men, their wrists bound by metal handcuffs, were led into the dock. Castro attempted to approach the magistrates. His path was quickly blocked by soldiers, who forced him to his seat. The three judges occupied the traditional raised bench at the front of the room. To their left in the corner sat the secretary, Raúl Mascaró Yarini, also on an elevated bench. Below the judges, with backs turned to the room, sat two stenographers. Along the flanks of the courtroom, on still more raised benches, perched the chief prosecutor and defense attorneys. Facing the bench in horizontal rows were the defendants, each row flanked by armed guards. Behind the defendants came the press, the families, and finally the general public.[15] (See Insert 2, Image 11.)

At exactly 10 a.m., a voice rang out from the dock: "Señor Presidente, señores magistrados!" Fidel Castro was on his feet. "I want to call your attention to something unusual here." The rights of the accused were already being violated thereby jeopardizing the trial's legitimacy. "You can't judge a person in handcuffs," Castro said, citing Cuban law, as his codefendants rattled their chains. The soldiers shifted uneasily. After an awkward pause, Nieto, the presiding judge, announced that the trial would be suspended until the handcuffs were removed. Nieto then upbraided the chief of the guard and retired to his chambers. Thereafter, a remarkable scene unfolded, Rojas recalls, with the chief himself removing Castro's handcuffs, as he stood bolt upright in his aquamarine suit ("red tie with black stripes, black shoes and socks"), arms extended and sweat flowing down his neck. An old caramel-colored belt pinched his trousers at the waist, evidence that he had thinned during his month and half in pretrial detention.

"Who is left?" a guard called out. When nobody answered, Nieto returned to the bench and signaled to the secretary to proceed with a roll call of the defendants. The secretary then read aloud the formal indictment followed by Colonel Chaviano's account of the attack. Chaviano's report, a litany of fabrications, undercut the government's credibility from the start. The attackers came bearing the most modern instruments of war, Chaviano alleged, including Remington rifles and fragmentation bullets. They were commanded by deposed president Carlos Prío, along with other Auténtico, Ortodoxo, and Communist Party officials (the illogic of such a coalition escaped the ignorant officer). The attackers had no scruples, no humanity, and made a mockery of the laws of war. There were foreigners among them, maybe Mexicans, maybe Guatemalans, maybe Venezuelans. Marks on their ammunition boxes revealed that their weapons originated in Montreal (thought to be Prío's base). The attackers perpetrated gratuitous, unspeakable crimes, which included storming the Civil Hospital with knives drawn, taking patients and staff hostage, and slitting the throats of hapless victims. All told, the assailants numbered in the hundreds, their devious plan to put Santiago to the gun repelled only by the loyal guardians of Batista's public peace.[16]

Looking on from his seat on the far left of the third bench from the front of the room, Castro struggled to restrain himself. He rose to his feet. Nieto signaled for him to sit down. When the court secretary completed Chaviano's report, Castro rose once more, announcing that he intended to exercise his right to assume his own defense. "In due course," Nieto responded curtly, as if already perturbed by the direction the trial had taken.

Jammed into the back of the courtroom with other journalists and the general public, Rojas remembers the atmosphere growing tenser with every jab and parry between the chief magistrate and the main defendant. With constitutional guarantees suspended and strict censorship in effect, nobody had dared to openly discuss the Moncada events in the lead-up to the trial, though privately many doubted the government's account. "For two consecutive months," Rojas says, "the only audible voice was the government's." The opening of the trial brought the government's monopoly to an end, and the significance of the moment was lost on nobody, including the presiding judge.

The examination of defendants began. As his name rang out, Castro (along with the nearby guard) rose to his feet. The chief of the guard approached Castro, his hand on the butt of his pistol, the silence broken only by the buzz of a low-flying plane. The prosecutor read the charges. Castro listened intently. The guards raised their bayonets. Chaviano had ordered the doors of the courthouse closed, and the room was suffocating. "Respond truthfully to the prosecutor," Nieto ordered. Did you participate in the attack on such and such a place on such and such a day, the prosecutor asked? "Yes, I participated," Castro replied. And those youngsters over there? "Yes," Castro replied again; "like me, they love the freedom of their country. They have committed no crime other than wanting what's best for their country, just as they were taught in school." Nieto interrupted with his bell. "Keep to the prosecutor's questions," he ordered. The prosecutor continued. Did Castro's followers really understand the extent of his plan? he wanted to know. Did they understand the political significance of the act and the risk they incurred? Please answer my questions, he went on, and spare us the political harangue. Politics was hardly the point, Castro shot back, "I seek only to reveal the truth."

The prosecutor thought to portray Castro as a bitter nihilist who coerced a group of innocent youth to join a scheme to overthrow a legitimate government. Castro rejected the prosecutor's portrait. He had coerced nobody, he said. The men, nearly all of them members of the Ortodoxo Party, shared his conviction that armed insurrection was the only solution to Batista. Why hadn't the rebels tried civil opposition? the prosecutor demanded; after all, hadn't Castro as a newly minted lawyer sworn to uphold the rule of law? The answer, Castro replied, was twofold: first, civil liberty no longer existed in Batista Cuba; second, he had indeed thought to marshal the rule of law in Cuba's defense, taking Batista to court in the days following the coup. The court could have sentenced Batista to over a hundred years in jail, Castro noted. Instead, the case was thrown out. With civil and legal recourse foreclosed, violence was the only option.

After a few hours of questioning, the prosecutor stood down, as if aware that the trial was not going how he had imagined. Then defense attorneys representing the political officials uninvolved in the attack lined up to clear their clients of complicity. Time after time, Castro denied anybody's responsibility for the attack besides his own and that of his fellow insurgents. "Nobody should worry about being accused of having been the intellectual inspiration of the Revolution," Castro announced emphatically, "because the only intellectual inspiration of the Moncada attack is José Martí, the Apostle of our Independence." The line elicited applause from some of Castro's men, which inspired yet another reprimand from Judge Nieto. The questions continued. Did you conspire with the communist leader so and so? With these ex-officials of Santiago de Cuba? With the FEU? No, no, no, Castro replied, before acknowledging that he had received help from individual FEU members, if not from the institution itself.

Baudilio Castellanos, general counsel to the defense, then posed a very leading question. In law school, Castellanos wanted to know, had Castro been "taught that the Constitution of Cuba should be defended?" Out of order! exclaimed one of the judges, prompting Castellanos to reword his question. More lawyers followed with more questions, allowing Castro to exculpate all but those who had directly participated in the attack. Finally, Nieto invited Castro to provide any details that might aid the court in exonerating those who had no direct or indirect role in the attack. Castro sensed an opportunity. Already on his feet, he paused for a moment, collecting his thoughts. He then began to speak, very softly at first, as if challenging the audience to attend his every word. "Señor Presidente, señores magistrados," he began, before repeating his readiness to accept full responsibility for masterminding the attack, to explain the steps he took to carry it out, and to exonerate innocent opposition leaders. He acknowledged that he had not informed all his fellow rebels about his plans in advance, inviting them to deny some culpability. At this point, he was cut off by a loud chorus of "NOs!" emanating from the insurgents. "Silence," bellowed the chief magistrate. "What I mean," Castro continued, "is that there might be some that understand their obligation to their country differently—" Again, he was cut off, as the insurgents shot to their feet in unison, answering with a resounding "Ninguno!" (none). Then an unfamiliar voice spoke out from the group, as clipped and hurried as Castro's was confident and measured: "All of us who participated in the attack are ready to say so expressly," Raúl Castro said, despite his brother informing some that the government lacked evidence against them. "We are going to tell the truth, even as they go about releasing others; we were the ones who fought."

The sound of a bell returned order to a proceeding, which, though barely begun, had already revealed so much. The opposition political leaders had all but been exonerated, Raúl Castro had made a name for himself, the young insurgents had demonstrated their continued loyalty to Castro, who had refuted Chaviano's depiction of him as a hapless, cowardly bully. At this point, Nieto asked Castro if he had anything more to say for himself. In fact, Castro had said just about all he had to say in this stage of the trial. He repeated his assertion that his group murdered no innocent people that day. He asked how seventy rebels could be dead when only nine died in combat. He complimented the soldiers who carried out their duty protecting the barracks, while repudiating those who killed his men in cold blood. He accused General Martín Díaz Tamayo of ordering the ensuing massacre. He then reiterated his desire to serve as his own defense counsel. The judges granted his wish. A clerk handed him a cloak. Castro sat down on the bank of seats flanking the dock reserved for defense counsel. Two more defendants were called, both maintained their innocence, and at exactly 12:20 p.m. the proceedings were suspended for the day.[17]

Day two of the trial proved perhaps the most riveting. The first rebel to be called after Castro was Andrés García Díaz, who had participated in the assault at Bayamo. García appeared pale and thin. Seven weeks after the attack, his shaven head was covered in scars and his neck was encircled by an abrasion that could only have been made by a noose. "Young man," the prosecutor began, "did you participate in the July 26 attack on the army barracks?" "Yes," García replied eagerly, as the audience rose to its feet. Amid gasps and murmurs, Nieto ordered the gallery to be seated. The prosecutor then asked García if he had joined the mission of his own volition. Absolutely, the defendant replied. "I'm done," the prosecutor said, as if convinced that the sooner García retreated from view the better. "With your permission," García addressed the bench, "I'd like to say something." The judge nodded, and García told the following story.

After fleeing the attack on the Bayamo garrison in the company of two rebels, he was spotted on a bus, apprehended, and taken to the town of Manzanillo, where he and his comrades were beaten. Returned to Bayamo in the early morning of July 27, the three were driven to a cemetery outside the town of Veguitas. There, they were smashed in the head with rifle butts, collared with nooses, and dragged to their deaths. Or so their captors thought. García regained consciousness just before dawn, awaking to find his friends lying mutilated alongside him, and his own neck ringed by a noose. Local peasants nursed García back to life and kept him secluded until, with yet another intervention by Archbishop Pérez Serantes, he could safely be turned over to the authorities and receive medical treatment. García raised a hand to his head to display a still open wound from the crack of a rifle butt. "And this bruise," he continued, pointing to his neck, "is from the noose with which they tried to hang me."[18]

When García, known hereafter as "The Living Dead," concluded, Nieto asked if any of the lawyers would like to cross-examine him.

Castro spoke up. "I would like to be allowed to examine the accused," he said. The judge agreed, and Castro asked García just who exactly committed those crimes. "Six or seven soldiers," García replied. "And did they act on their own authority or were they obeying orders?" Castro demanded. "They were obeying orders." Had García overheard any conversations to that effect? Castro asked. Yes, García replied. "One said that for every assailant killed he was going to be promoted a grade, and that by that count, he could already be made a captain." There were a few good apples among the bad, García allowed, describing a soldier who had appeared reluctant to carry out the orders. He was overruled by another who insisted that the order to finish off the captives had come down from Havana and that they had to comply. Chaviano himself had called to say that no rebels should be returned to Santiago alive.

García's story came to an end, and Castro paused as if to allow the gravity of it to sink in. Any other questions? the judge asked. Only that the court retain record of this testimony should the opportunity arise to prosecute the perpetrators, Castro replied. Noted, Nieto responded, ringing his bell to return García to his seat. With the silence broken, the courtroom filled with the murmur of hundreds of voices. Nieto called for order—"for the last time," he warned. It was only just after noon and two thirds of the defendants had yet to be called. As the soldiers stirred uneasily, and as the lawyers whispered among themselves, Nieto consulted his fellow judges. He then dismissed the trial until the following Thursday.

Each day in court began with a roll call of the scores of defendants, a tedious and seemingly unnecessary process to which nobody paid particular attention. When the trial recommenced on Saturday morning, September 26, after an extended break, the bailiff was making his way down the alphabet when he came to the letter C. "Fidel Castro," the bailiff intoned. Nothing. "Fidel Castro," the bailiff said a little louder. Still nothing. "Fidel Castro!" the bailiff exclaimed. Silence . . . accompanied by quizzical looks all around. The chief justice ordered the bailiff to proceed. The bailiff explained that Fidel Castro was not present. The trial must go on, Nieto responded. "The trial cannot proceed without the main defendant," Baudilio Castellanos insisted, as the judges eyed one another quizzically.

After an awkward silence, Nieto threw up his hands. Castellanos remained on his feet, arms extended on the defense attorneys' table, as if refusing to back down. His colleagues rose around him, with the guards quickly following suit. "Sit down," Nieto commanded, before summoning the army lieutenant in charge of trial security. Lieutenant Vicente Camps scurried up to the bench. Where was Fidel Castro? Nieto demanded. Camps handed him a letter, which Nieto read and then passed on to the two other judges. He had an announcement. "The principal defendant has not been brought to trial, owing to his having taken ill at Boniato prison." Accompanying the letter was a signed doctor's certificate confirming Castro's indisposal. Nieto prepared to go on.

"Fidel is NOT ill!" cried a voice from among the defendants. The voice belonged to Melba Hernández, one of the few female defendants in the dock. Hernández quickly made her way toward the judges' bench, while reaching beneath the scarf that covered her head to remove a small note concealed within the folds of her ample hair. Nieto ordered her back to her seat, as several guards moved to cut her off. "OK," she replied, "but first I have to deliver this letter from doctor Fidel Castro to the Tribunal." She dropped a slip of paper on the dais. One after another, the judges read the paper before passing it to the court secretary. Nieto told the lawyers that they could read the note at the end of the session. The lawyers protested, and Nieto called a ten-minute recess as the courtroom erupted in commotion.

In his note to the magistrates, Castro charged the authorities of contriving his illness to prevent him from exposing the egregious lies concocted by the government to conceal the massacre of Moncada prisoners. He was perfectly healthy, he told the judges, neither ill nor ailing in any way. He protested his isolation in jail since his arrest and claimed to be the victim of repeated assassination attempts, first by the pretext of the *Ley de Fugas*, then by poisoning and other means still unfolding. He asked the judges to dispatch a respected doctor from the University of Santiago de Cuba to evaluate him and confirm his health. He also demanded that the judges take responsibility for all the prisoners' safety hereafter by ensuring their transport to and from the courthouse for the duration of the trial. He was not alone, he said, in imagining the government staging a prisoner escape to simply finish the defendants off. Finally, he asked the judges to share his letter with colleagues throughout the country, including the National Lawyers Guild, the Supreme Court, and other civil society institutions, to inform them about the level of deception to which the government had stooped.

Typically, Castro concluded by emphasizing what he knew to be at stake here, both for the Urgency Court and for Cuba's judicial system. If the trial continued in its bastardized form, it would be thoroughly discredited, he warned. The eyes of the nation were on this courthouse. This was not a question of one man's life, but of the fate of the ideas of "right and honor."[19]

With the ten-minute recess approaching the twenty-minute mark, Nieto returned to the bench, saying that he had called Castro's jailers to account and dispatched a team of physicians to evaluate the defendant's health. Meanwhile, the trial would proceed. The owner of the Siboney farm was called. Did he know of the pending attack? He did not. Had he been to the farm when the rebels were present? He had not. Whom besides Abel Santamaría possessed keys to the house? Only Andrés Pérez Chaumont, aide to Colonel Chaviano. No one else. Next came the radio operator who had pulled out of the plan just before departing for Moncada. Had he refused to participate, the prosecutor asked? He had, indeed. Castro did not force you to go? "I would not be forced," he said, insisting that Castro had defrauded him and that he had wanted no part in the attack.

More innocent men were called. Nieto ordered another break. Heat and humidity hung over the courthouse like an electric blanket. The pace of the proceedings would have to be accelerated. When the court reconvened at 10:30 a.m., eighteen defendants testified within forty minutes, giving the audience hope that the trial might speedily conclude.[20]

Later that morning the prosecutor Mendieta approached the bench. He handed the judges a list of political leaders exonerated by Castro, requesting that they be granted provisional liberty. After a brief recess, the judges agreed, whereupon the trial was suspended to the following Monday. A long succession of rebels testified that day. Had they participated? Yes! Was their participation coerced? No! Had they used knives to attack innocent patients? Had they fired indiscriminately? Did they carry grenades? Were there foreigners among them? No, no, no. No! One by one, Chaviano's lies fell by the wayside in the face of testimony by young rebels with nothing to hide.

Judge Nieto granted Raúl Castro the final word of the day. He aired a fear common among the rebels that his brother's life remained in grave jeopardy, despite the intervention of the court. "Fidel still runs the risk of being assassinated at any time at Boniato prison," Raúl Castro announced, "the Court must recognize this." He went on to list examples of ongoing mistreatment of defendants, begging the court to treat a crime as a crime. Just as the defendants would not deny their role in the attack, so they would not be silent in the face of crimes committed against them. Raúl Castro's plea brought the day to an end.

Day after day of testimony followed in which prosecutor Mendieta tried vainly to confirm Chaviano's lies.[21] Finally on Monday, October 5, day nine of the trial, it came time for closing arguments. Nieto called the courtroom to order and invited Mendieta to have his say. The prosecutor began by asking the court to free the sixty-five defendants who had played no role in the attack, including the eleven who had previously been granted provisional liberty. After reading the names on this list, Mendieta then turned to the perpetrators. They invoked the doctrine of José Martí, the prosecutor observed. They said they wanted to liberate Cuba. But he doubted Martí would have endorsed "a war among brothers." It was true that "Martí preached war, but not among Cubans, rather against a foreign yoke. I don't think we should invoke Martí in response to these questions," he said.

Mendieta reminded the audience that at the beginning of the trial he had asked Castro why a "cynical" public would ever follow the likes of little old him. For the same reason Cubans followed Antonio Maceo, Manuel de Céspedes, and the other fathers of Cuban Independence, Castro had replied, namely, because the rebels shared their dream of Cuba Libre, of a Cuba free and independent of foreign rule. Ah, but these others had already proved themselves in war and civil society, Mendieta said now. The act before the court hardly merited comparison. The rebels were misguided. "They brought only mourning to their own households and to the households of their friends and soldiers," while "generating hatred among Cubans." Cubans were nobler than that.

Mendieta acknowledged that the defendants had comported themselves with honor, sincerity, and valor. He found their confessions "civically minded" and even suggested that they might one day fulfill their objectives (presumably by nonviolent means). By sparing the lives of soldiers in the very building in which the trial was now taking place, the attackers under Raúl Castro's authority had demonstrated a "nobility" no different from the soldiers they confronted. A people that behaves with such valor and nobleness should not succumb to fratricide, he said. He signed off by commending the principal defendant's "odd strength of character."[22]

The next day, Tuesday, came Castellanos's turn. He commended the magistrates for their professionalism. In a setting in which the legislature was shuttered, the press moribund, the Constitution destroyed, and the rights of man trampled, it was indeed a pleasant surprise to see a Cuban court uphold the rule of law and judges carry out their duty with professionalism befitting their station. If there were shortcomings in this trial, they were not entirely the fault of the magistrates, Castellanos observed, and he thanked them for providing security in the chamber. He then returned the prosecutor's courtesy, acknowledging that Mendieta "had acted according to the dictates of his conscience," no mean thing in the Cuba of Fulgencio Batista.[23]

Next Castellanos turned to the glaring absence in the courtroom—Fidel Castro, the main defendant. Castro's honorable bearing before the court jogged Castellanos's memory, and he told the story of witnessing Castro's first court case as a lawyer, when the tables were turned and Castro defended Castellanos against a charge of public disorder. In winning Castellanos's acquittal, Castro had impressed the presiding magistrate, who noted that the defense attorney had carried out his job with poise and polish unusual in one so young, pointedly telling Castro that Cuban law expected much from him. This was the person so feared by the Batista government that it had gone out of its way not only to banish him from the trial, but to try to assassinate him in the process. What was the government so afraid of?

Castellanos then proceeded to refute the prosecutor's suggestion that the Moncada attack owed little to the doctrines of Martí or the tradition of Cuba's founding fathers. Wasn't it interesting, he observed, that the prisoners asked for but were not allowed to read Martí's works at Boniato Prison during the trial? In the name of Martí, he continued, if there existed no similarity between the two, why in the world forbid the prisoners from reading the Apostle's books? He then cited Martí's own "Manifesto of Montecristi" (1895), which described war undertaken on behalf of liberty as the crucible of national solidarity and virtue. The prosecutor maintained that the Moncada attack could only promote disorder. Well, Castellanos asked the magistrates, what kind of order reigned in the Cuba of Fulgencio Batista? For every rebel on his way to jail, Castellanos warned, there were countless others ready to take his or her place, to support a war for liberty. It was not hatred the rebels sowed, nor hatred that inspired them. They offered up their lives for a better Cuba. And despite the best effort of Batista propaganda ministers "repeating and repeating and repeating" their lies, it was not hatred with which the country now regarded them.

Castellanos closed by asking the judges to acquit the defendants before them. They were not the ringleaders of the alleged crime but the rank and file. The ringleaders were either dead (Santamaría and Tasende) or absent (Castro). Moreover, it could be argued that the attackers had committed no crime. Crimes were acts against established law. There was nothing lawful or legitimate about Batista's government. There were any number of eminent legal authorities going back through history ready to defend the rebels' actions. Indeed, Cuba's own Constitution sanctioned armed resistance against tyranny. The Rights of Man of the French Revolution did likewise, even to the extreme of tyrannicide. Based on these and other law codes, the defendants were not guilty and must be granted liberty. There cannot be two kinds of justice in this world, Castellanos concluded, "one for Fidel Castro and another for Chaviano, one for God and one for the Devil."[24]

After a short recess, the judges announced the sentences for the confessed rebels (minus Castro). For their part in leading the assault, Ernesto Tizol, Oscar Alcalde, and Pedro Miret each received a sentence of thirteen years in prison. Curiously, Raúl Castro, by no means one of the principal planners of the attack (he had only recently returned from an extended trip abroad that June), was also sentenced to thirteen years. The majority of the foot soldiers—Juan Almeida, Jesús Montané, Andrés García Díaz (the Living Dead), and so on—received ten-year terms. A few others received three-year terms. Melba Hernández and Haydée Santamaría were sentenced to seven months at the Women's Correctional Facility in Guanajay, the hometown of Rosa Mier. The men were all supposed to be imprisoned at Havana's La Cabana fortress. At the last minute, they were rerouted to the National Men's Prison on the Isle of Pines.

With the majority of the rebels on their way to jail, there remained only the cases of those too sick or injured to appear in court: Castro, Abelardo Crespo, and Gerardo Poll Cabrera (two other accused, an injured rebel named Gustavo Arcos Bergnes, and the Communist Party leader, Juan Marinello, would be the last to be tried a few days later). To accommodate Crespo, who was bedridden from a bullet wound, the trial took place in a patient room at Santiago's Civil Hospital on Friday, October 16, 1953. The room measured a mere twelve feet square but somehow managed to accommodate a makeshift bench for the judges, desks and armchairs for the prosecutor, court secretary, and defense attorneys (including Fidel Castro), seats for six journalists (including Marta Rojas), Gerardo Poll, and Judge Mejías's niece (a recent law school graduate), and Crespo's bed. Armed guards occupied the meager standing space that remained. Last but not least, in one corner of the room stood a cabinet containing a life-size skeleton whose hollow eyes and ghoulish smile provided a fitting commentary on the state of justice in Batista's Cuba.

Castro entered the courtroom at 9 a.m., dressed in the same aquamarine suit, white shirt, and brown tie that he had worn on September 22, when he last appeared at the Palace of Justice. He was already bathed in sweat, though, as always, he did not seem to notice. Over the suit he wore a fraying black robe borrowed from the local Lawyers Guild. Observers divide the day into two parts: the conventional parade of accused and witnesses, including Castro, and a long address by Castro to the court (later published in expanded form as "History Will Absolve Me").

Castro had already assumed responsibility for the attack on the Moncada Barracks and exposed the government's lies. Hence this stage of the trial proceeded with relatively little drama. In one short but telling exchange, Castro asked Major Andrés Pérez Chaumont, second in command at Moncada and the person who, along with Chaviano, was thought to have ordered the massacre, how many rebels he had met in hostile encounters in the first three days following the attack. "There were many," Chaumont replied. "I went out on three such patrols." Could he remember the number of rebels killed on these patrols, Castro asked? Eighteen, Chaumont said. And on the army side, how many had fallen? One or two were injured, Chaumont replied. How could Chaumont explain eighteen deaths and no injuries among the rebels, and one or two minor injuries among his men? Castro demanded. "Had he used atomic weapons?" Chaumont erupted, forcing Nieto to intervene. Ultimately, Chaumont attributed the vast discrepancy in losses among the two sides to the "better aim" of his marksmen. Ah, Castro said, and stood down.[25]

Prosecutor Mendieta's summary lasted a mere two minutes. Poll should go free, the other two should be sentenced according to Article 148 of the Civil Defense Code. The law stipulated a sentence of between five and twenty years for those "who committed an armed uprising against the constitutional powers of the state." Mendieta asked the judges to sentence Castro to the full extent of the law: to twenty years plus six more for aggravating circumstances. Mendieta then took his seat without justifying his extraordinary sentence. A prosecutor would request a twenty-six-year prison sentence without bothering to explain himself? Castro could not conceal his astonishment. But it was not yet his turn to speak. First came a word from Poll's attorney and then from Castellanos on behalf of Crespo. Finally, the chief magistrate turned to Castro. Did he still intend to assume his own defense? That he did, Castro replied. The room fell silent as he asked to borrow Castellanos's copy of Cuba's legal code, along with a piece of paper and a pen. The clock on the wall read 11 a.m. The morning proceedings had taken two hours so far. Castro would hold his audience in place for two hours more.

Castro regarded his auto-defense as the opportunity to complete the task interrupted by his removal from the Palace of Justice, namely to defend the rebels' right to resist an unconstitutional government. He did not intend to inconvenience the court by engaging in "epic narrations," he said, before launching off on an epic narration. Much of what followed recapitulated testimony already aired during the formal phase of the trial. From there, Castro went on to lay out his revolutionary platform in the most detail to date. Had the rebels been successful, he said, they would have enacted a series of Revolutionary Laws to restore the 1940 Constitution, redistribute land, promote profit sharing, and recover stolen property. He pledged to align Cuban policy in Latin America "with the democratic peoples of this continent." Countries struggling against political oppression would find sympathy and support "in the land of Martí." Only then could Cuba become "a bulwark of liberty and not a shameful link in the chain of despotism."

This Castro—committed to social equity, regulation, and central planning—will be familiar to casual observers. Later in life, Castro responded to critics who accused him of ignoring individual rights by remarking that all individuals had the right to good medical care, education, housing, employment, and a decent standard of living, as if elevating social rights over civil and political liberties. But at this stage in his development, he remained a liberal constitutionalist and civil libertarian. If you do not like the person in office, he had scolded Batista after the coup, then vote him out.

So long, that is, as that person in office has been placed there legitimately. The most compelling part of this speech was Castro's detailed recitation of how Batista's conduct during and after his coup violated Cuban law. The people's liberties derived not from individual largesse but from natural right as expressed in institutions like the 1940 Constitution. That Constitution made military coups illegal, and in the face of such provided citizens with a "lifeboat"— the last remaining right that every individual everywhere possesses by virtue of his or her humanity—namely, the right to resist tyranny. Castro had done his reading, citing in support of the right to rebel not only chapter and verse of the Cuban Constitution but nameless ancient Greek, Roman, Indian, and Chinese philosophers, Montesquieu, John of Salisbury, Thomas Aquinas, Martin Luther, Philipp Melancthon, John Calvin, Juan de Mariana, François Hotman, Stephanus Junius Brutus, John Knox, John Poynet, John Althus, America's founding fathers, John Milton, John Locke, Jean-Jacques Rousseau, and Thomas Paine besides.

At stake here was Cuba's place in the constitutional pantheon. Bearing ideas like the social contract and the consent of the governed, revolutionary mavericks in North America and France overthrew inherited power. Those revolutions made possible "the liberation of the Spanish Colonies in the New World," Castro noted, "the final link in the chain being broken by Cuba." There remained much work to do. And so, rather than juxtaposing social rights to civil liberties, the writers of Cuba's 1940 Constitution codified what Castro called "the social function of private property and of man's inalienable right to a decent standard of living." Therein lay Cuba's contribution to liberal constitutionalism, he emphasized; it recognized "the socialist currents of our time." Read this way, the reform platform he championed in this and other speeches was not out of place among Western political philosophy but was simply the most updated articulation of it. Castro's future and the future of his Movement would depend on his being right.

———————

When Castro was picked up by Cuban authorities in the hills above the village of Sevilla a few days after his disastrous attack, he did not seem to have much going for him. Within less than three months, thanks to the astonishing incompetence of the Batista government, and to his own resourcefulness, he emerged from the ordeal triumphant, if not yet victorious, in the eyes of many Cubans. In the courtroom, he had conducted himself with dignity, professionalism, and respect. His intelligence and self-confidence made him formidable in the courtroom; combined with his memory, these rendered

many of the contests he entered unfair. The historical record contains no evidence of his knowledge or use of the law being called
into question by a fellow counsel, a prosecutor, or a judge. In Batista-era Cuba, his legal arguments were often overruled, but they
were rarely, if ever, refuted.

Looking back on this period knowing how things turned out,
it is easy to mistake the recklessness of a young firebrand for the
revolutionary to be. But little of what Castro argued for in his
self-defense was new to Cuban politicians. Years earlier, President
Machado himself had articulated a platform not so different from
Castro's, as had subsequent presidential candidates, including Fulgencio Batista. What made Castro radical, even revolutionary, was
that he meant what he said and was willing to back his words up
with force in a manner not seen in Cuba since the War of Independence. In mid-century Cuba, it would take a revolution to enact
sensible reforms, so entrenched were the interests of Cuba's professional politicians and their foreign patrons.

One hallmark of the ensuing struggle is the extent to which
Castro's early commitment to both civil and political liberties (freedom of expression and association, habeas corpus, the right to vote)
and social rights (the right to a good education, good health care,
a good job, a fair wage, a decent standard of living) yielded to an
emphasis on the latter at the cost of the former. This is a long story,
and it need not be rushed. Up to this point in his political development, Castro's campaign for national regeneration and Cuba Libre
depended on his being able to get the word out, to say and publish
what he wanted, where he wanted, to whatever audience was willing
to listen. Here, again, Castro's thrust was not all that radical. Addressing questions of liberty and justice, he appealed to a broad swath of
Cuban society that included middle- and upper-class Cubans like
himself (largely urban, educated, and accustomed to exercising their
rights in the press and at the ballot box) and lower-class Cubans
(renters and squatters, often rural, uneducated, and underserved).
The first constituency had more to gain from a defense of political

and civil rights and liberties, the second from talk of land, health care, and educational reform. But the two went together, Castro insisted, as reflected in the still largely aspirational 1940 Constitution. Once everybody enjoyed the social security of regular work, good housing, education, and health care, all would benefit equally from the civil and political rights so prized by intellectual and professional elites.

Castro's liberal constitutionalism was rooted in the bedrock of Cuban history. Revolution and resistance to tyranny were at the heart of what it meant to be Cuban, he told the magistrates. Since childhood, he had been taught that "to live in chains is to live in opprobrium," that "to die for the country is to live." Such teachings, and the rights and liberties they sustained were a "heritage from our forefathers."[26] Defending and extending that freedom was the very essence of patriotism. In choosing resistance over material comfort and political office, the rebels rose to the level of Céspedes, Maceo, Gómez, and Martí, Castro said, before going on to cite Jean-Jacques Rousseau's proposition that to renounce one's freedom was to renounce one's status as a man.[27]

chapter eight

THE GREAT BOOKS

On the evening of November 21, 1952, Naty Revuelta tidied her desk, turned out the light in her office, and descended the stairs of the Esso Building, headed for home, a thirty-minute walk. Typically, Revuelta arrived home around 6:30, giving her plenty of time to greet and feed her daughter, Tatín, before putting her to bed and then dining with her husband, Orlando Fernández, a prominent cardiologist. This evening Revuelta worked late, missing Tatín's dinner and her bedtime, too. There was word of a rally at the university commemorating the execution by Spanish authorities of eight Cuban medical students. Curious, Revuelta decided to take the long way home.[1]

The university looms over Central Havana like the Acropolis over Athens' Agora, providing the students a commanding setting from which to air their grievances. In their clashes with Batista's police, the students literally held the high ground. But the government controlled the power grid, and when news leaked out that there was to be a rally on the Escalinata, the magnificent granite steps leading up to campus, the government flipped the switch, plunging the neighborhood into darkness. Undeterred, the students spread out across the broad steps in little groups talking animatedly, surrounded by bottles of beer and wine.

A half block away, Revuelta sensed that something was awry. "It was too quiet," she recalled. "I thought I had missed the event." She couldn't have; it was still early. Had the police broken up the rally? she wondered. Was anybody hurt? Rounding the corner at the base of the stairway, Revuelta took in "a magnificent scene." Autumn evenings in Havana can be sumptuous. With the electricity down, the scene on the Escalinata became positively enchanting with groups of young men and women sprawled out on the stairs beneath the pale glow of a crescent moon. This is not how she remembered her education at a fusty boarding school outside Washington, D.C. At mid-century, the University of Havana was as much a political platform as an institution of higher learning. In the aftermath of Batista's coup, it was one of the few places in Cuba where political opposition could reliably be found.

Naty, I want you to meet someone; come with me. A friend grabbed Revuelta's hand and pulled her up the stairs where, near the top, ten or fifteen students listened attentively to a charismatic man, nattily attired, speaking with laserlike intensity. Revuelta and her friend came to a halt waiting for a chance to interrupt. *We must prove once and for all that we are not as they portray us—a shapeless mob of irresponsible youth. We are the offspring of a noble people with a glorious history and exalted ideas.* "Fidel Castro," Revuelta's friend whispered. Revuelta stared, entranced. The speaker stood out from those around him like a bolt of color in a world of black and white. "He was eloquent, authentic, authoritative." As he spoke, his audience appeared hardly to breathe. He finally stopped talking and looked up at the newcomers. "Fidel," her friend cut in, "I want you to meet Naty Revuelta."

Once met, Castro was hard to forget. Soon after, Revuelta made

a fateful decision, distributing house keys to three men she thought
capable of mounting a successful opposition to Batista, and who
might be in need of a secure meeting place: Roberto Agramonte,
Ortodoxo Party leader and favored candidate in the nullified 1952
presidential election; Emilio Ochoa, Agramonte's running mate; and
Castro himself. "Tell Fidel Castro that if he ever needs a safe place
to meet, he may do so at our house," she told a courier. A few
weeks later, Revuelta received word that Castro wanted to drop by
her home. That January, Castro came to dinner. The hosts served
maple-glazed ham, which Castro praised so extravagantly that Revuelta later sent him the exact same menu in prison.[2]

Revuelta and her husband listened sympathetically as Castro
explained the need for revolution. "We agreed to help him," she
said. "Over the next several months, we opened our home to him,
as well as our purses." Revuelta pawned jewelry to raise money for
weapons. "I never collected guns myself, but I helped hide weapons,
clothes, and cash, and sewed Cuban Army insignia on belts, jackets,
and hats." Revuelta's husband, Orlando, was completely on board.
Amid escalating repression and censorship, he shared his wife's impression that Castro had the vision and commitment the nation
needed. "We appreciated his desire to reacquaint Cubans with the
tradition of self-sacrifice embodied by the Mambises," she said, in
reference to the heroes of Cuban Independence. "We thought he
would set a shining example."

Revuelta was one of a very few people Castro trusted with
knowledge of the impending attack. Before departing for Oriente
that weekend, Castro asked two things of her: to make him a recording of music to be broadcast over the radio in Santiago de Cuba in
the event the attack succeeded ("I recorded . . . Beethoven, Prokof-
iev, Mahler, Kodály, Berlioz, and the national anthem," she said); and
to distribute the Moncada Manifesto to the press at the exact time
the attack took place. "That morning I woke up Orlando to tell
him I was running an errand for the Movement and would be back
in three hours." At the home of one of the editors, she learned that

the assault had failed. "I was suddenly desperate. I ran to our parish church in Vedado and prayed. For the dead."[3]

———————

On December 19, 1953, two months after arriving at the National Men's Prison on the Isle of Pines, Castro wrote Revuelta a letter. "Naty, what a formidable school this prison is! It is here that I am forging my vision of the world and can complete the task of giving my life purpose." The familiar tone reflects an epistolary courtship in the early stage of liftoff, but which would fast attain rocket speed. The catalyst for the exchange was a letter she had sent Castro's mother, Lina, during the Santiago trial. "I am taking the liberty of writing these lines," Revuelta explained, "because I know you must be going through anguished and terrible times, and I think that perhaps a few words of encouragement that you did not expect could help you find peace in your soul, and more pride for your son Fidel." Regardless of what Lina thought about her son's behavior, he needed "the moral and emotional support that only a mother can provide."[4]

A grateful prisoner first reached out to Revuelta on November 7. "An affectionate hug from prison," he began. "I remember you faithfully and I love you [*te quiero*] . . . although it's been a while since I've heard from you. I treasure and will always treasure the tender card you wrote my mother." In the immediate aftermath of Moncada, Revuelta had somehow avoided being swept up by Cuban intelligence. Castro was relieved that she was safe and grateful for her help. "If you have had to suffer because of me in any way," he wrote, "please know that I would happily give my life for your honor and well-being." He likened his image of her to the reward of personal sacrifice in a noble cause. "What the world thinks doesn't matter; what matters is what's inside our hearts. There are things in life that outlast our daily miseries—eternal things, like the image I have of you, which will accompany me to the grave."[5]

At the time of this letter, Castro and Revuelta had spoken privately a mere "two or three times." Though each found the other attractive, they apparently never considered their relationship amorous. In person, that is. In letters, the two let themselves go, as if finding in the epistolary form the freedom and exhilaration missing in their marriages and the workaday world. Sentenced to twenty-six years in prison, Castro would end up serving a mere twenty months of that, but he could not have known that at the time. For the first six of those twenty months, the two engaged in a largely secret love affair that produced over a hundred letters amounting to hundreds of pages. No one needs an excuse to fall in love. But Castro seems to have found in Revuelta the intellectual soul mate he never had at precisely the time he needed one most. If Revuelta was any less tickled than he by conundrums of moral philosophy, epistemology, and historicism, she never let on. As for her, she appears to have initiated this relationship in order to save the Revolution, only to find in its catalyst a passion and purposefulness the likes of which she had never met. Why the romance lasted a mere six months will become clear below, but a love this hot seems destined to burn out eventually. One can trace its trajectory not only in the letters themselves, but in the books he requested from her, which she dutifully tracked down and delivered as he went from simply biding his time and maintaining his sanity to finding his purpose in life, as he put it, and pursuing his one true love, the Cuban Revolution.

Who needs food and water when one has books to read? "When I read the work of a famous author, the history of a people, the doctrine of a thinker, the theories of an economist, or the preaching of a social reformer," Castro wrote Revuelta in December 1953, "I am filled with the desire to know everything that all authors have written, the doctrines of all the philosophers, the treatises of all the economists and the preaching of all the apostles." By this time, Castro had been on the Isle of Pines less than two months and was still getting used to it. The intellectual curiosity that Paquito Rodríguez recognized in his young playmate back in Birán comes through in these letters, but so, too, an immense (and expanding) political ambition, along with vertiginous mood swings, as the free flow of ideas collided with the walls of a prison cell. "Outside, I was restless because I did not have enough time," Castro wrote; "here, where there seems to be too much time, I am still restless."[6]

Castro and his fellow rebels occupied a hall approximately forty meters long by eight meters wide, with a floor of granite marble. There was a bathroom at one end, and a marble kitchenette at the other, equipped with a simple coffeemaker. Twenty-seven beds lined the hall in "perfect formation," their mosquito nets calling to mind army tents in which the rebels took shelter from the invading hordes. Halfway down the hall, a broad archway opened onto a colonnade and inner courtyard where, twice a day, the prisoners could stretch their legs and amuse themselves at games of volleyball. Within a few months, the men settled into a regular schedule. Rising before dawn, they breakfasted, attended classes, broke for exercise, ate lunch, held more classes, relaxed, supped, and attended yet another class, usually led by Castro, on the subject of political economy. At 9:30 p.m., amid strict silence, the prisoners returned to their beds. By 11 p.m., all were generally fast asleep.[7]

The classes were the prisoners' own design. Soon after arriving on the Isle of Pines, they established a school named after their fallen comrade, Abel Santamaría. Those with literary friends solicited books. Before long the Abel Santamaría Academy had its own library, which overflowed with titles like Manuel Grant's *Elementary Physics*, Salvador Massip's *Geography*, Hippolyte Taine's *Philosophy*, and Lamartine's *History of the Girondists*, along with books by Shakespeare, Dostoyevsky, Marx, Victor Hugo, José Martí, and many others.[8] For some of the prisoners, this school constituted their first and only brush with higher learning, and a few could not conceal their enthusiasm. "We have organized an academy for the purpose of raising our educational level," a rebel wrote a friend. "Our subjects are philosophy, world history, political economy, mathematics, geography, and languages. We have a very rigid class schedule, and we are all really motivated to learn."[9]

The most educated of the group, Castro oversaw the instruction. Every other morning, from 9:30 to 10:00, he taught a course in philosophy and world history. Other rebels chipped in with Cuban history, math, geography, and English. Twice a week, Castro led a class on public speaking. "I read to them for half an hour," he told Revuelta, "a description of a battle, such as Napoleon Bonaparte's infantry attack at Hougoumont, or an ideological topic such as Martí's plea to the Spanish republic or something similar." Designated participants then discussed the reading, with prizes awarded to the best speaker. Together with the valor the rebels had demonstrated at Moncada, the zeal with which they took up their studies led Castro to insist that they had earned the right to lead the Revolution. No one was glad to be there, he told Revuelta, but it was hard to imagine a more formidable training ground. "The life here, the discipline, the indomitable will, the education—everything is Spartan here," he wrote, and such was the men's "faith and unshakable firmness that it can be said of them, too, that they will conquer with their shields or die upon them."[10]

In the hostile environment of the prison, the rebels did not rely on goodwill to maintain social harmony. With the school and library in place, they turned their attention to forming a government, complete with constitution, officers, and regularly scheduled meetings. Pedro Miret, a natural leader, was appointed presiding officer. Oscar Alcalde, the accountant, supervised purchases and safeguarded the prisoners' savings. Pepe Suárez oversaw the distribution of supplies. Israel Tápanes served as secretary. Others chipped in as inclination or proficiency allowed. The constitution established protocols and rules of decorum designed to keep things moving smoothly. If decorum broke down, the rebels could fall back on Article 10, which vested the chairman with absolute power to "ensure the assembly's success."[11]

In short, though hardly a picnic, prison life was not that bad, Castro wrote his parents on October 27, 1953, ten days after arriving on the Isle of Pines. He had just been visited by Mirta and Fidelito, along with his sisters Enma and Lidia. Fidelito seemed bigger and stronger, he noted with pride. Visiting days were the third Friday of each month, from noon to three. The next visiting day was November 20, and he expected Mirta to meet all his and Raúl's requests. They wanted for nothing and needed no money, as there was scarcely anything to purchase.

After maintaining physical and psychological health, revitalizing the Movement was topmost on Castro's mind. The benefits of prison—the time to hone his political program, the proximity of the rebel leadership, the solidarity forged by adversity—could not make up for the threat prison posed of silencing him. In late 1953, he reached out to his friend Luis Conte Agüero, an influential journalist and cofounder of the Ortodoxo Party, for assistance in keeping his name and the rebels' example before the Cuban people. The letter, which Castro asked Conte to publish in the university newspaper, repeated the charge he made in court that the government had committed a massacre and then covered it up with lies. Why wasn't more being done to publicize this? he wanted to know. Silence amounted to complicity and only confirmed Batista's gambit that Cubans could be cowed by violence and intimidation. The minute the trial was over, Batista had reestablished constitutional guarantees and lifted the censorship. The ensuing calm made Castro wonder if a quid pro quo had been struck between the government and the press. Even so, it wouldn't hold, Castro warned. "All of Oriente knows" the truth, and "the entire country whispers it."[12]

The fact of his imprisonment forced Castro to try to mend fences with former adversaries, including advocates of civil resistance atop the Ortodoxo Party hierarchy. Castro needed that hierarchy now. The rebels' political program was fully in keeping with Ortodoxo principles, Castro told Conte. Had the attack succeeded, he planned to relinquish power to Agramonte and Ochoa. The rebels' first priority was to reestablish the 1940 Constitution, to be followed by land redistribution (indemnified by the state), a program of profit sharing, industrial diversification, the eradication of corruption, and the confiscation of misappropriated wealth. All this was to be achieved constitutionally, he emphasized, the party's ascendance ratified by a general election. "Speak with Agramonte," Castro urged. "Show him this letter." Tell him that those who fell in Moncada were followers of his friend Chibás. It was, after all, Chibás who taught the rebels "to die when the fatherland needed heroic sacrifice to raise the faith of the people and bring about the realization of its historic destiny."

Early the next year, Revuelta sent Castro a note describing Columbia University's core curriculum, which she had just read about in *Time* magazine. Her boss at Esso had graduated from Columbia, and he praised the program for immersing would-be poets, doctors, dentists, and engineers alike in the history and literature of the Western tradition. It was precisely the sort of general education that she herself lacked, she said. Wouldn't it be great if the two of them could introduce the core curriculum at Havana University? Castro responded enthusiastically, but the plan would have to wait. Meanwhile, the two did their best to fill the gaps in the Abel Santamaría Academy library.

In the beginning, Castro's reading list reflected the scattershot nature of the library's collection. He found himself drawn to French literature, with its unmistakable social and political lessons. Transported by Axel Munthe's *Story of San Michele* and Somerset Maugham's *Cakes and Ale*, he was mesmerized by Romain Rolland's *Jean-Christophe*. From Rolland, he told Revuelta, "I get the same feeling I had when reading Victor Hugo's *Les Misérables*; I did not want it to end." *Jean-Christophe* is the tale of an idealistic German musician caught between personal ambition and idealism and social and familial obligation. The hero endures hardship, persecution, and exile, before ultimately returning home in triumph. Castro sympathized with the hero's quest for meaning and alienation from his family; whether he himself would one day experience such a reconciliation remained to be seen.

A work of English literature, A. J. Cronin's *Keys of the Kingdom*, seemed equally momentous. Cronin provided an unforgettable model of "the man of true merit," who, upon seeing vain, selfish, and corrupt individuals constantly exulted by a misguided public, nevertheless sticks to his guns and to what he knows is right. Such examples helped Castro endure "days of unending torture and lonely struggle," making him "better and worthier." These and other stories confirmed Castro's growing conviction that life was meaningless unless devoted to some higher purpose. He came to identify that purpose in Cuba's unrequited dream of Cuba Libre. To his dismay, many of his contemporaries seemed deaf to this historical tradition, as if having been betrayed by one leader too many. For company, he plunged into literature and history, finding affirmation in the lonely heroes of Thackeray's *Vanity Fair* and Turgenev's *Nobleman's Nest*, among others, describing them as "immensely valuable."

Castro continued to lose himself in novels throughout his prison term. But his letters to Revuelta reveal an increasing interest in history and social theory, with deep dives into Marx's *Capital*, the Dean of Canterbury's *The Secret of Soviet Strength*, as well as works by Félix Varela, José de la Luz y Caballero, and the forefathers of Cuban Independence. "I'm studying Marx's *Capital* in depth," he told Revuelta in December; "five enormous volumes of economics, researched and set forth with the greatest scientific rigor."[13]

Capital was one of the first books Castro taught in his course on political economy. Teaching *Capital* is no mean feat. Volume I alone comprises a compendium of abstract concepts combined with page after page of vivid illustrations of industrial violence. Castro's marginalia to *Capital* reveal him wrestling with Marx's account of the transition from an economy in which commodities are exchanged to meet needs to one in which commodities are exchanged to make money (i.e., capital), as well as the method by which owners wring profit from labor by lengthening the workday, depressing wages, and introducing new technology. Competition, Marx notes, promotes innovation; innovation displaces workers (while increasing profits), thereby creating a "reserve army of the unemployed." The system leaves individuals fortunate to find work exhausted, maimed, and dehumanized, with Marx providing examples of working-class immiseration drawn from British newspapers.[14]

One heartrending example from the city of Nottingham caught Castro's attention. On January 14, 1860, local citizens came together to consider a petition to reduce the workday to eighteen hours. It was not adults whose fate was at stake here, Marx noted, but children in the lace trade who endured "an amount of privation and suffering . . . unknown in other parts of the kingdom, indeed, in the civilized world." Nine- and ten-year-olds were being "dragged from their squalid beds at two, three, or four o'clock in the morning and compelled to work for a bare subsistence until ten, eleven, or twelve at night, their limbs wearing away, their frames dwindling, their faces whitening, and their humanity absolutely sinking into a stone-like torpor, utterly horrible to contemplate." A local clergyman likened the conditions to "slavery—socially, physically, morally, and spiritually." Such stories reduced the voluble Castro to near silence. "Torpor," he wrote at the bottom of the page; "numbness."[15]

Cubans' own numbness in the face of inequality and injustice inspired Castro to call for a social revolution beyond an end to the Batista dictatorship. Cuba had seen one self-proclaimed reformer after another rise to the position of president only to succumb to self-interest and the culture of embezzlement. In the face of entrenched power, such reforms could only be won by revolution, Castro concluded, and Marx's tales of abuse sharpened his denunciation of half measures. In the Prologue to *Capital*, Marx dismissed as naive John Stuart Mill's conviction that one could reconcile management and labor through goodwill. "Sycophant," Castro wrote of the celebrated English civil libertarian; "informer, slanderer." Castro characterized Mill's political economy as a "a religio-philosophical system" that attempted to reconcile "irreconcilable doctrines." The result was "vacuous and empty."

The way out of the contradiction between the interests of capital and the interest of labor, Marx taught, was not Millian compromise but revolution. To Marx, and increasingly to Castro, history was the unfolding of such clashes, with landed elites overcoming a crumbling Rome to produce feudalism, then the bourgeoisie overcoming feudal elites to produce capitalism. Mill was a subtler thinker than Marx implied. But for both Marx and Castro, Mill stood in for nineteenth- and twentieth-century liberal constitutionalists—in Europe, the United States, and Cuba, alike—who believed that capitalism and republican government represented the culminating stage of human development, providing the essential foundations of the good life. From this perspective, the exploitation of lace workers in a city like Nottingham constituted an anomaly in the capitalist system. Marx insisted that the workers' fate was not anomalous but essential to capitalism. In one section heavily annotated by Castro, Marx argues that capitalism and republican government were but the latest stage in an unfolding historical evolution: individual liberties and justice today, social liberty and justice tomorrow—just as Castro had suggested in his self-defense and would argue again in the published version of "History Will Absolve Me," to which he turned his attention shortly after this encounter with Marx.

———————

Revolution was not the only thing on Castro's mind. He and Revuelta spent a lot of their time focusing on the fact of their unexpected infatuation, confessing their love, questioning one another's devotion, and salving wounds inflicted by the inconvenience of a dalliance that seemed destined to remain unsatisfied. Revuelta did not need Castro to tell her that falling in love is exhilarating. He did so anyway. For proof, he cited a book by the Cuban psychologist Emilio Mira y López, entitled *The Four Giants of the Human Soul: Fear, Anger, Love, and Duty*, writing out long passages by hand.

"There is no joy or satisfaction that can compare, in magnitude or quality, with what is felt in such moments," Castro quoted the author. "There are no words nor metaphors capable of describing that euphoria, that clashing of sweet welfare and passionate rapture, of pleasure and elation, of fullness and ecstasy, that characterizes the awareness of the correspondence, that is, the discovery of the 'echo' lover." Where once there were two individuals, now there is one. "The two lovers fertilize one another mentally and are enshrined in a world much more intimate and durable than the corporal world." The marvel, Mira y López goes on to explain, is that this "fusion and symbiosis" results not in loss of self, but in the fulfillment of the individual. "Without ceasing to become myself, I become more than myself. I exist in the other. I become in some manner him. I perceive, feel, and share what he feels and lives." Love reveals the other, as the lover's gaze penetrates and illuminates him. In the face of that gaze, the world acquires "a new dimension," exposing the "innermost precincts of personal intimacy."

Falling in love *in letters* adds a degree of complexity. Physical separation prevents the intimacy—the casual glances, the accidental touch, the rapturous embrace—essential to discovery and trust building. Fully half of the Castro-Revuelta correspondence is devoted to chastising one another for not writing enough. How else to read the gaps in communication other than as evidence of faithlessness? Not only did the letters take too long to arrive (up to three weeks for a letter to come full circle), but the context in which the one wrote was almost always different from the one in which the other read and, still later, responded. The result was recurrent fits of pique and pettiness.[16]

The period between Christmas and New Year's was hard for two lovers at the height of infatuation. *He* felt forgotten and left out, loath to imagine his beloved in the company of her husband and their friends—the very elite he blamed for destroying Cuba. *She* felt sad and conflicted, infatuated with her prisoner but forced to put on a good face for people she had grown weary of. The more commonplace these tiffs, the sooner the two got over them. Books proved a medium of repair. One Sunday in late January, Castro wrote a lavish letter which opened with a long poem by the Nicarguan Rubén Darío on the value of the book. Though never himself a prisoner, as far as Castro knew, Darío nonetheless captured the "humane mission" of all books, namely, "to sweeten sometimes to forgetting the bitter and somber hours of prison." Darío brought to mind Victor Hugo's biography of Shakespeare, where Hugo compares Christ's "multiplication of loaves of bread" to Gutenberg's "multiplication of readers." Gutenberg reinvented man as a reader, Castro wrote, "with an insatiable appetite for knowledge and with the desire for knowledge the ultimate human concern." What was once the province of scribes, priests, and intellectuals had now become obligatory, allowing the "immense human bible composed of all the prophets, poets, and philosophers to shine resplendent" in the world's schools.

Letters like this one confirmed Revuelta's sense that the key to Castro's survival was intellectual stimulation. She plied him with moral and philosophical conundrums. He wrote back with long and detailed observations of a playful, nimble, and penetrating mind. Examples abound, but one from later that spring comes especially to mind. One lazy Sunday afternoon found Castro tussling with Section One of Immanuel Kant's *Critique of Pure Reason*, entitled "The Transcendental Aesthetics of Space and Time." Castro confessed that Kant's dense and difficult text had put him to sleep ("space and time disappeared for a good while," he quipped). But not for long. The German philosopher's idea about the relativity of time and space reminded him of Einstein's formula for energy, $E=mc^2$. What was the relationship between these two apparently incompatible concepts? he wondered. Kant believed that he had identified the "definitive criteria that saved philosophy from being buried, beaten down by the experimental sciences," Castro explained. But had Kant met the same fate as Descartes, whose philosophy succumbed to the hardheaded proofs of Copernicus and Galileo? Kant was not offering an account of the "nature of things," but rather the process through which we arrive at knowledge—indeed, whether it was even possible to definitively comprehend nature. Kant's was "a philosophy of knowledge," not a theory about the objects of knowledge. Hence "there should be no contradiction" between the thought of these two giants.[17]

Kant's work called into question philosophy's attempt to establish the essence of things beyond individual perceptions. Does the individual's idea of the good, for example, correspond to some reality that transcends experience? Or is individual experience of the world—fickle, capricious, idiosyncratic—all there is? At stake here, Castro knew, was the possibility of agreement not just about philosophical puzzles but about the foundation of knowledge itself—and about history and policymaking. Kant's insistence that it was futile to look for the essence of things outside human experience made him radical in his day (and a progenitor of modern relativism). But Kant held out the possibility of agreement between individuals and peoples thanks to human intuition, which linked the mind to the surrounding world. Via the mechanism of intuition, Kant arrived at a (Newtonian) notion of space and time not so different from the philosophers he critiqued, and Castro was right to recognize a contradiction.[18]

Moreover, Kant did in fact meet the same fate as Descartes, as Castro put it, when Einstein disproved Newtonian physics, thereby exposing Kant's reliance on Newton. Put simply, despite his apparent relativism, Kant remained loyal to the universal aspirations of the Enlightenment, namely, to understand the world in its essence. Einstein himself did not escape the evolution of quantum physics. What happened to Kant would one day happen to Einstein. Confronting these issues, "along with the many others that constantly torment us," Castro was awed by both the limits and aspiration of human knowledge. He found the "relativity" of knowledge "saddening," he told Revuelta. How many theories, he remarked, "now outdated, were treated like the Bible! How dearly man has paid for the progress of humanity!"[19]

Castro's abstract ruminations had practical relevance. The contradictions in Kant corresponded to tensions within Castro's emerging worldview. On the one hand, Kant's acknowledgment that human understanding changes with context was consistent with Castro's belief in progress. On the other hand, Kant's insistence that some concepts endure (the categories of space and time, for instance), jibed with Castro's appeal to timeless virtues like nationalism, patriotism, and self-sacrifice. Revolutions are not driven by hypotheses, but by a single-minded vision that sweeps doubt aside. If Cuba were to progress, Castro argued, it would do so because there still flowed in the veins of some citizens the timeless virtues that had inspired the fathers of Cuban Independence. In the short term, the tension between Castro's progressivism and conservatism, his relativism and resolve, could be turned to tactical advantage.

On February 12, 1954, President Batista visited the prison. Nearing the infirmary where Castro and his men were confined, Batista heard some prisoners singing and believed the serenade to be in his honor. Upon edging closer, however, he discovered that the hymn was intended to humiliate him: the Moncada prisoners were at full throat, singing what would become known as the "Marcha del 26 de Julio," after the day of the Moncada attack. Batista flew into a rage and left the prison, vowing to take revenge. Two days later, on February 14, Valentine's Day, Castro and a few of the leaders of his group were removed from the common holding pen and placed in solitary confinement. Most of the men were soon released. Castro's confinement in solitary lasted until June 27, some 134 days.[20]

With fewer distractions, Castro bore down on his books, mining them for historical lessons and examples. "Now that I have no magazines or newspapers, no radio, nobody to talk to, I have fewer worries," he told Revuelta. Never had time passed more quickly. "The characters of history, the novels and ideas of great thinkers of all times make great companions, useful and unforgettable."[21]

In March Castro immersed himself in a series of novels from which he drew concrete historical lessons. One was *Doña Bárbara*, by the Venezuelan writer-politician Rómulo Gallegos. The novel explores the confrontation between urban development and rural traditionalism. Elected president of Venezuela for a brief term in 1948, Gallegos regarded modernization as indispensable to Venezuela's prosperity, while insisting that measures be taken to preserve the country's social and cultural traditions, a challenge on Castro's mind.[22] Another was A. J. Cronin's novel *The Stars Look Down*, a contrast of two young men from mining families whose growing consciousness of exploitation leads them in very different directions, with one fighting in Parliament for the rights of miners, the other ascending the ladder of mine ownership. Castro had confronted a similar choice after graduating from Law School in 1950, when his parents thought he might manage the family business.[23]

Then there was Somerset Maugham's *The Razor's Edge*, the saga of a disillusioned American pilot struggling to find the meaning of life in the aftermath of World War I. Apparently, Larry Darrell, the book's hero, reminded Castro of himself. It took an act of will, he told Revuelta, "not to devour it in one sitting." At the end of the war Darrell suffers from what today would be called PTSD. As he casts about for meaning, friend after friend counsels him to tighten the old belt, find a stable job, pull himself together. The more Larry resists, the healthier he becomes. Forsaking conventional happiness for authentic experience, he recovers his wits just as his friends and family endure one setback after another.[24]

In her relentless struggle to keep Castro distracted, Revuelta sent along newspaper clippings as well as books. One exchange reveals Castro's evolving criticism of the cultural elitism he met in secondary school in Santiago de Cuba and Havana. In late winter 1954, the conservative daily *Diario de la Marina* published an essay by the musicologist Orlando Martínez, lamenting what he called Cuba's "Cultural Tarzans," those middle-class professionals whose lack of sophistication and bad taste transformed Cuba into an intellectual and cultural wasteland. In response, the critic Rafael Suárez Solís accused Martínez of lamenting the symptom of a problem long in the making without identifying its cause—namely the detachment of the country's culture industry from its people. The debate generated a lengthy response from Castro on the problem of cultural production, just as Revuelta intended.[25]

"I read the articles," he wrote, "and much prefer Solís to Martinez." Where Solís was "popular, democratic, humane, and practical, Martínez was sour, resentful, exclusive, and vain." Not only did Martínez seem to be responding to "some secret wound," but he was condescending, as if looking down from some "cultural Sinai." Critiques of this sort required artistry, Castro observed, and he contrasted Martínez to his beloved Romain Rolland, whose light touch, absolute control, and geniality allowed him to engage an audience without offending it. Castro conceded that Cuban audiences lacked a certain sophistication, but whose fault was that? Surely not their own, as this "blue blooded intellectual" implied, looking out from his "ivory tower." Cultural coarseness was not a product of chance but a symptom of the "shameful sterility of Cuba's bereft, apathetic, and castrated upper classes."[26]

The solution was not to segregate the learned from the ignorant, but for artists to tap into the nation's cultural traditions. The ancient Greeks had long since demonstrated that theater, ballet, orchestra, and art would have no problem retaining an audience so long as it revealed something essential, new, and relevant about everyday life. This required no sacrifice of taste or sophistication. Once won, audiences could be educated as well as transported. But that would never happen by distancing art from the public, or by disdaining audiences eager to be entertained.[27]

An increasingly critical prisoner recognized similar condescension in Revuelta's philanthropic social circle, the topic of yet another pointed exchange. She was an active member of diverse philanthropic causes (the League Against Cancer, for instance, much in the papers that spring). What was behind the public obsession with "good service" he asked. Surely, in a nation with gross inequality like Cuba's philanthropy was necessary. But he was struck by the vanity of it all, the preening, posing, and partying that inevitably went with it. Moreover, addressing real social problems by charitable giving threatened "to aggravate or put off a long-term solution." He did not doubt that the money that Revuelta and company collected would go to the purchase of an appliance, the erecting of a building, or funding a room and improving treatment," just as they pledged. But what if it rained the day of the anti-cancer drive? What if the collection were poor and they lacked the money to carry out their good work? "The poor things will die," he said, as everybody throws up their hands and bemoans that "God is evil for commanding the rains!"[28]

In short, by this time, Castro had concluded that the nation's political, social, and cultural problems required real solutions beyond the reach of individual conscience, no matter how well-meaning. The crisis in housing, education, and health care were "problems for the state to resolve." The way to address inequality was not through philanthropy but by taxing "the owners of 5th Avenue and Country Club mansions, recreational farms, aristocratic clubs, inheritance, and luxury." Only then could Cuba ensure that no patient died because a rain shower had put off a fundraising drive, or because some soaking-rich countess had taken ill. It was past time for the very rich to lapse into extinction—"like Siboney Indian chiefs and manatees."[29]

———————

One Saturday in spring 1954 Castro asked Revuelta for a copy of Batista's legal statutes. He was apparently working on the revision of his Santiago trial speech. The following day was Sunday, and he promised to write her a proper letter. But Sunday came and went without his usual detailed note. He wrote her simply to say that he was too busy to write. Late that evening, he divulged the source of his distraction: he'd been juggling two volumes by Marx (*The*

Eighteenth Brumaire of Louis Napoleon and *The Civil War in France*) and one by Lenin (*State and Revolution*), all three related and of "incalculable value" to a prisoner wrestling with his vision of a future Cuba.[30]

The *Eighteenth Brumaire* took up the question of why the French bourgeoisie, vanguard of the Revolution of 1789, had become the brake on revolution two generations later, when, in December 1851, they joined hands with their old enemy, the landed elite, and conceded to the ascendancy of Louis Bonaparte, Napoleon's nephew. By this time, the biggest threat to bourgeois rule was no longer a wilted aristocracy, but working-class unrest. The nation's industrial leaders agreed to sacrifice political and civil liberty in exchange for order, a choice that would have been very familiar to Batista-era Cuba. To Marx (as increasingly to Castro), the once vaunted Republic had come to embody narrow commercial interests masquerading as the nation.

In March 1954, Castro still believed that republican government could be reformed (if only by "revolution"); Marx insisted it be overthrown, replaced by a government of the workers. This raised the question of the role of the peasantry in making revolution, and here Marx differed from Castro in relegating the peasantry to a secondary part beneath the urban working class. Small-scale agricultural production left peasants socially and geographically isolated from one another, Marx believed. On peasant farms, there was no division of labor to speak of, hence no specialization, no innovation, no stimulation of diverse talents. By proximity alone, peasants seemed to have more in common with landlords than with urban laborers. Just witness Louis Napoleon's France, where peasants comprised a solid bloc of conservative support.

Meanwhile, in *The Civil War in France*, Marx revealed how the new emperor tried to be all things to all people (except the workers). Peasants took pride in being told they were the heart of France, capitalists took heart in order and efficiency, the old landed elite swelled once more at talk of empire and invocations of national glory. Of course, this did nothing to address real working-class grievances, and workers rose up in Paris in 1870, ultimately speeding Louis Napoleon into exile. From March to May 1871, France was ruled by "a dictatorship of the proletariat" known as the Paris Commune. The Commune's successful, albeit brief, seizure of the reins of government led Marx and others to debate the role of the state in a proletariat revolution. Should the working class seize and appropriate state institutions, as Marx had argued in *The Communist Manifesto*? Should the state be crushed and dissolved, as Marx had come to believe as he looked on at events in Paris from London? And what about the standing army and the national police? The hallmark of the state is a monopoly on the use of force. Designed to promote the interests of capital, democratic republics entrust the monopoly to capitalism's police. The first act of the Paris Commune, Castro read, was to abolish the national army and replace it with a people's army, something Cuba's revolutionary government failed to do in 1933, as Castro would later note.

By the time he got around to Lenin's *State and Revolution*, Castro's faith in the state as a vehicle of progressive reform was under siege. In his *Discourse on Inequality*, Jean-Jacques Rousseau, one of Castro's favorite philosophers, exposed the rule of law (outside a social contract) as an instrument by which the propertied justified and protected its wealth from the un-propertied masses. Marx took Rousseau's criticism up a notch, describing the state as a tool of capitalist self-interest, designed to keep labor in its place. State bureaucracy made a mockery of the ideal of public service, as the state was simply not designed to serve the public. If this were true, then it would not suffice to simply seize control of the state, as the Paris Communards had imagined; the state, too, would have to be destroyed. Lenin suggested this be a matter of steps. In the first stage of revolution, once in the possession of workers, the state could serve as the guardian of society as a whole, taking possession of the means of production and abolishing class distinctions. By so doing it would eliminate its own reason to exist. With a government of (corrupt) people replaced by an administration of things, the state could be allowed to wither away.

Castro was transfixed. The state was the hammer of capitalist rule, democracy its subterfuge. Controlled by oligarchic elites, elections in so-called democratic states did not represent the will of eligible voters, much less that of the disenfranchised majority— women, laborers, racial minorities, the illiterate, and so on. At best, democratic elections confronted voters with a dispiriting question, namely, which representatives of the ruling class shall represent us? How much of this Castro believed at this time, he did not say. But it did not take a communist to recognize that fifty years of democratic rule had not brought Cuba honest, efficient, public-spirited government, or an economy balanced between agriculture and industry, imports, and exports, and capable of sustaining local, national, and international markets. Castro promised Revuelta that he would read these books to her one day. In fact, she told him, she was not all that interested in Marx. Among other things, she was skeptical of Marx's notion that conflict was the product of human institutions, regarding it rather as a remnant of animal aggression. Castro clarified that he had not written to endorse Marx's and Lenin's ideas, but simply to signal his pleasure in reading them in light of one another. Asked at his trial in Santiago what a book of Lenin was doing among Abel Santamaría's possessions on the eve of Moncada, Castro shrugged. "Anyone who isn't curious about such texts is an ignorant fool."

chapter nine

TRUE LOVE

Castro's plan to save Cuba was bolstered by the release from
prison in February 1954 of two trusted lieutenants, Melba
Hernández and Haydée Santamaría, the two women who
took part in the Moncada attack. Seasoned militants no less committed to a new Cuba than Castro, the two could expect to shoulder
great responsibility for revitalizing the dormant Movement at a time
when virtually all fellow members were either in prison, in exile, or
in hiding. With this responsibility came great pressure, as Castro expected Hernández and Santamaría to carry out his every command
with the devotion and intensity, even mania, with which he himself
would have done it. This, of course, was simply not possible. As a
result, his cajoling occasionally came off as abuse, raising questions
about his ability to delegate authority and work productively with
his peers in the Movement.

In mid-April, Castro wrote Hernández a note to discuss

strategy and explain how she could get in touch with him. Mirta had advised him about the good work that Hernández and Santamaría were doing, and he began to issue directions. Drawing on the lessons of his prison reading, he told Hernández to begin with propaganda, which he characterized as "the soul of the struggle." Political messaging must be carefully adjusted to the tenor of the circumstances, he had learned from a book about Napoleon. The obvious talking point of the moment was the illegitimacy and brutality of the Batista government. "We must not stop denouncing the assassinations," he said. Mirta, who was serving as a messenger, would fill them in on a brochure he was preparing of "decisive importance," a reference to the forthcoming "History Will Absolve Me." He also urged the women to organize a memorial for the first anniversary of Moncada. The event must be done with great "dignity," he advised, and include a demonstration on the Escalinata. If properly orchestrated with the FEU, and timed to coincide with similar events in Santiago de Cuba, New York, Mexico City, and Costa Rica, the demonstration could inflict a "terrible blow" on the Batista government.[1]

Castro warned Hernández that the fight was sure to become more difficult the closer the rebels came to their goal of overthrowing the dictator. He directed her to travel to Mexico to take the pulse of Raúl Martínez, Lester Rodríguez, and other militants who had eluded prison in the wake of the Moncada and Bayamo attacks. The question of coordinating the Movement's action with other groups was already proving tricky, and Castro cautioned her to be wary of those who would simply invoke the Movement's name to fulfill their own agenda, like José Pardo Llada, for instance. The rebels were in an enviable position, having distinguished themselves from the rest of the pack. It would be better for the Movement to "hoist the banner alone until the formidable boys that are imprisoned and who steeled themselves for struggle get out of jail." Patience was essential now, Castro observed, invoking Martí. "To know how to wait is the great secret of success."[2]

This would not be easy, Castro acknowledged. Hernández must not let others' envy and jealousy get her down. Appearances were everything. She and Santamaría should "offend nobody and smile at everyone." This was precisely the tactic he had used so successfully at trial ("defending our point of view without stirring the hive"). There would be opportunity soon enough to "crush the cockroaches." Be open to anyone who wants to help, he said, but "trust no one."[3]

With Marx and Lenin fresh on his mind, with two lieutenants free to resume the work, and with "History Will Absolve Me" nearing completion, Castro appeared at once distracted and steely. Revuelta could not help but notice. You don't write me anymore, she said at the end of April. He had not forgotten her, he wrote back, "it's just that I am completely submerged in my thoughts"—thoughts which had so recently been centered upon her. He still needed her. To get him books. He was moving on to history, he said, Cuban history. By returning to Cuba's past, he gained a clearer picture of "the paradise it might become." That, more than anything else, "is the question that consumes me now. I am more in love with Cuba than ever," he said, "like a suitor who blindly follows a woman regardless of the many setbacks." If Revuelta was not jealous now, she was not paying attention. Castro had found his true and only love—the Revolution—and there would never be another rival.[4]

In early May 1954, the inevitable happened. Letters Castro had written to Revuelta and Mirta crossed, with each ending up in the other's hands. Mirta called Revuelta to report the error and "exploded," Revuelta said. Distracted at that moment, she had inadequately explained herself, but she was mortified. She was fond of Mirta, at least she allowed Mirta to think so. Over the course of the preceding months, she had repeatedly sought out Mirta's and Fidelito's company, as if a substitute for Castro himself. Initially, Revuelta thought to forward her letter on to Mirta but had decided against it, as she did not know the "tone" Castro had used and did not want the contrast to be hurtful. She urged Castro to reach out to his wife, if only for her (Revuelta's) sake. Mirta accused Revuelta of "deceit and betrayal," threatening "to take revenge, by any means," if she continued to write him. Of course, Mirta had a right to defend what was hers, Revuelta said. She asked him not to second-guess his affection for his wife and begged him not to worry about her. "My conscience is at peace," she said a little unconvincingly; "the truth will come out in the long run."[5]

In fact, Revuelta's conscience gnawed away at her. In the days ahead, she tried to find consolation in the inspiration behind her originally reaching out to a married man, namely, to comfort him and thereby ease the isolation of prison. There was no dishonor in that. This need not have been kept secret from Mirta. Naively, Revuelta said that she never imagined an outcome as disagreeable as this, and suggested they cease their correspondence. She then repeated some previous advice: the only thing that could assuage Mirta was evidence that his love for her had not changed. Having come face-to-face with "the smoking volcano," Revuelta thought it in nobody's interest "to see it erupt." She pledged to return to her initial silence (though "without forgetting"). "Hasta que Dios quiera," she signed off, until it pleases God.[6]

Castro, now fully mobilized politically, interpreted the episode differently. This was not some regrettable, if inevitable, mistake, he wrote, but the result of a deliberate campaign to smear and silence him. Thanks to his special relationship with the censor ("a man incapable of such an oversight"), he knew that these letters had not passed through the usual mill but had been deliberately switched. Previous irregularities in the treatment of their correspondence now made sense, he said. He had been naive not to expect this of Batista officials. Revuelta was right to conclude that they must bring their correspondence to a halt. He hoped she would retain the faith that she had declared in him. He would still write her when he needed something, and when his doing so could not be turned by his enemies into something harmful. "Don't worry about me," he signed off, "I am fine."

Castro's letter to his wife is not in the public record. He was not a man given to apology and was not accustomed to accepting blame. But Mirta was too valuable to the Movement for him not to patch things up. On May 12, using the subject of Fidelito as an icebreaker, he wrote her a short note to say that he was thinking of her. He'd been looking at a recent photograph of Fidelito and was delighted to see how "big and strong" he had become. He worried lest Ángel be late in providing money to cover her and Fidelito's expenses and begged her not to waste any money on her prisoner. This was not a letter likely to buoy the spirits of a disheartened wife. "It's been raining here non-stop," he wrote; "I almost never see the sun, and rarely use the patio. When I do go outside it's only for a few minutes as it's even more boring there than in this cell." Promising to write again soon, he signed off with "many kisses" to her (and to Fidelito).

This letter was not as transparent as it seemed. Written between the lines of this note, in lemon juice (that old childhood trick!), which once dried faded from view, was another note for Mirta to pass on to Melba Hernández. When the paper was moistened, the hidden contents became visible. The coded letter explained that by this identical method, he would be smuggling out of prison the entire text of his speech at his Santiago trial. The document represented the rebels' revolutionary program. Nothing could be more important than presenting the Cuban people with a goal worthy of the ultimate sacrifice. Castro acknowledged that his was not the only opposition group at the time. His own members, like those Melba Hernández was to visit in Mexico, were itching for action, and Castro worried lest they fall under the influence of Carlos Prío's Montrealistas, now feverishly recruiting.[7]

With his epistolary affair all but over, Castro focused single-mindedly on the task at hand. When next he wrote Revuelta, in late June 1954, he described a "change of tactics." It was no longer enough for the rebels to act as an independent cell, he told her.

It was time to "close ranks with the people," by which he meant reach out to laborers, peasants, students, and disgruntled professionals. Prison was not a waste of time he said, reprising comments he had made to his brother Ramón. By providing an opportunity "to study, observe, analyze, plan, and shape the men," it advanced the cause immeasurably. "I know where and how to find Cuba's best. I began alone; now we are many."[8]

Indeed, Castro was no longer in solitary confinement. That same month, two marine convicts had been placed in his cell, to be followed soon by his brother Raúl. Prison officials had joined his cell to another with access to a large outdoor patio, open from sunrise to sundown. He now slept with the lights off and had access to electricity, food, and clean clothes ("for free"). He could follow any schedule he wanted. Come to think of it, he said playfully, "we don't pay any rent, and have visitors twice a month"; could life be any better on the outside? He could not say how long he would remain "in this paradise," but expected the presidential election, scheduled for November 1, would "leave a residue of dissatisfaction and discontent." Perhaps an amnesty could relieve "the tension."[9]

The mass mobilization to which Castro committed himself that month depended on getting the Movement's message out. Focus on propaganda! he had told Hernández in April. He now practiced as he preached, reaching out to Luis Conte, who boasted a loyal opposition following on Oriente Radio Network and had somehow managed to escape Batista's censors. In early June, Conte was to be celebrated at an event at Havana's Teatro de la Comedia. Mirta attended the event, reading aloud a letter by her husband ostensibly praising Conte while calling attention to his own fate and what it augured for the Ortodoxo Party's future.

Of all Ortodoxo officials, Castro wrote, Conte had been the most consistent defender of the rebel cause ("of those who do not resign themselves to be slaves in the thousand-times glorious motherland where today her children are even denied the right to be men"). Castro described the treatment he suffered in jail since being cast in solitary confinement the previous February. Conte himself had been recently jailed for speaking the truth and defending constitutionalism and the rule of law. Together the two made quite a contrast to the "traitors" who abandoned Ortodoxo principles to seek personal gain alongside Batista in a discredited Congress. It wasn't too late to make amends, Castro said. "Everything is saved if our principles are saved; from the depth of rot the redeeming ideal will rise, purified and clean."[10]

Castro followed up a week later with a personal letter to Conte commending his work and asking him to use his influence to mount an amnesty campaign for the Moncada rebels exiled in Mexico. Together with Mirta, Hernández, Santamaría, and perhaps even Roberto Agramonte, they could enlist the help of university students, the Cuban bar association, and other sympathetic groups to join the cause. Conte might announce the length of Castro's prison sentence day by day on his radio show. That would provide incalculable publicity. Naturally, Castro had other ideas to further the work of propaganda. If his friend agreed to devote just a little of his time and energy on this, together they could "attack the dictatorship in an area where it cannot defend itself."[11]

Hernández's trip to Mexico went better than expected. Through Mirta, Castro learned that his lieutenant had been warmly welcomed by the exiles, all of whom were doing well. Still, her visit confirmed his suspicion that other opposition leaders were also mobilizing. In Mexico, Hernández acquired a copy of a letter from Carlos Prío instructing his agents to "penetrate the Fidelista group," and vowing to eliminate it once coming to power, a warning Castro would never forget.[12] More worrying in the short term to Castro was news that Prío had approached Aureliano Sánchez Arango, founder of the action group known as AAA, insisting that it was time for the opposition to unite. To Castro's chagrin, Conte, Santamaría, and Hernández were inclined to agree with Prío. Two sharp letters to the two women, written in mid-June, reveal Castro's increasingly imperious management style.

There was no evidence to suggest that Auténtico Party leaders like Prío and Sánchez Arango had a solution to the problems besetting Cuba, Castro wrote. Nor had they demonstrated any competence as opposition leaders (as evidence, he pointed to reports that a list of Auténtico members had recently been discovered by police in a suitcase loaded with contraband). In fact, the Auténtico Party appeared to be in a state of meltdown, "lacking ideals and morale and compromised to the bone." But regardless of their current state, the women's inclination to ally with them constituted "an ideological deviation." If the Movement had not done so earlier when it was penniless and unknown, why would it do so now? "By virtue of what principle, what idea, what reason are we to lower our unblemished flag in their name?" he demanded. "What ideas, what history, what principles do they propose to join to ours?" Even if sincere, Prío's overture came two years too late. The Revolution's first order of business would be to clean out the nation's political stables to make room for "honest men."

The next most urgent task, Castro said, was to "mobilize tens of thousands of men." This would not be done clandestinely, as before, but openly, with the rebels making the case for change in propaganda distributed to the Cuban people. At this critical stage of the conflict, ideological clarity and consistency was everything, and there was simply no room for those "who change their political positions like they change their clothes." Who did this leave? Why, him and his fellow prisoners, whose self-sacrifice and discipline gave them (and them alone) the "right" to lead the Revolution. Just as the rebels had pride of place among the opposition, so he himself would lead the rebels. "I have reason to know about such things," he told the two, "because to me has fallen the task of searching and organizing and fighting against a million intrigues."

His lecture over, Castro turned to tactics. The biggest threat to the Movement at this time came from mercenaries ready to sell themselves to the first person able to put a gun in their hands, he said. Such people should be expelled at once, "just as those who cower in the face of battle should be shot." The Revolution had no room for "gangsters or adventurers." It wanted only "men conscious of their historical destiny, who knew how to work patiently for the well-being of their country." That had always been the Movement's guiding light. That was what motivated his fellow prisoners. "None of us are impatient," he said. The rebels knew how to wait. And they would be ready to strike when the time was right.

Castro then turned to the subject of "History Will Absolve Me," recently smuggled out of prison. He ordered Santamaría and Hernández to print and distribute 100,000 copies before the upcoming presidential election. With Conte Agüero's assistance, they should get copies to all major news outlets and to all important Ortodoxo leaders. This had to be done with absolute discretion, making sure that none of the production sites were discovered and that nobody was detained. They were to safeguard this document as if it were their own limbs. Mirta would help them in this. The very future of the Movement depended on this mission. Though written by him alone, the document "contained our program and ideology without which nothing else was possible."[13]

Stung by Castro's criticism, it took Santamaría and Hernández six weeks to write back. They accused Castro of committing the sort of errors that he had cautioned others against: trusting in hearsay, making assumptions about people's motivations, playing favorites, and promoting the very infighting he claimed to detest. He had said that things would be hard. Hard they were ready for, and for "firmness," too. What dismayed them, Hernández wrote, was when they looked to Castro for firmness and found him wanting. She raised the case of a recent incident in which Castro had accused her and Santamaría of pettiness in questioning the reliability of a new recruit. After everything the two had been through Hernández couldn't believe it. "You obviously don't know me very well," she wrote.[14]

In letters that summer, Castro urged Conte to appeal to Miguel Quevedo, editor of *Bohemia* magazine, to publicize the plight of the Moncada prisoners and join the call for amnesty. The July 12 edition of *Bohemia* suggests that Conte achieved his mission beyond Castro's wildest dreams. A four-page spread introduces readers to the National Men's Prison on the Isle of Pines. Photographs of the Moncada prisoners share the pages with images of soldiers convicted in various conspiracies against the military dictatorship. Due to the censorship in effect since the Moncada attack and subsequent trial, this constituted many Cubans' introduction to Castro's group. In these photos, the rebels do not seem like the diabolical murderers that Batista and Chaviano made them out to be. Indeed, it is hard to distinguish Castro's men from the professional soldiers. Castro was the inspiration for the article, and he was its main beneficiary. Two entire pages are devoted to photographs and commentary of and by him. These pages, too, belie the government's portrait of a young nihilist bent on cold-blooded murder.

At the time of this profile, Castro was one month shy of twenty-eight. The photographs reveal a solid, increasingly columnar young man, clean-shaven, crisply dressed, just beginning to boast a double chin. He looks well-fed, smokes a cigar, chats easily, and listens intently to questions posed by an interviewer. The images include a few photographs from earlier, happier times, showing Castro alongside Mirta and Fidelito, in something approaching familial bliss. The net effect is of a serious, reflective, and responsible leader, and this before you arrive at his words.

These were to be the first words that Castro could be sure would reach the Cuban public since his arrest, and he chose them carefully. He began by complimenting his jailers for their fairness and professionalism. "Despite being separated from my companions," he remarked, "I am being treated with the highest consideration possible given the circumstances." He was granted normal privileges and enjoyed regular visits from his family. The place was run by the book. He had never been mistreated. The food was good.

Pivoting quickly, he said that he hoped this interview would serve as a bridge allowing the nation to transcend the current fratricide. Asked for his thoughts about the state of the Ortodoxo Party, he said that it should unite to halt the upcoming presidential election, which was called to rubber-stamp the dictatorship. In fact, the party was badly split at this time, with some (Carlos Márquez Sterling and Federico Fernández Casas) calling for it to field a presidential candidate of its own, some (Emilio Ochoa) conniving with Carlos Prío and his Montrealistas, and some (Roberto Agramonte and Castro) insisting the party boycott the election and maintain its distance from other opposition groups. In the current political context, Castro told *Bohemia*, a free and fair election was impossible, hence all who participated in it would only legitimate electoral fraud and further entrench the dictatorship. In short, he was all for party unity, but only if the party lived up to the principles of its founder, Eduardo Chibás, and recommitted itself in the name of the Moncada fallen to the welfare of Cubans as a whole. "That is my opinion," Castro concluded, "and I say it knowing that it may win me a thousand enemies and five more years in jail."[15]

One of the photographs of the *Bohemia* spread stands out from the rest. It reveals Castro not in animated conversation, but seated alone, his face sober, his focus riveted on an article in the previous month's *Bohemia* about a social revolution not so different from the one he himself imagined for Cuba coming undone. GUATEMALA, blared the headline, its contents recounting the latest chapter in President Jacobo Árbenz's effort to raise the living standard of the nation's indigenous majority by redistributing land, expanding education, and broadening suffrage. As in Cuba, this initiative met fierce resistance from those with the most to lose, including the Guatemalan military (from which Árbenz himself had sprung), and U.S. companies accustomed to go about their business as usual. Throw in a few communists in government ranks, an escalating Cold War, and savvy opportunists all around (including in Washington, D.C.), and you have the potential for a big explosion. In June 1954, Guatemala exploded when a motley band of disgruntled officers backed by U.S. warplanes toppled Árbenz, persecuted, jailed, and assassinated progressive ministers and judges, and restored military dictatorship to the country under the command of a colonel named Carlos Castillo Armas.[16]

The caption accompanying this photograph does not refer directly to the incidents described here. But the lesson was not lost on Castro and other revolutionaries to be, including Ernesto (Che) Guevara, who, as a restless and peripatetic young physician, witnessed these events firsthand. Those who aspired to lead movements for national sovereignty and social reform in Latin America at the height of the Cold War would have to reckon with the opposition of the United States. In Cuba all the more so, given the two nations' intimate relationship.

Always a perfectionist, Castro refused to let well enough alone. After reading the profile, Castro dispatched his wife, Mirta, to *Bohemia*'s headquarters to correct a potential misinterpretation of his plight. This represented the last time the couple worked as a team. That month, their marriage suffered a shock graver than the revelation of Castro's epistolary love affair. Listening to his radio on the evening of Saturday, July 17, Castro caught news of Mirta being relieved of a position in the Batista government. Castro knew of her family's intimacy with Batista going back to their common roots in Banes. Mirta's brother and his old friend Rafael served as Batista's undersecretary of the interior (responsible for state security). But Castro couldn't imagine Mirta ever taking a job in the government of his sworn enemy—no matter how strapped she was for cash. The story implied that Mirta had done no work at all but was nevertheless receiving a government salary—a common form of corruption known colloquially as *la botella* (the bottle)—which, if true, could jeopardize Castro's credibility.

Unable to believe what he had heard, Castro assumed this was yet another government plot to destroy him. "Perhaps the government has forged your signature or perhaps someone has spoken in your name," he wrote his wife. That would be easy to find out. Meanwhile, he had already begun legal proceedings. If this were the work of her brother Rafael, she must demand that he take it back even if it cost him his job. "It is your name that's in play here," Castro said. Rafael could not avoid responsibility for slandering "his only sister, now motherless and fatherless, and with her husband in jail!" Now more than ever it was important for her to present the text of "History Will Absolve Me" to Miguel Quevedo and *Bohemia*. It was Batista, along with her brother, who invited the conflict. "I recognize your pain and your great sadness," he said; "you can count unconditionally on my confidence and love."[17]

Meanwhile, in a note to Conte, Castro characterized the "plot" as "ruinous, cowardly, indecent, and intolerable." Despite his reluctance to believe it, it appeared that Mirta was being "seduced" by her family. The event was "hard and sad beyond imagination," he said. The Revolution itself was at stake here, and Castro vowed to take appropriate action no matter how dire the consequences, even if this meant breaking with his wife. "Only a faggot like Hermida in the last stage of sexual degeneration" could have come up with such a cowardly plot, Castro said, referring to interior minister Ramón Hermida, Rafael's boss. Hermida deserved to be shot, Castro declared, before asking whether he might challenge the minister to a duel? Rafael, too, for that matter. "I am blind with rage, and can't even think." Conte had urged him to reconcile with Mirta; Castro reported that there would be no reconciliation. "On private matters, I have already made my decision," he said, "which I must take as a man who places duty to the homeland and the love of its ideals above all other sentiments." By this time, conjugal love was simply a distraction. Castro would file for a divorce.[18]

Later that same summer, Conte proposed that Castro and the rebels join a "civic" front, insisting that a disciplined, nonviolent attempt to oust the dictator had never been tried. Castro appeared open to the idea, despite having castigated Hernández and Santamaría for entertaining the idea themselves. "I agree wholly with you regarding that necessity," he replied. "You cannot imagine the long hours I have meditated on this and innumerable other ideas, based on my experience of the last few years." It is hard to say whether Castro was being sincere in this reply or simply trying to appear so in order to remain close to Conte and thereby exploit him for propaganda purposes. Regardless, he was prescient in anticipating the challenges such an alliance would present. Challenge number one would be reconciling the various egos that such a front implied, as there was an "excess of personalities and ambitions among the groups and leaders," his own included. The more experienced and respected the person, the harder it was for him to commit himself to a cause greater than his own.[19]

Conte's overture reminded Castro of Martí's attempt to corral Cuban independence fighters into a coherent force back in 1895. "Each one had his history, his glories, his individual expertise," Castro said; "each thought himself more entitled to a position of leadership than the next, or at least as equal." Through patriotism, patience, and persistence, Martí managed to bring these factions together. Of his many glorious feats, this was the most "gigantic." Had Martí failed, Cuba might be "a Spanish colony or Yankee protectorate" to this day.[20]

October was a difficult month for Castro. With election day fast approaching, any hope for a political amnesty faded away. That month Batista bestowed the Order of Carlos Manuel de Céspedes Medal upon Rafael Trujillo, the dictator of the Dominican Republic. The award mocked Céspedes's dedication to liberty and independence, Castro said. Meanwhile, at a meeting in Monterrey, Mexico, the old politicians convened to discuss Cuba's future, but without acknowledging the need for social and political reform.

On the other hand, "History Will Absolve Me" was at long last published and disseminated throughout the country—not, to be sure, in the volume Castro had imagined—but to enthusiasm and happy effect. A glossy edition of the pamphlet hit the street in New York City on October 30. The document publicized the plight of the political prisoners still languishing on the Isle of Pines. At the end of the month, while listening to a radio station out of Oriente, Castro learned firsthand that his message was getting through. At the end of a political rally meant to whip up support for Ramón Grau (who pulled out of the fraudulent election within days), Castro heard the crowd chanting his, rather than Grau's, name. "What a formidable lesson for the assembled elite!" a grateful Castro told his sister Lidia.[21]

In an uncontested election on November 1, 1954, Batista received just shy of 1.3 million votes. The election lent a veneer of legitimacy to Batista's dictatorship but did nothing to stop the violence and repression afflicting Cuba. The following January 28, Batista's police prevented Grau himself from honoring the birth of José Martí. The same day, the police attacked a group of students in Santiago de Cuba on the way to Martí's grave. Others were arrested across the island. Books were banned, dissidents intimidated, students beaten up, workers arrested.[22] Batista's inauguration on February 24, 1955, did not stop the murder, intimidation, and arrest of dissidents. But it did imbue the new president with a feeling of generosity that inspired him to take up the subject of amnesty for Castro and his companions. In his first letter from the National Men's Prison back in November 1953, Castro had told his parents that he expected his prison term to be short. His optimism was based on speculation surrounding Batista's announcement in October 1953 that he planned to hold a presidential election the following November. At the time of the announcement, many opposition leaders were in jail or in exile, and any thoughts Batista had about achieving electoral legitimacy depended on his enabling rival political parties to field a plausible candidate or two.

This prompted the talk of political amnesty. But an amnesty of whom? Of all political prisoners? An influential few? Over the course of the next few months, Batista granted amnesty to opposition leaders piecemeal—one here, a few there, talk of perhaps a couple more—before finally announcing a general amnesty on June 4, 1954, for all political opponents *except* the Moncada attackers, who had done nothing to improve their chances by serenading the dictator on his visit to the Isle of Pines the previous February.

The rebels' case was not entirely forgotten. On Saturday, May 15, 1954, the day before Mother's Day in Cuba, a group of parents of rebel prisoners calling itself the "Suffering Mothers" released a message to the country. The nation was about to celebrate its Independence Day (on May 20). But were Cubans truly independent? they asked. Were they happy? Had the nation "fulfilled the aspirations of the liberty struggle?" Of course, the answer depended on whom you asked. "We can't be happy while our boys are in jail." They called for amnesty not just for their own boys but all political prisoners. "Empty the cells," they demanded. "Open the gates. Grant liberty to those detained solely for their ideals."[23]

Batista's "election" relegated the question of amnesty to at best tertiary importance. But the idea was kept alive by the parents of Jesús Montané (from Nueva Gerona on the Isle of Pines) and Juan Almeida (from Havana's Poey neighborhood), who took advantage of the parade of friends and family members through the Montané household on visiting days to organize an amnesty committee. They produced postcards publicizing the prisoners' plight and pleading for "a generous amnesty" for Cubans jailed "because of their love for country and its freedom." In early December, the FEU picked up the cause, amplifying the families' message. By the end of the year 1954, the Montané-Bosque committee created an amnesty petition, with family and friends (and friends of friends) fanning out across the country, going door-to-door, visiting factories, shops, schools, and universities, collecting signatures, distributing pamphlets and telegrams, and writing articles for newspapers, magazines, and radio broadcasts.

The amnesty campaign provided a lesson in political mobilization that transcended its immediate cause. By its conclusion the following May, hundreds of thousands of Cubans had signed the petition. The heart of the campaign through winter and spring of 1954 coincided with the publication of "History Will Absolve Me," and Castro was becoming a household name. The Communist Party (PSP) was not the only group once leery of Castro to get on the amnesty bandwagon. In late February, a who's who of respected writers and politicians, including Carlos Márquez Sterling, José Pardo Llada, Luis Conte Agüero, and Max Lesnik, signed a petition, published in *Bohemia*, demanding "freedom for those imprisoned for political reasons and guarantees for the return of all those in exile, with no qualifications or exclusions."[24] Batista himself took up the subject that same day, telling journalist Marta Rojas that a new amnesty law should "be as broad as the people want it to be." He said he "would not be averse to approving an act of pardon passed by the Congress if it would bring the nation long-term peace." This could not be an unconditional amnesty, mind; he would grant "no exceptional benefits to those who have broken the laws of the republic so that these groups could then go on disturbing family life, the economy, our institutions, and the nation itself."[25]

As the amnesty campaign gained momentum, Castro and Revuelta's correspondence ground to a halt. The two exchanged nary a letter in the month of November. Castro wrote a brief note in early December on the subject of books. He had been reading with "extraordinary spirit," he told her. He loved Robert Sherwood's book on FDR, and asked her to get him the second volume. Curiously, he expressed interest in Simón Bolívar, as if encountering him for the first time. He wanted something beyond Thomas Rourke's *Man of Glory*, he said, wondering if Cubans had written anything about the man who had "liberated five countries." His ambition seemed to be swelling.

Back in October, he had said that it was time he and Revuelta moved beyond the scandal. December arrived and he himself had clearly not done so. The thing that kept it present, he explained, was the pain of not being able to express his love for her adequately— to write without holding himself back. Again, he refused to take responsibility for their predicament, blaming it once more on his enemies in the government.

There was one topic on which stoicism eluded him, namely, the well-being of Fidelito, now in the presence of those who had become his mortal enemies, the Díaz–Balarts (including Mirta). In late October, he had received news from his sister Lidia that his divorce was nearly settled, and that, according to his wishes, Fidelito would remain in school in Havana. At the end of November, however, Lidia informed him that Mirta had taken Fidelito to Miami without his consent. He planned to ask a judge to order the boy's return. "So deep is the chasm that separates me from these people," he told his sister, "that I resist even the thought of my son spending a single night beneath the same roof as my despicable enemies, receiving on his innocent cheeks the kisses of such miserable Judases."[26]

Revuelta counseled against his taking Fidelito away from his mother. The best place for a young child, she said, was in its mother's arms. Castro would not budge on this and wanted Revuelta to see the issue from his perspective. This was more than just a family affair; Fidelito had become the "mascot" of the Moncada rebels ("many of whom are no longer among us"). The boy would have to be rescued. A few weeks later, upon learning that a judge had denied him custody, Castro planned to appeal. If the court ruled against him because he was in jail for defending the integrity of Cuba, he told Revuelta, then he would consider defeat in this custody battle "an honor." An adverse ruling would "reaffirm my principles and my tireless purpose of struggling until death to live in a more respectable Republic. . . . I would not mind losing the case legally if I could win it morally."[27]

Just before Christmas, a little over a year after first taking up his correspondence with Revuelta, Castro wrote her one final letter from prison, the longest yet. In a previous letter, he had expressed his novel appreciation for Aphrodite, the Greek goddess of love. This long letter, really a brief for the defense, might be entitled, "Aphrodite Will Absolve Me." He held a photograph of her in his hand, "eyes big and beautiful, smile burning about me, mouth pretty and provocative (lips seeking a kiss, a million kisses!), gesture resolved, the features of someone talking eloquently about love." (See Insert 2, Photo 12.) How could he be expected to write "serenely" in the face of this? he asked. "You know that I adore you, and at times lose my mind with love."[28]

He had been thinking a lot about the two of them, recently, and also about the matter of honor. The word brought to mind "someone who would sacrifice the opinion of others for the love of another person . . . or who acts out of profound conviction" rather than egotism. Honor was not the same as selflessness or devotion to good; those inspired nobody, he said. He had become devoted to what was "noble, good, intelligent, and humane" in Revuelta. Loving that in her, he came to regard her "with delirium." There was nothing "impure" or shameful about that. On the contrary, their love for each other was entirely honorable. He went on, as if confessing for the last time what had been welling up in him since the previous May. He had found in her "spiritual essence," he said, "the feminine ideal." Her love for him calmed and fulfilled him, just as the psychologist Mira y López promised. What lay ahead he couldn't say, only that he could not "conceive anything better than to see my life one day united with yours in body and soul." That seemed unlikely, he allowed, before signing off: "I have much faith and faith makes miracles."[29]

Revuelta got the last word. She had just met a doctor who had examined Castro in prison and asked the doctor how the prisoner fared. Well, the doctor replied. And physically? Revuelta asked. Fine again, he said, notwithstanding the prisoner's concern about his son. The letter reads like an epitaph to unrequited love. "Get some sun," she counseled. "Take the vitamins I gave you. Take care of yourself." Yes, she was delicate just now, and her nerves were frayed. But she slept "like a rock," she said. "Time, long or short, and God, will help me get over my nervousness."[30]

———————

Meanwhile, the amnesty campaign gained momentum in the first several months of the new year, thanks to the efforts of the Montané-Bosque committee and its swelling ranks throughout the country. Indeed, the amnesty campaign had become so popular by late winter that former enemies and conservative politicians were coming on board. This made Castro and his allies on the outside suspicious. Looking down from his perch atop University Hill, FEU president José Antonio Echeverría denounced "the contemptible spectacle" of politicians tripping over each other to catch a train that had long since left the station, as if their sudden change of heart could redeem their participation in the recent elections. In March one of Batista's former cabinet ministers predicted that the amnesty would soon become a reality, "not only because it is supported by the citizens, but because the president of the republic and his cabinet fully share the people's feelings."[31] In early April, *Diario Nacional* registered the turning tide of national opinion with a front-page banner emblazoned, "All Cuba Calls for the Amnesty Law."[32]

Naturally, Castro had a lot to say about the subject. When, in early March, *Bohemia* suggested that he had agreed to curtail his political activity in exchange for his liberty, he wrote Conte that he would never agree to such conditions and would happily spend two more years in jail rather than "undermine" his "moral stature." Castro was still having difficulty wrapping his mind around the fact that his fate was in Batista's hands.[33] Once published, this sentiment earned Castro a hearing before the Administrative Council of the National Men's Prison at the end of the month. He was sentenced to thirty days in solitary confinement for smuggling a letter out of prison. The same sentence was levied against his brother Raúl, though without the benefit of a hearing. Predictably, the government's heavy-handed response only increased the call for amnesty.

On Monday, May 2, Cuba's House of Representatives passed an amnesty bill over the objections of Rafael Díaz-Balart, a newly elected congressman. The Senate approved the amnesty bill the following day. On Friday, May 6, Batista signed the bill into law.

That same Monday (May 2), with the amnesty law all but on the books, Castro wrote Lidia what is believed to be his last surviving letter from jail. The immediate need was a place to live. Lidia reported finding an apartment large enough for her liberated half-brothers, their sister Enma, now a resident of Havana, and herself. Adjacent to the apartment was another smaller residence that might serve as a haven from what was sure to be an onslaught of visitors. "I was thinking of turning one of the two apartments into a sort of office where I could take care of my affairs and leave the other exclusively as a residence for the four of us," Castro explained. "Otherwise one's home is constantly invaded, and it is impossible to have any kind of private life."

This he knew from experience, when, as a young attorney, he tried practicing law out of his own kitchen, before finally renting space in Old Havana. The alternative to separating one's public from private life, he observed, was to "end up tired of people and the world." There was too much work ahead for that. More than ready to leave prison, he would nonetheless miss a few of its conveniences. "I have a bohemian temperament, which is unorganized by nature," he told Lidia; "there is nothing more agreeable than having a place where one can flick on the floor as many cigarette butts as one deems convenient without the subconscious fear of a housewife, vigilant as a sentinel, setting the ashtray where the ashes are about to fall." He had learned the hard way that "domestic peace" was incompatible with the "frenetic energy of a rebel." It was wise to keep the two apart.

Castro pleaded with his sister to disregard material comfort in order to keep expenses to a minimum. He would have no means of making a living when he got out of jail. He also asked her to take great care of his books. These would be shipped to the new address, and he worried about their safekeeping and organization. Some were worn from use (Martí), some not, some missing, some still in the hands of fellow rebels. He had catalogued the books in his possession more or less by subject ("history, economics, literature, social and political questions, etc."). There followed talk of money, debt, and creditors, all of which made him wonder if he would not come "to miss the calm of prison." People were never satisfied with what they had. "Here at least, one is not bothered by creditors."[34]

The prisoners were to be freed on Mother's Day, Sunday, May 15, 1955. In preparation, families and friends made arrangements for one last pilgrimage to the Isle of Pines. Lina Castro traveled to the capital, where she awaited the return of her sons. Enma and Juanita Castro sailed to Nueva Gerona and took their place among the eager greeters who amassed outside the prison gates. "The Isle of Pines was like a beehive that morning," *El Crisol* reported. "Families and journalists teemed over the grounds just outside the Model Prison, overwhelming all the public establishments and hotels in town."[35]

Expected to be released at 11 a.m., the first of three groups of prisoners emerged onto the prison portico shortly after noon. It did not contain the Castro brothers, but that didn't stop the crowd from erupting. Forty-five minutes later, a second group of prisoners appeared on the portico, this time with Fidel and Raúl Castro among them. Their liberation is captured in an iconic photograph in which Castro walks toward the crowd flanked by Raúl, Juan Almeida, and Jesús Montané. The men are impeccably dressed. With broad smiles, arms extended, and suitcases in hand, they could be tourists arriving home from a cruise. Most of the men cannot conceal their jubilation. Having caught sight of his sisters, Raúl smiles contagiously. Only Fidel Castro, the rebel leader, withholds a smile. His arm, too, is raised, though less in greeting than in triumph, his expression calm, but purposeful, as if determined to impart a message to the

Cuban people: we are free, beholden to no one, and more than ever committed to the project for which we went to jail.

Castro's demeanor softened when the prisoners fell into the arms of their families and friends. Juanita Castro remembers experiencing something close to ecstasy as the four siblings came together amid "exploding tears."[36] Similar scenes unfolded throughout the grounds. The once disparate group of freedom fighters had become, for one sweet afternoon, a single family, and it was hours before the intensity subsided. By early evening the group retired to the Hotel Nueva Gerona to await the boat that would return them to the mainland overnight. Castro held a hastily convened press conference, in which he struggled to balance magnanimity and defiance. He distributed copies of a document titled "Manifesto to the Cuban People from Fidel Castro and the Combatants," which was published in Cuban newspapers the next day.

Cubans who put their faith in the rebels would not be let down, the document stated. "We leave prison without prejudice, either or mind or soul; neither insults nor calumnies can turn us toward hate or away from the path we are obligated to follow." And yet Castro was not the least bit contrite. He presided over the press conference like a commander in chief, poised on the edge of his seat, back rigid, index finger extended, punctuating his points with gesticulations and table banging. The journalists devoured his words like famished cadets. Would he go into exile? Had prison changed him? Had he forsaken the Ortodoxo Party? Had he cut a deal with Batista? "I will answer all of your questions," Castro said, imposing order. "I will speak only the truth."

First, he emphasized that he spoke not for himself but for the rebels collectively. The rebels would not go into exile. They had not abandoned the Ortodoxo Party. They would ally with the FEU. They had cut no deals and were prepared to be the test case of the government's guarantee to extend constitutional protections to all former prisoners and exiles. He was not naive, he insisted. He had already received word that Batista's henchmen had him in their sights.[37] He refuted what he labeled government lies circulated about him and his fellow rebels in advance of their release. He had no political ambitions once Batista was deposed and the Constitution restored. He disavowed the use of terrorism as a tactic in the struggle, but warned that if real political and civil liberties were not restored to Cuba, the opposition had no choice but to resort to violence.[38]

Rapturous crowds thronged the stations dotting the rail line between the port of Batabanó, on the Cuban mainland, and Havana. Local officials, laborers, policemen, soldiers, families, and children craned their necks to catch a glimpse of Castro and his men. The closer the train got to Havana, the thicker the crowds became. Upon arriving in the capital, the train was forced to stop as Castro was pulled out a train window, hoisted onto shoulders, and paraded out of the station, in his arms a Cuban flag presented by a group of mothers of Moncada victims. The well-wishers included FEU president José Antonio Echeverría and Luis Conte Agüero.

Batista was right to regard Castro as a threat. Cuba had a new symbol of hope. "That was a day of celebration for the thousands who were against the dictatorship of Fulgencio Batista," Juanita Castro remembered. To Juanita, who became a vehement critic of the Cuban Revolution, this was the pinnacle of her brother's prestige and her family's pride and happiness. "Looking back on that day," she wrote, "it is difficult to find words to describe it." Her brother appeared "larger than life, respected, heroic . . . after so much anguish and suffering. It seemed a dream to us, something unforgettable." Amid the excitement, Enma Castro was reduced to babble. "It's unbelievable," she said repeatedly; "it's unbelievable to be living all of this." In the face of that "human whirlwind," the Castro sisters recognized that this was not the time for intimate reunions. They retreated in the company of their mother to the elegant Hotel Bristol. That afternoon the Castro women set off on a triumphant stroll across a city the girls had come to love as students, now suddenly full of hope and good feeling. Later that night, Lina hosted a party for all comers at the family's favorite Chinese restaurant. But the Castros weren't buying that night. "This one's on the house!" the manager exclaimed.[39]

On Tuesday, May 17, a torrential rain forced the cancellation of rallies to support the Moncada rebels, stranding cars and flooding cellars across the city.[40] Castro took refuge in his new apartment just off Jardín le Printemps in Vedado.[41] As he predicted, the apartment was overrun by well-wishers, political allies, and journalists, including *Bohemia*'s Agustín Alles Soberón, who managed to steal a few minutes alone with the celebrity in the company of a staff photographer.

In May 1955, there was much talk in the city's newspapers about the state of peace and democracy not only in Cuba and Latin America but around the world. Alles opened by asking Castro about the prospect for peace in Cuba.[42] On the face of it, this was an easy question, as who in their right mind is against peace? In fact, Castro explained, the question was not so simple, as despots had long brandished peace as the means to preserve order and maintain power. The interview is notable less for what Castro said than for how he looked in the accompanying photographs. Castro was nearly twenty-nine now. As a child he had become accustomed to being photographed. As an athlete and aspiring student leader, he forced his way to the front and center of virtually every photograph he was ever a part of. When ranking pushed him to the background, he still managed to stand out from the crowd. For Castro posing was performance, the point to convey authority and gravity. By contrast, the photographs accompanying this article show Castro with his guard down and are among the most intimate photographs of him publicly displayed. They are not flattering. They humanize him, revealing him from angles that only a son, a wife, an intimate would know.

The first image reveals a mustachioed face seen from below. If prison had not dampened the rebel leader's spirit, as Alles suggested, it thickened his waist, neck, and chin, as these photographs attest. From inches away, Castro looks young, his features softened by baby fat that, paradoxically, was absent in childhood. His mustache is thin, his whiskers uneven. He remains as handsome as ever, his roman nose, thick eyebrows, and dark eyes providing the bulwark for the surrounding edifice. In the second image, Castro embraces the daughter of a comrade murdered in the aftermath of Moncada. She will never know her father. Castro's tenderness with the child recalls a prison photograph with Fidelito perched atop his father's lap. It was then that Fidelito asked about one of the fallen men, and, discovering his fate, dissolved in tears. "This moved me deeply," Castro had written Naty Revuelta; "from that day I loved him more because he has suffered from my ideas."[43] Fidelito was neither the first nor the last to have suffered so. Judging from the little girl's delight at being in the arms of someone she just met, Castro was as irresistible to young kids as he was to their parents and, indeed, to strangers.

Another image shows Castro seated on a bench, arms on thighs, leaning forward, head down, hands fidgeting, listening intently to someone or something outside the picture frame. This is not the strident, insistent, domineering attention seeker other photographs portray him to be. Here he appears thoughtful, reflective, sympathetic, even vulnerable (and, yes, exhausted). Still another image shows him lounging comfortably in an old armchair, one leg crossed across his lap. His right hand rests on a foot covered by socks so worn you can see his toes. A broad smile reveals teeth a little worse for the wear of cigar smoke, black coffee, and haphazard personal hygiene. Castro is typically depicted as a man without equals. These photographs reveal him as an ordinary guy, in conversation with peers and friends, now listening, now laughing, at all times relaxed. Even the one photograph where Castro looks directly at the viewer is less assertive than interrogatory, as if there remains something of the curious boy in the increasingly indomitable man. Castro seems to be asking for recognition and acceptance, his steeliness balanced by vulnerability.

The cease-fire did not hold. Within a fortnight of his release, Castro and the Batista administration were back at it, the catalyst Alberto del Río Chaviano, perpetrator of the Moncada atrocities and ensuing cover-up. With the rebels safely incarcerated, and despite overwhelming evidence of his incompetence, Chaviano was given command of Oriente Province. At the time of the amnesty, he was back in the headlines when two broadcasters from the dissident radio station CMKC in Santiago were tortured. Called to account for the bullying by the editors of *Bohemia*, Chaviano struck back not at the magazine but at Castro, reprising his spurious account of the Moncada events. One might imagine Batista officials counseling Chaviano to steer clear of Castro after he turned the tables on the commander at the Santiago trial.

Castro was an effective counterpuncher. He used the words of the government prosecutor in the trial at Santiago to rebut Chaviano. The revolutionaries had comported themselves honorably at the trial, the prosecutor had acknowledged. During the attack itself, they had spared the lives of those they might have killed. The government's own witnesses had refuted Chaviano's charges, making a mockery of the government's lies. Moreover, the people of Oriente had sided with the rebels during the trial, just as they had joined the recent campaign for amnesty.[44]

In late May, the government announced that Castro's rebuke of Chaviano would be treated as a provocation.[45] Tension mounted early the next month, when the administration propagated the unlikely story that Carlos Prío, just returned to Cuba from exile, intended to assassinate Castro. Castro interpreted this news in the only logical way possible: that the government planned to eliminate him and blame Prío partisans. "If something happens to me," he told readers of *La Calle*, "they and they alone will be responsible."[46]

With Castro outperforming the government spokesmen, Batista himself joined the fray at the renaming of a Havana boulevard in his honor ("twenty more years, twenty more years," the crowd chanted). He had tried to be patient with the amnestied prisoners—those "braggarts and bullies"—he assured the crowd. But his patience was not infinite, and his government would use force as well as "brains and hearts" to convince the public of its righteousness. Castro talked a lot about the rebels' courage, Batista noted. "The only one who has courage here is the one who rules close to the people with dignity and affection."[47]

Police and intelligence officials interpreted Batista's threat as a green light to target dissidents, just as Castro anticipated. Juan Manuel Márquez was picked up and severely beaten by police, prompting Castro to warn that government bullying only increased the ranks of rebels "ready to die to defeat the tyranny."[48] Violence did indeed breed violence, though not from Castro and his group. Yet. On June 10, dissidents unconnected to the Movement exploded seven bombs across the capital. Opposed to terrorism, Castro denied complicity, suggesting that the regime itself had carried out the bombing to justify the ensuing crackdown.

In a still more egregious example of state-sanctioned violence, former minister of the navy Jorge Agostini was brutally assassinated. Agostini was a member of Aureliano Sánchez Arango's AAA. In justifying his murder, the police explained that he had a pistol in his backpack, and that he was "meeting with subversives at his Vedado home." To Castro, this said just about all that needed to be said about how the Batista administration functioned. A respected naval officer riddled with bullets for carrying a pistol in his backpack. "Agostini was not a gangster," Castro said. "He never abused or killed anyone; he never stole." This was the logical result of Batista's recent threat. Who, Castro wondered, would be the next to fall?[49]

One reasonable answer was Castro himself. When this editorial campaign did not silence Castro, Batista turned the matter over to his minister of communications, Ramón Vasconcelas, who all but banished Castro from the radio, while threatening to close down *La Calle*, the pro-Castro daily (Vasconcelas would do so within a matter of weeks). It was a sad day, Castro remarked, for those who "recently left prison hoping to contribute to the civic solutions demanded by the country," only to be met by "a total absence of constitutional guarantees." Lacking such guarantees, amnesty became "a trap," and life itself "hung like a thread before the whims of paid assassins." Castro took heart in the evidence that the Cuban public sided with the rebels. He pledged to continue to exercise his civil liberties and "press on with his Martían mission."[50]

In mid-June, the government began to target individuals close to Castro, including his brother Raúl, who was falsely accused of bombing a city movie theater (at the time Raúl was visiting his parents in Birán, with credible witnesses to vouch for him), and his sister Lidia.[51] These threats led Castro to conclude that it was time to leave the country; it simply was "not possible to live here anymore."[52] With his mind made up, Castro and his colleagues came together to formalize their organization and appoint officers. The purposely nondescript "Movement" would now become the "July 26 Movement" (Movimiento de 26 de Julio), after the date of the Moncada attack. Besides Castro, the leadership included Pedro Miret, Jesús Montané, Haydée Santamaría, Melba Hernández, "Pepe" Suárez, Pedro Aguilera, Luis Bonito, Ñico López, Armando Hart, and Faustino Pérez. María Antonia Figueroa, a friend from Santiago, was named treasurer. Hernández's house, 107 Jovellar Street in Havana, became the center of activity, along with the old Ortodoxo office at 109 Prado. Miret, Pérez, and Suárez were charged with collecting weapons. López and Hart would take care of propaganda. Frank País, Vilma Espín, and Léster Rodríguez, among others, were already hard at work in Oriente, setting a standard of efficiency and effectiveness that would not be matched elsewhere.[53]

On July 7, 1954, Castro went into exile. "The doors of civic struggle are closed to the people," he told a crowd at José Martí Airport gathered to say goodbye. He said he no longer believed in general elections. He vowed to return with a revolutionary force capable of restoring Cubans' "right to liberty and a decorous living, without despotism or hunger." To fight for those rights was the essence of what it meant to be Cuban, he said, finishing his goodbye with words from the Cuban national anthem and José Martí.[54]

In abandoning Cuba for Mexico, Castro surrendered more than his son, Fidelito, and more than his country. He also sacrificed a short-lived love affair with Naty Revuelta, now finally consummated. Juanita Castro suggests that Castro enjoyed the company of several different women in the period between the amnesty and his departure for Mexico.[55] Revuelta described ten blissful days and nights in Castro's company in the confines of the small apartment attached to the larger space Lidia had rented. The two wasted little time asleep. Moving from coffee to wine then back to coffee, they pored through old letters, soothed old wounds, and clarified misconceptions. Castro, a passionate cook, re-created favorite recipes from prison, including paella, pulled pork, and garlic chicken, all devoured in the rosy glow of the rising sun. Enma Castro remembers surprising them one day and seeing Revuelta, seated at Castro's feet, staring adoringly into his eyes. Enma knew Revuelta was married and scolded her older brother. Revuelta said both she and Castro knew that this rhapsody could not last. Still, they wrung it for all it was worth, to the point of physical exhaustion.

Nine months later, Revuelta gave birth to a baby girl, living proof that those ten days were not a dream. And proof was needed by then, as Castro was on to other things and other women, Naty Revuelta for all intents and purposes discarded.[56]

chapter ten

EXILE

Most *days Antonio del Conde* left the front of his gun shop at 47 Revillagigedo (just off Alameda Central in the heart of Mexico City) in the hands of two salesmen. If needed, he could be found in one of the joinery, saddlery, or smithing workshops at the back of the store. On a lazy summer afternoon in July 1955, del Conde occupied the front counter when the door opened to a smartly dressed young man accompanied by two assistants. As the two took a seat, the man approached the counter and asked simply, "Do you sell gun parts?" Del Conde was (and remains) a fit, lean, angular man with a receding hairline and wire-rim glasses. He comes off as studious, if not professorial, and gives the impression of having seen it all. Having been in the gun business six years, he had certainly seen a lot, including jealous husbands and spurned lovers drop by to consult him on the possible means of revenge.[1]

He had never seen the like of this. Did he sell *gun parts*? A sign on the front door read, "Del Conde and Son—Rifles, Pistols, Shotguns." Separating patron and client was a showcase laden with gun parts (lock, stock, and barrel). Del Conde fancied himself a good judge of character. The stranger was polished, almost regal, a foreigner obviously, though from where exactly in Latin America del Conde could not say. The man's question lacked detail, so he was clearly not a collector or a professional hunter. Was he a revolutionary out to liberate his country? Perhaps. Whatever he was, he appeared out of his league.

Mind whirring, del Conde played for time. "Repeat the question," he said. "Do you sell gun parts," the stranger responded with an iron gaze. As del Conde struggled to make sense of the man, he had the feeling that the guy was reading him like a book. "He seemed to anticipate what I was going to say," del Conde explained, "as if he were clairvoyant. Later, I learned that an ability to read people was one of his greatest strengths." Del Conde felt himself falling under the stranger's sway. With a quick gesture, he ushered the man into his private office and closed the door. He then asked him to repeat the question once more. "Do you sell gun parts?" was all the stranger deigned to say.

By now del Conde concluded that the man was less naive than he had first thought. The stranger seemed to know what he wanted, and to be asking for help. To provide someone with weapons, del Conde knew, meant to provide him with more than that—with instruction in assembling, operating, cleaning, and storing the weapons, as well as with advice about where and when to conduct training and how to avoid the scrutiny that comes with such a sensitive operation. Something about the man's demeanor won del Conde over. "Look mister," he heard himself saying, "I don't know who you are or what you're up to. That doesn't interest me. But if you want, I will help you."

In identifying someone to provide him with weapons, Castro accomplished one of a daunting array of tasks involved in mobilizing not one but two revolutionary forces—the expeditionary army with which he promised to return to Cuba the next year, and a political underground ready to greet his return with a general strike. Castro had arrived in Mexico on July 7, 1955, traveling from Mérida to Veracruz, where he spent two days at the home of exiled Cuban artist José Manuel Fidalgo and his family, throwing together a memorable spaghetti marinara with shrimp and ground beef, an old standby. With his pockets full of contacts provided by Fidalgo, Castro boarded a bus to the Mexican capital. He was met by his brother Raúl and a Cuban émigré named María Antonia González, whose home a short walk from del Conde's armory served as welcome mat and meeting ground for the Cuban rebels. González's brother, Isidoro, was a member of the July 26 Movement back in Cuba. Isidoro had assured Castro that he would receive a warm welcome at his sister's house, and he wasn't kidding. Many of the rebels' most important alliances were forged over her dining room table. González provided the rebels regular meals, and before long some were bedding down on her living room floor. One evening she remembered tiptoeing around eleven of them.[2]

A convenient gathering place, González's apartment was not the place for discreet conversations. For this Castro relied on the largess of yet another Cuban exile, Orquídea Pino, sister of a former Cuban naval captain sacked by Batista, and her husband, Alfonso (Fofó) Gutiérrez, a Mexican engineer and entrepreneur. Besides furnishing Castro a secure location, the couple provided him with considerable financial support, as well as access to an elite circle of Mexican businessmen and politicians. Castro would later attempt to write the generous (and apparently too bourgeois) couple out of the history of the Cuban Revolution. His sister Juanita remembers the three forging a fast friendship. "Fidel employed his powers of persuasion with them," Juanita observed, "and they quickly became the hub of the organizational process." The couple not only "believed in him, they were captivated by his account of what was happening in Cuba. It was the source of their unconditional support." The Gutiérrezes treated the Castros like family. Before long Enma and Lidia Castro moved into their home in the exclusive Pedregal de San Ángel neighborhood of Mexico City. After a few nights at the Hotel Galveston, a centrally located boardinghouse where many rebels lodged upon arrival, Castro took a room at 9 Pedro Baranda, around the corner from the Gonzalezes. In simple accommodations with few distractions and fewer comforts, he set to work fomenting a revolution.[3]

Castro was hardly the only dissident conspiring to upend Batista at the time. Cosme de la Torriente, for one, a veteran of the Cuban War of Independence and founder of the Society of Friends of the Republic, attempted to corral senior Auténtico and Ortodoxo leaders into a "civic dialogue" with Batista. Carlos Prío, the deposed president, wavered between returning to Cuba to join the civic dialogue and attempting to overthrow Batista himself. Rafael García Bárcena, founder of the Revolutionary National Movement (Movimiento Nacionales Revolucionarias, or MNR) and mastermind of the failed countercoup of April 5, 1953, conspired with dissident military leaders. José Antonio Echeverría, president of the FEU, galvanized university students into a revived Revolutionary Directory. Frank País, a charismatic secondary school teacher from Santiago de Cuba, mobilized students and workers throughout Oriente Province. In short, in labor unions and women's groups, in teachers colleges and local clinics, in automobile repair shops, in secondary school institutes, even in the halls of Congress, Cubans of many different stripes debated alternatives to Batista, whose private payoffs and public works could not quite compensate for the brutality and corruption that characterized his dictatorship.[4]

The questions dividing the Cuban opposition had not changed significantly since the lead-up to Moncada. Was a civil dialogue with the dictator truly possible? Could Batista be overthrown violently? Was terrorism justified? What was the opposition's ultimate aim, after all, to restore the status quo ante Batista, or to revolutionize the country from stem to stern? Paradoxically, Castro's commitment to revolution made him a moderate among opposition leaders. Revolutions required the support, hence education, of the masses. They did not happen overnight. Revolutions also cost a lot of money, found more readily among sympathetic businessmen and professionals than among cash-strapped workers and peasants. Finally, a revolution could not afford to alienate the public through random acts of terrorism. In short, while the sympathy of young firebrands like País and Echeverría was indispensable, so, too, was the endorsement of established Ortodoxo leaders like Raúl Chibás, Luis Conte Agüero, and Max Lesnik, never mind the scores of Cuban émigrés overseas. In letters, pamphlets, and manifestos written throughout the summer and fall of 1955, Castro attempted to delineate a revolutionary platform capable of uniting these disparate constituencies.

Castro spent the first few weeks in Mexico acclimating himself to his second banishment from Cuban society in as many years. "It is hard to explain how bitter it has been for me to have to leave Cuba," he wrote Faustino Pérez, a former member of MNR and recent convert to the rebel cause. "I almost wept upon boarding the airplane. The lack of news these first days is maddening, but I have quickly recovered myself and have returned to work." Together with his brother and Maria Antonia González, he established a safe and efficient courier network between Mexico City and Havana. He reached out to Cuban émigrés in Tampa and New York. And he hurried to endear himself to sympathetic Mexicans. All the while he struggled to maintain as low a profile as possible in a city crawling with Cuban intelligence officials. "I occupy a small room and pass the time reading and studying," he told Pérez. He took his inspiration close to home, devouring histories of the Mexican Revolution and its leaders.[5]

On July 26, the second anniversary of Moncada, Castro ventured out publicly, laying a wreath at the Monument to the Child Heroes of Chapultepec (killed defending Mexico City from a U.S. invasion in 1847), before addressing a meeting of young Latin American exiles at the Spanish Athenaeum that night. "Everyone has a July 26," he told the crowd. He also produced a declaration to be distributed back home belittling Batista's claim to have restored the 1940 Constitution, which specifically prohibited second terms.[6]

It did not take long for Batista's agents to infiltrate Castro's circle. Long before Castro arrived, Cuban intelligence officers had been tailing militants belonging to various opposition groups. It was nothing to add Castro to the list, and by the end of July a naval attaché at the Cuban embassy wrote home proudly of having planted a mole in Castro's midst. Upon arriving in Mexico, Castro had reached out to Evaristo Venereo, former lieutenant of the University of Havana police. Posing as a bitter adversary of Batista, Venereo allied himself with Castro while "immediately contacting" the attaché, who ordered Venereo to update him about Castro's activities on a daily basis. This Venereo apparently did, as the Cuban embassy, through the Servicio de Inteligencia Militar (SIM), provided the Mexican Secret Police with a steady diet of Castro's plans and whereabouts. Castro and his colleagues were not oblivious to such a threat, and quickly came to suspect Venereo, feeding him false tidbits of information which he then turned over to Cuban officials. Within a few weeks of Castro's landing in Mexico, the intrigue was already well advanced.[7]

In early August, Castro addressed a letter to the July 26 Movement leadership, which established his essential talking points through the end of the year: the futility of a civic dialogue with Batista; the timeliness of violent insurrection; the need to broaden the Movement beyond the group of rebels to include peasants, industrial workers, and the general public; finally, the importance of sheer, unrelenting work in the face of persecution, exhaustion, and inevitable mistakes. Cuba was at a crossroads, he told his colleagues. Down one path lay misery, disenchantment, and cynicism, in short, more of the same; down the other path lay justice, hope, and a return to the soaring ideals of Cuba Libre. "This is our moment!" he exclaimed. Not since the U.S. betrayal of the Republic back in 1902 had Cuba been so ripe for revolution.[8]

Training an expeditionary force and laying the groundwork for a general strike entailed different kinds of work. Neither was possible without broad popular support, and Castro began drafting the first in a series of manifestos designed to put the Movement's platform before the Cuban public. The conditions in which he labored were less than ideal, he wrote Melba Hernández. He was out of money and had had to pawn his overcoat to raise the printing costs. Still, adversity suited him. "If I had to do the same with the rest of my clothes, I would not hesitate an instant," he said. The hour approached when the rebels would prove their "honor and faith" and "triumph or die for the country. If the road were easy, I would not feel so happy and alive."[9]

Castro identified someone to print the manifesto through the intervention of María Antonia González's husband, a former champion wrestler known by the name of "Kid Medrano." Medrano had a friend, also a former wrestler, named Arascio Vanegas, who came from a family of distinguished graphic artists. When the local Renaissance man wasn't coaching or giving lessons in physical fitness, he worked in his shop, binding books and periodicals and occasionally producing art of his own. Aware that Castro was working on a manifesto, Medrano introduced him to Vanegas. The two hit it off immediately and Vanegas invited Castro to dinner on August 16, Vanegas's birthday and the anniversary of Eduardo Chibás's death. Over quesadillas and mole verde provided by Vanegas's aunt, Castro apprised his new friend of his plan to "return to Cuba to defeat the dictator or die trying."[10]

Well and good, Vanegas replied, but what did Castro want from him? As it happened, Castro needed a manifesto produced that very night, as he had a courier ready to depart for Cuba the next morning. Vanegas spent the wee hours cajoling his less than stellar workforce into setting, printing, and revising the document. Producing the manifesto in record time was only half the challenge. How, Castro wondered, could they get the thing through Cuban customs? "As a book," Vanegas suggested, after a long pause. He would fold the manifesto into a jacket designed for Cervantes's *Don Quixote*, currently in production in his shop and thick enough to hold multiple copies. The irony of choosing *Don Quixote* to conceal the manifesto was apparently lost on Vanegas. Castro liked the idea. When the first copy appeared, he ripped out a pen and began crossing out paragraphs and correcting spelling and punctuation. "Ya, Fidel!" Vanegas exclaimed. The fact that the manifesto had been produced on such short notice was practically a miracle. There was no time to make changes. Nonetheless, changes in hand, Vanegas dashed back to his workshop where his staff initially refused to reset the type. With Castro at his back, Vanegas got the men to make the changes, and a second copy was produced. Out came the pen a second time. Vanegas beat him to it. "Enough already!" Vanegas said, snatching the pen from Castro's grip. "But it is missing a period!" Castro replied.[11] Just before sunrise, Vanegas handed the book to the courier, suggesting she carry it openly in one hand, an overcoat casually slung across her arm. A few hours later, courier, cover, and contents sailed through Cuban customs.

Dated August 8, 1955, and titled "Manifesto No. 1 of the July 26 Movement to the People of Cuba," the document defended the Moncada attack and explained Castro's decision to go into exile. It also laid out the Movement's revolutionary platform, much of it already aired in "History Will Absolve Me." There were a few items in the manifesto new to Castro's agenda. The Revolution would end "racial and sexual discrimination that lamentably exist in the field of social and economic life," Castro pledged, without explaining exactly how. If true, that would position it in the forefront of social revolutions across the Western world.[12]

Castro's letters from summer and fall 1955 betray mood swings similar to those he exhibited in prison. On the one hand, he was buoyed by the remarkable support demonstrated by Cubans throughout the country for the amnesty and for his decision to go into exile. On the other hand, he doubted that his lieutenants could be trusted to work as hard as he would have worked had he remained on Cuban soil. He had promised to return by the end of the following year, putting added pressure on all those allied with him. Melba Hernández suffered the brunt of his anxiety, with letters pouring in often at the rate of two a week imploring her and her colleagues to get on with the propaganda and fundraising efforts. Propaganda would be "decisive in this contest, as decisive as anything else," he nagged. "Our divided predecessors never understood this." Without a successful propaganda campaign there could be no fundraising. Without fundraising, there could be no weapons, no army, in short, no expeditionary force.[13]

Throughout late summer and fall of 1955, Castro calibrated the strength of the Movement by its success in clearing the ground of rival opposition groups. These rivals included the old guard in the Ortodoxo Party, most of whom had done little or nothing to thwart Batista's consolidation of power in the months and then years succeeding his coup. August was a big month for those who claimed to bear the mantle of Eduardo Chibás. August 16 was the anniversary of Chibás's suicide, and this year delegates planned to mark the event with a National Congress the preceding day, in advance of a memorial service at Colón Cemetery. Among the questions to be taken up by delegates was whether the party should participate in war veteran Cosme de la Torriente's civic dialogue. In a letter addressed to the delegates and read aloud by Faustino Pérez, Castro made his feelings known. The party's commitment to civic dialogue had accomplished nothing, besides inspiring its members to abandon ship. For three years, party leaders had proved themselves incapable of confronting the situation, directing their energy into sterile and endless quarrels, while taking no action. Castro called for delegates to quit this nonsense and embrace his program of violent resistance. A resolution in support of the armed insurrection and the July 26 Movement met with overwhelming support from the delegates, driving a permanent wedge through its ranks. "This was the last time all the elements that made up the Ortodoxo Party came together," noted Armando Hart. It marked the first time that one of Cuba's official political parties endorsed Fidel Castro and the July 26 Movement.[14]

———————

Arascio Vanegas was only one of many interesting people Castro met at the home of Maria Antonia González that summer. A few weeks after arriving in Mexico City, Raúl Castro introduced his brother to Ernesto (Che) Guevara, the Argentine physician and revolutionary fellow traveler who had come to Mexico from Guatemala the previous year after the U.S.-backed overthrow of Jacobo Árbenz. In the months and years ahead, Guevara would exercise outsized influence on the Cuban Revolution, but there is no evidence in the historical record that Guevara made a particularly strong impression on Castro initially. He met all sorts of interesting characters that summer. An unremarkable exchange of pleasantries with Guevara over González's table that evening gave way to an all-night conversation, hardly unusual for Castro. "There was nothing extraordinary about that first meeting," González confirmed. "They simply got to know each other . . . as any two people would after meeting. . . . The conversation lasted a long time."[15]

Guevara, by contrast, remembered being immediately taken by Castro. "I met him on one of those cold Mexican nights, and I remember that our first discussion was about international politics," he wrote. "Within a few hours—by dawn—I was one of the future expeditionaries."[16] The two crossed paths again on the second anniversary of Moncada, when Guevara and his not-quite fiancée (though soon to be wife), Hilda Gadea, shared another notable spaghetti produced by Castro in González's kitchen, this time with clams.

Like a good bottle of wine, Guevara revealed his secrets over time. Castro hit you square on the nose, and Gadea, too, remembered immediately falling under his spell. "He was young . . . light of complexion . . . tall . . . and solidly built," she wrote. "He could very well have been a handsome bourgeois tourist." It wasn't just his looks that caught her attention. "His eyes shone with passion and revolutionary zeal. . . . He had the charm and personality of a great leader, and at the same time an admirable simplicity and natural-ness."[17] A few days later, Guevara and Gadea invited Castro to their home for dinner. An inveterately tardy Castro foiled the couple's attempt to hook him up with Gadea's roommate, Lucila Velásquez. That did nothing to alter Guevara's growing esteem for the rebel leader. "Ñico [López] was right in Guatemala when he told us that if Cuba had produced anything good since Martí it was Fidel Castro," Guevara told Gadea. "He will make the Revolution. We are in com-plete accord. . . . It's only someone like him I could go all out for."[18]

They say that opposites attract. Castro was loud, boisterous, ex-troverted, gregarious, Guevara quiet, reserved, judgmental, circum-spect. Guevara hailed from an aristocratic family, lately down on its luck, Castro from a pair of peasants only recently raised from rags to riches. Their differences were complementary. "Without Ernesto Guevara," Velásquez wrote, "Fidel Castro would never have become a Communist. Without Fidel Castro, Ernesto Guevara would never have been more than a Marxist theoretician, an idealistic intellec-tual. . . . Fidel's Cuban passion and Guevara's revolutionary thoughts came together like a striking spark, with an intense light."[19]

Still, friendship needs something in common to keep it going. Castro and Guevara shared a few essential characteristics, includ-ing a taste for adventure, a love of books, a conviction that life was precious and had to be lived to the fullest, and, above all, a fierce sense of social justice. Both men also possessed extreme self-confi-dence. This inevitably led to conflict between the two of them and between themselves and fellow revolutionaries. There is no telling what would have happened to their relationship had Guevara not died in 1967, but Guevara, irredeemably peripatetic, seems to have recognized by that time that Cuba was not big enough for the two of them.[20]

Encounters with del Conde, Vanegas, Guevara, and other action-oriented figures drew Castro out of his room and provided an outlet for his energy and enthusiasm. His sex appeal proved powerful as ever in Mexico, as we shall see, but he allowed himself an occasional look back. One of his August letters to Hernández contains an intriguing postscript. "May I ask you a personal favor, Melba?" he wrote. "Speak to my friend N. [Naty Revuelta] who works in the International Office at Esso, and explain that I have not responded to her long letters due to the word I got that some of mine were intercepted. Tell her I received her last note (dated August 16) and ask her to write me a few lines telling me by what name and address I can write her securely." Whatever became of this request is not known. Revuelta never received it. "He never responded to the letters I sent him in Mexico," she said, besides sending a trinket to the couple's infant daughter, Alina, upon learning of her birth.[21]

Havana remained on the boil that autumn, thanks partly to provocations by Castro's friends in the Mujeres Martíanas, Echeverría, and others, and to the violence meted out by Batista's police. After much hand-wringing (and with Batista's permission), former Cuban president Carlos Prío returned to Cuba from the United States in August, ostensibly for the purpose of engaging in civic dialogue. In early October, Prío scheduled a demonstration of opposition groups committed to the values of family, peace, and civic engagement. Curiously, he invited the Mujeres to participate, and after considerable debate the group accepted the offer, thinking to turn the event in a militant direction. To represent them, they selected the young firebrand Aida Pelayo.

Pelayo would take up the subjects of family and peace, all right, but not quite in the way Prío imagined. After some late maneuvering, it was agreed that Pelayo would speak third. By the time she ascended the lectern at Havana's Plaza de los Desamparados (Plaza of the Forsaken) on a breezy evening in early October, the vast crowd had lost patience with those counseling yet more dialogue with the dictator. "Revolution! Revolution!" went the cries. Besides Castro, few in Cuba had been as committed to Batista's overthrow as the Mujeres. Pelayo began by recounting what Batista had done to the peace and economic well-being of Cuban families. She then reviewed his record on civil liberties, before recounting a seemingly endless litany of crimes and murders perpetrated by his regime. This was what peace meant to the dictator, Pelayo said. What, she asked the crowd, did it think of engaging a dictator with such a record in civic dialogue? "Revolution! Revolution!" roared the crowd. "Batista is a murderer! Down with the traitors! Revolution! Revolution! Revolution!"

Pelayo's remarks, and the uproar they generated, mobilized Batista's police, never far from the action. As Pelayo returned to her seat, Ramón Zaydín, next speaker in line, leaned over and whispered in her ear. "I was hoping you'd warm up the audience for me, not bring it to the boiling point! What am I to do?" Zaydín did the only thing he could do, throwing out his pacan to peace and harmony and replacing it with a call for revolution. Zaydín was not the only one forced to improvise that day. "Chica, you made me change my concluding remarks," Carlos Prío told Pelayo as the event came to an end. "I made you put some pants on," Pelayo replied, as Batista's police swept in. Pelayo was secreted away in a clutch of spectators. The police caught up with her the next day.[22]

People like a winner. The Movement's surge to the forefront of the opposition meant that it attracted to its ranks individuals with questionable pasts and dubious allegiances. In composing the core of his Moncada assault group, Castro had selected young, mostly working-class men free from the taint of money and politics. Later, in making the case for the July 26 Movement's leadership of the opposition, he celebrated the youthfulness and innocence at its core. Now, the Movement's growing popularity exposed it to taint by association, as even former Batista officials sought to ally themselves with Castro's band.[23] Suspicious of the opposition and determined to retain the rebels' sudden prominence at the forefront, Castro told Hernández and Santamaría to regard financial contributions as proof of people's commitment. This proved misguided in the end as Prío and his fellow embezzlers could throw money in several directions at once.[24]

By early autumn, there was talk of a fundraising mission to Cuban exile communities in the United States retracing José Martí's path three quarters of a century earlier. Impressed by Castro's idealism and staying power, some of these communities had reached out to him with offers of financial support. In mid-October, Castro flew to San Antonio, Texas, before moving on to Philadelphia and New York. From a base in Manhattan, he toured the vast metropolitan area, with stops in Newark, Elizabeth, and Union City, New Jersey, as well as Bridgeport, Connecticut, and Long Island City. In November, he flew to Miami, then visited Tampa and Key West before returning to Mexico City in early December. *Bohemia* reported the trip a success beyond Castro's wildest dreams. In New York, the magazine marveled, Castro was able to unite behind the banner of July 26 émigré groups which up to that point could barely share the same room, including Acción Cívica Cubana, Comité Ortodoxo de Nueva York, El Comité de Emigrados y Obreros Democráticos.[25]

The highlight of the trip was a meeting at New York's Palm Gardens theater on Sunday, October 30. Despite little advance notice and torrential rain, some eight hundred émigrés packed the facility, lured by an advertisement that distilled the aim of the July 26 Movement to three simple words: "liberty, dignity, bread." Up to this point in his life, Castro told the audience, the most moving thing he had ever experienced was at the Santiago trial when the gallery went from calling for the rebels' heads to embracing them as heroes after discovering the lies of the Cuban government. This turnout exceeded even that, Castro maintained, for what it suggested about the virtue and persistence of the Cuban people.

The show of support was all the more gratifying coming less than a day after Castro had been detained by FBI agents in Union

City, a welcome he attributed to the influence of the Cuban consul. Agents of the Cuban government had also tried to sabotage the Palm Gardens event, circulating rumors that U.S. immigration authorities would be on hand to check the exiles' papers. To no avail, Castro thundered. "We respect the laws of this country just as we respect the laws of our own country," he said. "Imagine if we had had a consul who looked after the interests of all Cubans and not just the rich and powerful."[26]

The day's crowd was the perfect response to skeptics who wondered how a penniless, defenseless, idealistic opposition could ever defeat a military dictator. This was the largest assembly of Cubans in New York since 1895, Castro claimed, proof that the Movement was winning Cubans' hearts and minds and would soon be as unstoppable as the Mambises themselves. Castro devoted considerable energy countering Batista administration propaganda. The July 26 Movement was not a criminal gang devoted to random violence. "We are against violence directed at individuals or opposition groups which differ with us, and we are totally opposed to terrorism and personal assassination," he said. The rebels aimed to provide "a decorous existence" to every citizen by ending Cuba's dependence on a sugar monoculture that left hundreds of thousands of workers unemployed for much of the year. Exploiting the nation's untapped agricultural and industrial riches, they would "end the tragedy whereby a man capable of work, wanting to work, cannot feed his family for want of a job."[27]

Always alert to the context in which he spoke, Castro summoned the U.S. founding fathers to lend the Movement legitimacy. By standing up to Batista, he said, the rebels were exercising the right "that Washington and other American liberators had exercised before them," when they stood up to the tyranny of Britain in order to defend their inalienable rights. Helpless in the face of Castro's patriotism, the crowd emptied its pockets. Men, women, and children marched down the aisles left, right, and center, depositing their savings into coffers labeled July 26 as Castro bellowed, "We are not rich! We are not robbers! We seek only humble contributions."[28]

"Men and women cried like babies," Castro's travel companion Juan Manuel Márquez wrote his friends back in Mexico City, describing overflow crowds at one speaking engagement after another. Newspapers commended the two for uniting opposition groups that had never before come together. Their reception was as warm in Tampa and Miami as it was in New York. In a few days, they were on to an engagement at Miami's Flagler Theater, Manuel Márquez explained, which they expected to be the most successful yet. In a postscript to this note, Castro described the public response as "beyond his wildest dreams." Coverage of their trip in periodicals like *Bohemia* and *The Miami Herald* was "priceless," he said; never before had he experienced such optimism or been "so confident of the triumph of our Revolution."[29]

The enthusiasm generated by the U.S. trip did not last. Pledges are easier to secure than money, and Castro became frustrated when contributions arrived in numbers far smaller that he had been led to expect. After nearly six months in exile, the Movement still operated on a shoestring and that thanks to the largess of individuals like the Gutiérrezes rather than a network of reliable supporters. This disappointment was compounded by evidence of success among competitors in the radical opposition. In December, FEU members Antonio Echeverría and Faure Chomón reestablished the old Student Directory, now committed to take out the dictator by any means necessary, including terrorism and assassination. The work of the Directory was not solely destructive, with members fanning out into local communities throughout western and central Cuba, galvanizing workers and peasants the way Frank País was doing in Oriente.

In early December, a Day of Popular Protest led by the Directory inspired a labor strike on behalf of fair pay for sugarcane cutters. "A violent large-scale strike has broken out from one end of the island to the other," journalist Carlos Franqui reported. "Twenty of the principal cities are closed, the workers have occupied churches, town halls, and many buildings. Streets are strewn with nails, highways closed and the railroads at a standstill." When police and rural guards moved in to break up the stoppage, the strikers hit back, engaging government forces in hand-to-hand combat. By the end of the strike, two sugar workers had been killed, twenty severely wounded, and thousands arrested. Despite protests from owners and managers, Batista announced a 4 percent raise. The strike had been successful. The Revolutionary Directory was on the map. Castro and the Movement had to get moving.[30]

Through autumn 1955 the number of Castro's forces in Mexico did not exceed twenty or so people. Early the next year the numbers began to grow, confronting the Movement with a new challenge of paying for and maintaining security at safe houses spread throughout Mexico City, which also served as storage facilities for weapons and other contraband. Rebels and recruits did not arrive all at once, but in batches, a few here, a few there, continuing right up to the day of embarkation on November 30, 1956.

The rebels took many precautions to avoid being identified and arrested by Mexican authorities or kidnapped by Batista's agents. They changed houses and apartments regularly, selecting those in discreet, secluded neighborhoods, with internal garages that allowed them to move their contraband out of sight. They used rental cars for transportation, exchanging them frequently. They traveled in pairs or small groups, never alone. They played tricks on their pursuers when they knew they were being followed. They engaged in counterintelligence, buying off the Cuban agents and émigrés hired to follow them.

Long a target of rivals, gangsters, and police, Castro had simple, practical guidelines for avoiding trouble. When new groups of rebel recruits arrived in the Mexican capital, he left a list of rules in every safe house. The rules went from the letter A to the letter Q, seventeen in all, beginning with the mandate that each recruit raise the money needed to sustain him (at this stage the recruits were men), and ending with the demand that the rebels comport themselves with discretion. "In each house shall reign the most complete order," Castro warned. "Each person must take care not to throw cigarette butts, ash and paper let alone spit on the floor. Absolute respect is expected for whatever person, man or woman, outside the house who is performing work on it." The location of the houses was to be kept entirely secret. No visitors were welcome. No mail was to be accepted at the safe houses. Spare time was not to be squandered but used for reading and studying "about matters of culture in general, but especially about questions of military and revolutionary techniques." The rules were designed not to inconvenience anyone, but to maintain safety and promote the success of "an ideal to which we have committed ourselves before the people and our consciences and which will leave us conquerors or dead."[31]

The rebels' training included target practice at a rifle range called Los Gamitos, five kilometers from the city center, along with calisthenics at Chapultepec Park supervised by the former wrestler Vanegas. At Los Gamitos, the men took aim at chickens, turkeys, bottles, and ceramic plates from distances of between two and five hundred meters. The charge was one peso per person per day. The men would arrive in groups of ten, starting at six in the morning, and continuing until eight at night. They shot rifles with telescopic sights provided by del Conde. Castro would have preferred to train with automatic weapons, of course, but automatic weapons were simply too expensive—and too likely to be traced. As a result, the telescopic lens became a Castro fetish.[32]

Castro expected the expeditionary force to disembark in southeast Cuba and use the Sierra Maestra mountains for protection. Knowing little or nothing about mountain training, Vanegas borrowed manuals and conducted training exercises in hilly neighborhoods just outside the city center. In spring 1955, Castro sought to raise the level of the preparation by re-creating the conditions of guerrilla life. When del Conde described a hunting ranch thirty kilometers southeast of Mexico City, Castro dispatched Guevara to check it out. Located in the town of Chalco and known to locals as San Miguel (the rebels called it Santa Rosa to disguise its whereabouts), the ranch happened to be for sale. As if aspirationally, Guevara told the owner that he worked for a military strongman from a neighboring country who liked the look of the place but wanted to test its suitability before committing to it. He proposed to bring in a team of fifty men to do just that; if all went well, they had a deal.

The owner accepted the terms and the rebels established two separate campsites on the premises, moving the men down to Chalco in mid-May.[33] Alberto Bayo, a veteran of the Spanish Civil War, conducted training, leading the men on all-night marches, teaching them how to shoot straight, to set explosives, and to fire a mortar. Bayo made his students go for days without food and water. He also taught them theories of guerilla warfare picked up fighting Franco in North Africa. The noise and the increased movement did not escape the locals, who alerted police. Inquries by the authorities were met by the owner's bland assurances that there was nothing unusual going on.[34]

Guevara distinguished himself in this training. As a physician and a reader who had traveled throughout Latin America, he was polished, sophisticated, and thoughtful in a way Castro appreciated. But it was Guevara's discipline and dedication to training that first caught Castro's eye. A notebook from the ranch includes evaluations of two dozen men. Among the names is a who's who of Moncada veterans and Castro's confidants, including Almeida, Jesús Montané, Melba Hernández, now in Mexico, and Calixto García. Guevara's evaluation stands out from the rest. "Excellent shooter," an instructor wrote. "Attended twenty regular sessions, shooting approximately 650 cartridges. Discipline excellent, leadership qualities excellent, physical stamina excellent." Guevara occasionally pushed back, with one instructor noting "a few minor errors in interpreting orders along with his wry smile."[35]

In fact, Guevara loved the outdoors, his famous asthma notwithstanding. The ranch was nestled in the foothills of the high mountains that girdled Mexico City to the south. These included the snowcapped volcano Popocatépetl, whose summit tantalized Guevara like Sisyphus's hill. Accounts differ about whether Guevara ever summited Popocatépetl (Castro, ever competitive, says he did not), but Castro admired the determination that drove Guevara to return to the mountain multiple times. "Cultured and politically conscious," he was also "disciplined, serious, and responsible," Castro told an interviewer. Guevara's daring and attention to detail qualified him for leadership of Santa Rosa ranch—to the chagrin of some of the Cubans. Catching wind of jealousy and prejudice against the "Argentine," Castro lowered the boom. Máximo Gómez, one of Cuba's greatest founding fathers, was himself from the Dominican Republic, Castro reminded the men. Guevara was putting his life on the line to secure Cuba's freedom, just as Gómez had done in 1895, and as many Cubans had done in Spain in the mid-1930s. To grumble about Guevara's origin was self-defeating and showed remarkably bad faith, as if Cuba's future was not tied to the fate of Latin America as a whole—indeed, to that of freedom-loving people everywhere.[36]

While the men trained, Castro continued to be distracted by political events back home. Despite having nothing to show for it, proponents of a civic dialogue continued their dalliance with Batista. To Castro's astonishment, senior Ortodoxo leaders remained open to the approach, leading him to finally break with the party in April.[37] April was a violent month in Cuba. On April 3, a group of army officers, led by Colonel Ramón Barquín López and known subsequently as Los Puros (the Pure Ones), were arrested in Havana for conspiring to overthrow Batista. On April 5, in Santiago de Cuba, two university students were arrested and brutally tortured by Batista's police. Two weeks later, men affiliated with the July 26

Movement struck back at police killing four patrolmen. Three of the attackers were wounded and taken to the hospital, where two of them were subsequently assassinated.[38]

That same day, back in Havana, militants affiliated with Aureliano Sánchez Arango's AAA stormed the Goicuría Barracks with truckloads of dynamite. The attack was repelled before the dynamite could be detonated. All fifteen attackers were killed, but not before loudly proclaiming their affiliation with the deposed president Carlos Prío, who had had nothing to do with the attack, but who nonetheless was forced back into exile in the aftermath. Batista dispatched the future chief of his notorious National Police to deal with the perpetrators. Photographers captured images of policemen in the company of one alleged perpetrator later shown to have "died in the attack."[39] The government's readiness to torture and assassinate protesters did nothing to stop the violence, leading many to conclude by summer 1956 that Batista had to be removed by any means necessary.

While these events unfolded, still another conspiracy was in the works, this one, too, emanating from within the military, though not among progressive ranks this time, but among a group of fascists concerned that Batista was too prone to engage the democratic opposition in discussion. Known as the *tanquistas*, after the tank group in which a few of these renegades rose to power, the men were said to be working in cooperation with the Dominican dictator Rafael Trujillo, a regional rival of Batista and someone who worried justifiably that a successful democratic revolution in Cuba led by the likes of Fidel Castro might one day turn its attention to him. Through summer and fall of 1956, Trujillo's navy made a series of successful weapons drops along the coast of Oriente Province. Castro detested Trujillo almost as much as he did Batista. But with little money and desperately in need of weapons, some M-7-26 leaders thought to help out with the collection of these weapons in exchange for a share of the booty, leading to some inevitable confusion.

The strain of this position is palpable in Castro's correspondence with Melba Hernández and Jesús Montané that June. On a visit to

Oriente, Hernández and Montané encountered M-7-26 members confused by talk of cooperation between the Movement and individuals linked to the *tanquistas*. Oriente lacked mature, unified leadership, Hernández warned. She asked Castro to resolve the confusion and bring Oriente in line with the rest of the Movement. Montané echoed Hernández's concern, calling on Castro to renounce the *tanquistas*. It was not just loosely affiliated members who were trucking with them, Montané observed, but Ñico López and Lester Rodríguez, two Movement stalwarts. Where some Oriente leaders had reluctantly said no to Trujillo's weapons, "Ñico had a different opinion." It was time to "let the nation know our opinion on Trujillo."

The problem was that Castro was not the only person calling the shots in Oriente Province. Many of the Movement's leaders there were also closely allied to Frank País, a young teacher and master organizer, as yet unaffiliated with Castro, who was bringing to Oriente a degree of discipline that other jurisdictions lacked. Less ideological than Castro, País was inclined to accept weapons regardless of their origin. That May, País was contacted by people associated with the *tanquistas*: a Dominican naval vessel was on its way to Cuba laden with weapons; could País help secure the weapons in exchange for a share of them? Only too happy to help, País contacted Rodríguez, the Movement's local coordinator. Rodríguez, in turn, assigned fellow members to the task. The weapons were unloaded, transported to Santiago, and neatly tucked away, thus compromising Castro's official line and confirming accusations made by the Batista government (and denied by the U.S. embassy) that July 26 was involved in the plot. País's and Castro's disagreement on colluding with Trujillo was only one of several important strategic and tactical differences to be worked out. It reinforced the impression conveyed by Armando Hart's support of Los Puros that affiliation among the various opposition groups was more fluid than Castro wanted to believe.[40]

Castro could not respond immediately to Hernández's and Montané's letters. By the third week of June, his attention was drawn to the Santa Rosa ranch, where discontentment simmered among the rebel recruits. Guerrilla warfare is often miserable, with hours of marching, hiding, and waiting around, amid few comforts, inadequate sleep, inconsistent meals, and little water. Measured by the rebels' misery and hardship, Vanegas and Bayo had done a good job of simulating combat conditions. The discontent was captured in the diary of Tomás Electo Pedrosa, a recruit. With little water to drink or cook with, the only possibility of relieving the "fatigue and lightheadedness" brought on by long marches was sleep, and yet sleep was impossible in the hills above the ranch, thanks to "a profusion of flies in the daytime and cold and rain at night." If it weren't for their hatred of Batista, no one would have put up with that, the writer observed; even then, the lack of basic sustenance left trainees "in a foul mood." Most blamed the ranch owners and not Castro for the neglect. Some blamed "the Argentine."[41]

Castro and the renegade rebels faced off at ranch headquarters at the end of the month. Castro was not the sort of person you wanted to confront face-to-face. He refused to countenance the attack on Guevara. But confronted by his ragged men (described by one witness as "something out of a concentration camp . . . with crusted, dirty feet, six or seven-day beards, physically exhausted, tired and hungry"), he conceded that the men needed a break. When he headed back to the city center that night, he left in the company of a group of trainees. Over the next several days, the Chalco camp was evacuated, the trainees brought to the city for a week's rest and recovery. Maria Antonia took charge of the sick. Meanwhile, other recruits would take their place in training; the evacuees would return once their spirits had recovered.[42]

The decision to return to the city proved fateful. On the evening of June 20, Castro dropped in on the men recovering at the safe house at 26 Kepler Street. With cars coming and going and with twelve new arrivals in the apartment, the rebels could not maintain their usual discretion. When Castro arrived with three more men, the party swelled to over sixteen, and it caught the attention of the

Federal Police. Another rebel, Ciro Redondo, soon showed up, insisting that he had left his car in a discrete location nearby. Not all that discreet, apparently, as within minutes of Redondo's arrival, a patrol car crawled by 26 Kepler, giving the building an uncomfortably long look. The inhabitants all dropped to their knees, as those with arms drew their pistols. Passing by the apartment the police patrol stopped at Redondo's car, taking note of its license plate.

The rebels took this as a sign to flee. Castro barked out directions. He told Guillén Zelaya to pick up his car, which was laden with weapons, and drive it to the nearby monument to the revolution, which Zelaya did. Redondo and Julito Díaz went to check on the car parked outside and were picked up by the police—not by the Federal Police, in this case, but by the Secret Police, which would turn out to be very unfortunate for them. Castro himself exited by a side door in the company of fellow rebels Ramiro Valdés and Universo Sánchez. The three headed down Copérnico Street, with Sánchez well out in front, Castro in the middle, and Valdés straggling behind. All three carried automatic pistols concealed in overcoats. They had barely made it two blocks when Valdés was apprehended by three Federal Police officers, who acted so quickly and so smoothly that his companions did not notice. Reaching the next intersection, Sánchez was surrounded by three police cars from which sprang more Federal Police, guns drawn. Seeing Sánchez apprehended, Castro ducked into a portico, where he reached for his weapon, only to be stopped short by the pressure of a gun barrel at the nape of his neck.

The Secret Police and the Federal Police were not working in tandem that night. Several months earlier, the Federal Police had learned of the existence of a group of Cuban dissidents operating in the city. At first their captain, Fernando Gutiérrez Barrios, was not overly concerned. Mexico City was chockful of dissidents from across Latin America. These Cubans, small in number and relatively anonymous, seemed unlikely to amount to much. News that the Cubans were amassing weapons to overthrow the government changed their profile, and the Federal Police began staking out the Cubans' apartments. Curiously, the men who picked up Castro, Valdés, and Sánchez did not recognize them, but assumed they were trafficking in narcotics. They drove the Cubans out of the city to an abandoned park where they began to interrogate them. Castro managed to convince the officers that he and his companions were not drug runners but Cuban freedom fighters, and the three were taken to Federal Police headquarters in the city center.

Why the Secret Police were in the neighborhood at that exact time is not clear. The Secret Police, long under the pay of Batista's agents, knew about some of the rebel hideouts, and may have learned of activity in the neighborhood over the radio. The fortunes of those in federal custody and those in the hands of the Secret Police were very different, the former run by a stern but disciplined professional, the latter by a collection of officers as cruel as they were corrupt. Picked up the Secret Police, González, Días, and Zelaya were taken to the headquarters in Calle Revillagigedo, across the street from del Conde's gun shop. When the Cubans would not talk, they were transferred to El Pocito, home of the First Mounted Police, where they were severely tortured.

There has been speculation that the U.S. government was behind Castro's arrest. Gutiérrez denied this. "I don't feel that the Americans exerted any pressure at all," he told an interviewer in the 1990s. Castro had been traveling back and forth to the United States; had the U.S. government been worried about him at that time they could have barred him from entering the country. "The Americans were never present" at the time of Castro's arrest, Gutiérrez noted. In his position at the Interior Ministry, he was in a position to know.[43]

The hasty departure of Castro and others from the safe house on Kepler Street made one remaining rebel uneasy. The sounds of zooming cars and screeching brakes sent Carlos Bermúdez into the streets to see what was going on. From two blocks away, he saw Castro and Sánchez seized. He then hopped a streetcar headed in the direction of the city center. Meanwhile, Gutiérrez's men set to work interrogating the rebels, inspecting their cars, and raiding the safe houses. At least one of the rebels had cracked. Other rebels were picked up that first night, among them Ciro Redondo and Reinaldo Benítez, who had driven off in Castro's weapon-laden car, managing to stash most of the contraband before joining Castro and the others at police headquarters.

For those on the outside, including Raúl Castro and Juan Manuel Márquez, the first order of business was to secure the men and women still at liberty, ensuring that they did not themselves fall prey. The second order of business was to continue the preparations for the expedition, something Raúl Castro and a few other leaders were able to do by transferring the operation to a ranch near Veracruz. New recruits continued to enter the country from Cuba, elsewhere in Latin America, and the United States. Much work remained to be done, including raising the money to feed and house the newcomers, as well as furnishing them weapons for training. The arrests had robbed the rebels of precious time and roughly a third of their guns and ammunition. This would be a real test for Raúl Castro and those who remained at liberty.[44]

At police headquarters, Castro struck up a cordial relationship with his captors. From documents confiscated at María Antonia's house, and from the snippets of information wrung from the captives, Gutiérrez knew that some of the rebels remained at liberty in a training camp in the vicinity of Mexico City. The captain tried to get Castro to concede this. He would not. On June 24, four days after first apprehending the Cubans, Gutiérrez approached Castro again with still more evidence of the Chalco ranch. The police would raid that ranch, the captain warned; was there anything that Castro might tell them to reduce the odds of somebody getting hurt? Aware that the game was up, Castro convinced Gutiérrez to let him accompany him down to Chalco. Castro would precede him into the ranch, explain the situation to the others, and convince them to lay down their weapons. Gutiérrez agreed, and the trip came off as planned, swelling the number of prisoners to twenty-six. The prisoners included Che Guevara and the men who had been tortured at El Pocito.[45]

Word of the Cubans' arrest trickled out slowly, as the Mexican government struggled to understand the full scope of the conspiracy. Castro had been picked up on Wednesday evening, June 20. That Saturday, the headline in Mexico's leading newspaper, *Excelsior*, blared: "SEVEN COMMUNISTS IMPRISONED HERE FOR CONSPIRING AGAINST BATISTA; WEAPONS SEIZED." While Mexican detectives went to work, the Cuban embassy hurried to fill the silence, insisting without a trace of irony that Castro and company were part of a large communist conspiracy determined to upend Latin American democracies. Anticipating this disinformation campaign, Castro sent *Bohemia* a short letter denying his group's connection to communism. "No one in Cuba is unaware of my position toward communism," Castro wrote; "I was a founder of the Partido del Pueblo Cubano [Ortodoxos] along with Eduardo Chibás, who never made a pact nor accepted any type of collaboration with the Communists." Nor was his group connected to Carlos Prío or any of the other militants conspiring to overthrow Batista.[46]

On Tuesday, June 26, Mexico's attorney general delivered his office's official report to President Adolfo Ruiz Cortines. The conspirators were part of a group of roughly forty men led by Fidel Castro of the July 26 Movement. Their aim was to overthrow Cuban president Fulgencio Batista. Comprised primarily of Cubans, the group included militants drawn from across Latin America, some of them veterans of the Spanish Civil War. The Cubans were not communists, the report concluded, nor were they conspiring with former president Carlos Prío. Still, the accusations of communism persisted, prompting Castro to publish yet another statement to the contrary in mid-July.[47]

For over a week, the prisoners were held without access to legal counsel or the press. On June 30, a federal judge demanded the Cubans be granted habeas corpus. Meanwhile, friends and colleagues rallied public support and hired a team of lawyers. As news trickled out of the Cubans' true intentions, many Mexicans began to regard the prisoners sympathetically, a reprise of events at Santiago. On July 2, *Excelsior* carried an interview with Castro published beneath the headline, "They Are Not Reds but Cuban Nationalists." On July 5, an editorial in the same paper defended Castro as someone Cubans "trust to free them from tyranny." How was it, the writer wondered, that Mexico, a country long regarded as a champion of "the politically persecuted," now appeared to be cooperating with Cuba's Secret Police? Likewise *La Prensa* interpreted the Cubans' arrest as "nothing but a powerful maneuver on the part of dictators to extend their underhanded persecution of their adversaries." The Cubans only wanted what Mexicans themselves took for granted, readers wrote President Ruiz Cortines, namely, to live under a constitution dedicated to the rule of law.[48]

Rumors abounded that the Cuban detainees were to be handed over to Cuban authorities and deported, which everyone knew would amount to a death sentence. That would violate international protocols of political asylum, a federal judge concluded. On June 2, the judge ordered the Interior Ministry to either release the prisoners in twenty-four hours or turn them over to a competent tribunal. The demand sparked a battle over jurisdiction that lasted the better part of a week. On July 5, the Interior Ministry conceded the prisoners' right to legal representation and visitation. That evening a large group of well-wishers swarmed into the courtyard of the Miguel Schultz prison for the first time.

Among the crowd was exiled Cuban writer-actress Teresa Casuso, veteran of the anti-Machado struggle and a person, in her own words, "in need of a dream." Hearing news of a group of Cuban revolutionaries languishing in a Mexican jail, Casuso showed up at Miguel Schultz the first night, describing her initial encounter with

Castro in vivid detail. "More than fifty Cubans were gathered in the large central courtyard of the Immigration Prison," she recalled. "In the middle, tall and clean-shaven and with close-cropped chestnut hair, dressed soberly and correctly in a brown suit, standing out from the rest by his look and his bearing, was their chief, Fidel Castro. He gave one the impression of being noble, sure, deliberate—like a big Newfoundland dog." Castro greeted Casuso with "restrained emotion, and a handshake that was warm without being overdone. His voice was quiet, his expression grave, his manner gentle. I noticed he had a habit of shaking his head, like a fine thoroughbred horse."[49]

Less sophisticated than he, Castro's companions "swarmed" around a beautiful young woman accompanying Casuso, as naive and transparent as he was reserved and circumspect. Castro and his fellow rebels were scaled differently, she observed. He stood out from "among them like a tower among hovels." This was the source of his "absolute authority" over them, she surmised, and "why he was able to impose an extremely rigid discipline upon them." Like others before and after, Casuso was struck by Castro's ability to make her feel like she was the center of the universe. Within minutes she found herself imbued with his sense of mission. Castro was not a narcissist, she emphasized. He did not speak about himself but plumbed her for information on the 1933 Revolution. The "fixed star of his faith," she said, was the Cuban people. In sum, Castro possessed "a serene firmness that was more convincing than if he had raised his voice in flaming grandiloquence." In the face of "such personal magnetism, there is, at first sight, no resistance possible."[50]

Two days after this encounter, the interior minister agreed to free the prisoners so long as they returned to their countries of origin, an offer that was promptly rejected. On July 9, unexpectedly, and without much information, twenty-two of the twenty-six detainees were freed after being warned to desist from their previous activities and ordered to check in with Mexican officials on a weekly basis. Despite all that had transpired, their visas were still valid, the Interior Ministry announced inscrutably, as if hoping the problem of the Cubans would simply go away. Only Castro remained in prison, along with Guevara, Calixto García, and Santiago Liberato Hirzel.

On the evening of July 22, 1956, leaders of Western Hemispheric nations signed the Declaration of Principles, pledging themselves to promote the liberty and economic well-being of all their people. Signees included Cuban president Fulgencio Batista and U.S. president Dwight D. Eisenhower, who remarked that "the time is past . . . when any of our members would use force to resolve hemispheric disputes." Two days later, with Mexican president Ruiz Cortines back from the conference, Mexican authorities released Castro. Castro was warned that he would be closely watched and was advised to leave the country as soon as possible.[51]

Once out of jail, Castro hurried to make up for lost time, meeting with the leaders of various dissident groups whose support would be crucial to the Revolution's success. On August 8, he welcomed Frank País, the young militant schoolteacher from Santiago de Cuba, whose support among students and workers throughout the east was the envy of rival opposition groups. Like everybody else in Cuba, País was aware of Castro's intent to return to Cuba and launch the Revolution by the end of the year. A canvass of Castro's organization in Havana and elsewhere, together with his own knowledge of Oriente, convinced País that neither the Movement nor the country as a whole was in any condition to rise up by December 1956.

This was the first time País and Castro met. País was one of the few people able to tell Castro what he did not want to hear, namely, that the country was not ready. That was not the case, Castro insisted, apparently convincing País of his argument, at least for the time being. Castro's plan called for an invasion to coincide with a general strike and disruption of the power grid and communication lines throughout the country. País had the influence in the east to lead a general strike and to organize both civilians and combatants to support the expeditionary force upon arrival. So long, he insisted, as Castro stopped draining militants from the east. The two agreed that País be left with both men and resources to carry out his end of the mission. By sunrise the following morning, they had come to terms, with País returning to Cuba a few days later. Castro seemed more convinced by País than País by Castro. "I confirm everything you told me about the magnificent organizational ability, valor, and capacity of F," Castro wrote María Antonia Figueroa, the treasurer of the July 26 Movement. "We understood each other very well. His visit has proved very beneficial."[52]

The meetings continued through the month. In mid-August, Castro welcomed to Mexico City representatives of a coalition of professionals and businessmen opposed to Batista, which would later become the Civic Resistance (not to be confused with de la Torriente's "civic dialogue"). These representatives included the mainstream economists Regino Boti and Felipe Pazos, who with Castro by their side produced a document of modest reforms entitled "The Economic Thesis of the Revolutionary Movement of July 26." This document contrasted markedly with a more radical statement produced simultaneously by Hart, País, and others (which included statements about labor being "the only source of wealth" and the individual's right "to a job and the income his ability and effort deserve"). Ultimately, Castro adopted neither, preferring to fall back on the program laid out in "History Will Absolve Me."[53]

At the end of August, Castro welcomed a still more important visitor, José Antonio Echeverría, president of the FEU and cofounder of the militant Revolutionary Directory. The Revolutionary Directory embraced strategy and tactics very different from M-7-26, not least the assassination of Batista and his minions and the use of terrorism. By this time, Castro had come to regard Batista and his cronies as a symptom of the economic and political distortions that had hobbled the Republic since its founding and which continued to breed corruption and injustice; assassinating Batista would not fix the problem. Castro also recognized that terrorism alienated the public and eroded popular support. Moreover, the Directory's ranks included former Castro adversaries from the university struggle, some of whom reprised old accusations of Castro's violent past (which seems a bit like the pot calling the kettle black).

Castro intended to launch the war against Batista from Oriente Province, the source of previous antigovernment campaigns successful and not. With his base at the University of Havana, Echeverría thought Havana should be the center of anti-Batista operations. Despite their differences, Castro was willing to cooperate with Echeverría so long as he agreed to submit to Castro's authority. Echeverría, meanwhile, was no less willing for the different organizations to pool their resources, so long as Castro agreed to submit to him. A conversation seemed in order.

The two men came together on the evening of Wednesday, August 29, in a small apartment in the Colonia neighborhood of Mexico City. Castro and Echeverría talked through the night. The following afternoon, they produced what became known as the Letter from Mexico, announcing Echeverría's pledge to support Castro's expeditionary force upon landing despite the two leaders' failing to resolve their fundamental differences. Both the Movement and the Revolutionary Directory were committed to Batista's removal, the letter declared. Both opposed partial elections proposed by Batista and warned that those who participated in them would be regarded as traitors.[54]

Castro had another interesting meeting that fall. Cuban communists, members of the Partido Socialista Popular (PSP), were also interested in talking to Castro, and, separately, dispatched two of their number to learn about Castro's plans. Like Echeverría and País, the two communists did not think the country was ready for revolution. They tried to convince Castro to push back his arrival date in the interest of generating a truly united front. Castro's chances for success would be much greater, they suggested, if his arrival coincided with a massive strike among sugar workers. That could only happen in January during the harvest. They asked Castro to get on board with this plan and issue one last call for a peaceful solution. If Batista rejected the call and the terms, then all Cubans would lend their support for Castro's landing together with a general strike. Castro conceded the reasonableness of the suggestion. He then rejected it, explaining that he had promised to return to Cuba by the end of this year and that his credibility depended on it. His stubbornness alienated his PSP counterparts, who went on to denounce his quixotic struggle against Batista when Castro returned to the country the next month.[55]

Of the many things standing between Castro and his promise to return to Cuba by the end of the year, money remained at the top of the list. Faced with the disappointing fundraising results earlier that year, Castro had charged his deputies in the United States to focus on big donors. When they, too, failed to deliver, he confronted the unpalatable decision of whether to solicit a contribution from his former nemesis, Carlos Prío. "You can't make a revolution with money stolen from the Republic," Castro had recently announced. The Revolution "would not knock on the doors of the embezzlers."

The opportunity to meet Prío came via his new friendship with Teresa Casuso, whom Castro visited at home just after his release from prison. Casuso and Prío were close. Knowing Castro's desperate straits, she raised the issue of a contribution from the former president. Casuso offered to travel to the United States to discuss the issue with Prío in person. Ultimately, Castro concluded that he had no choice but to accept the offer. "This was bitter and humiliating," he later recalled. He swallowed his pride and took the money "to save the Revolution."[56]

In retrospect, Castro claimed that everybody in the July 26 Movement hierarchy (referred to by its members as the Directorate) more or less conceded the need to work with Prío. Not everybody remembered it that way. Franqui recalls Movement leaders being divided. Hart thought the idea betrayed ideological slippage, along with a lack of faith in the Movement's fundraising ability. Faustino Pérez insisted that a decision be taken only after consulting the entire leadership. In fact, as in so many important decisions of this nature, Castro had long since made up his mind. Jesus Montané covered for him by insisting that cooperation with Prío did not signal slippage but merely evidence of the Movement's evolving alliances.[57]

In late August, Casuso visited Prío in Miami, where the former president readily agreed to provide Castro with money. Castro's passport remained in the possession of Mexican immigration authorities, and so a plan was hatched to bring the former adversaries together at the Casa de Palmas hotel in McAllen, Texas, just across the Rio Grande from Mexico. Alfonso Gutiérrez, the husband of Orquídia Pino and an engineer with oil interests in the northeast corner of the country arranged Castro's transportation. The plan called for Gutiérrez's people to deliver Castro to the banks of the river, which he would then swim across (a distance of some two hundred feet) to waiting horses, which would then take him to a waiting truck and then on to the hotel and, after a quick shower, his rendezvous with Carlos Prío. The meeting came off without a hitch on September 1. "We spoke a long time," Castro recalled. "I was there for several hours; we ate lunch together." Castro returned to Mexico via the nearby bridge, $40,000 swelling his pocket.[58]

Castro's work life left him little time for privacy and family life. Just months after returning from their honeymoon in December 1948, Mirta had complained of feeling abandoned. The arrival the next year of the couple's first child did little to keep Castro close to home. After leaving prison and before fleeing for Mexico, Raúl made sure to visit his family in Birán, where he said goodbye to his ailing father. Fidel promised to visit his father, too, but never made it home. In October 1956, while Castro was fundraising in New York, Ángel wrote his last letter to Raúl, updating him on his health and assuring his sons that he was following news of their whereabouts. "I have received your letter from which I gather that you both are in good health," Ángel wrote. "I heard on the radio that Fidel is in

New York." He himself was doing "a little better now," he assured
Raúl, a reference to a stomach ailment that would ultimately kill
him. Meanwhile, Lina was in the hospital in Santiago de Cuba, recovering from an infection. At eighty-one, Ángel knew that despite
all the attention he received from his devoted family, his was not an
encouraging situation. "Still, everything is fine here," he said, just
shy of convincingly. "I beg God to look out for your health and
tranquility; receive the benediction of your parents who always remember you with love and affection."[59]

To the surprise of everyone, Ángel made it another year. He
died on October 21, due to an infection after a hernia operation.
In Birán, Lina, Juanita, and Ramón presided over a flood of well-
wishers who stopped by Ramón's house where Ángel's body lay at
rest. Juanita remembers being overwhelmed by the response. "Never
could we have been prepared for the multitude that arrived like
waves to a wake." The guests included the North American managers from neighboring plantations, local peasants, and the Haitian
workers on the farm. Fidel Castro was staying at the Gutiérrez-Pino
home when he got the news. Juanita Castro reports that he was
oddly stoical where Raúl and Enma and Augustina were broken
up. Enma says that Fidel felt Ángel's death as much as anybody else.
Everybody responds differently to such events, she said. "Fidel had
so much work to do, it was natural that he went right back to it."[60]

This work included welcoming País and Echeverría back to
Mexico City at the end of October. The two returned with the
purpose of nailing down the final plans to launch the Revolution at
the end of the following month. País arrived first, and was delivered
to the Gutiérrez-Pino residence to await the meeting. País was a
man of many talents, including poetry and piano. When the hosts
returned to the room they found him seated at the couple's grand
piano, his revolver resting on the top, pounding out a tune with
ferocious mastery, as if to warn those within earshot that revolution
was not to be embarked on lightly.

País had plenty of men and women ready to come to Castro's

assistance, he explained, but they simply lacked the necessary equipment. And though País could boast great influence among the workers, much needed to be done if workers were to launch a general strike. Delay the expedition six months, País pleaded; at a minimum that would allow him to collect and distribute more weapons. Since ducking out of classes as a student at the University of Havana, Castro had never mastered the skills of give-and-take. Nobody knew the state of the militants' preparation better than País. If he said the country wasn't ready, it wasn't ready. But Castro had made a promise and he intended to stick by it. He rewarded País's candor by promoting him to a position atop the July 26 Movement leadership, while at the same time granting him virtual independence to support the landing and ensuing battle as he saw fit, which País would have done anyway. Castro then informed País of his intention to arrive along the coast of Oriente Province on November 30, at which point País should unleash simultaneous attacks on strategic governmental and military posts around the province.

If Castro's intransigence left País frustrated, there was no piano at Hotel Chulavista in Mexico City for País to express it when he got together with Echeverría a few days later. Echeverría's colleague Faure Chomón later summed up the rapprochement that the Directorate worked out with Castro, and which seems to have applied to País as well. The different approaches of the three groups need not be resolved at the moment, the parties agreed. Each would proceed with its own plans, with Echeverría and País timing their work to coincide with Castro's arrival in the east. Only one of the three leaders—País, by all accounts the most level-headed—seemed to understand what was in store for them, and he could barely get a word in.[61]

When not selling guns, Antonio del Conde ran a small guide service for wealthy sportsmen from the United States. Looking through a catalogue one day, he saw an advertisement for a decommissioned

World War II PT boat, eighty feet long, for sale on Chesapeake Bay. Knowing Castro was looking for a ride home, del Conde informed Castro about the boat, and he immediately ordered del Conde to travel to the United States and check out the boat in person. Del Conde did so and was favorably impressed. The boat cost $20,000 (including a down payment of 50 percent). Del Conde told the owners that he intended to buy the boat but needed to check with the boss. For reasons that are far from clear, the sale fell through, and del Conde continued on with his work.

Whether hunting, fishing, or gunrunning, del Conde often found himself traversing Mexico's Gulf Coast between Tampico, Veracruz, and beyond. One day in October 1956, he was headed south on Mexico 180, just east of the town of Tuxpan. Today, a bridge whisks drivers and passengers over the Río Pantepec. Back in 1956, the road ended at the river, leaving drivers with the choice of taking a ferry or hiring a launch to cross to the village of Santiago de la Peña and so continue on their way. Making the thousand-foot ferry crossing this time, del Conde noticed "a little white boat," nestled among the undergrowth, just upriver, on the opposite bank. Exiting the ferry, he drove his car along the riverbank, parked, and took off on foot to where he figured the vessel to be.

After a hundred meters or so, he came face-to-face with an abandoned boat with the name *Granma* emblazoned on its stern. Del Conde had a small boat of his own at this time that he used for onshore fishing. *Granma* was much bigger, sixty to seventy feet long, by his estimation (it turned out to be exactly sixty-three feet). Del Conde had long dreamed about buying a large pleasure boat to take clients fishing. The abandoned cruiser intrigued him, and once back in Mexico City, he traced the boat to an American couple by the name of Erickson, who had recently purchased it to fulfill an old dream.

Granma sat alongside a small parcel of land also owned by the Ericksons. On the parcel were a house, some apartments, and a small warehouse. A scary encounter with a band of robbers had cured the

Ericksons of their marine fantasy, del Conde learned, and they soon abandoned the coast for Mexico City. The couple intended to sell the boat, but a hurricane damaged it and they never got around to repairing it. When del Conde showed up talking about purchasing it, the couple quickly agreed to a price of $20,000 ($10,000 down, the balance to be paid in a couple months).

The damage was worse than del Conde had originally thought, and these were lean times. Castro owed him a lot of money. The boat had been scuttled in warm water leaving its bottom corroded. Its keel was cracked and would have to be replaced. The boat's bridge, cabin, and storeroom had been ransacked by vandals. The engines were unserviceable, the electrical system frayed, the gas tank rusted. At the shortest, del Conde estimated, the boat could be ready in six months. He bought the boat anyway, rounding up a crew to raise it out of the water and onto dry dock, then hiring a team of technicians and carpenters to do the work.

With most of his time consumed by Castro's mission, del Conde made it down to Santiago de la Peña only on the weekends. One day not long after purchasing the boat, del Conde received a new shipment of rifles. Lighter than the ones they had been using, del Conde suggested that Castro test the rifles in conditions similar to those he would find in Cuba, namely, in the vicinity of Tuxpan. According to an agreement struck with Mexican authorities, Castro was not supposed to leave Mexico City. But a simple disguise and some crisp bills was all it took to get him where he wanted to go. After a day of target practice, del Conde was driving his charges home when he stopped the car in Santiago de la Peña, saying only that he had to check on something, and that he would return "ahorita" (in a minute). In Cuban idiom, "ahorita," means more like "a while" than "a minute," and Castro's impatience got the better of him. He took off after del Conde, eventually catching up to him on his hands and knees inspecting a new keel. "What the fuck is this," Castro wanted to know, pointing to the boat. "Oh, this is my new boat," del Conde said.

Del Conde then recounted the story of the boat's provenance and how he planned to use it to take clients fishing when Castro cut him off. Silent for a moment, Castro said, "If you get this boat working for me, I will return to Cuba in it." Del Conde began to reply that the boat was too small, too damaged, too unsuitable when Castro cut him off again. "If you get this boat working for me, I will return to Cuba in it." By this time, del Conde knew better than to protest or to question Castro's seriousness. Silent, del Conde turned around and walked back to the car. He turned the keys over to someone else, opened the rear door, and sat down without saying a word. After a long pause of his own, he leaned forward, tapped Castro on the shoulder, and said. "I will do it."

And so del Conde's complicated life became more complicated still. He did not stay the night in Mexico City, but turned right around and drove straight back to Tuxpan, a six-hour drive. The first thing he had to do was inject some life into his repair crew. He told his foreman that he had decided to move the boat to a harbor secure from hurricanes. His six-month time frame had narrowed to less than a month. Given the expedited schedule, he would remove the engines from the boat and take them to the General Motors plant in the capital, where they would be rebuilt as if from scratch. Back at his workshop he began to construct the largest gas and water tanks that could be squeezed into the available space, and to repair the electrical system and battery. After a couple of weeks of non-stop work and no sleep, the boat was ready to be launched and put through its paces. Del Conde's growing role in Castro's preparations was confirmed around this time when a smiling Castro showed up simply to inform him that the Batista government had put a bounty on del Conde's head to the tune of $20,000. He should be flattered, Castro quipped; the Cuban government had valued his own head at merely half of that. "We've gotta get out of here," del Conde replied unamused; "there's plenty of people in this country who'd happily sell their mother for $20k."[62]

Del Conde was pleased by the boat's performance on initial

outings. The boat's agility on the river was matched by its confidence on the ocean, and the more del Conde asked of it, the more the boat delivered. He tested the boat by day, at night, and in rough seas. Some of the tests stretched eight to ten hours, allowing him to get a good feel for the engines, steering, and navigation. Once he was asked to help rescue some stranded pleasure boaters on the Isla de Lobos, a hundred miles round-trip. The boat performed beautifully. "*Granma* was *muy marinero, muy marinero*" (very seaworthy), del Conde told me. On one of these tests, he perceived the portside clutch to be slipping a bit. He asked an assistant if he felt it, too. The assistant did not, and the two moved on to other things.[63]

Castro set Sunday, November 25, as the day of departure. He expected the trip to take five to six days and to arrive at Cabo Cruz, the southwest tip of Oriente, at the foot of the Sierra Maestra, on Friday, November 30. That was the day that País would launch an attack on government positions across Santiago de Cuba. Del Conde spent that last week gassing up and stowing water, sacks of oranges, and biscuits. That Sunday, the expeditionaries arrived in Santiago de la Peña by car, ferry, and private launches. They massed at the house and apartments that Castro had purchased from the Ericksons. The day was cloudy with occasional rain showers. Around noontime del Conde received news that a storm was brewing and that the port would be closed, a cable strung across the mouth of the river. Thinking fast, del Conde told the port commander that he had important clients coming down from the capital, and that he could not let them down. The party included several celebrities, their schedules busy, the opportunity rare. The commander drew up a paper, called his staff at the mouth of the river, and ordered them to withdraw the cable.[64]

Del Conde remembers bidding goodbye to Castro "with a strong hug." Castro warned his friend not to pay attention when the Cuban government said that it had killed him ("they have supposedly killed me many times"). Castro ordered del Conde to follow *Granma*'s progress by land, up the Yucatán Peninsula, through the

Yucatán Channel, and into the Caribbean. "Don't talk to anybody," he said, "don't visit anybody you know until Frank País initiates the war in the streets of Santiago de Cuba, which will mean that we have arrived. Then you can return to your usual life." Del Conde accompanied Castro to the gangplank. Castro boarded without looking back. Del Conde pulled the plank away, cast off the lines, and looked on in amazement as *Granma*, with only one engine running so as not to draw attention, slithered out into harbor.

Santiago de la Peña lies fifteen kilometers up the Pantepec River from the Gulf of Mexico. Aboard the *Granma*, Faustino Pérez remembered an eerie silence prevailing as the overloaded boat chugged its way downstream, "with only one engine going at low speed and all her lights out." No matter what happens, do not stop, del Conde advised Castro and Onelio Pino, the former Cuban navy captain now commander of this once in a lifetime mission, before saying goodbye. Five rifles sat fully loaded if there was any trouble from the riverside. The river was tranquil, but those who knew boats and who were familiar with the sea listened intently to the sound of wind whistling past the lanyard. Early winter can be stormy along Mexico's Gulf Coast, as high pressure over Yucatán sucks in colder, heavier air from the rapidly cooling North American continent. When the conditions are right, this pressure pattern spawns punishing northeasterly winds known locally as El Norte. The first formidable El Norte of the year compelled the port commander to seal the entrance to the Bay of Tuxpan early that afternoon. The captain withdrew the cable at del Conde's request, assuming his quiet, confident friend knew what he was getting himself into.

As *Granma* cleared the sea wall where the Pantepec joins the Gulf, del Conde was beating his way toward the Yucatán Peninsula— by automobile. Witnesses describe the boat surging into the Gulf like a bull bursting its stall at a rodeo, as if trying to rid itself of all passengers aboard. People and possessions went flying, Juan Almeida recalled, as seawater inundated the main cabin. In the soft cabin light, the men exchanged worried glances, hearts hammering, stifled cries lodged deep within the throat. Che Guevara, the ship's doctor, went off in search of Dramamine. If only. Then some game fellow struck up a tune—"Marcha del 26 de Julio," followed by the Cuban national anthem—which buoyed spirits for a couple of minutes. The trip was scheduled to take five days. It wasn't long before one after another of the men succumbed to *mareo*, the seaman's curse, the great equalizer, which brings giants to their knees and transforms men into babies. There was nowhere to escape, barely space to lie down. If anyone left the cabin they would be washed overboard; open a window and seawater poured in. The boat's head became a vomitorium. "The whole boat assumed a ridiculous, tragic appearance," Guevara wrote: "men clutching their stomachs, anguish written on their faces, some with their heads in buckets, others lying immobile on the deck in strange positions, their clothes covered in vomit." To Castro, who wasn't sick, the scene called to mind "Dante's Inferno."[65]

The further from land *Granma* proceeded, the worse the weather became. It was not clear that the boat and passengers would survive. "We seemed to be making no headway," Pérez recalled. "She began to ship water and seemed in increasing danger of sinking," he said, in reference to the ship. To make matters worse, the bilge pumps were not functioning. "The water was rising instead of going down." Grabbing whatever containers they could get their hands on, Castro and some others formed a bucket brigade. Pérez sought out the captain. How far were they from Yucatán, he asked. Too far to turn back, the captain responded. "We're goners," Pérez mumbled to himself.

Before leaving for Cuba, Castro sent telegrams to Santiago ("Book ordered out of print"), and Havana ("Make reservation"), signaling that the expeditionaries were on their way and expected to arrive on Friday, November 30. According to the plan worked out in Mexico, País would strike government holdings in Santiago de Cuba and Echeverría in Havana, with the idea of engaging and distracting the government and thereby increasing the odds of a successful landing.[66] Despite misgivings about Castro's schedule, País prepared to put his end of the plan into effect, which included simultaneous attacks on the Moncada Barracks, the national police headquarters, and on the maritime police station on the bay.

On November 29, the day before *Granma* was scheduled to arrive in Cuba, Chomón and a colleague from the Directory met with the July 26 Movement's representative in Havana, Pepe Suárez, and a few Auténtico Party militants, to plan an attack on government positions around the city. Chomón was not impressed by Suárez's leadership. The Auténtico representatives had not heard of Castro's expedition. Later that day, at a meeting of Directory leaders, Echeverría scotched the idea of a joint endeavor. Suárez and the Movement had demonstrated no capacity for carrying out a successful strike, he said. July 26 lacked resources and had not distributed sufficient weapons. To dig in at the university against government troops would be suicidal. "We'd be sacrificing our men," he said. "I'm against both and accept full responsibility because we can't send a group of our comrades to certain death."[67]

Aboard the *Granma*, conditions began to improve by day four, as the weather system that generated the storm shoved off to the east. Amid falling winds and flattening seas, *Granma* split the Yucatán Straits, and advanced east-southeast in the direction of Grand Cayman Island. Some sixty miles north of Jamaica, it veered northeast toward Cabo Cruz, in far southwest Oriente, bound for its supposed landing ground near the town of Niquero. On Friday, November 30, Castro received news over shortwave radio that País had delivered on his end, attacking army and police headquarters in Santiago. Still days away, Castro was growing increasingly desperate. "I wish I could fly," he told Pérez. It was not just the weather that had slowed them down. The clutch of the portside motor was slipping, as del Conde had noted but failed to correct. The slipping clutch reduced *Granma*'s speed by roughly a third. Castro did his best to keep busy, cleaning guns and adjusting the telescopic sights on converted hunting rifles.[68]

It did not help Castro's mood any to hear reports of the deployment of air and sea patrols along the Cuban coastline. In fact, Batista's navy had been on the lookout for weapons drops from the time of the coup. Due partly to Castro's boast that he would return to Cuba with an expeditionary force (dead or alive) by the end of the year, the navy had been waiting for him since mid-October.[69] Early the next month, a top secret dispatch from the Defense Ministry warned local commanders to expect Castro's imminent arrival. The dispatch also warned of concerted attacks on local garrisons, training camps, and other military installations. A week later, on November 6, came yet another dispatch from the ministry, this one more urgent, warning of a conspiracy between Castro, Trujillo, and former president Carlos Prío targeting not just Oriente Province, this time, but "both ends of the island"—a warning that said more about the state of Batista administration intelligence than it did about Castro's intent.[70]

On December 1, the army chief of staff sent a telegram to colleagues across the island to be on the alert for "a white, 65-foot yacht, without a name and with a Mexican flag and a railing that surrounded almost the entire boat." The vessel had left the port of Tuxpan in the state of Veracruz, Mexico, on the evening of November 25, the telegram said. The government had great interest in its pursuit and capture. Early the next morning, as the expeditionaries neared the coast, an army telegram identified the name of the expected boat as *Granma*. A few hours later, still another telegram ordered all stations on high alert, and announced the suspension of constitutional guarantees in Pinar del Río Province in the far west, in Las Villas and Camagüey in central Cuba, and in Oriente.[71]

Aboard the *Granma*, Castro did not receive these messages, of course. But he could not mistake the scrambling of Cuban naval and air force jets and spotter planes. The mission's welcome was sure to be less than friendly, its disembarkation urgent. Nerves were already unsettled since the previous evening, when a helicopter passed over the boat before turning around and heading back to Cuba, prompting lookouts to be posted through the night. Around 2 a.m., Felix Roque, a former naval officer, mounted the cabin top to get a better look of the approaching coastline. Upon descending, Roque lost his footing and plunged into the sea. A frantic search yielded muffled cries but no castaway, and the search was called off. Then Castro ordered one final circle. Roque was spotted struggling in the waves. A line was thrown and a shaken Roque was hauled aboard.

Just before sunrise, a lookout spotted the lighthouse at Cabo Cruz, off the starboard bow. *Granma*, nearly out of gas, made for the coast. As the boat neared land, there was confusion about navigation buoys and the exact destination. Captain Pino made three passes, causing consternation among the men and prompting Castro to ask if he was sure this was the coast of Cuba. The tide was ebbing, making a treacherous shoreline more formidable still. When Pino replied in the affirmative, Castro ordered him to make for the coast at full throttle. A hundred yards offshore, *Granma* plowed into a sandbar, sticking fast. The lifeboat was lowered and a party headed off to identify a suitable landing spot. Overloaded, the little boat capsized, plunging its occupants into the sea. With water up to their chests and rifles held above their heads, they headed for land. Castro ordered everybody to follow, as *Granma* was unceremoniously abandoned, along with all the heavy weaponry collected at great cost throughout the previous year.

The men came ashore at an inhospitable swamp just south of the town of Las Coloradas. It is hard to imagine a less favorable landing place, the rebels' only advantage a predawn arrival, which gave them an hour or so head start on the Cuban military. By the time they made it one hundred yards to what looked like land, they came face-to-face with an impenetrable belt of mangrove, just shy of a mile wide. Castro's men could be forgiven for thinking that

God had it in for them. With great restraint, Faustino Pérez described the challenge ahead as "rough going." The men labored on. Someone climbed a tree. What did he see? More mangrove, then more water, with mangrove beyond. "We thought we had landed on a key in the middle of the ocean," Pérez said.[72]

It would have been one thing to confront the mangrove when strong and healthy. Weak from seasickness, poor nutrition, and lack of water, the men quickly became exhausted. Finally, after what seemed like hours, the men reached dry ground. Eventually, they came upon the home of a local peasant named Ángel Pérez Rosabal, who was not part of the official welcoming party, and who was bewildered by the arrival of seventy-four ravenous and waterlogged guests (eight of the men, including Juan Manuel Márquez, were missing). A leery Rosabal provided the stowaways with water and what little food he could scrounge up. He slaughtered a pig and had just started a cooking fire when the sound of gunfire from the direction of the abandoned boat sent the expeditionaries dashing for the nearby woods. Castro was visibly perturbed. "It wasn't a landing, so much as a shipwreck," someone muttered. "We had landed days behind schedule and in the wrong place," Pérez said. "Everything had gone awry."[73]

Despite his doubts that Cuba was ripe for revolution, Frank País had done his part, staging attacks on the Moncada Barracks, the police headquarters on Intendiente Hill, and the maritime police station, located on the bay. The assault on Moncada fizzled from the start thanks to a malfunctioning mortar round. The attack on the relatively small maritime police headquarters was successful, leaving four dead policemen, no casualties among the attackers, and a prize of twenty rifles. The attack on police headquarters in the center of the city was the most ambitious and carefully planned, and stood the fairest chance of success. It began in the early morning of November 30, just after the changing of the guard. It ended in chaos, with the police building ablaze and two rebels and five policemen dead. "The city woke up under heavy fire," the rebel Félix Pena later recalled. "Weapons of every caliber were spitting fire and lead." It seems a stretch to say that anything positive was accomplished, though the inevitable reprisals further alienated the Batista government from the local population. Over the course of the next several days, from Thursday to Sunday, the people of Santiago harbored the attackers and tended to their wounds, suggesting where their allegiances lay.[74]

In Havana, Carlos Franqui recalled, the Movement leadership was incapable of mounting a serious disturbance. Left to their own devices, Franqui and some others tried to blow up electric, gas, and telephone lines, to no effect. At Camp Columbia, Franqui dropped homemade bombs down manholes connected to the electrical grid, while warning pedestrians to run for cover. He needn't have bothered. "None of our bombs went off that night," Franqui admitted. "Mine was discovered years later, still intact." In the end, there was "lots of smoke and small fires easily put out by the fire department."[75]

In retrospect, the operations meant to coincide with the arrival of the expeditionaries off Cabo Cruz on November 30, 1956, appear as quixotic and ineffectual as the landing itself, revealing little more than Castro's power to convince a few individuals, at least, to undertake ludicrous activities on his (and Cuba's) behalf. Still, the work undertaken by País, Celia, Sánchez, and others to build support for the Revolution among workers, peasants, and professionals alienated by Batista's corruption and bullying was significant, providing the foundation of a guerrilla operation so long as Castro and his fellow expeditionaries could make it off Playa las Coloradas alive.

chapter eleven

TO WAKE THE NATION

T he *Sierra Maestra can be* a jealous host. Just ask the men
of the 22nd Battalion, 1st Division, Rural Guard "Antonio Maceo." In a day and a half of combat against inexpe-
rienced, outmanned, and ill-equipped guerrillas, they had suffered
some thirty killed, seen as many taken prisoner, and surrendered
a trove of guns, mortars, ammunition, and radio equipment. By
nightfall on the evening of June 29, 1958, about the only thing the
soldiers could look forward to was a good night's sleep, as the guerrillas were thought to lack the wherewithal for a frontal attack. By
late June, most of Cuba is unbearably hot and humid. In the deep
canyons of the high Sierra, nights remain comfortable well into
July, and in their camp beside the garrulous Yara River, just outside
the hamlet of Santo Domingo, the men of the 22nd Battalion had
drifted off to sleep.[1]

Just after midnight their sleep was shattered by a hail of mortar and artillery fire discharged from weapons only recently their own. The guerrillas were on the front foot, and the hunters had become the hunted. In terror and disbelief, the soldiers grabbed their weapons and dashed for battle stations. If overconfident, the 22nd was not naive. It, too, had dug in on the steep slopes overlooking Santo Domingo, and taking aim not so much at human targets as at flashes of gunfire, the regulars repelled the guerrillas' assault, eventually fighting the enemy to a standoff.

Then Castro unleashed his secret weapon. Over the cacophony of gunfire ricocheting off the valley walls rose the swell of live music, crackly at first, then crystal clear and ebullient: the Cuban national anthem, the "Marcha de 26 de Julio," followed by a parade of Cuban favorites, all calculated to unnerve the young men who comprised the 22nd and make them pine for home. "The Revolution needs all the weapons at its command," Castro had told the five teenage boys of the Medina family who approached him, days earlier, guns in hand, hoping to come to the defense of their neighborhood. Castro had discovered the musical Medinas the year before when one of his lieutenants happened by their hillside home. "We will defeat the enemy," Castro told the eager boys, "but we will do so with guitars as well as guns."

As the 22nd Battalion headed off to bed, Castro ordered the Medinas to the crest of a nearby hill named El Sabicú where rebel technicians had set up a portable sound studio, complete with microphone and loudspeakers placed several hundred yards apart. There the Medinas, hereafter Quinteto Rebelde, made their public debut, projecting the gospel of the 26th of July over the Yara River valley and into the minds of enemy troops: *We are alive and well. We are here to stay. We will fulfill the unrequited dream of Cuba Libre.* "We were told the rebel army was a bunch of savages, with no resources, no leadership, and no weapons," a captured soldier marveled a few days later. "And yet here you were with your music, culture, and technology, blasting it over the valleys."[2]

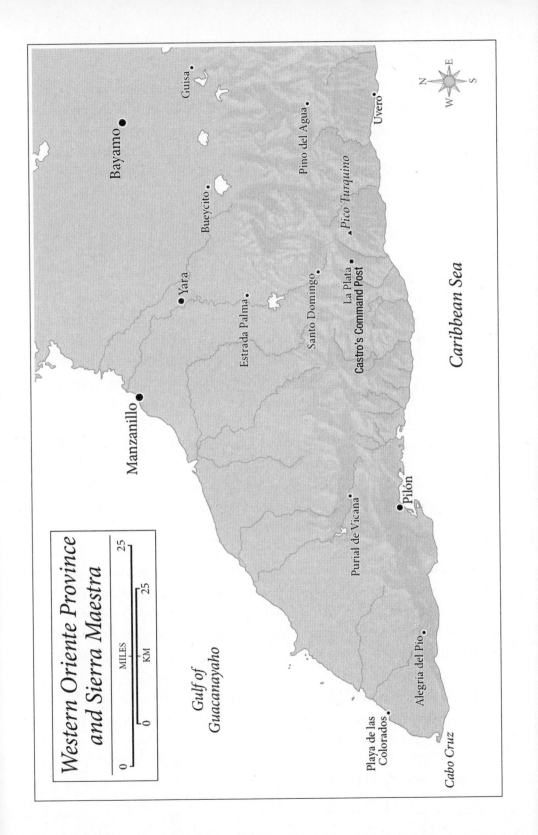

Western Oriente Province and Sierra Maestra

MILES
0   25

KM
0   25

Gulf of Guacanayaho

Caribbean Sea

Bayamo

Guisa

Pino del Agua

Uvero

Bueycito

Pico Turquino

Yara

Santo Domingo

Estrada Palma

La Plata
Castro's Command Post

Manzanillo

Purial de Vicana

Pilón

Playa de las Colorados

Alegria del Pio

Cabo Cruz

N
E
W
S

The standoff at Santo Domingo was the first significant clash between Castro's guerrillas and government forces in Plan Fin-de-Fidel (Plan F-F, as it became known), a massive Cuban military offensive launched in May 1958, whose title concisely conveys its aim. In fact, thanks to the sort of improvisation that Castro displayed in harnessing the young Medinas, the rebels proved impossible to dislodge, and this battle marked the beginning of the end not of Castro but of Batista, an outcome unimaginable a year and a half earlier when eighty-two weak and demoralized men clawed their way through the mangrove at Playa Las Coloradas.

It is hard to imagine a less auspicious beginning to Castro's campaign to oust Batista than that botched landing. Arriving two days late, the rebels were met not by sympathetic locals but by the Cuban military. Flushed out of the home of Ángel Pérez, the rebels took cover in a nearby wood, where Che Guevara remembered a sense of doom descending on the group. With no one to greet them, the rebels did not know whom to trust or where to seek shelter. "We had lost almost all our equipment," Guevara recalled, "and wearing new boots had trudged endlessly through saltwater swamps. Almost the entire group was suffering open blisters on their feet."[3]

Over the course of the next three days, the rebels more or less marched in circles, hunted by air force spotters, tracked by government forces, getting by on little more than sugarcane pulp. On the afternoon of December 4, the rebels pitched camp in the neighborhood of Alegría de Pío, not five miles from where they had disembarked. The next morning, betrayed by a local guide, they were ambushed by government soldiers and forced to disperse. A few rebels died in the ambush, many more were seized, most of those summarily executed. The survivors fled in three separate groups led by Castro, his brother Raúl, and Guevara. Over the course of the next two weeks, the groups made their way east toward the Sierra, narrowly avoiding capture thanks to a network of local residents organized by a farmer named Crescencio Pérez. Rumors of executed captives and a few survivors punctuated the rebels' footsteps east. Passed from one peasant to another, the three groups united on December 21 at the home of Pérez's brother, Ramón, outside the town of Purial de Vicana. Purial sits at the western margin of the Sierra Maestra, twenty-five miles from where *Granma* ran aground nineteen days before.

Legend has it that upon reuniting with his brother and the others, Castro exclaimed, "Now we will definitely win the war!"—a paraphrase of Cuba's founding father, Carlos Manuel de Céspedes. Knowing Castro, he just might have. But only a fool would have put his money on the rebels at the time. The survivors numbered fourteen men in all: Castro himself, Faustino Pérez, and Universo Sánchez; Raúl Castro, Armando Rodríguez, Efigenio Ameijeiras, René Rodríguez, and Ciro Redondo; Che Guevara, Almeida, Benítez, Camilo Cienfuegos, Ramiro Valdéz, and Pancho González. Between them, they had fifteen rifles and a pistol, not the stuff of which revolutions are made.[4]

And yet appearances can be deceiving. Guevara kept a diary of the Revolution. On December 21, he reported that the fourteen survivors possessed ten weapons in total. The next day, "a day of almost complete inactivity," he noted the arrival of new arms. Suddenly "everyone" had a weapon. The following day, December 23, the guerrillas were engaging in combat exercise. "People arrive from Manzanillo," he wrote, "bringing 3000 .45-caliber bullets," along with "nine dynamite cartridges." Now the rebels were "almost completely equipped," with "sufficient medicines for small ailments." Two days later, Christmas Day, the rebels conducted a training exercise, but only after enjoying "a sumptuous pork banquet." In short, just days after their cataclysmic landing, the tiny rebel band was being amply provided for by a network of peasants and July 26 Movement members who remained behind the lines and out of sight. Early the next year, Castro would inflate the size of his guerrilla band to fool visiting journalists. But it was never as small as some would make it, and only seems that way if one ignores the countless organizers, gunrunners, couriers, farmers, teamsters,

guardians, guides, and cooks organized by Crescencio Pérez, Frank
País, and Celia Sánchez, among others, who, doubling as commissary and quartermaster, made the guerrilla war possible.[5]

Once safe in the fastness of the high Sierra, the rebels turned to
making their presence known. On the eve of *Granma*'s departure
from Mexico, Castro had warned del Conde not to believe it when
the Batista government announced that the rebels had been wiped
out. Sure enough, on the afternoon of the rebels' landing, the government announced that the expeditionaries had been annihilated.
"Cuban planes and ground troops wiped out a force of forty exiled
revolutionaries who landed on the coat of Oriente Province to-
night," the Associated Press reported on December 2. "Government
military leaders said Fidel Castro, leader of the revolt against President Fulgencio Batista, was among the dead."[6]

On January 17, the rebels launched their first attack, surprising
a small garrison of soldiers and capturing weapons, ammunition,
sausages, and rum (the last of which was strictly off limits to the rebels but made attractive gifts). The Battle of La Plata, as this became
known after a local river, was a modest success, but success it was,
and the rebels took heart. Guevara noted wryly that with twenty-
two rifles on hand, the guerrillas had more guns than soldiers, a luxury that would not be repeated until the end of the war. A few days
later, the rebels scored another modest victory, surprising a company
of soldiers on the move in an adjacent river valley.[7]

However gratifying these small victories, the calamitous landing
had left the insurrection on life support, and Castro knew it. In late
December, he dispatched Faustino Pérez, a trusted lieutenant, to
Santiago de Cuba to strategize with Frank País and other members
of the urban underground about replenishing his guerrilla force. He
knew there would be no more money, guns, or new combatants
unless he could prove that he and the Revolution were indeed alive.
In early February, Pérez and País went to Havana to round up an

influential foreign journalist willing to come to the Sierra Maestra to interview Castro in person. At mid-month, the two returned to Oriente for a meeting between leaders of the guerrilla army (hereafter to be referred to as "the Sierra") and leaders of the urban underground ("the Llano"), the first such get-together since Castro's return the previous December. The meeting took place on the weekend of February 16–17 at a farm in the foothills of the Sierra, halfway between La Plata and the city of Manzanillo. It coincided with the arrival in the region of *New York Times* journalist Herbert Matthews, editor of the paper's Latin America desk, whom Pérez had arranged to interview Castro.

The meeting between the Sierra and the Llano came at a pivotal moment in the insurrection, with the Movement leadership at loggerheads. Practical and cautious, País thought it ridiculous to proceed with plans to overthrow a military dictatorship with a force of two dozen men. Castro was absolutely essential to the success of the Revolution, País argued. It was senseless to risk his life in an impractical venture that could not be won. País urged Castro to abandon the country yet again and rebuild his army from a position of safety. Meanwhile, he, País, would do for Cuba as a whole what he had done in Oriente, namely, organize students, workers, and professionals into a disciplined, legitimate underground, complete with labor union and local militia support.

Castro would not hear it. Never one to doubt his ability to triumph in the face of insurmountable odds, he worried about ceding the initiative to rival opposition groups like Echeverría's Revolutionary Directory or Prío's Auténticos. He had promised to return to Cuba to defeat the dictator by the end of 1956. He had made the down payment on that promise. To go into exile again would jeopardize both his reputation and the Revolution itself. As Herbert Matthews made his way toward the rendezvous, Castro convinced País to send him a contingent of new recruits to replace those lost at Alegría de Pío.[8]

Castro and Matthews came together at mid-morning on the

17th. They talked for three hours interrupted occasionally by stage-managed visits from Castro's men, who returned repeatedly—in changes of clothes and with different men reporting—to fool Matthews into believing that the guerrilla force was larger than it really was. The ruse worked. Castro told Matthews what he thought Matthews wanted to hear. Matthews dutifully reported what Castro said. The result was a public relations coup for Castro and the Revolution that rankles Castro critics to this day.[9]

One week later, on Sunday, February 24, 1957, *The New York Times* published the first of three articles by Matthews. The veteran journalist began by touting his own accomplishment in penetrating Batista's censorship. Until now, Matthews boasted, "no one connected with the outside world, let alone with the press, has seen Señor Castro except this writer. No one in Havana, not even at the United States Embassy with its resources for getting information, will know until this report is published that Fidel Castro is really in the Sierra Maestra." Though fooled by Castro's misdirection about the size of the guerrilla force, Matthews captured the insurrection's character up to that time. He described Castro's program as nationalistic, socialistic, and anti-American, and said that it promised "a new deal for Cuba, radical, democratic and therefore anti-Communist." Like many before and after him, Matthews fell head over heels for Castro. "Castro was quite a man," Matthews wrote, "a powerful six-footer, olive-skinned, full-faced, with a straggly beard. He was dressed in an olive gray fatigue uniform and carried a rifle with a telescopic sight, of which he was very proud." His personality was "overpowering." Like Casuso, Matthews sensed that Castro was adored by his men. "He has caught the imagination of the youth of Cuba all over the island. Here was an educated, dedicated fanatic, a man of ideals, of courage and of remarkable qualities of leadership."[10]

Regarded in terms of Castro's eventual embrace of communism, Matthews appears naive. But regarded in terms of what Castro had been saying for years, there was little that was new here. Castro's was "a political mind rather than a military one," Matthews wrote. "He has strong ideas of liberty, democracy, social justice, the need to restore the Constitution, to hold elections." Where Castro was vague, Matthews acknowledged it. "He has strong ideas on economy, too, but an economist would consider them weak." Castro told Matthews that the July 26 Movement harbored no ill will toward the United States or its people, though he did complain about Batista turning U.S. weapons intended to promote hemispheric security on Cuban citizens (a violation of the 1952 Military Assistance Program, also known as MAP). Nor did he begrudge the Cuban Army in general, the rebel leader insisted; it was only Batista and his treasonous cronies that he promised to depose.

The publication of Matthews's piece caused a sensation, providing not only irrefutable proof that Castro was alive, but a rare sympathetic account of the rebel leader. Up to this point, the little outsiders knew of Castro came from Batista propaganda, which branded Castro and the Movement "communist." When, a few days prior to its publication, news of the interview leaked to the government, Batista's defense minister challenged Matthews to produce a photograph. Matthews happily complied, the *Times* emblazoning an image of Castro, signed and dated, on its front page. Despite the photograph (and in contradiction of its own evidence from the battle zone), the government continued to plead ignorance of Castro's whereabouts—and about whether he was even alive.[11]

Before returning to the States to compose his articles, Matthews also interviewed Antonio Echeverría and other members of the Revolutionary Directory. Those who knew Echeverría believed him to be Castro's equal in terms of charisma, intelligence, and organizational ability. Matthews was not impressed, taking Echeverría's word that his group was in "no position to start" a revolution (though it was ready to join one). In fact, less than three weeks after Matthews's articles appeared, and doubtless partly because of them, the Revolutionary Directory fulfilled *its* promise to strike at the head of the dictatorship, launching a calamitous attack on the

Presidential Palace, home to President Batista. Castro was not the only Quixote around.[12]

With Castro safe in the mountains, Batista's military and police treated Oriente Province to scorched-earth reprisals meant to dissuade the local community from joining the rebels. The violence had precisely the opposite effect. On January 2, 1957, the people of Santiago de Cuba awoke to news that a fifteen-year-old boy had been found dead in the street, his body grossly disfigured. The murder inspired a spontaneous demonstration the following day in which an estimated three thousand women marched through the main boulevards of the city in complete silence, while the men of Santiago lined the sidewalks. The scene moved many to tears, Armando Hart wrote his family. "Stores closed their doors, and I saw an officer of the U.S. Army, eyes wide open, overcome with emotion." Soldiers dispatched to break up the crowd were immobilized by grief. "Many of them were as young as us," Hart observed, and "their souls were shaken in the face of right and justice."[13]

The city's support for the guerrillas comes as no surprise. Like much of Oriente, Santiago was less developed than the rest of Cuba, more independent, more set in its ways. Grateful for the region's support, Castro and his fellow rebels would come to equate the Revolution with the world of Oriente—and to project that world onto Cuba as a whole. This would complicate things down the road as these two regions faced very different challenges. "The civic quality of the people of Oriente is exceptional," Hart noted. "The wealthy classes, certainly the most reluctant, will understand us. Here they are practically linked to the fight for freedom." In Oriente, Hart discovered "the essence of what it means to be Cuban." In Havana, opposition toward the current regime tended to target individuals rather than social conditions. In Santiago, by contrast, popular indignation created psychological conditions indispensable for "revolutionary upheaval."[14]

Their first months in the mountains proved trying for a group of city slickers adjusting to the hardship of guerrilla life while being targeted by a modern military. In two separate incidents in January and February 1957, the rebels very narrowly escaped strafing by government air and ground forces, facilitated by a traitor in their midst. In typical understatement, Guevara described these days as "not particularly happy." New recruits continued to come and go, every departure increasing the risk of more betrayals and more attacks. The rebels were in no condition to take the offensive. Hunger, exposure, and lack of sleep made things difficult, Guevara observed, but that was nothing compared to the psychological toll of living "constantly under siege." Some of Guevara's descriptions are almost comical. One new recruit "began to shriek, there in the solitude of mountains and guerillas, that he had been promised a camp with abundant food and antiaircraft defenses." Such episodes inspired Castro to declare "defeatism" punishable by death.[15]

Things looked up a bit in mid–March, when the contingent of new men promised by País showed up in the Sierra one week late. The group included three boys from the U.S. naval base at Guantánamo Bay, Charles Ryan, Victor Buehlman, and Michael Garvey, nineteen, seventeen, and fifteen years old, respectively. The arrival of País's men raised the possibility of launching a third attack. Castro insisted the men were not ready, and the guerrillas spent the rest of March and most of April marching and developing ideological discipline. It was not just war they were preparing for, Guevara reported, but "the life after it."[16]

Ryan remembered being astounded by what he and his two friends found there. Castro's band comprised a "strange little group," he said. They were very disciplined, never raising their voices above a whisper. "They didn't curse. They didn't drink. They ate little. They smoked cigars." Castro's men thought of themselves as guerrillas more than rebels, the word rebel suggesting a casualness that their professionalism belied. Ryan confirmed that Castro had a way with people. He got along as naturally with campesinos as he did with intellectuals, professionals, and students. He did not condescend to or bully the peasants. As a result, they trusted him implicitly. It was a good thing, too, as the guerrillas depended on a network of primitive stores supplied by mules from nearby towns bearing rice, beans, butter, sardines, milk, lantern oil, among other necessities. The peasants and the mules were Castro's lifeline. Ryan could never understand why Batista did not think to isolate those mule trains. The peasants also taught the outsiders how to light fires in the rain, to make fires that did not smoke, and to preserve and transport embers—fire, along with water, the sine qua non of outdoor survival. In short, Ryan said, the peasants "turned the rebels into Boy Scouts."[17]

On May 19, 1957, a vessel named *Corinthia* loaded with weapons procured by Prío's group departed Florida's Biscayne Bay bound for Cuba's northeast coast. The aim of the expedition was to open a second front against the dictator in the Sierra Cristal mountains, thereby ensuring that Castro and his guerrillas were not the only fighting force. Four days later, on May 23, the expedition was intercepted by the Cuban military, with sixteen of its twenty-seven members captured and assassinated.[18] The twin disasters of the *Corinthia* and the Revolutionary Directory's failed assault on the Presidential Palace created an opportunity for Castro and his group to prove their mettle. By mid-May, the number of guerrillas exceeded 130. The anxiety bred by the occasional desertions was mitigated by the arrival of weapons, ammunition, and food. The swelling numbers, new weapons, and ample nourishment hardened the guerrillas' resolve, and Castro set his sights on the coastal military barracks at El Uvero, thirty-five kilometers east of La Plata.

On the evening of May 27, eighty rebels grouped in the hills above El Uvero, home to a large sawmill and the site of a garrison some fifty men strong. The garrison sat on a coastal plain, its front to the sea, its rear and flanks vulnerable from the mountains. Six guardhouses, little more than felled trees, protected the periphery, as if the garrison expected to be invaded from the sea. Beyond the guardhouses were residences belonging to the mill owners and local townsfolk. Castro had intended to launch the attack in the dark of night, but dawn was breaking by the time the report from his rifle stirred the guerrillas into action. Over the course of the next three hours, the sides exchanged heavy gunfire, with the guerrillas ultimately outlasting their adversary. By the time the last shot was fired, the army suffered eleven dead and nineteen wounded, the rebels seven dead and eight wounded. Among the army prisoners was the garrison doctor, an elderly man recently graduated from medical school. The man confessed to Guevara that he knew little or nothing about medicine. That never stopped him, Guevara quipped, before stepping into the breach to nurse the wounded. To secure their safety the rebels departed the battlefield with over thirty captives along with forty-five new rifles, six thousand rounds of ammunition, clothing, and other essentials.[19]

The rebel victory sealed the fate of the remaining isolated government outposts. It also introduced the army prisoners of war to a novel way of treating enemy captives, namely, with dignity and respect. In the years since Moncada, Castro emphasized that the Movement had nothing against ordinary soldiers. He consciously targeted the rank and file with propaganda promising them better treatment and a happier life upon the triumph of the Revolution. There was no surer vehicle of propaganda, Castro knew, than the soldiers themselves. The rebels released their prisoners on the condition that they return home and spread the word about the professionalism of their adversary.[20]

The string of modest victories in the first six months of the year provided the guerrillas some breathing room, compelling them to impose law and order, while raising questions about who best to lead a rebel government and other complicated issues. It was a natural time for opposition groups to feel out one another again. Besides resulting in untold murders, the government dragnet that followed the Revolutionary Directory's attack on the Presidential Palace landed hundreds of opposition figures in jail, including Carlos Franqui, arrested for violating the censorship regulations. Ecumenical in its repression, Batista's police succeeded in doing what no one else had been able to do, namely, bringing the members of Cuba's diverse opposition into extended conversation at Havana's El Príncipe prison. There Franqui was able to glean the sentiment of the opposition as a whole, which he shared with Frank País. "There are two hundred of us in prison," Franqui wrote. "Over a hundred from the 26th of July, about forty from the RD [Revolutionary Directory], about twenty from the Auténtico groups, about ten Communists."

Franqui informed Hart that the communists did not endorse the tactics of the July 26 Movement or the Revolutionary Directory, both of which they regarded as "putschist, adventurist, and petit bourgeois." Though claiming with their emphasis on mass mobilization to be the only adults in the room, the communists came off as disengaged; they did not "understand the nature of tyranny and do not believe in the possibility of revolution." Meanwhile, the Auténticos comprised a "mixed" group, Franqui remarked cryptically, before expressing sympathy for the Revolutionary Directory, only recently decimated. The Revolutionary Directory shared his concern about Castro's "bossism" (evidenced by his unilateral decision to return to Cuba the previous December despite what everybody knew to be unfavorable conditions). Franqui counseled Hart to make common cause with the Revolutionary Directory, the only other "serious fighting, revolutionary group in the country."[21]

While Franqui patched things up with the hard-liners, País worked to manage Castro's image among groups whose endorsement was indispensable for the Revolution to succeed. These included diplomats at the U.S. consulate in Santiago de Cuba (more sympathetic than their colleagues in Havana) and members of the country's professional and political classes untainted by corruption or proximity to the dictator. In early July, País sent Haydée Santamaría and Javier Pazos, son of Felipe Pazos, former president of the National Bank of Cuba, to Havana to see if respected members of civil society, increasingly alarmed by the government's heavy-handedness, would be interested in allying with the July 26 Movement. On July 5, without any warning, País brought Raúl Chibás, Roberto Agramonte Jr. (son of the former Ortodoxo presidential candidate), and Enrique Barroso (leader of the Ortodoxo Youth) to meet with Castro, forcing them into discussion. Felipe Pazos himself arrived a few days later. País believed that the presence of these moderates within the Movement would assuage U.S. concerns about Castro. Anticipating Castro's opposition to such a meeting, País did not give Castro the chance to say no. A clever strategist, País also sent along a team of journalists from *Bohemia*, knowing Castro could never resist a little attention from the press.[22]

If surprised by País's initiative, Castro did not let on. The very day Chibás and the others arrived, he wrote Celia Sánchez that the newcomers were already well acclimated and that it was essential that news of the alliance be broadcast in Havana. He sent along some rolls of film depicting visitors and hosts united in amicable conversation. He noted that it "would be highly positive to form a Revolutionary Government presided over by Raúl Chibás," brother of the late Ortodoxo founder, though he worried that Chibás was too scrupulous to accept the offer.[23]

Castro's future tilt to the left makes it tempting to exaggerate the differences between the Sierra and the Llano at this stage of the revolutionary struggle.[24] But except for the timing of Castro's return to Cuba, there does not seem to be much daylight between him and País as reflected in their correspondence from the period. If Castro evinces frustration at times, it is directed not at País but at the Gods of War for sending him poor recruits and for turning him into a bullet counter. Consumed by the challenge of simply staying alive, he was dependent on País for provisions and organization, and he appeared fully aware of that. Castro trusted País (and País alone) to gauge the cost and benefits of striking new alliances. "I have absolute confidence that he is clearly focused on the possible implications," Castro told Sánchez; "he understands our duty, and I delegate full authority in him, without consultation, and in every-thing related to this matter."[25]

At this point in the struggle, Castro believed that the com-bined efforts of the Sierra and Llano were paying off. Thanks to Sánchez, País, and their network, the guerrillas were "marvelously well." Through discipline and selectivity, they were "becoming a real army." Nor was the hard work and risk borne by comrades in the Llano lost on the guerrillas, he said. This letter to Sánchez coin-cided with the death of País's brother, Josué, who was murdered by Batista's police. That tragic event provided yet another reminder of "the heroism displayed by our brothers in the underground," Castro wrote. The relative safety of the mountains made him feel "ashamed." At this stage of the war, the Llano was where the most critical work was being carried out. "To be there has much more merit than to be here."[26]

Evidence suggests that País's cultivation of the moderates and U.S. consular officials was paying off. After the victory at El Uvero, Castro sent Lester Rodríguez, one of his trusted lieutenants, to País, in the hope that he could help Rodríguez get to Miami in order to whip the exile Movement into shape. País delivered thanks to the assistance of the U.S. consul in Santiago. "The consul took him per-sonally," País reported triumphantly, "and the papers, letters, maps that he needed were taken out in a diplomatic pouch. Good ser-vice." Castro did not respond to this delightful tidbit, but he had to have been impressed. País was proving as invaluable as everybody said he was. Good service, indeed.[27]

In early July, País informed Castro that he and Armando Hart had taken it upon themselves to streamline the Movement leader-ship. There were simply too many cooks, he said. The Llano's role was expanding. Besides providing the guerrillas with food, arms, and new men, it was organizing and training workers and militias across the island. A National Workers Directorate had been established to bring industrial and agricultural laborers into the fold. He and his colleagues had established another new office called the National

Directorate of Civilian Resistance comprised of professionals, businessmen, and industrialists. He was reaching out to other opposition groups, as Castro knew, and he was thinking of establishing a strike committee comprised of diverse elements, which, if not "an organ of 26th of July," might nevertheless help launch a strike "at the time we consider propitious." This was never a pleasant process, País allowed. He and Hart had "had to work a little highhandedly," doling out orders "and becoming rather strict."[28]

País also suggested it was time to put some meat on the bones of the Movement's ideological skeleton. Despite Castro's stream of manifestos over the years, the Movement still lacked a feasible, "clear and precisely outlined program," País said. Without that, the Movement would not gain traction among establishment figures essential to its success. Thanks to Castro's persistence and the groundswell of anti-Batista sentiment, Batista's days were numbered. What concerned potential allies was "the quality of the engineers that the 26th can mobilize to construct the new edifice."[29]

If Castro was upset by País's initiatives, he did not show it. In letters to Conchita Fernández, an old friend from Ortodoxo days, and Celia Sánchez, he reported that all was good in the Sierra. The rebels lacked for nothing, were content, and were better manned and equipped than "ever before." Moreover, the guerrillas enjoyed "the complete respect of the peasants." Meanwhile, Chibás and Pazos were thriving in the mountains. Castro suggested Conchita Fernández pay them a visit. It was much safer there than in the Llano.[30]

On July 12, 1957, Castro, Pazos, and Chibás published the Sierra Maestra Manifesto, announcing the creation of a "civic-revolutionary front" committed to constitutionalism, the rule of law, civil rights and liberties, and social justice, including educational and agricultural reform. Promising to name a provisional president independent of political party affiliation, the manifesto repudiated outside meddling in Cuban affairs and rule by military junta. Hereafter, the military would be kept strictly separate from and under civilian control. Vague and formulaic, the manifesto could not have slaked País's appetite for specifics. But it succeeded in associating the Movement with the moderates Pazos and Chibás while getting the attention of the Civic Resistance. U.S. officials also noticed. If true, the embassy observed, a coalition between Castro and Chibás "would be quite significant, as both men have large followings."[31]

Though fond of Chibás and Pazos, Castro found the act of reaching out to former adversaries distasteful. The publicity made it worth it in the short run, which seems to have been what he and País had counted on. The conflicting interests could be addressed later. Still, amid the document's bland verbiage came a clarion call in Castro's voice confirming the rebels' success in the mountains. "No one should be deceived by the government propaganda concerning the situation in the mountains," the manifesto concluded. "The Sierra Maestra is already an indestructible bulwark of liberty which has taken root in the hearts of our compatriots, and here we know how to honor the faith and confidence of our people."[32]

A few weeks later, Castro took time to respond to País's recent letters. He began by acknowledging the death of País's brother. Everybody admired the grace with which he had handled the grievous loss. Referring to País as a beloved friend, Castro assured him of his "pride and contentment" at having him at the helm of the Movement, "directing all the work." When it came time to write the history of the war in the Sierra, Castro remarked, two names would stand out: Frank País and Celia Sánchez.[33]

In one of his letters, País had suggested that Cuba was still not yet ripe for a general strike. By this time, Castro had come to agree completely. He himself had always emphasized the need to raise public consciousness. That is why he never endorsed the coup attempts of Rafael García Bárcena and Ramón Barquín, and why he consistently opposed the Revolutionary Directory's attempt to assassinate Batista. All these initiatives seemed to assume that the country would simply fall in line. The population had to be educated and brought to consciousness. Organization was essential to this process, so, too, propaganda, as he had been preaching since prison. Overwhelmed and overstretched by the challenge of raising an expeditionary force from Mexico, Castro now conceded that the Movement had not achieved the level of organization and consciousness raising that a successful revolution demanded. The guerrillas would continue the war of attrition in the mountains, while País and company proceeded with the political organizing. Indeed, "so clearly" did Castro understand the need for time, he told País, "that if I were asked to choose between a victory on November 30 and victory a year from now, I would prefer without doubt the victory that is brewing by means of this formidable awakening of the Cuban people."[34]

Coming from someone who always seemed to be in a hurry, this statement is remarkable, and reflects Castro's evolving sense of the peasants' role in the Revolution. Upon landing on the coast in December 1956, Castro regarded his peasant hosts as saviors of his revolutionary project. Six months later, he had come to associate the Revolution with the peasants themselves. What had changed? The answer is that the peasants embodied the revolutionary consciousness that orthodox Marxists believed could only emerge from the industrial proletariat. Unlike the rest of Cuba, the peasants did not need to be woken up. They were awake and alert and had joined the revolutionary struggle with barely a nudge on his or anybody else's part. Old abstractions like "revolutionary consciousness" and "the people" vanished in the face of the peasants' resolve to keep the guerrillas supplied, Castro told País. The Revolution inhered in "the invisible force that surrounds us, in those caravans of thirty or forty men, illuminated by torches, descending those slippery slopes, at two or three in the morning, with seventy-pound sacks on the shoulders, delivering our supplies."[35]

What was the source of that willpower and sacrifice? Castro marveled. Who organized those trains? "Where did they acquire such ability, such shrewdness, such valor, such sacrifice?" Not from books, not from party membership, not from cajoling by activists. The peasants organized themselves "spontaneously," he observed. Such was the dedication of those men that when the animals collapsed under the weight of those loads, the men stepped in to complete the job. Nothing could stop the peasants now, he said. Batista's army would have to kill them all, which was impossible, as "the people are awakening to that fact and become day by day more conscious of their immense power."[36]

It was from witnessing such sacrifice firsthand that Castro came to speak of the Cuban Revolution as a revolution of peasants. Critics accused him of mistaking a part of Cuba for the whole, of misreading the nature and needs of less isolated, less rural municipalities and provinces. Rightly or wrongly, living in the Sierra, surviving thanks to the peasants' ingenuity and support, Castro came to regard the local population as the true revolutionaries and the real rebel army. "Our armed force is nothing, insignificant, compared to the immense and terrible army that is the people," he told País, "men, women, old and young who admire the revolutionaries like characters in a fable." The respect was mutual, the trust building and social interaction reciprocal. The peasants taught the guerrillas the meaning of "true revolution." That was the news from the Sierra. If País could do for the rest of Cuba what the guerrilla struggle was accomplishing in the mountains, then Castro and his fellow fighters were happy to wait. País was right. The Revolution could not be rushed.[37]

Before signing off, Castro took up País news that U.S. vice consul Robert Wiecha wanted to talk to the rebel leader. Castro had no objection to speaking to a U.S. or any other diplomat, he said. Such a visit would constitute U.S. recognition that a state of belligerence existed in Cuba and be "one more victory against the tyranny." Contact with the Americans was not in and of itself compromising, Castro observed, so long as Movement representatives remained steadfast on the issues of "DIGNITY AND NATIONAL SOVEREIGNTY." Control was everything. If the Americans made demands, they would be rejected. If they wanted to know what the Revolution stood for, Castro would be happy to explain. If they were ready to befriend a "triumphant Cuban democracy?

Magnificent." On the other hand, given the history of U.S. intervention in Cuba, there could be no U.S. mediation in the current conflict, no matter how well-meaning. There was no need to repeat this, Castro said; it was all there in the Sierra Maestra Manifesto.[38]

That was the last recorded exchange between the two young mavericks. On the afternoon of July 30, 1957, País was gunned down by Batista's henchmen on the streets of Santiago de Cuba. Vilma Espín, a friend and fellow dissident, had spoken to País by telephone not ten minutes before he died. "He spoke rapidly," she told Franquí. "I realized he was in a hurry." In fact, País was trapped in a house with no escape. The noose had tightened, and he seemed to know the end was near. Espín heard the shots that killed her friend, the perpetrators confirmed by a conversation that rebel agents had taped between police chief Rafael Salas Cañizares and his assassins. "It's done," Laureano Ibarra told his boss. "We put a bullet through him," at which point another voice cut in to claim his 3,000 pesos.[39]

The murder of Frank País robbed the Revolution of the only person of comparable stature to Castro, if boasting different skills. País was irreplaceable, and Castro knew it. He greeted news of País's death with outrage. "I can't even begin to express my bitterness, my indignation, the endless sorrow that overwhelms us," he wrote Celia Sánchez. País's killers had "no idea of the intelligence, character, or integrity of the man they murdered." Vitriolic toward the murderers, Castro was equally unsparing of the political passivity that made such events possible. It was time for "every decent and dignified human being, no matter what institution he or she represents, or what party or organization he or she belongs to," to unite to depose Batista and his government.[40]

On August 31, the day after País's assassination, Santiago erupted in peaceful protest, completely shutting the city down. René Ramos Latour, País's colleague in the Llano (and the person pegged to fill his role), described the "general strike" in a letter to Celia Sánchez. "There were no conservatives or radicals, rich or poor, blacks or whites," Ramos wrote. The people came together in a show of unity and defiance. "All businesses, movies, cafés, banks, factories, professionals, in a word, all of Santiago shut its doors, and came together in one of the greatest outpourings of sorrow in memory." The city was "ours." Citizens did not hesitate to declare their solidarity with the Movement. Santiago remained paralyzed the following day, with "employers as well as workers . . . ready to prolong the stoppage as long as necessary."[41]

Movement leaders hoped that the Santiago strike would precipitate similar stoppages in other cities. It did not, leading to finger-pointing that did not bode well for life after País. Within hours of his death, the Directorate took up the task of divvying up the innumerable tasks that País had somehow managed to do himself. The immensity of the challenge was not lost on them. Formally, País's burden was divided among Sánchez, Hart, and Ramos, with the Sierra and Llano retaining their separate roles. "Ultimately," Castro wrote Sánchez, he and she would have to shoulder the responsibility. And not for a want of "valiant comrades," but because País's "authority, initiative, and experience" could not be acquired on the run.[42]

Just a few weeks earlier, at País's suggestion, Castro divided his forces, creating what would become known as Column 4, under the leadership of Che Guevara, recently promoted to commander. Numbering roughly a hundred strong, Guevara's column left the La Plata area for the territory east of Pico Turquino, in the municipality of Buey Arriba. The idea behind the split was to make it harder for the army to concentrate its forces on a single target. Meanwhile, Castro stayed put atop the La Plata River valley, writing letters, conducting business, and raiding isolated garrisons. Through summer 1957, the army's effort to take the battle to the guerrillas can only be called halfhearted. Instead of avenging the rebel victory at El Uvero, it avoided the Sierra Maestra, allowing the rebels to consolidate their positions, recruit new men, and acquire new weapons. In late July,

Castro and Guevara grew restless, scanning the exposed army out-posts at the base of the foothills for ripe targets. Castro raided the garrison at Estrada Palma, taking it without firing a shot. *Bohemia* took advantage of a short window without censorship to chronicle the event, converting a trivial skirmish into a major rebel victory won by over two hundred men. The number in Castro's band was far smaller. Delighted by the publicity, Castro did not quibble about the numbers.[43]

In mid-August, Guevara's command received its initiation, de-scending the hills for an early morning raid on the army garrison at Bueycito, where the greenhorns out-battled the garrison's twelve men. "My debut as a major was a success from the point of view of victory and a failure as far as the organizational part was concerned," Guevara informed Castro. His column continued to succeed despite itself. A few days later, a company of Cuban soldiers under the lead-ership of Colonel Merob Sosa snaked its way up the El Hombrito valley and into the mountains where Guevara set an ambush. The guerrillas opened fire just as one of the regulars was overheard de-scribing the advance as "a picnic." Inexperience converted what might have been a smashing rebel victory into something close to a draw, demonstrating in Guevara's words, "how ill-prepared for com-bat our troop was, unable to fire accurately at a moving enemy line from close range."[44]

In the end, Sosa and his men retreated, allowing the rebels to count this a success. An important, if obvious, new tactic was com-ing into view. "This battle showed us how easy it was, in certain conditions, to attack columns on the march," Guevara remarked. Amid the mountain fasts, if you aimed at the head of an approaching column, you could bring it to a halt. "Little by little, this tactic crys-talized and finally it became so systematic that the enemy stopped entering the Sierra Maestra."[45]

These little triumphs forced the rebels to confront the challenge of governing a liberated territory just as the coming and going of untested recruits raised tension between the Sierra and the Llano about vetting practices. Moreover, despite Castro's glowing account of peasant consciousness, the local inhabitants of the Sierra Maestra had no political experience whatsoever and could not be counted on to help build a political movement. "The political development of its inhabitants was still superficial," Guevara conceded, "and the presence of a threatening army made it difficult for us to overcome these weaknesses." Looking back on this period after the triumph of the Revolution, Guevara also noted the intriguing relationship between strength and mercy. Crimes committed that first year of war were dealt with severely, he said. With the rebels untested and enemy aggression on the rise, it was simply "not possible to tolerate even the suspicion of treason." Early in a war, when an army is very weak, or late in a war, when it is confident and strong, perpetrators might expect a degree of leniency. Guevara told the story of one poor devil whose crime "coincided precisely with the point at which we were strong enough to mete out drastic punishment, but not strong enough to sanction him in another way, since we had no jail or any other type of confinement."[46]

Castro told an interviewer that the rebels executed very few people during the war ("not more than ten guys in twenty-five months"). Guevara suggests otherwise. There was this one for treason, that one for murder, another for rape, two more for spying, all in the span of a month or so. Those for whom capital punishment was deemed extreme could be treated to "mock execution," among other measures. "In retrospect, this method . . . might seem barbaric," Guevara allowed. In real time, there were no other options, such were the challenges of stamping out "the seeds of anarchy" in areas outside the rule of law.[47]

These were temporary exigencies. After the Cuban Army withdrew from El Hombrito, Guevara set up camp there, creating a press, a radio station, a small hydroelectric plant, a bakery, a hospital, and a school, with farms and other industries to come in the next year. The seeding of institutions meant that the guerrillas had more to protect, and so Guevara and his troops dug in on the roads and rivers leading up the valley, in the manner of a true army. The Cuban Army did not stay away for long. It returned to the mountains that fall, launching a scorched-earth campaign not so much against the guerrillas, but against their peasant hosts, with the aim of robbing the rebels of subsistence.[48]

With the rebels consolidating their dominion over the Sierra, rival opposition leaders convened in Miami in mid-October 1957 to discuss a post-Batista government. The Cuban Liberation Junta, as the rebels referred to it derisively, consisted of representatives of the old Auténtico and Ortodoxo parties, including Carlos Prío and Roberto Agramonte, members of the Revolutionary Directory, among them Faure Chomón and Alberto Mora, along with delegates from the Cuban Labor Confederation (CTC) and Independent Democrats. Felipe Pazos, signatory to the recent Sierra Maestra Manifesto, was present, too, though by whose authority it was not exactly clear, as was Lester Rodríguez, the July 26 Movement's representative in the United States, who attended without Castro's authorization. The conference was closely watched by the U.S. State Department. Its unstated purpose was to limit Castro's role in a post-Batista government.[49]

On the face of it, the resulting document, known as the Miami Pact, was not groundbreaking. Signatories committed themselves to oust Batista, reestablish constitutional democracy and the rule of law, and restore civil rights and liberties. There was talk of a provisional government, free and fair elections, curbing corruption, monetary stability, and civil service, agrarian, industrial, and educational reform. The pact called for the United States to end its military support of the Batista government and to recognize the signatories, who now referred to themselves as the Liberation Council. It also promised to curb the influence of the military in civilian life, while inviting the armed forces to "unite with us [in] the common objective of obtaining freedom."[50]

Though not officially signed until November 1, the pact was leaked to the U.S. press in late October. The July 26 Movement Directorate got word of the Miami meeting when Luis Buch, a member of the Civic Resistance, hand-delivered a draft of the agreement to the Llano leaders later that month. Anyone could see that the Junta hoped to capitalize on the work being done by the rebels, and Armando Hart and the others vociferously denounced it, as did Faustino Pérez in Havana. Hart and Pérez instructed Buch to return to Miami to make the Movement's opposition clear, and to inform Pazos that his role must be as an observer only. They would leave it to Castro to provide the public condemnation.

Condemn it Castro did in mid-December, after six furious weeks dodging Batista's military, which had increased its pressure on the guerillas. In principle, Castro explained, the rebels were not opposed to an alliance with the opposition. He reminded the Junta of how it was that they could now entertain the thought of a post-Batista Cuba. He said that news of the accord had reached him on a day in which his command engaged in three pitched battles in a mere matter of hours.[51] He noted the irony of receiving a *document* from Miami when what he desperately needed was *arms*. The Junta's tactlessness in sidelining the Movement was galling in the face of its passivity. But the thing that rankled most was its suggestion that the revolutionary army would simply dissolve into the Cuban armed forces at the end of the war. The lack of an independent revolutionary army able to stand up to Batista in January 1934 had doomed the 1933 Revolution, Castro pointedly observed. The rebels were not about to repeat that mistake. Moreover, he demanded, just whom did the Junta expect to include among the armed forces once Batista had been deposed? Former police and military people now desperate to distance themselves from their past? Individuals who had stood by with their arms crossed while the rebels put their lives on the line? In short, what was to prevent the corruption, gangsterism, and abuse that had made a revolution necessary from raising its head anew?

Castro's denunciation arrived in Miami at the end of the month. Junta leaders pleaded with Movement representatives not to publish the document. The Junta was willing to concede all points, it said, insisting that Castro's criticism would only help Batista. But the Junta was in no position to bargain, and their plea fell on deaf ears. Castro's repudiation was published for all to see.[52]

It did not take publication of the Miami Pact for Castro to recognize that he had competition and that that competition was working with some in the U.S. government to ensure he never came to power. The pact was more significant for revealing the growing division between the Sierra and the Llano in the aftermath of País's death. Helpless to vanquish the Junta or restore País to life, Movement leaders turned on one another, competing to see who could condemn the pact the fiercest. Busy defending himself from the government's reinvigorated military campaign, Castro remained aloof from most of the rancor. But he surely knew about it and, one thinks, might have done more to nip it in the bud. Castro possessed many traits of a successful leader—charisma, idealism, daring, self-sacrifice, and attention to detail, to name a few. But his ability to hold together a team of talented and devoted subordinates remained to be seen.

Dependent on the Llano for men, money, and arms, the Sierra bristled about the timing, quantity, and quality of everything that came its way. Meanwhile the Llano chafed at what it perceived as the guerrillas' lack of discipline and refusal to uphold a chain of command. There was a reason for the betrayals and desertions hampering the Sierra, the Llano pointed out; the guerrillas were too casual about welcoming unknown entities into their ranks and about allowing just about anyone to serve as couriers. Well and good, the Sierra shot back. They were simply trying to make the best of a near impossible situation.

Both groups endured tremendous risk and saw many of their

members fall. In early November, for example, Armando García, captain of one of the action groups in the Llano, was removed from his house in the middle of the night and tortured—"his testicles crushed, his ears burned with cigars, his body and feet stabbed"— before being finished off by a bullet in the street.[53] While País was alive, the tensions between the Sierra and the Llano seemed manageable, as he and Castro respected one another's contributions and distinct gifts. Once País was gone, the tensions came out in the open, with Castro himself occasionally succumbing to pettiness.

Many examples come to mind. Guevara dismissed his colleagues as incompetent. Castro complained about the Llano. Ramos accused Castro of a lack of sympathy. Hart charged Sánchez with bad faith. Hart, Ramos, and Guevara bickered about who was more radical, and so on.[54] An exchange between Guevara and Ramos conveys the substance and tone of these aspersions. On December 9, Guevara wrote Castro with an update from the battle front that included a forceful indictment of the Llano. He refused to accept any more notes about whom to accept weapons from, and whom not, with the lives of his men in jeopardy (he wrote with a bullet lodged in his instep, he noted). Back in Mexico, Guevara's elevation to a position of leadership caused resentment among the rebel rank and file. Guevara suspected something similar at work in Hart's and Ramos's reprimands for not abiding by the Directorate's protocols. "My suspicions have reached the point that I think there is direct sabotage against this column or, more directly, against me," Guevara wrote Castro. Either he would strenuously fight back or surrender his column. As evidence, he pointed to instances in which his "urgent requests" were met by "three-page letters that latch onto one paragraph of mine, in which I did nothing but carry out orders given to me by passing visitors."[55]

Not about to quit, Guevara lashed out at Ramos the next week, just as Ramos was writing a conciliatory letter explaining that he was doing his best to meet Guevara's needs ("200 coats, 75 pairs of woolen underpants, 150 pairs of socks, the new mimeograph, and some other things" were on the way). The inconveniences of the postal service. The reason he engaged strangers peddling ammunition, Guevara explained, was because, um, he needed ammunition! The Miami Pact was unforgivable, he noted, as if Ramos had had anything to do with it. "I belong to those who believe that the solution to the world's problems lies behind the so-called iron curtain," he went on, seemingly off subject, "and I see this Movement as one of the many inspired by the bourgeoisie's desire to free themselves from the economic chains of imperialism." Guevara said that he had once regarded Castro as the epitome of a "leftist bourgeoisie," before realizing the "extraordinary brilliance that set him above his class." Guevara arrived in Cuba expecting to do no more than assist the nation in its liberation, expecting to depart when the Revolution veered to the right, that is, "toward what all of you represent." He was dumbstruck that Castro could sign on to the Miami Pact, before learning that it was not Castro's work but that of the Movement leaders in the Llano, whose responsibility amounted to betrayal. "If this letter pains you," Guevara continued, a tad presumptuously, "because you consider it unfair or because you consider yourself innocent of the crime and you want to tell me so, terrific. And if it hurts so much that you cut off relations with this part of the revolutionary forces, so much the worse. One way or the other, we'll go forward since the people can't be defeated."[56]

Ramos was every bit Guevara's match.[57] When Guevara suggested the Sierra let the Llano go, Castro said that he was not ready to go that far. He conceded that some in the leadership had behaved naively. The Directorate's ambiguous role in the pact had caused a breach. He had chosen not to emphasize the breach, he told Guevara, so as not to make the situation worse. He said that the events surrounding the formulation and publicizing of the pact had led him to cut off communication with the leadership (which was not quite true, as Armando Hart was at that very moment in the middle of a month-long stay in the Sierra). However bitter it was to see his name exploited fraudulently, Castro said, it was worse to see the

Movement looking so "chaotic and undisciplined" at the moment when the Revolution was "half-way home." The Llano was already reversing direction and realizing its blunder. In the end, there would be no Revolution without the money, food, and weapons it supplied, however inadequate, and equally important, no political organization. The Llano still had an important role to play.[58]

Viewed from a distance, 1957 had not been a bad year, all things considered, despite País's death and subsequent bickering. Castro's band of fifteen men had not only survived, it had expanded and was beginning to thrive, even extending the rule of law over what would soon be declared the Liberated Territory of Cuba. One could even regard the machinations of the Miami Junta as a sign of the Movement's strength. If Castro and his fellow rebels had not proved they were for real, the Cuban opposition (and the U.S. government) would not have been so eager to find an alternative to Batista. The intrigue across the Florida Straits had not caught Castro off guard. "I am terrified by these conspirators," he wrote Celia Sánchez earlier that year. "It exasperates me to think of these supposed comrades one thousand miles away, putting useless plans into effect."[59] A few days later, having wearied of expecting others to come to the rebels' assistance, he allowed that maybe "destiny has insisted on making this a tough and difficult fight, in making us undergo this test without the help of anyone."[60] Ever and always alone.

In fact, others were stepping up. The July 26 Movement had expanded its reach. With an injection of energy provided by País, Hart, Pérez, and others, the Movement had established labor, student, and civic associations across the country, and was recruiting and training local militias. Although the impromptu strike that erupted in Santiago de Cuba after País's murder had not caught on, citizens of Santiago and elsewhere had witnessed firsthand the power of collective action. "Everyone has begun to think about strikes," Castro wrote Sánchez, "and have seen in them a terrific weapon of the people."[61]

Meanwhile, Castro had learned lessons and carried out policies that would extend into the new year. Since first arriving in the Sierra, he took pains to explain his actions and policies to the local residents. When, for example, in November 1957, the rebels launched a cane-burning campaign to rob the government of profits and distract the army, Castro reached out to growers, acknowledging the inconvenience and promising to compensate their losses. "I implore you to forgive us for the sacrifice that we have caused for the benefit of the motherland," he wrote one plantation owner. "Before the tyranny can put these riches at its disposal to assassinate and oppress our brothers, it is preferable to burn them." He promised to return and repay the damage with interest. Producers could be sure that the product of their "sweat would not be used to pay assassins or purchase homicidal weapons."[62]

By late autumn 1957, Castro was using the liberated territory as a hothouse for future revolutionary projects. In mid-November, he sent money to a woman named Nancy Reyes, who had come to the Sierra to help educate children. Castro had long prized education and regarded educational reform as a top priority. "Tomorrow's teachers will be the best soldiers of freedom," he said. "In our schools, we must cultivate the land that we liberate from oppression, and the work must begin now." A pencil and pen could go a long way not only in defeating the tyranny, but in vanquishing "the conditions that made tyranny possible."[63]

Castro had begun to reach out to enemy soldiers. After the rebels' first battle at La Plata at the beginning of the year, Castro regarded prisoners of war as ready-made propaganda. By treating them well and then sending them home, he delivered a message to soldiers, friends, and family alike: "the rebels admired the soldiers' valor; this wasn't a battle against them, but against those who took advantage of them to enrich themselves at the soldiers' and civilians' cost."[64] The rebels also provided medical care for wounded adversaries. Those whose wounds were too grievous were provided with passes to facilitate their transport to hospitals in Santiago de Cuba.

In exchange, the prisoners were expected to testify that "in no moment had they been maltreated by their hosts in words or deeds."[65]

Finally, Castro spent as much time as possible cultivating his relationship with the peasants. Of all the offenses that beset the guerrilla army, he tolerated exploiting peasants the least. In early September, he received word that some of his men were "commandeering arms" from the farmers of the Sierra. In a letter to one of the victims, he insisted that the "the Rebel High Command" had "never authorized, nor will it ever authorize" such appropriations. Measures were being taken to ensure it never happened again. The guerrillas had made it a point to distribute land seized from the government. When the government responded with its own promises of land, Castro warned his neighbors not to be fooled. That was too little too late, he said. The land already belonged to the peasants "thanks to our arms, which have never permitted nor ever would permit the despoiling of peasant farms."[66]

chapter twelve

KEEPING ORDER
IN THE HEMISPHERE

The new year began on a sour note. "Get moving and do it
fast," Army Chief of Staff Francisco Tabernilla ordered his
subordinate, Alberto Chaviano. By "it," Tabernilla meant
the assassination of Armando Hart, Javier Pazos, and Tony Buch,
who had been picked up by the army on their way down from the
Sierra Maestra after a month with the rebel commander in chief.
"These degenerates mobilize quickly and they mustn't learn of this,"
Tabernilla remarked. Chaviano should stage an incident to cover up
the murders.[1]

But the rebels had learned of the arrest as it was occurring over
phone lines tapped by agents working at the Cuban Telephone
Company. They quickly notified Pazos's father, the banker, who contacted Batista and insisted he ensure the captives' lives. Meanwhile,
the rebels commandeered the radio station at Vista Alegre (in the
hills above Santiago), and announced the government's intention to

commit murder. Within minutes, rebel agents intercepted another call from Tabernilla to Chaviano, ordering that Pazos's life be spared while demanding that the others be dispatched quickly ("Armando like a dog"). Too late, Chaviano replied. The news was already out. The men were on the way to Boniato prison.

Castro experienced Hart's arrest "like a bomb going off." Not only was he fond of Hart, more valuable to the Movement than ever after País's death, but Hart possessed a letter from Castro to Guevara on the subject of Guevara's communism. Castro and Hart had had a few long conversations on the topic in the mountains, and Castro wanted to share Hart's objections to the Argentine's theories. The letter also mentioned Raúl Castro's communist leanings, making it a propaganda bonanza for the Batista government, which wasted no time putting it to good effect.[2]

Looking back on the event years later, Hart recalled Haydée Santamaría being asked by one of her contacts at the U.S. consulate why Hart appeared so agitated about communist infiltration in the Movement if its leaders were averse to communism, as they had so strenuously maintained. Hart was criticizing Soviet communism, not Guevara's, Santamaría responded unpersuasively. In retrospect, Hart claimed that Guevara was simply ahead of the curve in anticipating Cuba's future direction. His own difference with Guevara was not about socialism, he insisted, but about whether existing models of communism addressed the problems of Latin America. Castro seems to have remained neutral between his two friends, as if his own mind was not yet made up.[3]

Much ink has been spilled about the nature and timing of Castro's conversion from liberal nationalism to communism. There is no evidence that this conversion took place before the triumph of the Revolution on January 1, 1959. "If you ask me whether I consider myself a revolutionary at the time I was in the mountains," Castro told journalist Lee Lockwood a few years later, "I would answer yes, I considered myself a revolutionary. If you asked me, did I consider myself a Marxist-Leninist, I would say no, I did not consider myself a Marxist-Leninist. If you asked me whether I considered myself a Communist, a classic Communist, I would say no, I did not consider myself a classic Communist."[4]

Asked in the Sierra by the Spanish writer Enrique Meneses his opinion about the Soviet Union, Castro replied, "I hate Soviet imperialism as much as Yankee imperialism. I'm not breaking my neck fighting one dictatorship to fall into the hands of another." Anticipating that some might think the rebel leader was simply playing him, Meneses explained that he had been at Castro's side for nearly six straight months by the time of this statement, too long to be fooled. When, in 1961, an Italian reporter requested that Castro characterize the Revolution, a frustrated leader responded, "you wish to write that this is a socialist revolution, right? Write it, then." The aim of the Revolution was to banish a "tyrannical system," along with its "philo-imperialistic bourgeois state apparatus, the bureaucracy, the police, and a mercenary army." Targeting privilege, aristocracy, and exploitation, the revolution comprised a national liberation program that included agrarian reform—much like that recently carried out by the United States in Japan. The "Americans and priests" might call that communism, Castro quipped; he knew "very well that it is not."[5]

Finally, Lucas Morán (no friend of the Revolution), who once fought with both Fidel and Raúl Castro, wrote that he never detected any attempt on the part of Castro or his fellow leaders "to indoctrinate the rebel footsoldiers politically." In not a single case, Moran insisted, had the rebels established schools dedicated to anything more than reading, writing, and arithmetic. Nor had he ever seen the rebel commanders "examining the texts of Marx, Lenin, Engels, or other Marxist intellectuals."[6]

U.S. officials' surprise at discovering evidence of communism among Movement members reflected a consensus in the U.S. intelligence community that Castro and the Movement were neither fundamentally communist nor pro-Soviet. U.S. intelligence agencies had been tracking Castro for some time. The earliest known

reference to Castro in CIA files dates to 1948, when, after his participation in the Bogotazo, he was described as someone "who manages to get himself involved in many things that do not concern
him"—a reference that says more about the United States' sense of
itself as a regional arbiter than it does about Castro.[7]

U.S. attention to Castro heightened as his reputation grew.
In May 1955, the U.S. embassy in Havana followed the polemic
between Chaviano and the recently amnestied Castro in *Bohemia*
magazine, where Castro demolished Chaviano's version of the
Moncada attack. While acknowledging Castro had the better argument, the embassy could not disguise its disdain for the young
firebrand. "Ever since he emerged from jail under political amnesty,"
the memo noted, "Fidel Castro has lost no opportunity to further
his pretensions as a martyr to freedom and a patriot seeking to overthrow tyranny and oppression." If this kept up, he would surely find
himself in trouble again, the report suggested, before conceding that
"Castro's rebuke of Chaviano was "justified."[8] The Americans liked
their colonial dependents pliant.

By the mid-1950s, Cuba had become a pawn in the Cold War.
In April 1955, CIA director Allen Dulles traveled to Havana to preside over the establishment of the Bureau for the Repression of
Communist Activities (known by the acronym BRAC). BRAC relied on information provided by Batista's own Servicio de Inteligencia Militar (SIM), hardly a source of dispassionate analysis. Early
the next year, a U.S. embassy official dismissed a SIM report entitled "Antidemocratic Antecedents and Activities of Fidel Castro" as
nothing more than a summary of previous allegations. The Batista
government was determined to "make Castro a 'Rojo,' but the result
is a rather poor one," the official observed.[9]

U.S. intelligence followed Castro into exile in Mexico. In January 1956, an embassy dispatch noted that Castro had been tying
himself to the tradition of José Martí. Castro had plenty of "will and
enthusiasm," the dispatch noted, but he lacked "the means for a successful revolution." A month later, an official from the U.S. embassy

in Mexico met with a reporter who had just filed a long interview with Castro for United Press. The reporter found Castro "sincere, ambitious, confident, even cocky." He was "convinced of the justice of his cause and expected early success."[10]

Castro's return to Cuba and the ensuing violence brought the U.S. diplomatic corps to high alert by autumn 1957. In early September, naval officers at the port of Cienfuegos arose in mutiny, prompting brutal government suppression that included bombers, tanks, and ammunition provided by the United States. Responding to a query from Secretary of State John Foster Dulles about the role of U.S.-supplied weapons in suppressing the revolt, Ambassador Earl E. T. Smith, in office since the preceding June, explained that all the bombers deployed in the government attack on Cienfuegos had been supplied by the United States, though some before the Mutual Defense Assistance Agreement of March 1952, which mandated that U.S. munitions provided by the United States not be used on Cuban citizens. Meanwhile, no U.S.-supplied ammunition was used in the reprisal, though "a few" U.S.-supplied machine guns may have been involved. Smith then acknowledged that the Cuban Army had used U.S.-supplied equipment in its campaign against the rebels in recent months.[11] The negative public perception of this would haunt Ambassador Smith to the triumph of the Cuban Revolution. Smith, a former businessman (and head of the Florida Republican Party) with no experience in diplomacy, immediately ingratiated himself to President Batista, becoming one of his staunchest defenders.[12]

By late 1957, the U.S. government appeared increasingly determined to bring Castro's insurrection to a halt. The question was not whether but how best to do so. In mid-November, CIA Inspector General Lyman Kirkpatrick suggested sending a U.S. national peripherally connected to the government to mediate between the parties. Given Cubans' wariness of outside intervention, this would have to be done discreetly, Kirkpatrick noted, without fanfare or publicity. A week later, the State Department approached Adolf Berle, an expert on Latin America bound for Havana, to see what he might do to bring the Cuban war to an "orderly conclusion," as if both the State Department and CIA had not read the Sierra Maestra Manifesto and subsequent pronouncements on the subject of U.S. intervention—or, perhaps more likely, simply did not take Castro seriously. Berle acknowledged Cubans' sensitivity to outside interference, before concluding that "we are responsible for keeping order in the hemisphere."[13]

In January 1958, William Wieland, the director of the State Department's Office of Middle American Affairs, proposed trading U.S. military equipment for a pledge by Batista to end the state of emergency and curtail the "excessive brutalities" and most "violent and sadistic officers of the army and police," as if confirming the accusations of opposition groups.[14] Ambassador Smith regarded Castro as virtually the sole source of instability and violence on the island. While on a visit to Washington in mid-January, Smith was asked if the United States would ever be able to do business with Castro. Smith, who had never met the man, replied, simply, no: "The United States Government can only do business with a government that will honor its international obligations and can maintain law and order." Surely, if those were the conditions of legitimacy, then it was Batista, not Castro, whom Washington should be wary of. In the Sierra Maestra, where the rebels were in charge, law and order reigned, as any visiting journalist, local resident, or U.S. consular official could attest.[15] By late January, State Department officials were becoming so uncomfortable with the Cuban government's escalating violence that they advised Smith to ask Batista to keep word of the receipt of U.S. arms to an absolute minimum.[16]

The next month, the State Department identified yet another bargaining chip Smith might use in discussions over U.S. weapons deliveries: a commitment to general elections. In conversations with Wieland, Felipe Pazos, only recently a Castro confidant and a signatory of the Sierra Maestra Manifesto, expressed a willingness to negotiate with Batista and take part in a prospective election. State would do everything in its power to publish what it called "the other side of the Castro story," drawn from the perspective of U.S. businessmen.[17] Over the course of the next several weeks, Smith responded with contradictory reports expressing, on the one hand, the urgency of the U.S. not withholding military aid to the embattled dictator, and on the other hand, his belief that the insurrection was near its end. "Fidel Castro is losing prestige," Smith reported on February 10, citing no evidence. Smith's dispatches caused head-scratching in Washington ("there seems to be an increasing amount of violence throughout Cuba," assistant secretary of state for Inter-American Affairs Roy Rubottom wrote back on Valentine's Day) and contrasted notably with more balanced reports of Daniel Braddock, an embassy staffer.[18] By the end of the month, Smith was grasping for straws. "President Batista appeared convinced at meeting February 19 that Communists actively supporting Castro," as if Batista would say anything else. In fact, Cuban communists remained leery of Castro through the triumph of the Revolution.[19]

In late January, Castro told Guevara that he had been approached about possible peace terms with the government. Would the rebels agree to turn over Oriente Province, with all the rebel arms, in exchange for an honorable election? If Batista won the election, the rebels would stand down. If the rebels won the election, they would take over control of government. "What do you think?" he asked Guevara. "It's possible that an emissary will arrive on Sunday." Of course, he would remain skeptical, Castro told his skeptical friend. Still, this would provide "a good opportunity to feel out the regime." Meanwhile, the fight would go on. "There is no truce," he said, "nor will there be, nor will we concede one." He attributed the regime's interest in discussions to concern about the morale of its soldiers."[20]

In early February, the rebels entertained some distinguished guests: Senators León (Nené) Ramírez and Eduardo (Lalo) Roca, from Manzanillo. The two traveled to the Sierra apparently on their own initiative to engage Castro on the subject of a cease-fire. Journalist Enrique Meneses, from *Paris Match*, was with the rebels at this time and remembers seeing formal arrangements being made and suspecting that something big was in the works. For the first time since his arrival, the air was perfumed with the aroma of sweet cooking, and "the rebels were polishing their boots and cleaning their arms with more care than usual." By this time, Castro claimed to be presiding over the Liberated Territory of Cuba, and he wanted the event to have the trappings of a state dinner. Ramírez dutifully played the part of honored guest, arriving with a Christmas present (a brand-new pistol) for Celia Sánchez, the daughter of a family friend.[21]

After dinner, the group got down to business. Castro repeated his terms. Batista must depart, the Constitution must be restored. The rebels would then lay down their arms. An interim government would be named, its only mandate to ensure order and hold elections within six months. The agreement would be ratified by the current government handing over control of Oriente Province, including its armed forces, to the rebels. Representatives of the July 26 Movement would not serve in the provisional government, their only function to oversee an honest election. Only later, with constitutionalism restored, would the July 26 Movement establish a new political party and promote its program of revolutionary reforms. Castro assured his guests that he and his Movement were unassociated with Carlos Prío and his followers, on the one hand, and with communists, on the other (the communists stood "for an imperialism worse than the Yankees'," he said, "and just as foreign to our customs and beliefs"). How then, it is fair to ask, could he account for the presence of people like Guevara in his midst? "Anyone who wants to help us is welcome to do so," he said, only "without strings."

Meneses reported that the meeting went smoothly until Ramírez asked Castro if he meant that there would be a "period of transition without Batista, with a military junta" during the transition. "We shall never accept that!" Castro interjected. Cubans were tired of "tin-pot generals." Ramírez returned to Havana and a warm reception from the press. Batista officials greeted him coldly. His fellow senator Rolando Masferrer challenged him to a duel, presumably for taking Castro seriously.

The flow of journalists to the Sierra continued. That same week, *Look* magazine published an interview by Andrew St. George, in which Castro provided an update on the state of the Revolution. Rebel territory had expanded, he said. The Cuban Army had virtually abandoned the Sierra and was now ringing it with a blockade designed to starve out the rebels. Government planes were strafing peasant communities. Unable to hurt the guerrillas, soldiers showed up in towns, shooting suspected sympathizers. In a recent case, Castro alleged, forty-seven "simple farmers" were "rounded up and shot . . . their deaths announced as those of 'rebels' killed in combat."[22]

St. George asked Castro why the rebels were burning sugarcane when "the island's economic life depended on it?" For exactly that reason, Castro explained: to deprive Batista of the income by which he purchased his weapons of war. The Castro family farm in Birán would not be spared. Burning the cane fields was "a *hard* step. But it is a legitimate act of war." Cuban freedom fighters had done the same thing in the wars of independence. The Americans, too, for that matter, he reminded St. George—when they emptied the king's tea into Boston Harbor.

Was Castro merely telling a U.S. audience (and government) what he thought it wanted to hear? Perhaps. Castro made this overture from a position of strength. The rebel army had not only proved its staying power, it had expanded its territory. That February, Castro promoted his brother Raúl and Juan Almeida to the title of commander, assigning them companies of their own and readying them for new battle fronts in the Sierra Cristal and the Santiago region, respectively. The same month, Castro published a set of criminal and civil codes for the Liberated Territory written by the Movement's newly appointed judge advocate general, Humberto Sorí Marín, a respected lawyer. Castro established a system of civil administration that included graduated taxation. The rebels were building hospitals and schools. For the first time since March 1952, a rebel victory seemed not only possible, but likely, and Castro did not want anything to get in its way.[23]

———————

Success made Castro ecumenical. In mid-February, he reached out to enemy commanders, imploring them to avoid violence and switch sides. The first to hear from him was a captain by the last name of Guerra who commanded the garrison at Pino del Agua, at the foothills of the Sierra, where Guevara's troops were engaged. We have you surrounded, said Castro to his "compatriot." No one was coming to his rescue as the rebels had cut off access routes. The commander and his men were defending an unjust cause, Castro declared. His soldiers were poised to die defending the interests of people far away who cared nothing for them and shared no interests in common. The rebels were more than ready to take the garrison by force. But they had nothing against the rank and file and would much prefer to negotiate the garrison's surrender. Castro promised to respect the lives of the soldiers, which was "always our custom." He even promised to put the men at liberty within twenty-four hours; those who feared retaliation from their superiors were welcome to join the rebel ranks.[24] Guerra ignored Castro's overture at some cost. In two, ultimately indecisive days of fighting, Guerra lost some twenty killed and a similar number wounded, while surrendering thirty-three rifles, five machine guns, and considerable ammunition. The rebels suffered losses of their own, with three deaths and as many wounded. But they once again proved that they could hold their own, and the enemy noticed, sending reinforcements to ensure that the isolated garrison was not entirely overrun.[25]

A few weeks later, Castro made an emotional appeal to Ceferino Rodríguez, another army commander and a former childhood friend from Oriente. Actually, Rodríguez had been the first to make contact, sending Castro a note acknowledging their common past and seeking a way out of an impending showdown. This was an "extraordinary moment," Castro wrote back, a rare time when individuals stood face-to-face with destiny, and in which only the rare ones distinguished themselves. He urged Rodríguez to step up to the moment and join the side that was fighting not for narrow self-interest but for the glory of Cuba as a whole. Were he to do so, Castro assured his friend, Rodríguez would not have to confront his fellow members of the military. It was the example, not Rodríguez's fighting, that would tell. Government troops were demoralized, tired of fighting for an ignoble cause.[26]

By engaging enemy officers in this way, Castro was not simply trying to avoid bloodshed, though that was reason enough. Rather, he was looking for a bridge to an alliance with the army rank and file capable of defending a triumphant Revolution. This was a lesson hard learned by supporters of the Revolution of 1933. When the push for much needed social reforms collided with U.S. and Cuban business interests backed by Batista, the revolutionary government had nowhere to turn—no political apparatus to rally the people, no army to defend the Revolution. Castro would not repeat this mistake.

In a young army lieutenant named Aquiles Chinea, Castro believed he found a solution. Conditions are "extraordinarily favorable," he wrote Chinea in the middle of March. All that was lacking was for an influential figure to emerge from the army to declare that enough was enough. By rejecting the idea of a military junta taking over after Batista's removal, Castro did not suggest that the military had no role to play in the ensuing Revolution. Given the interests already amassed against the Revolution, an "insurgent military" able to march "shoulder to shoulder with the people" was indispensable to its success. By allying with a younger officer like Chinea, Castro intended to sidestep officers implicated in machinations like the Miami Pact. And for the record, he told Chinea, a revolutionary government would not needlessly antagonize the U.S.

embassy; there was no need to worry about that. The North Americans would retain the rebels' respect so long as they kept their noses out of Cuba's internal affairs.[27]

Castro regularly set aside time to correspond with those he seemed to regard as future constituents. In early March, for example, he reached out to the mother of one of his prisoners, as if remembering his own mother's grief when he and Raúl were jailed after Moncada.[28] Another note addressed a widow whose husband had died in combat. She was now sewing uniforms for Castro and his men, and he wanted her to know that her sacrifice and continued work did not go unnoticed.[29] Castro's letter writing extended to the children of his commanders, as if thinking of his own son, Fidelito. He told Faustino Pérez's son, José Ramón, that his father would "soon be able to spend his nights at home and you will see him every day. He will spend Sunday with you and play with you and your friends." There were brighter days ahead, Castro promised. The boy's father had many fascinating stories to tell that the son could pass along to his classmates. Oh, and Castro had a present for the boy, the exact nature of which he would not divulge, but promised to deliver soon. "Take care of your mama," he signed off, "and behave yourself!"[30]

While Castro bided his time in the Sierra Maestra, the Batista government's indiscriminate crackdown on the opposition mobilized professionals, businessmen, and clergy throughout the island. Just the previous autumn, the National Medical Association asked the Supreme Court to do something to put an end to the government's torture and murder of physicians for simply fulfilling their duty to save lives.[31] In late February, the Cuban Episcopate added its voice, urging Batista to sit down with Castro. Just as negotiations looked set to proceed, Castro pulled out, saying that "no decent Cuban can sit down at the table presided over by Fulgencio Batista."[32]

Next to step up was a group of judges, who asked the Havana Court of Appeals, one of the country's preeminent legal authorities, to call a halt to Batista's atrocities. The rule of law and administration of justice hung by a nail, the judges wrote, citing a litany of atrocities carried out on judges themselves by government agents. Judges' own families were threatened, their homes subjected to bombs and gunfire, developments unprecedented in Cuba's tumultuous history. Rather than operating as instruments of the law, the police were terrorizing the nation. Cuba's Supreme Court colluded in the abuse, ordering prisoners turned over to the police, who later assassinated them. Elsewhere, government officials charged with cracking down on prostitution and gambling conveniently looked the other way in exchange for a cut of the profits. The judges went on, describing similar conditions throughout the country, with death by "gunshot, torture, and hanging" an everyday event. In a nation where judges themselves made a mockery of habeas corpus and the rule of law, there could be no public order, no administration of justice, no constitutionalism and civil liberty. What, the judges demanded, did Cuba's highest magistrates propose to do about it?[33]

The next week brought a still vaster collection of professional and recreational societies to the fore, when a group calling itself the Civic Institutions issued a clarion call for Batista's overthrow via a general strike (it claimed to lack the means to overthrow the government by force). Coming from a sector of society that had long clung to the belief that dialogue with Batista was still possible, the group's intervention was significant. For six years since the coup, they explained, idealistic young Cubans had spilled their blood to awaken the conscience of the nation. For six years, their "heroism and sacrifice" was met with nothing but brute force. "The moment has arrived," the Civic Institutions said. The government must go, if not by violence, then by general strike—a right "of free men granted by the Constitution."[34]

The idea of a general strike was also on the minds of Faustino Pérez and fellow members of the July 26 Movement leadership, which broached the idea with Castro at a meeting in the Sierra.

This seemed like a good time for a strike, the visitors said. The Cuban public appeared to be openly turning against the dictatorship. Weapons were arriving in the Sierra courtesy of Costa Rican president José Figueres, among others. Two new fronts had been established in the Sierra Cristal and on the outskirts of Santiago de Cuba. The Movement had published a new legal code and proposed a new provisional president. The Sierra Maestra was all but "clean" of enemy troops. Militias trained by the Movement were in position to conduct sabotage on public utilities, highways, and police throughout the country, including in the capital. Laborers organized by the Cuban Confederation of Workers were poised to conduct a walkout and only awaited notice. The Civic Resistance was on board. The Revolutionary Directory too. What did Castro have to say?

The call to strike surprised him. There had not been a successful general strike in Cuba for over twenty years, he noted. Reports of the Movement's organization in Havana and other cities were far from glowing. Preparations for a general strike threatened to rob the Sierra of desperately needed resources (men, weapons, ammunition), while relegating it to a secondary status behind the urban militias. This time Pérez prevailed. On March 12, against his better judgment, Castro signed off on what became known as the Total War Manifesto, calling for a general strike backed by intensified military operations throughout Oriente and Las Villas provinces.[35] Castro was not the only doubter. The latest manifesto received a cool reception from two stakeholders crucial to the strike's success, the Cuban Confederation of Workers and the Communist Party, sidelined by Pérez. Moreover, contrary to what Pérez and the others had told Castro, the Revolutionary Directorate declined to partake in the sabotage activity, insisting that the time was not yet ripe.[36]

Pérez intended to launch the strike on March 31, amid widespread frustration over yet another suspension of constitutional guarantees. By the time he finally got around to it ten days later, the public agitation had dissipated. The announcement of the strike was delayed until 11 a.m., when most workers were already at work. As a result, few if any workers walked off the job, leaving the strike in the hands of enthusiastic but inadequately armed urban militias who were no match for Batista's army and police. In Havana, where Pérez's organizational prowess was on the line, the strike fizzled out within a matter of hours, but not before scores of young bodies piled up in the city morgue. The government gleefully publicized the Movement's ineptitude, while pointing to its brutal suppression of the militias as evidence of its enduring strength.[37]

Bad for the Movement as a whole, the failed strike was cataclysmic for the Llano, which never recovered. The strike was a big moral defeat, Castro told Celia Sánchez, leaving him no choice but "to assume responsibility for the stupidity of the rest." Under the pretext of combating his alleged caudillismo (or heavy-handedness), "everybody was doing whatever they wanted." No more. In early May, amid fierce recrimination and finger-pointing, a war council of Movement leaders convened in the Sierra and named Castro commander in chief of the revolutionary forces and secretary general of the National Directory. This new role made him responsible not only for carrying out the guerrillas' war, as before, but for the provisioning and distribution of weapons and ammunition down to the last bullet.

For the first time since returning to Cuba in December 1956 Castro had undisputed control of the Movement.[38]

chapter thirteen

PLAN FIN-DE-FIDEL

T he failed strike ushered in a new phase of the war. Up to this point, the government's only real success on the "battlefield" (as measured by body count) was in the cities, where the police shot (tortured, mutilated) first and asked questions later. Except for occasional forays into the foothills of the Sierra Maestra, the Cuban military had all but abandoned the territory to the rebels by March 1958, prompting Castro to declare the Liberated Territory of Cuba and the war all but won.

NOT. SO. FAST.

Inspired by the apparent disarray in rebel ranks, the Cuban Army announced Plan Fin-de-Fidel, prompting Castro to unleash the Medina boys, who soon made a name for themselves as Quinteto Rebelde. Besides targeting Castro's command post atop the La Plata River valley, Plan Fin-de-Fidel included a campaign against Raúl Castro and his column in the Sierra Cristal, the countryside above Birán. Until this time, the army's forays into the mountains seemed halfhearted and incompetent, costlier to local residents than to the guerrillas.[1]

Looking southeast from Miami after the failed strike, members of the opposition junta also sensed an opportunity. José Miró Cardona, former member of de la Torriente's Society of Friends of the Republic, approached Haydée Santamaría to say that former president Carlos Prío would join forces with Castro in exchange for "equal participation in decision-making in wartime and power sharing in post-Batista government." Too little too late, Santamaría replied. If Miró and Prío really expected Castro to hand over leadership of the insurrection at this time, they had not been paying attention.[2]

Washington's response was measured. Addressing a meeting of the National Security Council on April 14, Secretary of State John Foster Dulles said that in the aftermath of the failed strike he expected Castro to retreat to the Sierra to weigh his options. "It would be very difficult to dislodge him," Dulles allowed. Still, with the rebels reeling, the Cuban Army appeared to have the advantage, forcing the enemy to adopt "a new tack." In passing, Dulles noted that he had not seen any evidence connecting Castro to communism.[3]

Indeed, through much of the preceding winter and into that spring, Washington had worried more about the Cuban government's use of U.S.-supplied weapons than about Castro. Congress continued to needle the Eisenhower administration about Batista using weapons furnished by the United States against a homegrown uprising.[4] This, in turn, led to tension between the State Department and Ambassador Smith, who, despite his protestations to the contrary, served as apologist in chief for the Cuban dictator.[5] In mid-March, Smith wrote to Washington about a recent meeting with Batista in which he had raised the subject of alleged brutalities perpetrated in Oriente Province by Colonel Jesús Sosa Blanco. Batista was "grieved and shocked to hear the allegations," Smith reported, and promised to look into the matter. Smith then quickly changed the subject to the spread of communism in Cuba, which, in turn, led to a discussion of Batista's plan to drive the civilian population from the Sierra to starve the rebels of support. Of course, Batista did not want to inconvenience those families, Smith said. The action was necessary strictly to eliminate Castro. The meeting concluded with the American ambassador feeling "gratified and impressed by [Batista's] sincerity, his desire to be fair, and his willingness to cooperate."[6]

On March 29, 1958, over the strenuous opposition of its ambassador, the U.S. government suspended arms shipments to Cuba. The U.S. government also insisted on the withdrawal of U.S.-trained military personnel (including Cuban Air Force pilots) from the battlefront.[7] The U.S. Congress and the American public were not the only ones compelling this policy, with consular officials across Latin America reporting mounting discontent over the North Americans' coddling of dictators.[8] In the ensuing weeks and months, Smith campaigned tirelessly for weapons shipments to resume. When the State Department ignored his counsel, he played his trump card: military support for Batista was justified, Smith insisted, because the Cuban government was "combatting elements in league with communism."

The more the State Department ignored Smith's charges, the harder he pressed them, until his accusations became a self-fulfilling prophecy. Castro was communist therefore the U.S. government had to prevent his taking power; the U.S. government later tried to prevent his taking power, compelling Castro to seek support from the Soviet Union.[9] Smith was hardly the only one making such claims. There were plenty of U.S. and Cuban businessmen around to confirm them.[10] But Smith commanded a bully pulpit, and with a bit of training and an open mind, he might have forestalled the conflation of nationalism with communism so common at this stage of the Cold War.

———————

The grand staircase, or Escalinata, at the University of Havana, which Castro entered in autumn 1945 as a first-year law school student.

Arriving at the university, Castro first tried his hand at sports. Outmatched, he soon turned his attention to university politics, winning election as a class delegate to the Federación Estudiantil Universitaria in the spring of 1946.

3

Castro passes a paraffin test. University politics was a dangerous affair, and Castro often found himself on the wrong end of the law, although he always managed to elude the government's charges.

In autumn 1947, the notoriously corrupt administration of President Ramón Grau tried to appropriate Cuba's Liberty Bell, struck by Carlos Manuel de Céspedes in 1868 at the start of the Ten Years War. Castro led the student protest, bringing him to the attention of the nation's press corps for the first time.

Castro, at left, en route to a student congress in Bogotá, Colombia, in 1948. Only twenty-one at the time, he already saw his fight for reform in Cuba as part of a larger hemispheric, even global, struggle for democracy and social justice.

Castro and his bride, Mirta Díaz-Balart, at their wedding celebration at the American Club in the United Fruit Company town of Banes on October 11, 1948. The couple honeymooned in New York City.

Castro confronts Cuban Army General Quirino Uría López at a student demonstration in January 1951. Castro's family hoped that marriage and the arrival of a son, Fidelito, would lead to his domestication. It did not; Castro's involvement in national politics deepened.

In March 1952, Fulgencio Batista overthrew the government of President Carlos Prío. Dismayed by the nation's passive response to the coup, Castro led these men in an audacious attack on the nation's second largest military barracks in Santiago de Cuba on July 26, 1953.

Individuals captured in the Moncada attack were assassinated on the spot, their bodies scattered across the barracks in a sloppy attempt to cover up the atrocity. Here, one of the photographs taken by Panchito Cano and smuggled out of Santiago de Cuba by Marta Rojas.

Picked up a few days later, Castro was interrogated by Colonel Alberto del Río Chaviano, who tried to implicate Carlos Prío, Cuban communists, and other political opponents in the attack. Seen here, Castro explains that he alone is responsible for the attack.

11

No photographs were allowed inside the courthouse where the Moncada attackers were tried that September. Castro, seen in this illustration rising to his own defense, turned the tables on the government so effectively that he was soon banished from the proceedings.

12

Castro was sentenced to twenty-six years in prison for his leadership of the Moncada attack; he would serve twenty months. Prison proved a useful time for Castro to hone his political program and study guerrilla warfare, with books provided by his friend Naty Revuelta.

13

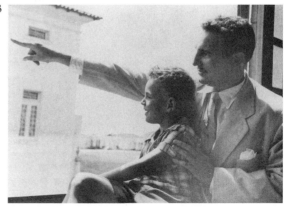

Castro looked forward to visiting days as much as any prisoner, and no visitor provided more solace than his son, Fidelito, here seated on his father's lap at the Model Prison on the Isle of Pines.

14

Thanks to a nationwide amnesty campaign, Castro and his fellow Moncada attackers were released from prison on Mother's Day 1955.

Returning to Havana from prison, Castro was pulled from the train by a jubilant crowd, hoisted on their shoulders, and paraded through the city.

15

16

In his first press conference upon leaving prison, Castro made clear that he intended to continue his protest against Batista's coup with all the rights and privileges guaranteed by the 1940 Constitution (then suspended).

Castro had a voracious appetite and loved to cook. Forced into exile in Mexico in July 1955, he is seen here with fellow conspirators enjoying one of his specialties, spaghetti marinara.

In December 1956, Castro returned to Cuba to begin the guerrilla war, against the advice of allied dissident groups. Arriving on the southeast coast with 82 men aboard a boat built for eight, Castro ran aground, losing most of his equipment and some of his men in a mangrove swamp a mile wide.

Fourteen men survived the botched landing, eventually making their way to the nearly impenetrable forests of the Sierra Maestra. With the Sierra providing cover and local peasants acting as commissary and quartermaster, Castro waged a successful war of attrition, defying seemingly impossible odds. Urged by his men to stay out of danger, Castro led the war from a command post high atop the La Plata River valley, often betraying frustration at the inconveniences of guerrilla war.

20

Batista fled the country early in the morning on New Year's Day 1959. On January 2, Castro began a week-long march to Havana from Santiago, during which he convinced a hitherto largely indifferent Cuban public that he, they, and the Revolution were one and the same.

On May 8, 1958, a Cuban expeditionary force disembarked at the coastal neighborhood of Macho, some eight miles west of where the La Plata River enters the sea. Plan F-F was in motion. A few days later, a second government offensive began in the Sierra Cristal, where Raúl Castro and his commanders were handing out bullets to their men a few at a time. From his perch in La Plata, Castro received reports of government forces massing in the towns at the base of the mountains. In anticipation of the onslaught, he summoned his commanders back toward his headquarters, which now included a radio station, a hospital, a commissary, a weapons depot, an airfield, workshops, and other operations essential to waging war.

Despite the modest successes of the previous fall and winter, the guerrillas were still desperate for arms and ammunition—and as dependent as ever on local residents for survival. The ad hoc, improvised nature of the recruitment, communication, and weapons dispersal that had so annoyed País and Ramos and hobbled guerrilla operations in the early stages of the war could now prove deadly, as the military concentrated its resources on an area not ten miles square. Castro marked this new stage in the war by ordering all commanders, platoon captains, and squadron lieutenants to pay scrupulous attention to weapon readiness, to the exact number and location of their troops, and to the meticulous maintenance of guard posts. Every single bullet was to be accounted for, any unnecessary discharge or misplacement of ammunition strictly avoided. Leaders were to put their troops through their paces "without discharging any weapons." Commanders were to continue their instruction in "reading and writing to illiterate *compañeros*, along with other free lessons." And they were to maintain cordial relations with their neighbors. "Teach good manners to the men," he wrote, "so that they don't bother the families without good reason." Finally, there was to be no intoxication—"not a single sip of liquor"—in the theater of war.[11]

Having consolidated leadership in the Sierra, Castro found himself saddled with more responsibilities than an ordinary person could accomplish. He wanted the guerrillas to be able to keep the

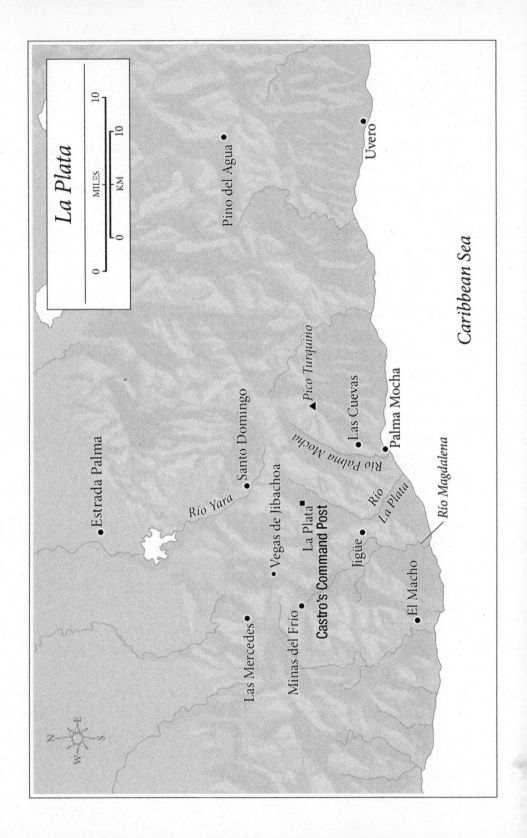

nation informed about the war's progress, which meant establishing a radio station along with effective means of record keeping.[12] Unusually observant as a child, he continued to focus on the details. Frustrated one minute by arguments about the distribution of bullets, the commander in chief cum quartermaster and commissary was delighted by a "café con leche" provided him in a nearby village the next. There were five families in the town, he told Sánchez. All had milk because two had cows, with one of the farmers providing milk to two neighbors. The town's good fortune meant that it was attracting refugees, and he asked Sánchez to send along two more milk cows and six steers to the inhabitants, thereby leaving them with milk and meat for three months. Sánchez must not "leave any of the barrios without meat," neither the farmers living in the settlements, nor the neighbors living along the roads. "No family should be forgotten by mistake," he said.[13]

Through much of May, Castro honed his skill at multitasking, now calling for "mines, grenades, ammunition of all classes," now ordering a redeployment of troops to a key mountain pass, now asking Sánchez to expedite delivery of money to the sick mother of a captured soldier ("make it happen," he ordered).[14] Being good at multitasking does not make it enjoyable. Susceptible to mood swings, Castro rebelled against the endless administrative tasks that fell his way as a result of his inability to delegate authority. He longed to be out doing the fighting ("how I miss the days when I was a real soldier," he told Sánchez), but did not trust others to exercise leadership in his place. In public, he kept his chin up and always exuded great confidence; in private, he confided to Sánchez that the war had become "a miserable and meaningless bureaucratic slog." He was fed up "with being the boss, running around like a chicken with its head off, forced to attend to one trivial thing after another because someone forgot this or overlooked that." Surely a solipsistic micromanager had brought this on himself.[15]

He had another weak spot. Having grown up amid plenty, Castro was unaccustomed to the deprivation of guerrilla life. Even in prison he could count on a minimal level of comfort and good food provided by family and friends. And so a commander in chief who could not countenance other people's complaints occasionally succumbed to complaining himself. "I'm eating very poorly," he wrote Sánchez in early May. "There's no attention paid to food here—none. When six o'clock arrives, after 12 hours of work, I am completely scatterbrained." More reliant on Sánchez than ever, he grew petulant at gaps in their communication. "Yesterday I received no word from you," he wrote. "I won't write any more as my mood is foul." Two weeks later, things had not improved. "I have no tobacco," he wrote, "I have no wine, I have nothing. In his refrigerator, Bismarck's kept a bottle of rose, sweet, Spanish. Where is it?"[16]

There is nothing like a military invasion to take one's mind off life's inconveniences. Self-pitying at times, Castro displayed laserlike focus when conditions called for it. Up to this point in his military career, Castro's leadership had been characterized more by daring and audacity than by strategic and tactical acumen. Though he read heavily in wars and revolutions, he never received any formal training. His comfort in the mountains equipped him to elude and harass small parties of government soldiers, but that stage of the war had ended, and the guerrillas were destined to confront the closest thing to pitched battles that the Sierra Maestra would allow. As he prepared for this, Castro was not without resources of his own, principal among them his authority over his men, his long-recognized intuition, and his photographic memory. All of these would prove invaluable in the difficult days ahead.

On May 8, the first troops of Plan F-F arrived in the Sierra. At the insistence of his own men, Castro had long since retreated from the front lines, and was now issuing orders from on high. He had a lot of territory to protect and too few people to protect it. It fell to an indefatigable captain named Ramón Paz to establish simultaneously two posts over twelve miles and four thousand vertical feet apart on opposite sides of the mountain below the rebel stronghold on the same morning. His notes to Paz suggest that Castro expected the enemy to approach from three directions at once: from the south (the coast), up the La Plata and adjacent river valleys; from the northeast, where the village of Santo Domingo afforded access to Castro's doorstep via a dependable road; and from the northwest, where a series of small villages served as stepping-stones leading up the high Sierra, just behind his back. Naturally, Castro wanted to engage the invaders as far down the mountain as possible. He ordered Paz to defend the territory by posting snipers, laying mines, and setting ambushes "at every turn in the road." This was a "decisive moment," he said. "We must fight as never before."[17]

In fact, the 18th Battalion did not advance from its position along the coast for over a month, as if afraid to enter the Sierra Maestra on its own. This allowed Castro to continue his public relations campaign and prepare the local citizens for battle. In mid-month the *Chicago Tribune's* Jules Dubois took advantage of the pause to visit Castro and evaluate his ideological development. The Cuban government insisted Castro was a communist; what had Castro to say about that, Dubois wanted to know. He was not now nor ever had been communist, Castro told Dubois. He blamed the talk of communism on Batista, who promoted the rumor in order "to continue to obtain weapons from the United States."[18]

Later that month, Castro convened a peasant assembly in the village of Vegas de Jibacoa, northwest of La Plata. With residents pouring in from towns throughout the region, he warned of the violence and hardship to come and discussed measures to safeguard the Sierra's lucrative coffee harvest and alleviate the effects of the military blockade. Israel Rodríguez Serano, one of fourteen children from a local peasant family, remembers attending the meeting with his father. Acknowledging the people's sacrifices, Castro asked attendees to keep their eyes on the prize: land, education, and health care reform, reliable work, better housing, and an economy dedicated to the welfare of Cubans as a whole. "My family was not overly cultivated," Serano said, "but we understood what Fidel meant when he said that too many people lived like animals." The young Serano found Castro courteous and down-to-earth. "He always treated peasants with the best manners," Serano explained, "as if they were members of his own family."[19]

Battle broke out in the neighborhood of Vegas de Jiboaca that very day, when the 17th Battalion, commanded by Pablo Corzo and backed by tanks, aerial bombardment, and mortar fire, advanced on the village of Las Mercedes, some ten miles northwest of Castro's headquarters. Adopting tactics that had proved effective in the first stage of the war, Castro's men lay concealed in the forest, as Corzo's column wended its way into the hills. After several hours' march, relieved not to have encountered any opposition, the 17th Battalion lowered its guard, stopping at a natural resting place on the outskirts of town. The rebels opened fire, taking out the advanced guard and pinning down the enemy for several hours. Eventually Corzo steadied his troops, and, exploiting his advantage in firepower, forced the rebels back. The 17th pushed on, its complacency banished by the grim reality of stepping over the bodies of fallen comrades.

The next surprise for the 17th came not from the woods but from a fifty-pound bomb planted in the roadway. The explosion obliterated the head of the column, sowing panic among the green recruits and forcing Corzo to corral his troops once more. The rebels made his task extremely difficult, pelting the soldiers with fire from the cover of the woods. For thirty-six hours, the battle continued: the army advancing, the rebels lying in wait, an ambush unleashed, the advance guard taken out, the rebels falling back, Corzo and company forging on, now thoroughly disheartened. In the end, the 17th suffered seven deaths and many injured, the rebels no deaths and one injury. With few men and scarce resources, the rebels were unlikely to win these battles. But they served their purpose of putting the enemy on notice and slowing its advance. In this case, seven losses were enough for Corzo, who decided to pause at Las Mercedes and convert the village into his base, which he did only after setting fire to peasant houses and murdering local men and boys thought to be collaborating with the enemy. The dismembered body of one young boy was found slung over a bridge in the nearby village of Calambrosio as a warning to local residents.[20]

Gratified by the rebels' stand, Castro had no illusions about the scale of the task ahead. Exponentially outmanned (his entire force is said to have numbered under three hundred troops, the government close to ten thousand), he nevertheless liked his chances of repelling an unpopular army from a territory he knew well—so long as he had the guns and ammunition. Over a year and half into the war, ammunition remained a pressing problem, and Castro's consolidation of power put that problem squarely in his own lap. "The imperative of the moment is to save bullets," he told commander Horacio Rodríguez on June 3. "Day in and day out, our worst enemy is not the Army, but the idiots who fire their guns for pleasure." A few days later, he told Celia Sánchez that he was by and large pleased with the state of the rebel defenses. "The problem that worries me most," he said, "is that the troops don't realize in a battle of continual and escalating resistance, you can't expend in two hours ammunition that has to last a month." Nothing was more crucial to the rebels' success, he told Sánchez, than marshaling scarce resources effectively. "I will not give a single bullet to anybody if it's not a question of life or death, as truthfully there will be no bullets left." This problem "is our Achilles heel."

In mid-June Castro continued to summon his commanders back toward the Santo Domingo/La Plata zone. "I need you here with all the good arms that you can muster," he told Camilo Cienfuegos; a huge battle was about to take place as the government was concentrating its forces on the guerrillas' command post.[21] On June 12, the enemy was amassing in the three directions that Castro had anticipated. "There is a veritable sea of soldiers descending on us," he wrote Ramón Paz.[22] By June 18, the battle looked imminent, and Castro positioned his troops with pinpoint precision. He clearly relished the chess game. "The enemy's main objective on the coast is to take La Plata, since they surely know we have an airfield there," he told Paz. The 18th Battalion was likely to advance via Palma

Mocha, he said, which was "a terrific spot for us to trap them." In issuing orders, Castro relied on his photographic memory of the local terrain, down to the last footpath and peasant home. "Cuevas should position himself on the banks of the Palma Mocha," Castro wrote, "the side closest to La Plata, by the footpath leading down to the river, and entrench himself there against the frigates and airplanes, so as to control the banks and the plains of the river's mouth." That way, the rebels would be "able to surprise and drive off any troops that arrive there." With another group of men upriver and five more men between Palma Mocha and Las Cuevas, the rebels would stop reinforcements coming to the soldiers' defense. Those last five should occupy "the upper part of the pass," Castro emphasized, "taking care not to be trapped between the road and the sea."[23]

After Cienfuegos, the next to be summoned home were Ramiro Valdés, Juan Almeida, and Guillermo García. Castro greeted them with the same warning he had greeted the others. This next stage in the war would be long and hard, he said. But when it concluded, Batista's end would be nigh. Batista was all too aware of this, Castro advised, and "for that reason he'll risk anything." The army possessed greater numbers and better firepower. The rebels knew the terrain and had local support. They would exploit that as long as possible, thereby "bleeding and exhausting the army." From a succession of modest victories, the rebels would harvest the resources necessary to launch a counteroffensive of their own, just as the enemy began to crack. In the meantime, he urged his friends to check their pride, fall back, concentrate their forces, and maintain an impenetrable nucleus. "These are bitter measures," Castro acknowledged, "like all measures adopted in difficult times."

He told the men to bring along food and other supplies needed to sustain them, including their livestock. Some would have to be slaughtered and smoked, some should "be kept alive to provide fresh meat." The same was true for grains and other supplies. And they must take every precaution in establishing their new camp, including constructing "reinforced tunnels for antiaircraft shelters." Again,

Castro's detailed memory of the local terrain informed his commands. "If the enemy manages to reach the hill at La Maestra by way of Santana," he warned, "you must withdraw the squads protecting the area of El Hombrito and Alto Escudero. Order them at once to take the road from La Gloria to the little house of the boy from Villa Clara in the Maestra, and to dig trenches on the road to Santana up to La Nevada." There, they should establish entrenched gun positions "along the hill at the cemetery to protect the approach to Malverde." Meanwhile, Paz and Miret would protect them from the sea. They should also identify the absolute best positions from which to ambush the approaching soldiers, protecting their supply depot and headquarters at all cost. This was do or die, he said; the rebel command post must not be taken under any circumstances. If Valdés, Almeida, and García were successful here, they would have to retreat no further. With the peaks of El Turquino on one side and La Maestra on the other, and Castro's column protecting them from the side, it would be impossible for the army to overrun the guerrillas.

Castro signed off like a worried parent telling a child to wear her seatbelt. Don't neglect the trenches! he warned; they must be "real excavations" capable of standing up to anything, "not just ridiculous little holes, which is what the vast majority tend to do." Proper defenses could stop the army in its tracks. Just look at what his column did at Las Mercedes, he said, where seven rebels "with 350 bullets" halted an entire brigade, before concluding "that seemed like a lot of bullets to me."[24]

———————

Fighting erupted on the morning of June 19. With the enemy advancing on the La Plata valley from three directions, Castro felt isolated and exposed. He would later refer to the government offensive as "D-Day." The live fire interrupted his supply lines, cutting off communication with his commanders. "I have nothing but my rifle here to confront the situation," he wrote Guevara, who arrived in the region around noon. Early that morning, Castro had ordered

Guevara to send him men, and had long since despaired of waiting. "I absolutely need the men I asked you for this morning if we are even going to make an attempt to save the La Plata zone," he said. Meanwhile, he had heard nothing from Paz, who was all that stood between the command post and the 18th Battalion, Major José Quevedo in charge. Castro had incorrectly anticipated Quevedo's route, allowing the Cuban commander to dodge Paz and Miret and dash up the west side of the Palma Mocha River, leaving Paz (and all seven of his men) in a frantic chase to catch up. Castro's scouts had lost track of Quevedo, and the whole territory looked to be in jeopardy.[25]

Again the Sierra came to Castro's aid. It simply did not lend itself to an assault carried out by large columns of soldiers advancing en masse. When Paz discovered Quevedo's gambit, he dispatched several of his fittest men to parallel Quevedo's move up a local peak named Naranjal, until they arrived at terrain suitable for setting an ambush. Meanwhile, the others followed as fast as they could to at least slow, if not repel Quevedo's approach. The plan worked. The 18th Battalion stopped, with Quevedo ultimately digging in for the night, thereby sealing his fate—and not just for the next day but permanently. Quevedo's halt allowed Castro and Guevara and others to send reinforcements, which ultimately stalled the offensive while cutting off Quevedo's retreat. The rebels had similar success on the other side of the mountain, with sets of well-placed troops stopping the 11th and 22nd Battalions in their tracks. If not exactly a victory—the 11th and 22nd occupied the village of Santo Domingo—this was a major accomplishment, imbuing the rebels with confidence while sowing doubt in the minds of the mostly young men who comprised the army rank and file.

Castro did not sleep that night, recalling it as "one of the worst in the entire war." The next day, having learned of Paz's success, a relieved commander had warm words for the young captain. "You have no idea how valuable it is right now that you repelled the guards on this road," Castro wrote. "I congratulate you, and the brave comrades accompanying you, both on your decision and your action."[26] This was just the beginning of the engagement however. Castro ordered Paz to hold the line, Miret to reinforce Paz. It was absolutely crucial, Castro wrote Miret, that they protect their own escape route. If the enemy got behind them, their retreat would be cut off, their columns wiped out, with the invaders gaining unimpeded access to La Plata. Patience and discipline, Castro counseled; this was not the time to take the battle to the enemy. The two must fortify and improve their trenches. The imperative now was simply to live to fight another day.[27]

The men did as they were told. When Quevedo's troops tried to outflank the rebels early the next day, they were greeted by withering fire resulting in many casualties. "Luckily you always make the right decisions when you have to resolve anything because you keep calm at all times," Castro wrote Paz. As a reward, Castro sent along some special treats—"a little packet of tobacco" for him, "a big one for everybody in your squad"—before asking Paz to check in on his neighbors. "Make sure the people from Palma Mocha and Las Cuevas who had taken refuge don't go hungry," Castro ordered. "Have some cattle killed for them."[28]

From the army's perspective, this was an inauspicious start to Plan F-F. Castro predicted that frustrated commanders would force their men up into the hills, which is exactly what they did. There was grave danger in this for Castro and his men; if Quevedo's battalion breached the rebel lines, Castro's command post would be overrun. But there was also opportunity. With only so many routes for the soldiers to advance, the rebels converted the Sierra into a death trap, inviting the soldiers into the few good mustering points before systematically cutting them down. By the end of "D-Day," the rebel defense had gone about as well as Castro could have wished. The rebels had successfully stalled the advance and secured their command post, radio station, weapons depot, hospital, and airfield. Perhaps more significantly, Castro had established a defensive line running from east to west atop the Sierra Maestra, thereby cutting

off the coast from the towns and cities to the north, effectively iso-
lating Quevedo and all but ensuring his end.[29]

Castro could not have known it at the time, but June 19 was the
last time that the rebels would face simultaneous attacks from the
south (the coast), the northeast (Santo Domingo), and northwest
(Las Mercedes/Vegas de Jibacoa). Though hardly decisive, the rebels' resistance that day succeeded in casting doubt in the minds of
Batista's commanders, many of whom paused in their camps as
if unsure of how to proceed in an environment that favored the
enemy. Repelled by an ambush along the Yara River just outside his
headquarters in Santo Domingo, for instance, Colonel Ángel Sánchez Mosquera, commander of the 11th Battalion, simply hunkered
down, awaiting backup from yet another entire battalion (the 22nd),
which arrived outside Santo Domingo on the 28th.

With Sánchez Mosquera's blessing, and apparently without a
word of warning, the 22nd Battalion took the same route that Sánchez Mosquera's advance guard had taken weeks earlier, marching
straight into the path of a massive land mine followed by an ambush
that wiped out the better part of two companies, while scattering a
third in an undisciplined retreat. The following day Quinteto Rebelde
made its debut, but only after Sánchez Mosquera sent yet another
company to its doom up the same bank of the Yara River where it
was met by yet another land mine. Besides leaving the rebels with a
cornucopia of automatic weapons, ammunition, mortars, and other
spoils of war, the army's folly in dispatching full companies up steep,
deeply wooded mountain paths confronted the rebels with a new
challenge, namely, managing large numbers of prisoners. In three days
of fighting outside Santo Domingo at the end of June, the rebels captured over thirty enemy soldiers, while inflicting numerous casualties.

Two weeks later, confronting Quevedo's 18th Battalion on the
other side of the mountain, the rebels deployed similar tactics to capture over two hundred men. Meanwhile, with Sánchez Mosquera

licking his wounds in Santo Domingo, the rebels tightened the noose on the 18th Battalion stranded since June 20 in the neighborhood of Jigüe, at the juncture of the La Plata and Jigüe Rivers. On the 11th of July, the 18th tried to break out and escape to the sea, only to be cut off by Paz, Miret, and others, losing its radio equipment in the process. Three days later, now without air support, the 18th tried to escape again, suffering still more losses. On the 15th, Major Quevedo managed to sneak a messenger through enemy lines, notifying the High Command of his desperate straits and pleading for aerial assistance. Assistance arrived the following day in the form of napalm. Still the rebels' circle held, with two amphibious battalions, meant to rescue the 18th, turned away on July 17 and 18, also at great cost to men, morale, and equipment.

The drama and scale of the rebel victory at Jigüe is captured in a series of letters that Castro sent to Quevedo over the course of the week. Castro had met Quevedo at the university. When he realized that it was this same Quevedo cornered in the valley below, he reached out on July 10, the day before the fighting broke out to see if bloodshed could somehow be averted. It was hard to imagine that two university chums would one day find themselves at opposite sides of a war, Castro said. It was all the stranger given that the two men undoubtedly shared the same aspiration for their country. Castro conceded that he had spoken harshly about the military in the course of the war, but he had nothing against honest officers. As evidence, he pointed to the aftermath of El Uvero, when the rebels released thirty-five prisoners, all of whom reported being well treated and some of whom had actually returned to battle. If Quevedo and his colleagues had something to worry about, it was surely crooked and incompetent officers like Sánchez Mosquera, who were notorious for ordering young men into unwinnable situations, while punishing those who refused to take part. But Castro wrote not to harangue, simply to salute an old classmate—"on the spur of the moment, without telling you or asking for anything, only to greet you and to wish you, very sincerely, good luck."[30]

On July 14, Castro reached out to Quevedo's soldiers directly, via a script recited aloud over Radio Rebelde accompanied by music from the Medina boys. The point was not simply to inspire doubt among the impressionable youth that comprised Quevedo's force, but to deprive it of sleep. The rebels were friends of the army, not foes, the announcers read. They wanted for Cuba only an end to violence and corruption and the restoration of constitutionalism and the rule of law. The rebels would unilaterally hold their fire the next day at noon for three hours, giving time to the soldiers to surrender. Soldiers who laid down their guns would be treated well, officers allowed to retain their weapons.[31] Castro continued to reach out to Quevedo over the course of the following several days. The rebels had his men dead to rights, he warned. There was no chance they would escape. He offered Quevedo a "decorous and dignified surrender," repeating his previous terms. Quevedo and his men would be treated with respect, he and his officers would be allowed to keep their guns.[32]

Four days, two battles, and many dead and wounded later, Castro tried yet again. Was Quevedo aware of what was happening? a mystified Castro wanted to know. "Company G-4 of your Battalion, which was on the beach, was completely destroyed by our forces when it tried to advance." Quevedo's men were being wiped out. What was the point of this? The route to La Plata was "like the pass at Thermopylae"; it couldn't be taken no matter how many thousands of soldiers the army dispatched. Castro was loath to inflict more harm. He had his own men to look out for. The rebels had captured hundreds of enemy soldiers, some fourteen of whom were gravely wounded but could not be safely evacuated to a hospital amid a raging battle. Unequipped to manage the hundreds of prisoners falling into rebel hands, Castro had contacted the Red Cross, which agreed to come collect the wounded soldiers in a few days. If Quevedo had any doubts, he could send along the battalion's physician to see things for himself.[33]

Quevedo may have been ready to surrender. His superiors were not. The following day, July 20, the Cuban Air Force treated the rebels to a seemingly endless bombardment that cost four lives and left four men wounded, two of them grievously. The bombing accomplished little more than that, however, and the Battle of Jigüe came to an end at 1:30 a.m. on the morning of July 21 when the 18th Battalion capitulated en masse. On the eve of the conflagration, Castro told Lalo Sardiñas that "this battle could mean the triumph of the Revolution." Looking back years later, Castro referred to Jigüe as the turning point in the war, the rebels' smashing victory demoralizing Batista's troops while investing the July 26 Movement with legitimacy it had heretofore lacked. "From then on," Castro recalled, "the fate of [Batista's] force was sealed, and with it perhaps—everyone thought—the fate of the Batista tyranny itself."[34]

The rebels' success was ratified by yet another compact, the Pact of Caracas, signed in the Venezuelan capital on July 20, 1958, by a Castro agent, along with Carlos Prío, Enrique Rodríguez Loeches (Revolutionary Directorate), David Salvador (Labor Unity), Lincoln Rodon (Partido Democrata), José Puente (FEU), Captain Gabino Rodríguez Villaverde (an ex-army officer), Justo Carrillo (Montecristi), and Ángel María Santos Buch (Civic Resistance), among others. The Pact of Caracas established a new civilian revolutionary front on the terms Castro had set out in the Sierra Maestra Manifesto the previous year.

The text, written by Castro, acknowledged the belated entry into the war of the Revolutionary Directory and Prío's Auténticos, while giving the rebels pride of place. "In each corner of Cuba," Castro wrote, "a struggle to the death is taking place between freedom and tyranny, while abroad numerous exiles are making every effort to free the oppressed Fatherland." Up to this time, he noted, the different factions had fought more or less independently. From here on out, they would marshal their resources in common, "aware that the co-ordination of human efforts, of war resources, of civic forces, of the political and revolutionary sectors of the opposition, including civilians, the military, workers, students, professionals, the commercial classes and citizens in general," could finally force Batista out.

The Pact of Caracas made a special demand of the North Americans: "cease all military and other types of aid to the dictator," while respecting the "national sovereignty and the nonmilitary, republican tradition of Cuba." The pact concluded with a plea for unity among all Cubans innocent of Batista's crimes. None of the opposition groups engaged with Batista forces had any enmity toward the soldiers, the signatories said. Everyday soldiers and honest officers were as essential to the new Cuba as "workers, students, professionals, businessmen, sugar plantation owners, farmers and Cubans of all religions, ideologies and races." Cuba's destiny, the fulfillment of its natural resources and human capacity, was within reach.[35]

Back in the Sierra Maestra, buoyed by his victory at Jigüe, Castro went on the offensive at Santo Domingo, first trapping the 11th Battalion in its camp, then cutting off the 22nd, which had been sent to the rescue from nearby Providencia. In three days of endless fighting in late July, the rebels cleared Santo Domingo of enemy troops. The Second Battle of Santo Domingo was costly for the rebels, with nine killed and eight wounded. But it was devastating to the army. Sánchez Mosquera, commander of the 11th Battalion, was wounded in the head and had to be evacuated by helicopter. Including prisoners, dead, and wounded, the army lost another 150 men over three days. At Jigüe and Santo Domingo combined, the rebels recovered some three hundred weapons and over 100,000 bullets, allowing them to outfit hundreds of volunteers languishing in training camps across the Sierra Maestra.

The government offensive was not over. Castro had defeated two of the three prongs of Plan F-F from the sea and the Santo Domingo valley. There remained the problem of the territory to the northwest, just over the mountain from La Plata, along a line running between the villages of Vegas de Jibacoa, Las Mercedes, Arroyón, and El Cerro. Of the three approaches to La Plata, this one provided the deepest access to the government's heavy artillery, including T-17 and Sherman tanks. Over the course of eight exhausting days in late July, early August 1958, the rebels squared off against elements from the 10th, 12th, 17th, 19th, 20th, 21st, and 23rd Battalions, amid unremitting aerial and artillery bombardment.

While the rebels absorbed the first blows of Plan F-F, Ambassador Smith continued to debate the merits of the U.S. arms embargo with his bosses in Washington. In mid-June, Smith insisted that the Cuban government, in deploying Military Assistance Program–acquired weapons against the rebels, had not violated the restriction against the government's using such weapons against their own people because Batista was combating "elements in league with Communism."[36] This conclusion put Smith far out ahead of colleagues both in Cuba and in Washington, who, if aware of the presence of some communists in the rebel ranks, did not regard the insurrection as fundamentally so. In a State Department memorandum dated June 26, Roy Rubottom, assistant secretary of state for Inter-American Affairs, cited "incontrovertible evidence that Cuba had failed to adhere to the MAP agreement."[37]

Rubottom was not alone in concluding thus. On June 28, Raúl Castro, infuriated by evidence that Batista was skirting the embargo and that his bombers were refueling at the U.S. naval base at Guantánamo Bay, captured a busload of U.S. marines on liberty outside the boundary of the naval base. Two days later, Castro contacted Ambassador Smith, pledging to release his U.S. captives if the United States ceased all military shipments (MAP-related or not) to the Batista government and stopped allowing the Cuban Air Force to refuel at Guantánamo. That same day, U.S. Admiral R. B. Ellis, commander of the naval base, wrote a memo to Chief of Naval Operations Arleigh Burke outlining U.S. options. Among the actions contemplated were an airlift of marines to Guantánamo ("accompanied by full fanfare"), a roundup of Cubans sympathetic to the rebels on the base, a threat to support Batista's counterinsurgency, and finally the expulsion of Cuban workers from the naval base. Ellis conceded that the last three options were likely to backfire on a base already unpopular among many Cubans. The first would likely be inconsequential.[38]

The kidnapping, undertaken without Fidel Castro's authorization (in late June, he was fighting for his life above Santo Domingo), achieved its intended effect. Unsure of where the captives were being held, the U.S. government demanded Batista halt the bombing raids. Raúl Castro brandished a U.S. requisition for rocket heads and fuses bound for the Cuban military as evidence that the embargo was being violated. The State Department insisted that the shipment was meant to replace an erroneous delivery antedating the embargo. The rebels also possessed photographs of a Cuban aircraft refueling at the base, prompting the State Department to concede that Commander Ellis had allowed one Cuban bomber to refuel at the naval base on account of its being low on fuel.

Meanwhile, Castro's men paraded the hostages, along with Park Wollam, the U.S. consul at Santiago de Cuba, around the Sierra Cristal, showing them incontrovertible proof of the damage wrought by Batista's bombers. Wollam had gone up to the mountains to negotiate the hostages' release. Among the evidence he was shown were fragments of U.S.-manufactured bombs and victims of napalm firebombing. "The Cuban bombing affects mainly civilian population," Wollam wrote Ambassador Smith. "Rebels themselves have lost few men by this but claim that many civilians have suffered." The sound of airplanes sent the local people diving for cover, Wollam reported, and for good reason; he himself had been forced to take shelter during "a similar incident in vicinity of a small church." The Cuban Army was being its "own worst enemy."[39]

Pressured by his brother, the commander in chief, Raúl Castro released the American hostages on July 18, but not before Ambassador Smith and Chief of Naval Operations Burke called for a forceful U.S. intervention to teach the rebels a lesson, prop up Batista, and preserve U.S. credibility in the region. But it was precisely to enhance U.S. credibility that the State Department adopted the arms embargo in the first place. By the late 1950s, the U.S. government's tendency to elevate anticommunism above economic development and democratic politics did not sit well among many citizens of Latin America. Vice President Richard Nixon found this out firsthand that April and May when, on a goodwill tour of the region, he was met by audiences frustrated by his government's apparent sympathy for dictators.

Nixon's rude reception in Latin America and the region's mounting hostility toward the United States was on the minds of State Department officials confronting escalating hostilities in Cuba. On June 3, 1958, Smith assured the State Department that Batista had things fully under control. The following day, Consul Wollam reported nineteen unidentified bodies dumped at the cemetery in Santiago de Cuba. The next month, another U.S. consular official described the inflationary calculus whereby every army officer killed yielded "three, four or more youths . . . shot dead the next morning beside a road outside the locality" where the original offense occurred. Summary arrests, executions, and torture were commonplace, the official reported. The country was unraveling. "A whole generation of Cuban youth has been sidetracked from normal pursuits to plotting and killing." Parents sent their kids into exile for fear of their becoming "the innocent victims of slaying by the police or the armed forces." The rule of law had all but disintegrated, with nine judges suspended for protesting police interference with the administration of justice.[40]

Amid evidence of the government's increasingly arbitrary behavior, some in the State Department began to build the case against Castro not as a communist but as a potential dictator, as if the U.S. government had a problem with dictators. As early as July 24, 1958, State Department opinion appeared to turn against Castro as a potential replacement for Batista, with one report citing former Castro friends referring to him as "a Frankenstein" and suggesting that some of his proposals "would make him as much a dictator as

Batista." An internal State Department memorandum written July 25 concluded that from the perspective of U.S. interests the gravest danger appeared to stem from "a successful revolution by the forces of the July 26th Movement which, so far, has given no indication of political or moral responsibility."[41]

The charge that Castro and the Movement lacked a sense of political and moral responsibility seems ignorant given the work that the rebels were doing in the Sierra Maestra to establish the rule of law and civil administration, as well as to build schools and hospitals, among other institutions, and suggests a diplomatic corps hopelessly ill-informed. But with Smith relying on Castro's sworn enemies (the editor of the conservative *Diario de la Marina*, for instance, and Eusebio Mujal, Batista's labor commissioner) for information about Castro, it is no wonder that some U.S. officials continued to misread him. Concern about order and stability conducive to moneymaking deafened Smith and others to Cubans' cries for real change. In late July, Smith called on the State Department to revisit the arms embargo and so "enable Batista to step up his offensive against the Communist infiltrated rebel elements in Oriente Province, whose elimination is essential for the restoration of normalcy in Cuba."[42]

In August 1958, José Miró Cardona, secretary general of the Pact of Caracas, wrote a letter to the White House on behalf of the so-called Cuban Civilian Revolutionary Front, which consisted of representatives of Cuba's political parties, the United Labor Organization, and the FEU, imploring the U.S. government to withdraw its support for Batista.[43] The White House ignored Miró Cardona's appeal. Three weeks later, William Wieland, director of the State Department's Office of Caribbean and Mexican Affairs, informed Miró Cardona that the accord authorizing the U.S. military missions in Cuba remained in effect and would not be withdrawn. This prompted yet another letter from Miró Cardona warning Wieland that the United States would bear "tremendous historic responsibility" for whatever fate befell Cuba upon the inevitable fall of

Batista. If the U.S. government did not take action soon, he wrote, the "fighters of today" would become the "rulers of tomorrow."[44]

―――――――――

By August 1958, the civil war had accelerated. Death and destruction exacted such a toll on both sides that there was talk of a negotiated truce. Confident that things had turned his way, Castro amplified his critique of Batista, expressing sympathy toward government troops who he believed to be deceived by the dictator's mischaracterizations about the state of the war. Flush with enemy captives taken during the recent battles, Castro spent much of August negotiating their release with the Red Cross. The rebels' successes left him at once optimistic and melancholy. As his ranks swelled and the ferocity of military engagements mounted, so, too, did the list of rebel casualties. These included the deaths of the capable Ramón Paz and the irrepressible René Ramos Latour, who, having exchanged the Llano for the Sierra that summer, was felled by a howitzer near Las Mercedes on July 30, 1958, one year to the day of the assassination of Frank País.

Success confronted Castro with a series of new challenges, or rather, with old challenges on a new scale. The trove of weapons harvested by the rebels in the Sierra that summer meant that they could finally outfit the hordes of volunteers gathering in Oriente. But that only raised the vexing problem of just who these volunteers were and what their motivation was. The last significant infusion of recruits back in March 1957 created discipline problems. Rebel victories that summer left Castro with weapons sufficient to outfit some five hundred new recruits, many of whom had never fired a shot and some of very dubious reputation.

The rebel victories galvanized the Miami-based opposition, now more determined than ever to ensure that Castro did not replace Batista. The U.S. government shared their alarm, engaging the Junta in frequent discussions about an alternative to Castro. Castro, of course, was well aware of these developments. He vowed that the rebels would not stop fighting until Batista was gone and a pro-visional government installed free of any taint of the old political parties and of U.S. influence. At the same time, he invited members of the still largely spectatorial opposition truly devoted to revolu-tionary change to join the final stage of battle.

In August, Castro began a correspondence with General Eu-logio Cantillo, commander of Cuban forces in Oriente Province. Cantillo was a rarity among Batista's High Command, enjoying a sterling reputation not only among army officers and the rank and file, but among rebel commanders and even the local peasantry. The rebel victory at Las Mercedes in early August left Castro with over a hundred prisoners of war, a few of them gravely injured. Castro wrote Cantillo to suggest that he dispatch a helicopter to pick up the injured prisoners. The Red Cross could be on hand to make sure that things went smoothly. Cantillo rejected Castro's offer, in-sisting that he turn over Lieutenant Colonel José Quevedo, captured at Jigüe. Castro refused to surrender a prized bargaining chip, ex-plaining his position in a long letter.[45]

Castro hoped to use Cantillo as a wedge to split the Cuban of-ficers in Oriente Province from the High Command at Camp Co-lumbia, and thus bring the fighting to a close. Despite government propaganda to the contrary, Castro insisted that the rebels were not communists or anarchists, but patriots committed to nothing so much as the unrequited dream of Cuba Libre—much like Cantillo himself. Consider the evidence, Castro urged: in nearly a year and a half of fighting, the rebels had treated their adversary with only the utmost respect, providing scrupulous care for enemy wounded—often at considerable risk to rebel troops. The contrast with Batista's treatment of rebels and peasants alike did not bear repeating.[46]

Castro warned Cantillo that time was running out to get on the side of right, and by doing so play a hand in determining the war's outcome. Once upon a time the rebels would have been eager for a negotiated settlement. Had Batista the "slightest fore-sight, intelligence, and historical sensibility, he could have nipped the Revolution in the bud" by cutting a deal, resigning his office, and leaving the country with all his ill-gotten gains. After all, Castro remarked, Cubans were "a forgiving and peaceful people." Some, like Castro (and perhaps Cantillo), would have decried such an outcome, but there was ample precedent for that in Cuban history. No longer. The tables had turned, and what "might have seemed a victory a year ago, would satisfy no one today." Cantillo faced a clear choice between joining the popular Revolution now or overseeing the "disintegration" of the Cuban Army.[47]

Hearing nothing from Cantillo, Castro assured the general the next month that joining the rebels would not mean relinquishing his command. The point was not to disband the army, but to redeem it by "inspiring a revolutionary action in its heart." Castro wanted to facilitate this end. Together, the forces of right could conquer Oriente, occupy its cities, and commandeer its garrisons, leaving Batista with no choice but to step down. The Revolution was going to triumph, Castro said. The only question was whether the intervention of a military man of Cantillo's stature could prevent the descent into violence that greeted the fall of Machado.[48]

Cantillo did not respond to these letters either. Castro was not fazed. He was confident that the rebels' march down out of the mountains, across Oriente, and soon (he hoped) into Camagüey and Las Villas would force Cantillo to the table soon enough.

When he was not pestering Cantillo, Castro continued to establish legal and administrative control over the Liberated Territory of Cuba. In early September, he heard reports of rebel soldiers exacting weapons and taxes from local businesses without authorization. In response, he announced new regulations governing the rebels' relationship with the local community, which included the warning that anyone found guilty of extorting the neighbors would be treated "like assassins."

Back in February 1958, with the assistance of the acting legal counsel Humberto Sorí Marín (a former Auténtico Party member), Castro published the First Law of the Sierra Maestra, which included penal, civil, and administrative codes designed to discipline the rebels' swelling ranks. In early October, he was back at it, issuing a series of decrees setting prices and establishing taxes on commodities like sugar, rice, tobacco, soap, and cooking oil. He also announced strict penalties for production, distribution, and consumption of marijuana, evidently a burgeoning industry in farms throughout the Sierra.

On October 10, 1958, the ninetieth anniversary of the Grito de (or Shout of) Yara, which launched the Cuban War of Independence against Spain, Castro published Laws 2 and 3 of the Liberated Territory of Cuba. Law No. 2 forbade citizens of Oriente Province from participating in the upcoming presidential election, which Castro considered a fraud for proceeding in a climate of intimidation solidified by the suspension of constitutional guarantees. Any politician running for office picked up in Oriente would be sentenced to death, Castro warned; ordinary citizens visiting the polling places would be banned from political or military service for years.

Law No. 3, entitled "On the Right of the Peasants to the Land," put muscle on the skeleton of the agricultural reform program that Castro first announced in "History Will Absolve Me." Cuba's economic progress depended on the expansion of industry, Castro explained. Rich in natural and human resources, the country was being held back by its dependence on sugar. Law No. 3 promised to diversify Cuban agriculture and industry by offering incentives, tariff protection, and credit to stimulate private enterprise. Castro pointed to United Nations studies to back up this law. Exports, he explained, were essential to foreign exchange, without which there could be no imports, no consumption, and hence no improvement in Cubans' standard of living.

The principal impediment to this vision of a flourishing, diversified, government-supported private economy was "the misery of the rural areas," the law declared. Despite progress made by the Sugar Coordination Act of 1937, many Cuban farmers did not own their land. Law No. 3 cited 1953 census figures showing that some

200,000 farmers operated as tenants, sharecroppers, settlers, and squatters on land owned by absentee landlords. Insecurity bred by this arrangement inevitably stifled productivity, as individuals who did not own the land they farmed had little incentive to improve it—"as universal experience demonstrates."

The 1940 Cuban Constitution based "the legitimacy of private property on its social function," Castro said. Insisting that "Revolution is the source of right," Law No. 3 promised to make things right for the peasant population that Castro had come to admire during the war. Peasants had comprised the rank and file in the War of Independence, the law said; peasants bore the brunt of the ongoing contest with Batista. The 1940 Constitution included promises, largely unmet, to provide land to squatters, tenants, and sharecroppers. With this new law, Castro vowed to deliver on past promises by divvying up state land, purchasing and dividing private property, setting fair prices, and ensuring small producers access to grinding mills and markets.[49]

The details of the Agrarian Reform Law would be left to the conclusion of the war. By mid-October, Castro saw signs that the end was near. The previous month, he dispatched Camilo Cienfuegos and Che Guevara and their two separate columns into central Cuba. On October 9, Cienfuegos sent word that he had arrived in Santa Clara after a harrowing forty-plus days slog through swamps and rain, with little food and less sleep, all the while dodging government troops who this time lay in wait for *them*. All the advantages they had come to take for granted in the Sierra Maestra, above all local support, were wanting on the journey. News of their arrival with their columns largely intact seemed miraculous to Castro. "I can't describe the emotion I felt in rereading your report of the ninth," he wrote Cienfuegos. Surely, this ranked among the feats of the great Mambises. "With the invading columns lies our prestige, our motivation, our history, our people," he wrote. "Nobody but nobody can stop us now."[50]

The Cuban Army was not the only adversary Cienfuegos and

Guevara had to dodge along the way. In Las Villas Province, the July 26 Movement had a small rebel force under the command of Víctor Bordón. Bordón had been fighting alongside another group of guerrillas commanded by Eloy Gutiérrez Menoyo, a member of the new Second National Front of the Escambray, which had splintered off from the Revolutiony Directory. When Guevara arrived in Las Villas, Bordón announced that he was going to combine his forces with those of his fellow Movement member. Gutiérrez Menoyo objected, arresting Bordón and seizing his weapons.

Gutiérrez Menoyo's treatment of Bordón surprised and dismayed Castro. Of course, there had been disagreements between the Movement and the Directory about strategy and tactics, he told Cienfuegos. But when members of the Directory first landed in Northern Oriente the previous year, Castro had tried to come to their assistance by launching a diversionary attack along the southern coast. The Movement would accept no other leader in Las Villas than Guevara, Castro said. The Movement's record of sacrifice and success gave it and it alone the right to call the shots. This was no time for stupid "quarrels and division." Castro counseled Cienfuegos to be "tactful and delicate" in dealing with Menoyo. The rebels should resort to force only in self-defense, or when "a vital revolutionary necessity was at stake." In that case, they must act "drastically and decisively," resolving things once and for all. The rebels must never succumb to infighting. The closer the Revolution came to triumph the more traps would be thrown in its way. By always acting with dignity, they would win the confidence and support of the masses.[51]

When not playing the part of peacekeeper, Castro was assuming the role of head of state. In mid-October, he learned that Britain had agreed to provide arms to Batista. In Law No. 4 of the Free Territory of Cuba, he denounced the deal as an act of war, declaring an embargo against British goods, while appropriating British property wherever he could. He gave British citizens ten days to leave Oriente Province, after which they would be subject to arrest and detention. What in the world had England to gain by exercising its power over tiny Cuba? he asked.[52]

At the end of the month, Castro was given the opportunity to demonstrate his statesmanship once more after word reached him from the region of northeast Oriente Province that the U.S. seemed to be seeking a pretext to intervene in the war on the side of Batista. First, the army withdrew troops from the Yateras River, source of the water supply for the U.S. naval base at Guantánamo Bay. This forced the U.S. Navy to dispatch marines to secure the site, thereby engineering a potential showdown with Raúl Castro's men. Then, two U.S. citizens were detained by the rebels after inadvertently walking into a rebel ambush. Finally, Batista withdrew troops from the U.S. nickel plant near the town of Nicaro, inviting the rebels to occupy the plant. As if on cue, U.S. State Department spokesman Lincoln White railed against alleged Castro aggressions. In response, Castro explained that U.S. citizens were not the only ones inconvenienced by the ongoing war. Responsibility for the current conflict lay not at the rebels' feet but at those of the "tyranny itself, which for the last seven years oppresses our people while retaining the support of the North American ambassadors."[53]

chapter fourteen

FIN-DE-FULGENCIO

Through *August and well into* September and October, Ambassador Smith kept up his denunciation of Castro and the rebels, imploring his bosses to end the military embargo and thereby allow Batista to face the rebels with gloves off. Failure to act promptly, he said in late September, would only invite "chaos and loss of U.S. property and life."[1] There were at least two problems with this argument. First, the lamentable state of the Cuban government's battle against the Castro insurgency could not be attributed to a disadvantage in weaponry; the army faltered thanks to a combination of incompetence and demoralization in the ranks and to Batista's unpopularity (never mind the rebels' surprising military prowess). Second, the rebels' descent from the Sierra Maestra into the plains of Oriente Province had occasioned no episodes of violence against civilians. The rebels wanted to tax local profits not appropriate U.S. property. In fact, the rebels retained stable working relations with businesses throughout Oriente Province.

On November 3, 1958, the Cuban people went to the polls to elect a president to succeed Fulgencio Batista. The election took place in a climate of suspended constitutional guarantees and voter intimidation, some of it carried out openly by Castro's rebels, some of it covertly by Batista's army. In Oriente and Las Villas Provinces, under partial rebel rule, Castro had announced that individuals who went to the polls would be treated like criminals. Agents of the July 26 Movement engaged in sabotage throughout the country, cutting electrical lines, setting cane fields ablaze, littering highways with nails. To good effect, apparently. In Oriente and Las Villas, an estimated 80 percent of eligible voters stayed away. Elsewhere the turnout was not much higher, with some estimates putting the national tally of eligible voters at a mere 30 percent. In advance of the voting, the Batista government produced a counterfeit set of returns in favor of its candidate, Andrés Rivero Agüero, who "defeated" former president Ramón Grau (Auténtico) and Carlos Márquez Sterling (Free People's Party), by an improbable 70 percent to roughly 15 percent and 12 percent, respectively. The electoral fraud was not lost on anyone, including the U.S. State Department, which refused to honor the results.[2]

In early November, anticipating the collapse of Batista's army, Castro warned his lieutenants to beware of a military coup, which would mean the end of the Cuban Revolution. In the event of a coup, he told his commanders, the rebels must seal off Oriente to prevent weapons from getting out. Meanwhile, with each successive victory and expansion of the Liberated Territory, Castro took on more of the trappings and function of a chief executive. In early December, he told the citizens of Oriente that they should not worry about where their next meal would come from. "You will have what you need," he said. He was particularly concerned that the people not be idle, promising that they would soon be able to "invest their time in work useful to society."

On November 9, Castro contacted Cantillo again, proposing to release captured Cuban Army officer Nelson Carrasco Artiles in exchange for jailed Army Major Enrique Borbonet, imprisoned on the Isle of Pines for allegedly participating in a coup attempt. Learning there would be no deal, Castro released Carrasco anyway. "The General Staff disgusts me," he said. Later that month, Gustavo Arcos, a Movement organizer in Las Villas, reported receiving queries from Cantillo and Archbishop Pérez Serantes about whether Castro could accept a provisional government different from the one he had proposed if Batista resigned. There is no record of Castro's response, but he had always insisted that the rebels would not lay down their arms until Manuel Urrutia Lleó, a federal judge who had upheld the rebels' right to protest back in 1957, occupied the provisional presidency.[3]

A few days later, Castro gathered together the men and women under his command and set out on what would become a seven-week march on Santiago. The guerrillas were as outgunned as ever, but few besides the U.S. ambassador would have bet against them by this time. Castro and his forces spent the first ten days of the counteroffensive winding uncontested through the little towns that lay between their old home atop the Sierra Maestra and the plains of the Cauto River delta to the north. On November 20, just outside the town of Guisa, the rebels' procession halted, when one of their companies engaged a rural guard patrol just after 8:30 a.m. By 10:30 that morning, the air over Guisa buzzed with spotter planes and bombers. By late afternoon, the army's heavy artillery arrived, with army and rebel batteries transforming the once quiet town into a shooting gallery. In the exchange of gunfire, the rebels destroyed a light tank, forcing the government to retreat. For the next several days an uneasy quiet settled over the region as the rebels hastily entrenched.

On November 26, the army returned with more spotters, more bombers, more light tanks. Again, the rebels fought the enemy to a standoff. Again, the army retreated, returning the next day with heavier (Sherman) tanks and still more airpower. After yet another standoff, the army paused for a day to marshal its resources, unleashing a two-day assault on November 29–30, consisting of two companies, four battalions, and fierce aerial bombardment. The rebel lines held, and the army retreated, effectively marking the beginning of the end of the battle for Oriente. Over the course of the next month, the rebels marched inexorably on Santiago, surrounding and taking the towns along the way. The fighting remained hotly contested through the end of the year. But the odds were now overwhelmingly in Castro's favor, with the question flipped: *how long could Batista's forces hold out?*

U.S. officials regarded these developments with alarm. Smith became increasingly desperate, trafficking in ludicrous reports that Castro suffered from a "syphilitic inheritance" and was bent only on destruction. Meanwhile, officials at the U.S. State Department and CIA reached out to Cantillo, Archbishop Pérez Serantes, and others in a last-ditch attempt to forestall the inevitable.[4] In mid-December, Washington tried a more direct approach, sending William D. Pawley, former U.S. ambassador to Peru and Brazil, to Havana to offer Batista a way out. The idea for Pawley's mission originated in a meeting in Miami late the previous month, attended by, among others, William Pennell Snow, deputy assistant secretary of state for Inter-American Affairs at the State Department and J. C. King, chief of the Western Hemisphere Division of the CIA Directorate of Plans. Everyone in attendance agreed that something must be done to stop Castro, Pawley later remembered. "I told them that we should . . . see if we can go down there to get Batista to capitulate to a caretaker government unfriendly to him, but satisfactory to us, whom we could immediately recognize and give military assistance to in order that Fidel Castro not come to power."

Pawley had spent some of his childhood in Cuba, later returning there as a business executive. He was friends with President Eisenhower and the powerful Dulles brothers, Foster and Allen, secretary of state and CIA director, respectively. In early December, Pawley presented his plan to Eisenhower and Foster Dulles, both of whom signed off on it. Foster Dulles was sick at this time, and his stand-in, Acting Secretary of State Christian Herter, insisted that Pawley proceed to Cuba as an "independent citizen" rather than as a representative of the U.S. government. Ambassador Smith was not informed of the initiative and was recalled to Washington to clear the way for Pawley, who arrived in Havana on December 7. Two days later, he presented Batista with the following deal: in exchange for his stepping down and relinquishing power to a caretaker government, he could retire to Daytona Beach, Florida, with his friends and former colleagues free from reprisals for at least eighteen months. Batista was many things, but stupid he was not. He refused to entertain a solution not officially sanctioned by the United States government.[5]

A few years later, in the aftermath of the Bay of Pigs invasion, CIA Chief King told a Board of Inquiry that the Pawley mission was one of two operations conducted by the agency in late 1958 designed to prevent Castro from coming to power. The other transpired just a few weeks before, when King's agents approached Justo Carillo, founder of the Montecristi Group, about orchestrating a coup led by army Colonel Ramón Barquín.[6] By contrast to Batista and his U.S. patrons, most Cuban officers recognized that there could be no solution to the conflict at this stage that did not involve the rebel leader. This included General Cantillo and Castro's old nemesis Chaviano, who reached out to Castro via intermediaries toward the end of the month. Would Castro be willing to partake in a civil-military junta, they wanted to know, combining forces with the jailed officers Barquín and Borbonet, along with Urrutia and two other civilian leaders to be chosen by Castro himself. After taking control of Oriente, the junta would march on the Cuban capital and install Urrutia at the head of a provisional government. In exchange, the mutineers wanted only that Chaviano and other former Batista stalwarts be allowed to leave the country. The U.S. embassy was fully on board, Castro was informed, and was prepared to recognize the junta. Time was short, the messenger emphasized.

The Revolutionary Directory was more bent than ever on assassinating Batista and seizing control of Cuba. Batista's chief of staff, Francisco Tabernilla, was rumored to be contemplating a coup of his own.[7]

A U.S. government endorsement was not the key to Castro's heart. Nor was he willing to grant immunity to perpetrators of the crimes that had rent Cuba since Batista's return to power. On Christmas Eve, Carlos Franqui responded to this overture on behalf of the National Directorate of the July 26 Movement. Any North American–supported junta was unacceptable to the rebels, he said. The following day Castro reiterated Franqui's rejection in a note to the emissary. If Cantillo was serious about seeking an end to the violence, he should come see Castro in person.[8] Cantillo agreed, with word arriving the next day that Cantillo would be contacting the rebel leader through a priest. By Christmas 1958, Castro could taste victory. For the first time since returning to Cuba, he visited the family home in Birán, accompanied by his brother Raúl and Celia Sánchez.[9] Ramón Castro, the eldest son, and their mother, Lina, prepared a festive Christmas dinner, complete with a twenty-pound roast turkey, a Castro favorite.

The closer victory approached, the more determined Castro became not to let it slip away. As impressed as he was by Guevara's and Cienfuegos's success in central Cuba, he was astounded to hear that Guevara was sharing command of Las Villas with members of the Revolutionary Directory, thus compromising his "authority, prestige, and power." The war was "won, the enemy in free fall," he wrote Guevara on the day after Christmas. "In Oriente we have ten thousand troops surrounded. Those in Camagüey have no escape." This victory was a result of one thing and one thing only, Castro said: "Our work." It made no sense at this point to give a leg-up to individuals and groups whose ambitions the Movement was all too aware of—and who were sure to be a source of difficulties down the road.[10]

With this problem in mind, Castro made some strategic and

tactical adjustments. He established a National Executive with himself, Pérez, Franqui, and Aldo Santamaría (Haydée's and Abel's brother) in charge. The leaders had rethought the role of a general strike. At the beginning of the guerrilla war, with the rebels confined to a remote section of the Sierra Maestra, Castro and his lieutenants regarded the general strike as decisive and military operation as symbolic—as simply a sign that the spirit of the Mambises lived on. Now, with the Cuban Army disintegrating and the rebels occupying major swaths of the country, the military operation had become the focal point and the general strike a means of consolidating a military victory.

The previous February, Castro had told the visiting senators Nené Ramírez and Lalo Roca that he and other members of the July 26 Movement would not serve in a provisional government at the triumph of the Revolution. They would help oversee honest elections and the restoration of the 1940 Constitution, then constitute a new political party devoted to revolutionary reforms. Castro repeated this pledge to Andrew St. George of *Look* magazine that same month in an interview designed for a U.S. audience. By the end of the year, with victory in sight, and with the U.S.-sponsored competition circling like vultures, Castro altered his message. The July 26 Movement would remain in power after the triumph of the Revolution. In the face of recent developments, surrendering power seemed both modest and naive. "The National Executive has agreed that the provisional government will be a revolutionary government," Castro announced. Members of the Movement would head government agencies. Limiting the rebels' role in a transitional government would mean "wasting a unique opportunity to realize the Revolution for which we have fought so hard."

Was this Castro's plan all along? To seize power and never let it go? Maybe. It is easy to claim that power is not your aim when power is out of your grasp. But there was plenty of evidence by this time that a change was called for. The machinations of the Liberation Junta did not cease with the Movement's denunciation of the Miami Pact the previous year. The United States government seemed more determined than ever to ensure Castro's demise, and he was justified to wonder just who among his interlocutors was operating in good faith. Not Batista, not the U.S. government, not the former government officials, ministers, and rival opposition groups conspiring in Miami, not supposed allies like the Revolutionary Directorate, not the ostensibly honorable military officials who had their own designs on the reins of power now that Batista's end seemed nigh. Castro did not say the rebels alone would comprise the government, only that they would not now walk away. They needed the help of honest professionals and experts in every field and Castro had been talking to such people for years.[11]

Moreover, despite the insistence of U.S. intelligence officials, there was plenty of evidence from the Sierra Maestra that the Revolution was taking seed. Since consolidating control of the territory in summer 1957, the rebels had been establishing schools and hospitals and distributing land to peasants. The rebels continued to use the territory as a hot-house for revolutionary projects through the following year, establishing a legal code, a taxation system, and other rudiments of state administration. Perhaps to their own surprise, the rebels turned out to be rather good at governance, at least in the Sierra Maestra. Many of these initiatives cut against the grain of recent Cuban history and conventional political priorities. They would have to be protected—and enhanced.

By late December, Castro's command was knocking on the door of Santiago de Cuba, having overcome the last-ditch resistance of the Cuban Army at Jiguaní, Maffo, and Palma Soriano. The question confronting General Cantillo was whether to capitulate or defend Santiago, and at what cost. By this time, much of the navy and no few of Cantillo's own officers had approached Castro secretly and asked to switch sides. The last Castro had heard from Cantillo there had been talk of Archbishop Serantes sending a priest to arrange a parley between the two commanders. That priest, Father Francisco Guzmán, finally arrived at Castro's mobile headquarters at Central América, the large U.S.-owned sugar plantation outside the town of Contramaestre, on the morning of the 28th. A meeting between Castro and Cantillo was scheduled for later that day.

The two men came together at Central Oriente, formerly Central Miranda, which bordered the Castro family estate to the south. Cantillo had the endorsement of Batista's chief of staff, Tabernilla, though not of Batista himself. Castro was in the driver's seat. He was accompanied by, among others, his brother Raúl, Raúl Chibás, and José Quevedo, his former schoolmate and recent adversary in the battle of the La Plata River valley. Assisting Cantillo was Colonel José María Rego Rubido, second in charge at Santiago and commander of the other garrisons in the province.

Cantillo began by repeating his earlier suggestion that Castro join a military junta and that Batista and his closest associates be allowed to leave the country. Castro refused. Cantillo was in no position to object. In the end, Cantillo agreed to cease fighting and combine forces with Castro beginning at 3 p.m. on the afternoon of December 31. The combined forces would occupy the three eastern provinces while Cantillo proceeded to Camp Columbia in the capital to arrest Batista. As the men talked, reports circulated of government and rebel troops exchanging hugs and well wishes and toasting the end of the war.

That same day, some three hundred miles to the northwest, Che Guevara's column departed the town of Caibarién, along the north-central coast of Las Villas, headed for Santa Clara, the provincial capital, fifty miles distant. Along the route, Guevara and his men were greeted by rapturous crowds, with government resistance melting away. Late on the afternoon of the 28th, Guevara arrived at the university on the outskirts of the city. There he divided his column in two, sending one group toward the southern margin of the city to engage the army, while the other hurried to cut off a government train laden with arms and reinforcements. On December 30, using earthmoving equipment commandeered from a local agricultural school, the rebels tore up the railroad tracks northeast of the city, overturning the train and capturing its contents and crew, including millions of dollars of precious weaponry and an estimated 350 officers and enlisted men. The spectacle caught the imagination of the local citizenry, making legends of Guevara and his men and effectively signaling to Batista that the game was up. When the hostilities ended at Santa Clara on New Year's Eve, Batista's bags were packed, his plane revving its engine on the tarmac at Camp Columbia.

Meanwhile, back in Santiago, on December 31, Cantillo sent Castro a note from Havana saying that the capitulation of Santiago had to be pushed back a week; something had come up. Castro smelled a rat. He responded by upbraiding Cantillo's second-in-command, Colonel Rego Rubido. There would be consequences for Cantillo's backpedaling. The rebel attack on Santiago would proceed. Cantillo's decision to postpone the handover of Santiago was "ambiguous and incomprehensible," Castro wrote Cantillo the following day. "You have made me lose faith in the seriousness of our agreements."[12]

In Washington, the latest National Intelligence Estimate revealed U.S. officials still struggling to get a bead on Castro. U.S. business interests on the island now wanted *both* Batista and Castro out of the picture. More sober minds acknowledged that if Batista was unable to dislodge Castro with all of Cuba's consolidated military might at his disposal, then it was unlikely that any self-appointed military junta would succeed at doing so. Unsure what to do, the U.S. intelligence community was clear where it stood on the subject of the rebel leader: Castro must be stopped. Failing that, "a prolonged period of instability and disorder, like that which followed the fall of the Machado regime in 1933, would almost certainly ensue, with consequent peril to American and other lives and property."[13]

President Eisenhower was surprised by how quickly things had come to a head. How had the rebel forces gained strength so rapidly?

he asked a meeting of the National Security Council on December 18. The answer, of course, was that they hadn't. The rebels had been growing stronger day by day since the previous winter, with Batista's incompetence and brutality enabled by an inept U.S. ambassador. Five days later, at another meeting of the National Security Council, Allen Dulles announced that the United States must prevent Castro coming to power, with a grave Eisenhower noting that this was the first time such a statement had been made in that setting.[14]

U.S. officials would later insist that that they had initially supported the anti-Batista opposition and even Castro's campaign for social and political reform. A State Department report released in April 1961, just days before the Bay of Pigs invasion, maintains that Washington "rejoiced at the overthrow of the Batista tyranny, looked with sympathy on the new regime, and welcomed its promises of political freedom and social justice for the Cuban people." With rare individual exceptions, the historical record emphatically contradicts this. Initial U.S. government opposition to Castro derived not from a consensus that he was communist but from fear that a social revolution would threaten U.S. political and economic hegemony on the island. In short, long before Castro nationalized American property or committed himself to communism, the U.S. government decided that the Cuban Revolution needed to be suppressed.

Rewriting this history enabled U.S. officials to claim that Castro, not they, betrayed the Cuban people. "It is not clear whether Dr. Castro intended from the start to betray the pledges of a free and democratic Cuba," the State Department report stated, "to deliver his country to the Sino-Soviet bloc, and to mount an attack on the inter-American system." In fact, it was perfectly clear that he had *not*—doing so in response to U.S. interference in the Revolution as early as autumn 1958.[15] Despite the noble rhetoric, the U.S. government had never put Cuban interests first—not when standing idly by as Cuban patriots waged an unsuccessful war of independence in 1868, not when intervening in the Spanish-Cuban-American War when it was all but won, not when making Cuba safe for capitalist exploitation during the U.S. military occupation, not with the Platt Amendment, not with the Reciprocity Treaty, not in helping crush the 1933 Revolution, not when propping up Batista, and not in December 1958 when it declared Castro and the Revolution dead. U.S. officials' claim to have done otherwise was plausible only in a country with a credulous public and no historical memory.

On the evening of December 31, 1958, as Guevara mopped up in Santa Clara, as Castro exchanged notes with Colonel Rego Rubido, and as U.S. intelligence officials continued to denigrate Castro's ability to govern effectively, Fulgencio Batista affected an air of business as usual, ringing in the New Year at several Havana casinos, before heading to the airfield at Camp Columbia, where his family and close associates awaited, their bags long since stowed aboard a fleet of Cuban passenger planes. At 2:30 in the morning of January 1, 1959, Batista turned over control of Cuba's armed forces to Cantillo. Civil authority was put in the hands of Supreme Court justice 'Carlos Modesto Piedra y Piedra. Batista then departed Cuba for Santo Domingo.

Confirming the U.S. role in this, Cantillo, now in command of the Cuban military, kept in close touch with Ambassador Smith throughout the night. Smith dispatched his first cable after Batista's departure to the State Department at 6 a.m. Approximately two hours ago, Batista, along with "top members of the GOC," abandoned the country, Smith wrote. Cantillo was now in charge of the armed forces, with Piedra set to assume civilian control. Cantillo hoped to enlist the support of Archbishop Pérez Serantes and pledged to reach out to the Castros. Early that afternoon, in another cable, Smith reported that Cantillo had agreed to "fly all asylees out as soon as possible," and was "ready to turn over authority to whoever should have it." At 6 p.m., Smith noted that Justice Piedra had declined the position of provisional president, thus leaving Cantillo in control of the country. At 8 p.m., Smith reported that the rebels had declared a general strike and that this time the strike was holding. Travel and communication throughout the country was paralyzed. American tourists were trapped. Then came this news, directly contradicting Smith's prediction of chaos: the rebels had taken to the radio and called for order. The people had listened. For the first time since March 10, 1952, the country was at peace.

At 9 p.m., Smith posted his last wire of the day. Colonel Ramón Barquín had been released from prison on the Isle of Pines and was now at Camp Columbia, where Cantillo relinquished power to him. Barquín summoned Castro to the capital. Barquín was the U.S. government's military strongman of choice. His step into the breach soothed nerves at the U.S. embassy. "Military vehicles now patrolling disturbed areas of city with military police to maintain order," Smith noted. The possibility of cooperation between the rebels and the armed forces was an "encouraging development," which "strengthens position of the military vis-à-vis rebels."[16]

Castro was not so naive as to show up at Camp Columbia and present himself to an army against whom he had been waging war for over two years. Surely, it would arrest and (finally) execute him and announce the Revolution over. Nor would he allow Cantillo, Piedra, or Barquín to call the shots. Instead, he ordered Cienfuegos and Guevara to the capital to secure the nation's arsenal, with Cienfuegos taking command of Camp Columbia, Guevara La Cabaña fortress. Simultaneously, Castro confirmed the general strike and declared Santiago de Cuba the transitional capital of Cuba. Urrutia would be sworn in as provisional president the following day.

At mid-afternoon on New Year's Day, Castro emerged on the balcony of Santiago City Hall, overlooking Parque Céspedes, to make the biggest speech of his life. For nearly seven years, he had worked tirelessly to oust the perpetrator of the March 1952 coup d'état and restore the 1940 Constitution. Along the way, he came to embrace a social program focused on improving rural Cubans' access to land, education, and health care. On this day, in the heart of Santiago, he largely eschewed talk of the revolutionary program.

He had more urgent work to do, namely, to convince the assembled crowd, along with Cubans huddled around radios throughout the country, that the rebel victory was really *their* victory, and to regard him, Fidel Castro, as the embodiment of the popular will. In this speech and in many statements leading up to it, Castro insisted that he himself did not seek political office. At this point, he still seems to have meant it. In his message that day, he did not claim that he was the state (*L'état c'est moi*), but that he spoke for the people (*Les peuple, c'est moi*), which was as presumptuous as it was crucial to his future success.

It is hard to know for sure how many Cubans outside the Sierra Maestra identified with the Revolution in early 1959. Until recently, the rebel army had been isolated from much of the Cuban population, with membership in the July 26 Movement numbering in the low thousands. The failed strike of the previous April demonstrated that the reach of the July 26 Movement did not extend much beyond the Sierra Maestra and certain neighborhoods in Havana and Santiago, along with a few isolated pockets in small cities and towns throughout the country. If this was really to be a people's revolution, as Castro claimed, he would have to make it so overnight.

This made for interesting, sometimes twisted logic, starting with his explanation of the Revolution's first act—unilaterally declaring Santiago de Cuba the provisional capital of Cuba. He had done so, he said, by authority of a "Provisional President," who had not yet been inaugurated, as well as that "of the rebel army and the people of Santiago," which was also a stretch. Castro allowed that some listeners might "be surprised by" the move. They would have to get used to it. For such was the way with revolutions, which did "things that have not been done before." Castro then announced that Manuel Urrutia, a former judge, would be inaugurated provisional president the next day in Santiago by virtue of his being "elected by the people." Of course, the Cuban people had not elected Urrutia to be the president of anything, unless, that is, the people and Castro were one and the same.

Ever since his rise in university politics, Castro had insisted that none of Cuba's political parties, past or present, truly represented the interests of Cubans in general. In Parque Céspedes that day, he tried to settle this debate, using the story of Cantillo's alleged deception and "coup d'état" to convince his audience to regard opposition to the new revolutionary government as a personal affront to each and every Cuban citizen. By setting aside his pledge and heading off to Havana, Castro said, Cantillo had "prepared a coup behind the backs of the people, the backs of the Revolution," in order to "cheat the people of power."

Castro assured the crowd that he had not been naive in his negotiations with his army counterpart. The lessons of 1898 (when Shafter insulted Calixto García) and 1933 (when Batista betrayed Grau and Guiteras) were fresh on his mind, he said. Cantillo had presented himself as a "Paladin of liberty." In a conversation witnessed by his fellow officers and by Raúl Chibás and other dignitaries, Cantillo had seemed to concur with Castro that Batista and his cronies must not be permitted to flee, that Urrutia would assume the provisional presidency, that war criminals would be prosecuted, and that rebel soldiers would join the armed forces on equitable terms. Above all, Castro said, "I told Cantillo that . . . the people and only the people have conquered their liberty"—that "the military will answer to the people and only the people and the Constitution and the laws of the Republic."

Cantillo's duplicity was more than simply dishonorable. By letting Batista, Tabernilla, and other fugitives escape—"with three or four hundred million pesos of stolen money"—Cantillo ensured that the battle for the soul of Cuba had not, in fact, at long last ended but had only just begun. "This is going to cost us heavily," Castro observed clairvoyantly. Batista and his fellow criminals were headed for "Santo Domingo and other countries, from which they will launch propaganda against the Revolution, stirring up as much trouble as possible." Castro predicted that this menace would last for the "foreseeable future, threatening our people, maintaining us in a constant state of alert, and paying for and contriving controversies among us."

Castro then turned to the subject of justice and reconciliation. After years of repression and abuse, the public was understandably keen on revenge. But if temporarily satisfying, revenge could never restore peace and prosperity to Cuba. He pleaded with his listeners to exercise restraint. Upon coming to power, the revolutionary government would appoint a joint commission of army and rebel officers to try accused perpetrators. So long as justice was meted out scrupulously, nobody would oppose it, neither the victims, nor the army, who more than anybody wanted to restore its integrity. Castro acknowledged that some listeners would be disappointed by these words. He assured them that the rebels would not betray the people's confidence.

The problem with erecting a political regime on people power, Alexis de Tocqueville and others had long since observed, is that the people's desire for equality does not always jibe with liberty, toleration, and minority rights. Careful listeners might have detected tension between Castro stoking popular enthusiasm ("What is legal right now is what the people say is legal"), while counseling restraint. If the Revolution and the Cuban people were one and the same, then criticism of the Revolution was unpatriotic, even treasonous. "I hope there will be no resistance," Castro remarked ominously. Resistance would be futile anyhow—"smashed in an instant"—as it would defy "the law, the Republic, and the will of the Cuban Nation."

Castro promised to once and for all deliver the peace and prosperity, the sovereignty and independence, for which Cubans had fought for nearly a century. This would be a world governed not by personal whimsy but by constitutional guarantees, in which peasants and workers no less than politicians and professionals enjoyed a full complement of civil rights and civil liberties. Liberty and justice, in turn, would generate economic prosperity, with tax revenue going not into military equipment but into new infrastructure conducive to industrial and agricultural development. Of course, change and innovation do not come easily. The hard work had only begun. "We will make mistakes," Castro allowed, before insisting that the one thing that would never be said about the revolutionary government is that it "robbed, bribed, exploited, or betrayed the Movement."

This had been a long struggle and Castro seemed to be relishing the moment. "We can say with jubilation that in the four centuries since its founding, for the first time we are entirely free and the work of the Mambises is complete," he exclaimed. Still, he had to get to Havana. In a fit of inspiration, he decided to proceed there not by air, but by road, sometimes literally on foot, stopping at one town after another, repeating his Parque Céspedes address almost verbatim. By doing so, he figuratively (and in some cases literally) brought the Cuban people along with him. By the time he arrived in Havana on January 8, he had done his job: the people had adopted the Revolution as its own, for now, anyway, regarding Castro as its personal embodiment. Resistance now seemed impossible.[17]

EPILOGUE

I n early January 1959, U.S. television host Ed Sullivan traveled to Cuba to interview a victorious Fidel Castro. Mainstream newspapers and periodicals had depicted Castro and his
followers as a band of communist thugs. Sullivan wanted to see for
himself. "Freedom is everybody's business," he told his New York
studio audience. Sullivan caught up with Castro in the town of
Matanzas at two o'clock on the morning of January 11, three days
after Castro led his triumphant army into Havana.[1]

Nestled in a thicket of gun–toting soldiers, the dapper variety
show host put five questions to a soft–spoken, deferential, and clearly
exhausted Castro: Are you Catholic? Weren't you once a baseball
player? How many people did Batista torture? How do you plan
to put a permanent end to dictatorship in Cuba? Finally, what do
you think of Americans? Castro, speaking very passable English, answered dutifully: yes, yes, many thousands, institutional reform, and

I have "great sympathy" for the people of the United States, who through "hard work" built a nation, which, comprised of "all the people of the world," "belongs to all the people of the world," serving as a refuge "to those who could not live in their own country." Gratifying answers all.

But in truth, Sullivan seemed less concerned with what Castro had to say than in putting his own spin on developments in Cuba. Castro's army was not a band of "communeests," Sullivan told the folks at home, but a "wonderful group of revolutionary youngsters who wanted to make corrections"—and who even "carry bibles." He sought to assure Castro that, notwithstanding the negative press coverage, "the people of the United States have great admiration for you and your men"; after all, Castro was in "the real American tradition of a George Washington, of any man who started off with a small body and fought against a great nation and won." Americans "like you," Sullivan insisted, "and we want you to like us."

The interview ended with Castro insisting that the feelings were mutual and promising to work on his English. Sullivan's studio audience was delighted. Amid thunderous applause, Sullivan signed off by observing that Castro was "a fine young man, and a very smart young man. With the help of God and our prayers, and with the help of the American government, he *will* come up with the sort of democracy down there that America should have."

In fact, despite the United States's recognizing the revolutionary government on January 7, there was little sympathy between Castro and an Eisenhower administration that had only recently tried to prevent his rise to power. News out of Cuba the first week of the new year did not help any. "When you have a revolution, you kill your enemies," CIA director Allen Dulles told the Senate Foreign Relations Committee in late January 1959. Dulles, who knew a thing or two about taking care of enemies, was in the unusual position of trying to ease U.S. senators' concerns about reports of summary executions carried out by the revolutionary government. In Law No. 1 of the Sierra Maestra, announced the previous February, Castro had warned that government soldiers, police, and paramilitary who committed atrocities during the war would face the death penalty upon the event of a rebel victory. He and his lieutenants believed that delivery on this promise was all that stood between an orderly transition and the mayhem that attended the fall of Machado. Even as Castro addressed the crowd in Parque Céspedes on New Year's Day, his soldiers were at work excavating mass graves, exposing government torture chambers, and rounding up alleged perpetrators. The irrefutable evidence of Batista's crimes only increased public demands for vengeance.[2]

As Castro headed off toward Havana, he left behind his brother Raúl to do the dirty work. During the first week in Santiago, Raúl Castro and his men carried out over one hundred executions. Within ten days, courts-martial presided over by rebel officers had been instituted across the country. There remained cause for concern about the rigor and fairness of the ensuing tribunals. In one notorious episode broadcast on U.S. television, some seventy alleged perpetrators were tried in Santiago's Palace of Justice, where the Moncada trial took place. Comprised primarily of Rolando Masferrer's private army, the accused were found guilty, transported to a nearby field, and shot in pairs by the side of a trench. In a still more notorious incident, Castro responded to mounting disquiet among the public and press corps by holding the trial of reviled Army Colonel Jesús Sosa Blanco at the seventeen-thousand-capacity Sports Palace on the outskirts of Havana. If the world wants transparency, we'll give it to them, Castro threatened, waving away comparisons of the proceedings to a Roman Circus. By the end of January, the list of executed is said to have reached two hundred; by the end of March, the number had climbed to around five hundred.

Not everybody tried was found guilty, nor were all the guilty put to death. The *Chicago Tribune*'s Jules Dubois was probably right that Castro could have avoided the criticism by doing what other

revolutionaries and liberated countries had done since time imme-
morial, namely, "mow down a thousand suspected torturers, killers
and informers" without making a public spectacle of it. Alarm over
the kangaroo courts poured in from all quarters, including Latin
America and Europe. Predictably, Castro tolerated U.S. criticisms
the least, asking where the North Americans had been all this time
when Batista was terrorizing Cuba.[3]

The outcry over the executions was only the first in a series
of disagreements between the new revolutionary government and
U.S. officials over the course of the year. Sabotage and terrorist attacks against the revolutionary regime began almost immediately,
just as Castro had anticipated. In February 1959, Castro replaced
José Miró Cardona as prime minister (Castro was making all the
decisions anyway, Miró Cardona concluded, so there was no point
in pretending otherwise). In March, Castro nationalized the Cuban
Telephone Company (ITT), reducing phone rates by 50 percent.
In April, while on a trip to Washington, D.C., Castro alarmed U.S.
officials by never bringing up the subject of U.S. aid, as if he had
another source of economic assistance in mind.

Castro's trip to the United States in April 1959 was the brain-
child of journalist Herbert Matthews and was intended to coun-
teract the negative press that the fledgling revolution continued to
earn. The trip included meetings with State Department officials, a
few congressional committees, and Vice President Nixon, though
not, notably, President Eisenhower, who fled Washington, D.C., just
before Castro arrived so as to avoid a face-to-face meeting with a
leader thought to be conspiring with communists.

In spring 1959, the Cuban economy was in free fall and the
revolutionary government in desperate need of economic assistance.
Castro refused to kowtow to U.S. officials and bankers, hoping that
by taking his message directly to the U.S. people they could pre-
vail on their representatives to provide the coveted loans. On day
three of his tour, Castro visited Mount Vernon, Arlington National
Cemetery (where he laid a wreath on the Tomb of the Unknown

Soldier), and the Lincoln and Jefferson Memorials. He was visibly moved by his encounter with Jefferson, reciting in broken English the words descending the memorial's southeast wall: *I am not an advocate for frequent changes in laws and constitutions. But laws and institutions must go hand in hand with the progress of the human mind. . . .We might as well require a man to wear still the coat which fitted him when a boy as civilized society to remain ever under the regimen of their barbarous ancestors.*

Administration officials greeted Castro with skepticism. Nixon found him "slavishly subservient" to public opinion. Nixon also described Castro as "naive" on communism and utterly lacking in "the most elementary economic principles." Secretary of State Christian Herter described him as "a most interesting individual, very much like a child in many ways, quite immature regarding problems of government, and puzzled and confused by some of the practical difficulties now facing him." Meanwhile, Florida senator George Smathers thought him devious and evasive. "There is serious trouble brewing in the Caribbean area," Smathers warned, "centered in Cuba."[4]

Others found their meetings with Castro encouraging. "I feel reassured about a number of matters I've been concerned about," said Louisiana senator Russell Long. "I was neutral and suspicious before, but today I was very favorably impressed," added Pennsylvania representative James G. Fulton. "I think we should help him." Even Nixon conceded that Castro possessed "those indefinable qualities which make him a leader of men. Whatever we may think of him," Nixon concluded, "he is going to be a great factor in the development of Cuba and very possibly in Latin American affairs generally."[5]

The American public ate him up. Fifteen hundred greeted him at the airport in Washington. Twenty thousand people showed up at New York's Penn Station and forty thousand flocked to Central Park to hear him speak in Spanish on the problem of hemispheric development. And it wasn't just youth who rallied to him, though university students swarmed him at Princeton and briefly at

Columbia, while 8,700 squeezed in to see him at Harvard's Soldiers Field. The Harvard visit, where Castro was hosted by dean of the Faculty of Arts and Sciences McGeorge Bundy, who would soon head John Kennedy's National Security Council and try to overthrow Castro, provided the comic highlight of the U.S visit, when Castro was understood to have said that he made this journey to the United States in order to appeal to the Jews. The young audience scratched its head. *Appeal to the Jews?* Castro's translator, Teresa Casuso, noticed the confusion. A brief conversation ensued, followed by a broad smile on Castro's face. To the *JOUTHS!* Castro emphasized, to the *YOUTHS!,* pronouncing the English word "youth" in classic Latin style.[6]

As Castro departed for Canada at the end of the month, *The New York Times* provided a postmortem. How had Castro fared? He had given reassuring answers to questions about supporting the United States over the Soviet Union, democracy over communism, and he confirmed a commitment to free enterprise. But it was the people-to-people contact that caught the paper's attention. "The reception Premier Castro received here was so friendly that he will surely return feeling better about the United States than when he arrived. By the same token it seems obvious that Americans feel better about Fidel Castro than they did before." One could only hope for good and long-lasting results. "This first visit was of great importance," the *Times* remarked. "It must not be the last."[7]

Nearly two years later, one month before the Bay of Pigs invasion, President John F. Kennedy introduced the Alliance for Progress, a Marshall Plan for Latin America. Designed to undercut support for communist Cuba, the Alliance for Progress promised economic assistance to nations willing to undertake significant social and political reform. Criticized by some for its idealism and overreach, the program won the praise of many, stoking Kennedy's reputation as a visionary while auguring a new chapter in hemispheric relations.

Largely missed in all the fuss was the fact that Castro himself had anticipated the Alliance for Progress by two years. Before returning to Cuba from his U.S. tour, he flew to Buenos Aires to attend a conference of the economic ministers of the Organization of American States. Widespread underemployment and a lack of private property deprived Cubans and Latin Americans in general of the power to participate in the marketplace, he explained. With no markets, there could be no profit making, no surplus, no investment—in short, no economic development. The solution was to stimulate purchasing power by redistributing land, diversifying agriculture, and establishing new industries. All of which took commitment, to be sure, but above all money—something the countries of Latin America simply did not have.

Castro estimated the cost of ushering Latin America into the modern age at "thirty billion dollars" to be paid out over a period of ten years. There was only one country in the world that could conceivably come up with that kind of money in 1959: the United States. Turning to the U.S. delegation, Castro emphasized that Latin America was not looking for a handout ("We don't ask for donations of capital, we don't want gifts of money"). What the region needed was loans, which the beneficiaries would repay "with interest." The United States had as much to gain from such a program as its southern neighbors, Castro argued. Greater purchasing power throughout Latin America would mean a larger market for U.S. goods, along with new opportunities for investment. By creating "internal markets in each country, we can create a common market among all." But markets and economic development were only the means to a higher end: fulfillment of the "democratic aspiration and the most cherished dreams and hopes of this Hemisphere."[8]

Castro's plea for help went unanswered, compelling him to turn to the Soviet Union for economic assistance, and leaving President Kennedy to take up the plan two years later at the exclusion of Cuba. Meanwhile, tensions between the two countries continued to escalate. In mid-May 1959, Castro introduced the Agrarian Reform

Law, which limited farmholdings to under a thousand acres, directly threatening U.S. sugar producers on the island, some of whom owned 400,000-plus-acre estates. In February 1960, he signed a trade agreement with the Soviet Union, by which the Soviets agreed to purchase five million tons of Cuban sugar over five years, while providing Castro with $100 million of credit and crude oil— an agreement calculated to displease North American refineries on the island. The following March, Castro accused the United States of blowing up a French freighter (*La Coubre*) packed with small arms in Havana Harbor. All of which prompted President Eisenhower to declare that Castro "is going wild and harming the whole American structure."[9]

It took until just after the Bay of Pigs fiasco of April 1961 for Castro to fully tie Cuba's fate to the Soviet Union, which in a speech the following December he characterized as a "natural" alliance ("there is no half way between socialism and imperialism," he thundered; "anyone maintaining a third position is, in fact, helping imperialism").[10] If Cuba's alliance with the Soviet Union troubled U.S. officials, it unsettled Castro, too. However much Cuba needed money and protection, it was never his intention to trade dependence on one imperial juggernaut for dependence on another, and Castro soon learned that condescension and a lack of reciprocity were not the province of Americans alone.

In summer 1962, the Soviet Union thought to give the United States a taste of its own medicine by increasing Soviet influence in the region and installing intermediate-range nuclear missiles on the U.S. doorstep. The crisis was diffused only when Soviet premier Nikita Khrushchev agreed to remove the missiles in exchange for the United States secretly withdrawing its Jupiter missiles from Italy and Turkey. To people around the world, this was a satisfying resolution to a cataclysmic threat. To Castro, by contrast, Khrushchev's readiness to negotiate with Kennedy without seeking Cuban input was evidence of imperialism not so different from that which Cuba had come to expect from the United States. Castro was livid,

Khrushchev bemused. "We believe the aggressor has suffered a defeat," Khrushchev wrote Castro. "It was preparing to attack Cuba, but we have stopped that, and forced [the aggressor] to acknowledge before the world that it will not do so in the current stage. We judge this to be a great victory."[11] What more did Cuba want?

––––––––––

In 1978 Max Lesnik, Castro's old friend from Ortodoxo days and one of the few Cuban exiles respected on both sides of the Florida Straits, returned home for the first time since departing just after the triumph of the Revolution. Why had Lesnik left Cuba? Castro wanted to know. Because he didn't like the communists or the Soviet alliance, Lesnik replied. Well, Castro continued, if Lesnik had been in his place, what would he have done? Would he have turned to the Soviet Union to help save Cuba's sovereignty? In retrospect, Lesnik believes that Castro had no choice. "Fidel was entirely correct . . . and I was wrong. If we had done what I wanted, that is to say, keep Cuba from forming an alliance with the USSR, the Revolution would have been wiped out by Washington."[12]

It seems fitting to leave the final word on Castro to his idol and fellow countryman, José Martí. Attending the dedication of the Statue of Liberty in New York Harbor on October 28, 1886, Martí testified to the agony of living in the grip of an oppressive political regime (at that time, colonial Spain). Overwhelmed by the pomp and circumstance among French and U.S. officials and journalists, Martí withdrew from the crowd to address Lady Liberty in private. "For him who enjoys thee not, Liberty, it is difficult to speak of thee," Martí confessed. "His anger is as great as that of a wild beast forced to bend his knee before his tamer. He knows the depths of hell while glancing up toward the man who lives arrogantly in the sun. He bites the air as a hyena bites the bars of his cage. Spirit writhes within his body as though it were poisoned."[13]

Despite a comfortable upbringing and privileged education, Castro grew up seeing the world from deep within that cage. He was a rarity in that he wanted for others the privileges that he enjoyed. It was never his intent to destroy the liberal institutions that undergirded those privileges. He had long insisted that national sovereignty, civil liberty, and social justice were compatible, so long as people were willing to settle for their fair share, a principle he applied simultaneously to individuals and nations, to Cubans and foreign nationals. When fairness toward Cuba collided with U.S. interests and Cold War realities, the imagined alignment between sovereignty, liberty, and justice disintegrated and Castro responded like a caged animal. With sovereignty in danger, liberty would have to take a backseat. But surely not for long. Either the Revolution would be smashed, or Cuba's self-determination acknowledged. Or so everyone imagined.

ACKNOWLEDGMENTS

This book is dedicated to my children, Nathalie, Julian, and Oliver. You are are my pride, joy, and inspiration.

The most gratifying part of writing this book has been the friendships forged in Cuba along the way. The book would not have been possible without the generosity and support of René González Barrios at the Instituto de Historia de Cuba, Eugenio Suárez Pérez and Elsa Montero Maldonado and their colleagues at the Oficina de Asuntos Históricos del Consejo de Estado, Gladys María Collazo Usallán at the Consejo Nacional de Patrimonio Cultural, Eusebio Leal Spangler, Historiador de la Ciudad de La Habana, Eduardo Torres Cueva, Director of the Biblioteca Nacional José Martí, Ambassador Jorge Bolaños, whom I first met in Washington, D.C., and Rafael Hernández of TEMAS. I am hopelessly indebted to you all.

Life and work on my many visits to Havana and Cuba was made both fruitful and fun thanks to Edelso Moret, Rainer Schultz, Giselle

Odette, Alberto Magnan, Fidel Rivero Villasol, Carlos Alzugaray, Tomás Diez Acosta, Elvis Raúl Rodríguez, Servando Valdéz, Belkis Quesada, Ángel Jiménez González, Marilú Uralde, Tomás Rodríguez, Pablo Armando, Javier Miyar Ibarra, Manuel de Jesús Céspedes Fernández, Caridad González Fernández, Nilo Julio García, Ricardo Torres, Yelsy Hernández Zamora, José Andrés de León Cruz, Israel Jesús Figueredo, Armando Gómez Carballo, David Camps Rodríguez, Jorge Pérez Soria, Gilberto Morales Pardo, José Angel Cardosa Pullú, Roberto Fonseca, and Carlos Cristóbal Márquez, among many others.

At the Cuban Interests Section (now Embassy) in Washington, D.C., I received timely assistance from Ambassadors Jorge Bolaños and José R. Cabañas Rodríguez, Consul General Llanio González Pérez, First Secretary Warnel Lores Mora, and Second Secretary Saylín Martínez Tarrío. In Mexico City, Enma Castro, Antonio del Conde, and Sergio Silva Castañeda were generous with time and information. In Miami, I benefited from conversations with Max Lesnik, Alfredo Duran, Salvador Lew, Mitchell Kaplan, Uva de Aragón, Carol Rosenberg, Jaime Suchlicki, Gustavo Godoy, Osvaldo Soto, and Juanita Castro. In Washington, Emilio Cueto shared his infectious enthusiasm for literally every single thing Cuban.

Young Castro was Richard Fox's idea. This is my third book written with Richard's help and I can't imagine what I would ever do without him. Jim Kloppenberg provided encouragement, sage advice, and close readings along the way. Sayres Rudy is always there at the ready and always understands better than I do what my books are about.

At Harvard, I continue to benefit from the intellectual stimulation and sustenance of the Committee on Degrees in Social Studies, my home, where Richard Tuck, Jim Kloppenberg, and now Eric Beerhbohm lead (or have led) a group of teachers and scholars as lively and talented as I could ever imagine being a part of. Sincere thanks to Peter Marsden, Claudine Gay, and Laura Fisher for facilitating and extending my presence there. Jorge Domínguez, Alejandro de la Fuentes, and my colleagues in the Cuban Studies Program at the David Rockefeller Center for Latin American Studies provided an audience and criticism for the early stages of this work on several different occasions. I am grateful for the hard work and support of the David Rockefeller Center staff, especially June Erlick, Cary Aileen García Yero, Alina Salgado, Edwin Ortiz, and Monica Tesoriero.

This book was supported by research and writing grants from the David Rockefeller Center for Latin American Studies and the National Endowment for the Humanities Public Scholars Program. Professor Joaquim-Francisco Coelho, Roger Lane, and Jim Kloppenberg read early drafts of the manuscript cover to cover. Mario Carretero read a chapter. Nelson Valdes made some valuable corrections. My old book group—Jane Kamesky, Michael Willrich, Dan Sharfstein, Seth Rockman, Steve Biel, and Conevery Valencius—was just gentle enough with a rough sample of the book that I did not throw it in the trash. Miriam Psychas and Edelso Moret provided expert and timely research assistance. Max Lesnick, Dick Cluster, and Ángel Jiménez González read the penultimate draft of the manuscript, redeeming it from a number of errors and infelicities.

For indulging, sometimes encouraging my obsession with Castro in various forms, honorable mention goes to Jeffrey and Jennifer DeLaurentis, Tom Palaia, Rudy Bednar, Daragh Grant, Jack Coleman, Doris Casap, Paul Farmer, Ophelia Dahl, Jorge Pérez Ávila, Jim Sloman, Maria Zuckerman, Thomas LeBien, Bob Mnookin, Dale Mnookin, Julie Dunfey, Anthony DePalma, Tom Miller, Jim Rasenberger, Bruce Schulman, Jim Johnson, Kate Anable, Katelyn Greene, Michael Lavigne, Lisa White, Scott Tromanhauser, Jennifer Shaw, Ann Stack, Lynn Shirey, Suzanna Lansing, Janet Moore, and Karen Lee Wald.

Wendy Strothman, my agent, remained steadfast throughout early incarnations of this project and countless delays. Wendy's wisdom and intuition are rivaled only by her perspective and good cheer, as those lucky to get to work with her know. At Simon & Schuster, Priscilla Painton is patient, persistent, and exacting. As a writer herself, Priscilla knew precisely where and how to needle to make the book accessible to a public audience. Megan Hogan has an eagle eye of her own and was always courteous with her demands and quick with answers to my questions. Philip Metcalf proves that at Simon & Schuster, at least, copyediting is not a lost art. His feat here was heroic. Any remaining errors are my responsibility alone.

Finally, boundless thanks to my wife, Anne, whose love and friendship are essential to this and all my work (and play).

NOTES

ABBREVIATIONS USED IN THE NOTES

FCP   Fidel Castro Papers, Oficina de Asuntos Históricos del Consejo de Estado (Office of Historical Affairs of the Council of State), Havana, Cuba.

FRUS *Foreign Relations of the United States*

NRP   Naty Revuelta Papers. Private Collection.

TSC   Tad Szulc Collection, Cuban Heritage Collection, University of Miami.

INTERVIEWS CONDUCTED BY AUTHOR

Victor Buehlman, Telephone, October 14, 2009.

Maria Dolores Capote, Guisa, Cuba, January 21, 2014.

Enma Castro, Mexico City, August 28–29, 2014.

Christina Cortine León, Birán, Cuba, January 20, 2014

Antonio del Conde ("el Cuate"), Havana, February 28 and March 1, 2014.

Alfredo Duran, Coral Gables, FL, July 11, 2012.

Fermín Flores, Miami Cuba, April 17, 2013.

Juan Gonzáles Castillo, Santo Domingo, Cuba, January 23, 2014.

Barbara Gordon, Georgetown (D.C.), March 5, 2012.

Sergei Khrushchev, Cranston, RI, April 24, 2015.

Alcides La O Zamora, Las Mercedes, Cuba, January, 23, 2014.

Rubén La O Zamora, Las Mercedes, Cuba, January 23, 2014.

Max Lesnik, Coral Gables, FL, July 11, 2012.

Francisca López Civeira, Havana, May 5, 2015.

Marita Lorenz, LaGuardia Airport, NY, February 11, 2015.

Charles Maier, Cambridge, MA, October 18, 2014.

Damián Medina Antolín, Las Mercedes, Cuba, January 23, 2014.

Alcibíades Medina Muñoz, Las Mercedes, Cuba, January 23, 2014.

Alejandro Medina Muñoz, Las Mercedes, Cuba, January 23, 2014.

Eugenio Medina Muñoz, Las Mercedes, Cuba, January 23, 2014.

Rosa Mier, Havana, June 19, 2014.

Leonardo Nieto Cabrales, Buey Arriba, Cuba, January 24, 2014.

Cosme Ordoñez, Havana, June 20, 2014.

Naty Revuelta, Havana, October 29, 2013.

Pedro Pasqual Rodríguez Rodríguez, Birán, Cuba, January 20, 2014.

Israel Rodríguez Serano, Buey Arriba, Cuba, January 24, 2014.

Marta Rojas Rodríguez, Havana, October 30, 2014.

Charles Ryan, Telephone, October 8 and 9, 2009.

Luis Ángel Seguro Castillo, Santo Domingo, Cuba, January 23, 2014.

Wayne Smith, Washington, D.C., March 4, 2013.

Osvaldo Soto, Miami, April 16, 2013.

EPIGRAPH

1 Castro quoted in Tomás Borge, *Un grano de maíz* (La Habana: Oficina de Publicaciones del Consejo de Estado, 1992), pp. 23–24, 26.

PREFACE

1 Castro to Naty Revuelta, April 4 and 15, 1954, Naty Revuelta Papers; hereafter NRP.

2 Castro to Ángel Castro, April 3, 1948, Fidel Castro Papers, Oficina de Asuntos Históricos del Consejo de Estado (Office of Historical Affairs of the Council of State), Havana, Cuba; hereafter FCP.

3   See, for example, José Álvarez, "Cuban Agriculture Before 1959: The Social Situation," and "Cuban Agriculture Before 1959: The Political and Economic Situations," University of Florida, Institute of Food and Agricultural Sciences, 2004.

chapter one - LIKE FATHER

1   Katiuska Blanco Castiñeira, *Ángel, la raíz gallega de Fidel* (La Habana: Casa Editora Abril, 2008), pp. 13–24. The literature on Fidel Castro and his family is at once sparse, contentious, and polemical. Even ordinary birth dates are the source of heated debate. Some writers say Ángel Castro was born the evening of December 4, 1875, some say early the next morning. The morning of December 5 seems a safe bet.

2   This speculative account of Ángel's trip to Madrid is based on James Simpson, *Spanish Agriculture: The Long Siesta, 1765–1965* (Cambridge: Cambridge University Press, 1995), pp. 34–45; Narciso de Gabriel, Introduction, *Leer, escribir y contar: escolarización popular y sociedad en Galicia, 1875–1900* (A Coruña: Ediciós do Castro, 1990); V. Fuster, "Extramarital Reproduction and Infant Mortality in Rural Galicia," *Journal of Human Evolution* 13, no. 5 (July 1984): 457–63; Luisa Muñoz Abeledo, "Women in the Rural and Industrial Labor Force in Nineteenth-Century Spain," *Feminist Economics* 18, no. 4 (2012): 121–44; and Bernadette O'Rourke, "Conflicting Values in Contemporary Galicia," *International Journal of Iberian Studies* 16, no. 1 (March 2003): 33–48.

3   Blanco Castiñeira, *Ángel, la raíz gallega de Fidel*, pp. 43–54.

4   Jone Tone, *War and Genocide in Cuba* (Chapel Hill: University of North Carolina Press, 2008), pp. 40–41; Jesus Cruz, *The Rise of Middle-Class Culture in Nineteenth-Century Spain* (New Orleans: Lousiana State University Press, 2011), chapters 1 and 5.

5   Blanco Castiñeira, *Ángel, la raíz gallega de Fidel*, 53–68.

6   Cruz, *The Rise of Middle-Class Culture in Nineteenth-Century Spain*, pp. 3–10.

7   Ibid., pp. 5–8.

8   Tone, *War and Genocide in Cuba*, p. 106

9   Ibid., p. 103.

10 Ibid, pp. 104–9.

11 Ibid, p. 107.

12 See documents pertaining to Regimento Isabel II, No. 32 from Madrid's Archivo del Servicio Histórico Militar, in Blanco Castiñeira, *Ángel, la raíz gallega de Fidel*, pp. 266–92.

13 Louis A. Pérez, *Cuba Between Empires, 1878–1902* (Pittsburgh: University of Pittsburgh Press, 1998), p. 81.

14 Blanco Castiñeira, *Ángel, la raíz gallega de Fidel*, pp. 99–100.

15 Tone, *War and Genocide in Cuba*, pp. 123–35.

16 Louis A. Pérez, Jr., *Cuba: Between Reform and Revolution* (New York: Oxford University Press, 1995), p. 165.

17 *Wheeling* (West Virginia) *Register*, January 19, 1896, p. 1.

18 See Jonathan M. Hansen, *Guantánamo: An American History* (New York: Hill & Wang, 2011), chapters 1 and 2.

19 *Bismarck* (North Dakota) *Daily Tribune*, December 31, 1897, p. 1.

20 Hugh Thomas, *Cuba, or the Pursuit of Freedom* (New York: Da Capo, 1998), pp. 360–62.

21 Pérez, *Cuba: Between Reform and Revolution*, pp. 176–78; Thomas, *Cuba, or the Pursuit of Freedom*, pp. 372–81.

22 Thomas, *Cuba, or the Pursuit of Freedom*, p. 376.

23 Lars Schoultz, *Beneath the United States: A History of U.S. Policy Toward Latin America* (Cambridge: Harvard University Press, 1998), p. 139.

24 Estrada Palma handed Janney a $2 million Cuban bond (6 percent interest), which discounted in the U.S. was worth half that. See Thomas, *Cuba, or the Pursuit of Freedom*, p. 376; David F. Healy, *The United States in Cuba, 1898–1902: Generals, Politicians, and the Search for Policy* (Madison: University of Wisconsin Press, 1963), pp. 26–27; and John Offner, *An Unwanted War: The Diplomacy of the United States and Spain over Cuba, 1895–1898* (Chapel Hill: University of North Carolina Press, 1992), p. 189.

25 Louis A. Peréz, Jr., *The War of 1898: The United States and Cuba in History and Historiography* (Chapel Hill: University of North Carolina Press, 1998), pp. 39–40; and Peréz, *Cuba: Between Reform and Revolution*, p. 179.

26 Calixto Garcia to William Shafter, July 17, 1898, quoted in Philip S. Foner, *The Spanish-Cuban-American War and the Birth of American Imperialism, 1895–1902*, Vol. II (New York: Monthly Review Press, 1972), pp. 369–70.

27 Alvaro Armero, ed., *Fragmentos del 98: prensa e Información en el año del desastre* (Madrid: Consejería de Educación y Cultura, 1998), p. 156.

28 *El Heraldo de Madrid* (September 2, 1898), in Armero, ed., *Fragmentos del 98*, pp. 161–62.

29 *La Correspondencia Militar* (undated), in ibid., pp. 144–45.

30 Armero, ed., *Fragmentos del 98*, pp. 155–56; Blanco Castiñeira, *Ángel, la raíz gallega de Fidel*, pp. 115–22.

31 Louis A. Pérez, Jr., "Insurrection, Intervention, and the Transformation of Land Tenure Systems in Cuba, 1895–1902," *The Hispanic American Historical Review* 65, no. 2 (May 1985): p. 239.

32 The fullest accout of this migration is Louis A. Pérez, Jr., *On Becoming Cuban: Identity, Nationality, and Culture* (New York: Ecco Press, 1999), chapter 2. See also Robert B. Hoernel, "Sugar and Social Change in Oriente, Cuba, 1898–1946," *Journal of Latin American Studies* 8, no. 2 (November 1976): p. 220; Carmen Diana Deere, "Here Come the Yankees! The Rise and Decline of the United States Colonies in Cuba," *Hispanic American Historical Review* 78, no. 4 (November 1998): pp. 733, 738–39; as well as Louis Pérez, Jr., "Politics, Peasants, and People of Color: The 1912 Race War in Cuba Reconsidered," *Hispanic American Historical Review* 66, no. 3 (August 1986): pp. 509–39.

33 Máximo Gómez, *Diary* (January 1899), available at http://www.historyofcuba.com/history/gomez.htm.

34 Wood to Roosevelt, October 28, 1901, in Leonard Wood Papers, Subject File: Cuba [1898–1902], Library of Congress, Washington, D.C.

35 *Diario de la Marina*, November 28, 1898, p. 1; December 10, 1998, p. 1; December 12, 1998, p. 1.

36 *Diario de la Marina*, November 28, 1998, p. 2.

37 William Jared Clark, *Commercial Cuba: A Handbook for American Business* (New York: Charles Scribner's & Sons, 1898). There were many such books. See also Willis Fletcher Johnson, *The History of Cuba*, Vol. 5 (New York: B. F. Buck, 1900), p. v and passim.

38 Clark, *Commercial Cuba*, p. 38.

39 Ibid., pp. 39–42.

40 Cuba's provincial system dates from 1879, when the Spanish colonial government created six provinces: Pinar del Río, La Habana, Matanzas, Santa Clara, Camagüey, and Oriente. In 1940, Santa Clara became Las Villas. This nomenclature held until 1976, when the six were broken up into thirteen: Pinar del Río, Havana, Matanzas, Cienfuegos, Villa Clara, Sancti Spíritus, Ciego de Ávila, Camagüey, Las Tunas, Granma, Holguín, Santiago de Cuba, and Guantánamo. In 2010, yet

one more division was made, with Artemisa and Mayabeque broken off from La Habana, leaving the current total of fifteen provinces plus the "special municipality" of the Isla de la Juventud (or Isle of Youth, formerly, the Isla de Pinos, or Isle of Pines).

41 Compare Juanita Castro, *Fidel y Raúl, mis hermanos: la historia secreta* (Doral, FL: Aguilar, 2009), p. 42, and Enma Castro interview, Mexico City, August 28–29, 2014.

42 Hoernel, "Sugar and Social Change in Oriente, Cuba," pp. 221–22, 225–29; Deere, "Here Come the Yankees!," pp. 735–38; Pérez, *On Becoming Cuban*, pp. 221–24; Pérez, "Politics, Peasants, and People of Color," pp. 509–12.

43 Hoernel, "Sugar and Social Change in Oriente, Cuba," pp. 229–39.

44 Clark, *Commercial Cuba*, p. 267.

45 *American Sugar Industry and Beet Sugar Gazette*, Vol. 7, p. 365. See also Joshua Henry Nadel, "Processing Modernity: Social and Cultural Adaptation in Eastern Cuba, 1902–1933" (UMI Microform, 2007); Oscar Zanetti and Alejandro Garcia, *United Fruit Company: un caso del dominio imperialista en Cuba* (Havana: Editorial de Ciencias Sociales, 1976); *The American Sugar Industry and Beet Sugar Gazette*, Vol. XI, No. 1 (Chicago, 1909), p. 233; Juan Carlos Santamarina, "The Cuba Company and Eastern Cuba's Economic Development, 1900–1959," in Michael V. Namorato, ed., *Essays in Economic and Business History*, Vol. XIX (Chelsea, MI, 2001), http://www.ebhsoc.org/journal/index.php/journal/article/view/439/287287297.

46 Blanco Castiñeira, *Ángel, la raíz gallega de Fidel*, pp. 130–31.

47 Ibid., pp. 152, 158–59.

48 Juanita Castro, *Fidel y Raúl, mis hermanos*, pp. 43–45.

49 Marco Antonio Ramos, *La Cuba de Castro y despues . . . entre la historia y biografia* (Nashville: Thomas Nelson, 2007), pp. 61–74.

50 Nadel, "Processing Modernity," pp. 51–54.

51 Ramos, *La Cuba de Castro y despues*, pp. 68–69; Juanita Castro, *Fidel y Raúl, mis hermanos*, pp. 59–67; Pedro Pasqual Rodríguez Rodríguez interview, Birán, Cuba, January 20, 2014.

chapter two - MORNINGS ON HORSEBACK

1 Katiuska Blanco Castiñeira, *Fidel Castro Ruz, guerrillero del tiempo: conversaciones con el líder histórico de la Revolución Cubana*, Tomo I (La

Habana: Editora Abril, 2011), p. 71; Fidel Castro and Ignacio Ramonet, *My Life: A Spoken Biography* (New York: Scribner, 2007), p. 44; Frei Betto, *Fidel & Religion: Conversations with Frei Betto on Marxism & Liberation Theology* (Melbourne: Ocean Press, 2006), p. 78.

2 Blanco Castiñeira, *Fidel Castro Ruz*, I, pp. 18–19.

3 Ibid., pp. 15, 18–19, 71–72; Betto, *Fidel & Religion*, p. 87.

4 Betto, *Fidel & Religion*, pp. 116–18; Fidel Castro and Ignacio Ramonet, *My Life*, p. 42; Blanco Castiñeira, *Fidel Castro Ruz*, I, pp. 22–23.

5 Enma Castro interview, Mexico City, August 28–29, 2014.

6 Fidel Castro and Ignacio Ramonet, *My Life*, p. 44.

7 Blanco Castiñeira, *Fidel Castro Ruz*, I, pp. 22–23.

8 Pedro Pasqual Rodríguez Rodríguez interview, Birán, Cuba, January 20, 2014.

9 Luis E. Aguilar, *Cuba 1933: Prologue to Revolution* (Ithaca: Cornell University Press, 1972), p. 228.

10 Jules R. Benjamin, *The United States and the Origins of the Cuban Revolution: An Empire of Liberty in an Age of National Liberation* (Princeton: Princeton University Press, 1990), p. 80.

11 Juan Carlos Santamarina, "The Cuba Company and Eastern Cuba's Economic Development," *Essays in Economic and Business History* (Chelsea, MI: *The Journal of the Economic and Business Historical Society*, Vol. XIX, 2001), pp. 83–85; Carlos Franqui, *Diary of the Cuban Revolution* (New York: Viking, 1976), p. 29; Aguilar, *Cuba 1933*, pp. 49–60; Benjamin, *The United States and the Origins of the Cuban Revolution*, pp. 80–86.

12 Joshua Henry Nadel, "Processing Modernity: Social and Cultural Adaptation in Eastern Cuba, 1902–1933" (UMI Microform, 2007); pp. 275–76, suggests that some Cuban businessmen in the east prided themselves on being generous in their business decisions; Pedro Pasqual Rodríguez Rodríguez interview.

13 Enma Castro interview.

14 Betto, *Fidel & Religion*, p. 79.

15 Blanco Castiñeira, *Fidel Castro Ruz*, I, p. 105.

16 Ibid., pp. 51–59.

17 Pedro Pasqual Rodríguez Rodríguez interview.

18 Betto, *Fidel & Religion*, p. 89; Enma Castro interview.

19 Enma Castro interview. See also Fidel Castro and Ignacio Ramonet, *My Life*, pp. 26–31, 41; and Betto, *Fidel & Religion*, pp. 85–88.

20 Blanco Castiñeira, *Fidel Castro Ruz*, I, pp. 128–30.

21 Rodríguez interview.

22 Patrick Symmes, *The Boys from Dolores: Fidel Castro's Schoolmates from Revolution to Exile* (New York: Random House, 2007), pp. 87–88, 286–88.

23 Marco Antonio Ramos, *La Cuba de Castro y despues . . . entre la historia y biografia* (Nashville: Thomas Nelson, 2007), pp. 68–69; Pedro Pasqual Rodríguez Rodríguez interview; Enma Castro interview; Juanita Castro, *Fidel y Raúl, mis hermanos*, pp. 56–57.

24 Compare Blanco Castiñeira, *Fidel Castro Ruz*, I, p. 55, to Symmes, *The Boys from Dolores*.

25 Pedro Pasqual Rodríguez Rodríguez interview.

26 Rodríguez interview.

27 Fidel Castro and Ignacio Ramonet, *My Life*, p. 31.

28 Ibid., pp. 33–34.

29 Christina Cortine León interview, Birán, Cuba, January 20, 2014; Pedro Pasqual Rodríguez Rodríguez interview; Enma Castro interview; Fidel Castro and Ignacio Ramonet, *My Life*, pp. 30–36.

30 Antonio Iraizoz, *Outline of Education Systems and School Conditions in the Republic of Cuba, 1924* (Havana: Motalvo, Cardenas & Co., 1924), p. 19.

31 Castro to Naty Revuelta, January 1954, NRP.

32 *Problems of the New Cuba: Report of the Commission on Cuban Affairs* (New York: Foreign Policy Association, 1935), pp. 129–39; Fidel Castro and Ignacio Ramonet, *My Life*, pp. 33–34.

33 Esteban Ramírez Alonso, "La primera maestra de Fidel" (interview with Engracia Perrand), p. 3, FCP.

34 Castro to Naty Revuelta, January 1954, NRP.

35 Blanco Castiñeira, *Fidel Castro Ruz*, I, p. 101.

36 "Analysis hecho del Registro de Asistencia de la Escuelita de Birán," December 2, 1985, FCP; Feliú testimony in *Revolución*, February 19, 1960, p. 3.

37 Ramírez Alonso, "La primera maestra de Fidel," p. 3.

38 Ibid.

39 Esteben Ramírez Alonso, "La vez que Juan de la Cruz salvo la Revolución," pp. 2–3, FCP.

40 Ibid.

41 Rodríguez interview.

42   Ibid.

43   Blanco Castiñeira, *Fidel Castro Ruz*, I, pp. 45–51. See also Fidel Castro
     and Ignacio Ramonet, *My Life*, pp. 41–45, 57; Betto, *Fidel & Religion*,
     pp. 78–82.

chapter three - SCHOOL DAYS

1   Esteban Ramírez Alonso, "Viejos compañeros del Colegio Dolores
    hablan de Fidel," pp. 28–30, FCP.

2   Castro to Naty Revuelta, April 11, 1954, NRP.

3   "Analysis hecho del Registro de Asistencia de la Escuelita de Birán,"
    December 2, 1985, FCP; Frei Betto, *Fidel & Religion: Conversations
    with Frei Betto on Marxism & Liberation Theology* (Melbourne: Ocean
    Press, 2006), pp. 85–95; Katiuska Blanco Castiñeira, *Fidel Castro Ruz,
    guerrillero del tiempo: conversaciones con el líder histórico de la Revolución
    Cubana*, Tomo I (La Habana: Editora Abril, 2011), pp. 101–10, 119–
    21, and Fidel Castro and Ignacio Ramonet, *My Life: A Spoken Biogra-
    phy* (New York: Scribner, 2007), pp. 46–59.

4   Fidel Castro and Ignacio Ramonet, *My Life*, pp. 46–53; Blanco
    Castiñeira, I, *Fidel Castro Ruz*, I, pp. 107–10; Betto, *Fidel & Religion*,
    pp. 85–95.

5   Betto, *Fidel & Religion*, p. 85; "Analysis hecho del Registro de Asisten-
    cia de la Escuelita de Biran," December 2, 1985, FCP.

6   Fidel Castro and Ignacio Ramonet, *My Life*, p. 59.

7   Betto, *Fidel & Religion*, pp. 93–98; Fidel Castro and Ignacio Ramonet,
    My Life, pp. 65, 70–75; Blanco Castiñeira, *Fidel Castro Ruz*, I, pp.
    138–45; 150–56.

8   Betto, *Fidel & Religion*, p. 93.

9   Fidel Castro and Ignacio Ramonet, *My Life*, p. 64; "Cronología de la
    vida escolar de Fidel," FCP.

10 Blanco Castiñeira, *Fidel Castro Ruz*, I, pp. 145–154; Fidel Castro and
    Ignacio Ramonet, *My Life*, pp. 70–75; and Betto, *Fidel & Religion*,
    pp. 97–98.

11 Ibid.

12 Ibid.

13 Ibid.

14 Ibid.

15 Ibid.

16 Fidel Castro and Ignacio Ramonet, *My Life*, pp. 75–80; Blanco Castiñeira, *Fidel Castro Ruz*, I, pp. 158–67.

17 Betto, *Fidel & Religion*, p. 118; Blanco Castiñeira, *Fidel Castro Ruz*, I, p. 134; Fidel Castro and Ignacio Ramonet, *My Life*, pp. 76–77.

18 Blanco Castiñeira, *Fidel Castro Ruz*, I, pp. 135–37.

19 Fidel Castro, *My Early Years* (Melbourne: Ocean Press, 20014), pp. 58–59; Carlos Franqui, *Vida, aventuras y desastres de un hombre llamado Castro* (Barcelona: Planeta, 1988), p. 32.

20 Ramírez Alonso, "Viejos compañeros del Colegio Dolores hablan de Fidel," pp. 12–13.

21 Ibid., pp. 13–14.

22 Castro to President Franklin Delano Roosevelt, November 6, 1940, FCP.

23 Blanco Castiñeira, *Fidel Castro Ruz*, I, p. 201; Symmes, *The Boys from Dolores*, pp. 64–66.

24 Ramírez Alonso, "Viejos compañeros del Colegio Dolores hablan de Fidel," pp. 12–13.

25 Ibid., pp. 24–25.

26 Ibid., p. 38.

27 Ibid., p. 40.

28 Interview with José María Patac, *El Comercio*, Gijón (Asturias, Spain), March 13, 1988, pp. 40–41, FCP.

29 Ramírez Alonso, "Viejos compañeros del Colegio Dolores hablan de Fidel," pp. 43–45.

30 Ibid., p. 41.

31 Castro to Revuelta, February 12, 1954, NRP; Ramírez Alonso, "Viejos compañeros del Colegio Dolores hablan de Fidel," p. 42.

32 Castro school reports, FCP.

33 Blanco Castiñeira, *Fidel Castro Ruz*, I, pp. 251–53.

34 Ibid.

35 Ibid.

36 Blanco Castiñeira, *Fidel Castro Ruz*, I, pp. 222–23.

37 See also Symmes, *The Boys from Dolores*, p. 83; Ramírez Alonso, "Viejos compañeros del Colegio Dolores hablan de Fidel," pp. 21–23.

38 Blanco Castiñeira, *Fidel Castro Ruz*, I, p. 225.

39 José Ignacio Rasco interview, Lois J. Botifoll Oral History Project, Cuban Heritage Collection, University of Miami.

40 Blanco Castiñeira, *Fidel Castro Ruz*, I, p. 226.

41 Ignacio Rasco interview, Botifol Oral History Project.

42 Ibid.

43 Ibid.

44 Ibid.

45 José Ignacio Rasco interview, Tad Szulc Collection, Cuban Heritage Collection, University of Miami; hereafter TSC.

46 Betto, *Fidel & Religion*, pp. 113-114. See also Blanco Castiñeira, *Fidel Castro Ruz*, I, pp. 227-231.

47 Betto, *Fidel & Religion*, pp. 109–10; Blanco Castiñeira, *Fidel Castro Ruz*, I, pp. 258–61; Fidel Castro and Ignacio Ramonet, *My Life*, pp. 67–68.

48 "Doble debate científico-pedagógico," *Diario de la Marina*, March 24, 1925; Emeril, "Estupendo Show!," *Hoy*, March 24, 1945; Juan Emilio Friguls, "En Debate de Belén," *Información*, March 24, 1945, p. 12; *Ecos de Belén, 1944–1945* (La Habana: Colegio de Belén), pp. 154–57.

49 Blanco Castiñeira, *Fidel Castro Ruz*, I, pp. 263–63; *Ecos de Belén*.

chapter four - QUIXOTIC (IN THE FINEST SENSE)

1 *Ecos de Belén*, Año VII, Junio 1945, p. 148; *El Mundo*, November 28, 1946, p. 20.

2 Humberto Vázquez García, *La expedición de Cayo Confites* (Santiago de Cuba: Editorial Oriente, 2012), p. 259.

3 Ilan Ehrlich, *Eduardo Chibás: The Incorrigible Man of Cuban Politics* (Lanham, MD: Rowman & Littlefield, 2015), p. 113.

4 *New York Times* journalist Rudy Hart Phillips described the university climate thus: "It is politics first, last and always; studies are merely incidental. They are divided into Rights and Lefts, the Lefts being a little more Communistic and radical than the Rights, although the difference is very little. They stage demonstrations, hold fiery political meetings, plant bombs, call strikes, make demands on the government; in short, meddle in the nation's affairs." R. Hart Phillips, *Cuba: Island of Paradox* (New York: McDowell, Obolensky, 1959), p. 139.

5 Carlos Franqui, *Vida, aventuras y desastres de un hombre llamada Castro* (Barcelona: Planeta, 1988), pp. 40–42; Jules R. Benjamin, *The United States and the Origins of the Cuban Revolution: An Empire of Liberty in an Age of National Liberation* (Princeton: Princeton University Press, 1990), pp. 80–86; 98–99; 104, 109; Hugh Thomas, *Cuba, or the Pursuit of Freedom* (New York: Da Capo, 1998), pp. 809–11.

6 Enrique Ovares interview, TSC. *Times* journalist Phillips confirms the prevalence of arms not just among university students, but among students in general: "From thirteen years upward they all carry revolvers." Phillips, *Cuba*, p. 138.

7 Ovares interview.

8 Alfredo Guevara interview, TSC. Guevara's account of young Castro is confirmed in Fermín Flores interview, Miami, April 17, 2013.

9 Katiuska Blanco Castiñeira, *Fidel Castro Ruz, guerrillero del tiempo: conversaciones con el líder histórico de la Revolución Cubana*, Tomo I (La Habana: Editora Abril, 2011), p. 312.

10 Note dated March 10, 1946, FCP.

11 Blanco Castiñeira, *Fidel Castro Ruz*, I, pp. 269–70, 318–19.

12 Rasco interview, TSC.

13 "Discurso del comandante en Jefe Fidel Castro Ruz," Universidad del Habana, September 4, 1995, http://www.cuba.cu/gobierno/discursos/1995/esp/f040995e.html; on the corruption of Grau and Alemán, see Ehrlich, *Eduardo Chibás*, p. 156.

14 Rasco interview, TSC.

15 Diaz-Ballart quoted in Ann Louise Bardach, *Cuba Confidential* (New York: Vintage, 2003), p. 240. Castro's participation in the incident is confirmed by Pablo Llabre interview of Leonel Gómez, Miami, Florida, December 24, 2017, shared with author, and Szulc, Ovares interview.

16 Francisca López Civiera interview, Havana, May 5, 2015.

17 López Civeira interview; Antonio Rafael de la Cova, *The Moncada Attack: Birth of the Cuban Revolution* (Columbia: University of South Carolina Press, 2007), p. 13; Marco Antonio Ramos, *La Cuba de Castro y despues . . . entre la historia y biografía* (Nashville: Thomas Nelson, 2007), p. 32.

18 *Prensa Libre*, January 12, 1947, pp. 1–8; *Diario de la Marina*, January 17, 1947, p. 3.

19 *Bohemia*, May 4, 1947, p. 40.

20 *Diario de la Marina*, April 24, 1947, p. 12.

21 *El Mundo*, April 29, 1947, p. 24; *Prensa Libre*, April 27, 1947, pp. 1–2, 8.

22 *Carteles*, May 11, 1947, p. 45; *Prensa Libre*, June 5, 1947, p. 1; *Diario de la Marina*, June 6, 1947, p. 12; *El Avance Criollo*, June 6, 1947, pp. 1–16.

23 R. Henry Norweb to Secretary of State, October 17, 1947, Serial 4434, General Records of the Department of State, Record Group 59.3.3, National Archives.

24 Pichirlo would serve as first mate on *Granma*, the boat on which

Castro returned to Cuba to launch the Revolution (see Chapter 10). The best account of Cayo Confites is Vásquez García, *La expedición de Cayo Confites*; see pp. 250–52, 345; Franqui, *Vida, aventuras y desastres de un hombre llamada Castro,* pp. 49–52, 256.

25 "La Dirección Nacional del Comité Cubano por la Liberación de la Republica, Dominica, 1947," FCP.

26 *El Mundo*, November 16, 1946, p. 24.

27 Juanita Castro, *Fidel y Raúl, mis hermanos: la historia secreta* (Doral, FL: Aguilar, 2009), pp. 85–88.

28 Ibid.

29 R. Henry Norweb to Secretary of State, October 17, 1947.

30 Vásquez García, *La expedición de Cayo Confites*, pp. 344–45; Blanco Castiñeira, *Fidel Castro Ruz*, I, pp. 404–11. Franqui, *Vida, aventuras y desastres de un hombre llamada Castro*, pp. 49–50, 257, disputes this account, calling Castro's claim to have swum to shore a myth.

31 R. Henry Norweb to State Department, October 17, 1947.

32 Fidel Castro and Ignacio Ramonet, *My Life: A Spoken Biography* (New York: Scribner, 2007), p. 114; Blanco Castiñeira, *Fidel Castro Ruz*, I, pp. 378–79.

33 Blanco Castiñeira, *Fidel Castro Ruz*, I, pp. 414–15.

34 Evidence for this and the following six paragraphs comes from José Martínez Matos, ed., *Antes del Moncada* (La Habana: Editorial Pablo de la Torriente, 1981), pp. 25–32 ; and "Sobre el Incidente de la Campana de la Demajaua en 1947," FCP.

35 Jesús Soto Acosta, "Cuando Fidel estuvo in Artemisa en 1947," *Juventude Rebelde*, July 26, 1987.

36 Arturo Alape, *El Bogotazo: memorias del Olvido* (Bogotá: Planeta, 1983), pp. 193–203.

37 Ibid., p. 168; Roland Bonachea and Nelson P. Valdes, eds., *Revolutionary Struggle: Selected Works of Fidel Castro* (Cambridge: The MIT Press, 1974), pp. 24–25.

38 Alape, *El Bogotazo*, pp. 168–69; Ovares interview, TSC; De la Cova, *The Moncada Attack*, pp. 18–19.

39 "Conferencia de prensa de Fidel Castro," *Diario de la Marina*, February 26, 1948, p. 25, in Bonachea and Valdes, eds., *Revolutionary Struggle*, p. 133; Blanco Castiñeira, *Fidel Castro Ruz*, I, pp. 388–89.

40 "Primeros pasos del movimiento latinoamericano," *Bohemia*, March 17, 1957, pp. 62–63.

41 Castro to Ángel Castro, April 3, 1948, FCP.

42   "Discurso dirigido al pueblo panameño," March 30, 1948, FCP.

43   Testimony of Álvaro Menéndez Franco, in Eugenio Suárez Pérez and Acela A. Caner Román, *Fidel Castro: Birán to Cinco Palmas* (La Habana: Editorial José Martí, 2002), p. 62. See also "Declaración de Fidel Castro sobre el Congreso Estudiantil de Bogotá," March 30, 1948, Panama, FCP.

44   To Ángel Castro, April 3, 1948.

45   Ibid.

46   Alape, *El Bogotazo*, p. 196.

47   Ibid., p. 172; Ovares interview, TSC; Alfredo Guevara interview, TSC; Blanco Castiñeira, *Fidel Castro Ruz*, I, pp. 441–42.

48   Alape, *El Bogotazo*, p. 173.

49   Blanco Castiñeira, *Fidel Castro Ruz*, I, pp. 445–448, 452–473; Fidel Castro and Ignacio Ramonet, *My Life*, pp. 98–99.

50   Guevara quoted in López Civeira interview.

chapter five - SALAD DAYS

1   Max Lesnik interview, Salim Lamrani, Conversations with Max Lesnik (courtesy of Salim Lamrani).

2   Ilan Ehrlich, *Eduardo Chibás: The Incorrigible Man of Cuban Politics* (New York: Rowman & Littlefield, 2015), pp. 11–12, 17–20.

3   Max Lesnik interview, TSC.

4   Ibid.

5   Lesnik Interview, TSC. In fact, MSR had decided to eliminate Castro and Justo Fuentes long before Castro made this speech, according to a statement by MSR member Rubén Hernández in *Bohemia*, November 13, 1949, pp. 78–79.

6   Juanita Castro, *Fidel y Raúl, mis hermanos: la historia secreta* (Doral, FL: Aguilar, 2009), pp. 87–88.

7   Ibid., p. 88.

8   Jack Skelly, *I Remember Cuba: Growing Up American-Cuban, A Memoir of a Town Called Banes* (Morgan Hill, CA: Bookstand, 2006), p. 19.

9   Wedding invitation, FCP.

10   Juanita Castro, *Fidel y Raúl, Mis Hermanos*, pp. 89–90.

11   Blanco Castiñeira, *Fidel Castro Ruz*, I, p. 519; Franqui, *Vida, aventuras y desastres de un hombre llamado Castro*, p. 48.

12   Franqui, *Vida, aventuras y desastres de un hombre llamado Castro*, p. 49.

13 *Problems of the New Cuba: Report of the Commission on Cuban Affairs* (New York: Foreign Policy Association Incorporated, 1935), p. 131.

14 Blanco Castiñeira, *Fidel Castro Ruz*, I, pp. 519–20.

15 Juanita Castro, *Fidel y Raúl, mis hermanos*, p. 92; Lesnik interview, Lamrani; Lesnik interview, TSC.

16 Barbara Gordon interview, Georgetown (D.C.), March 5, 2012; Skelly, *I Remember Cuba*, pp. 151–52.

17 Skelly, *I Remember Cuba*, pp. 151–59.

18 Juanita Castro, *Fidel y Raúl, mis hermanos*, p. 92.

19 Ibid., p. 93.

20 Ibid., p. 98.

21 Ibid., p. 93.

22 Ibid., p. 100; Enma Castro interview.

23 Castro's complete university file can be found in FCP.

24 Castro to Naty Revuelta, December 13, 1954, NRP.

25 Juanita Castro, *Fidel y Raúl, mis hermanos*, pp. 94–95. This account is confirmed in Blanco Castiñeira, *Fidel Castro Ruz*, I, p. 534, and Jorge Aspiazo interview, File No. 1280, FCP.

26 Aspiazo interview, FCP.

27 See Aldo Isidrón del Valle, "Patriotico ¡Yo Acuso! de Fidel Castro," ed., *Antes del Moncada* (La Habana: Editorial Pablo de al Torriente, 1986), pp. 143–164.

28 Pérez Leiva quoted Isidrón del Valle, "Patriotico ¡Yo Acuso! de Fidel Castro," pp. 151.

29 Ibid., pp. 149–53.

30 Ibid, pp. 155–56.

31 Fidel Castro, "To the People of Cienfuegos," *La Correspondencia*, November 15, 1950, FCP.

32 Ibid.

33 Ibid.

34 Isidrón del Valle, "Patriotico ¡Yo Acuso! de Fidel Castro," pp. 158–60; Suárez Pérez and Caner Román, *Fidel Castro*, pp. 120–23.

35 Benavides quoted in Isidrón del Valle, "Patriotico ¡Yo Acuso! de Fidel Castro," p. 163.

36 Blanco Castiñeira, *Fidel Castro Ruz*, I, pp. 540–41.

37 Suárez Pérez and Caner Román, *Fidel Castro*, pp. 86–87; Acta de la Asamblea Nacional del Partido del Pueblo Cubano (Ortodoxo), 28 de enero de 1950, FCP.

38 Suárez Pérez and Caner Román, *Fidel Castro*, pp. 87–88.

39 Ibid., pp. 112; 120–23; Matos, ed., *Antes del Moncada*, pp. 140–42.

40 Undated flyer in FCP (1951–1953), pp. 6–8, FCP.

41 Note card, February 23, 1952, FCP.

42 Lesnik interview, TSC.

43 *Alerta*, August 18, 1951, p. 2.

44 Published vow by the leaders of the Partido del Pueblo Cubano (Ortodoxos), August 17, 1951, FCP. The warning is repeated in Fidel Castro, "Porristas and Lamebotas," September 21, 1951, FCP.

45 Lesnik interview, TSC.

46 Juanita Castro, *Fidel y Raúl, mis hermanos*, p. 101.

47 Enma Castro interview; Juanita Castro, *Fidel y Raúl, mis hermanos*, pp. 99.

48 Juanita Castro, *Fidel y Raúl, mis hermanos*, p. 100.

chapter six - WE FINALLY HAVE A LEADER

1 Marta Rojas Rodríguez interview, Havana, October 30, 2014.

2 Jorge I. Domínguez, *Cuba: Order and Revolution* (Cambridge: Harvard University Press, 1978), p. 113; Louis A. Pérez, *Army Politics in Cuba, 1898–1958* (Pittsburgh: University of Pittsburgh Press, 1976), pp. 126–28.

3 In 1950, the New York Stock Exchange was formally known as the New York Curb Exchange. See https://en.wikipedia.org/wiki/NYSE_MKT.

4 *Report on CUBA. Findings and Recommendations of an Economic and Technical Mission* organized by the International Bank for Reconstruction and Development in collaboration with the Government of Cuba. Francis Adams Truslow Chief of Mission (New York: World Bank, 1950); hereafter Truslow Report. See also *Problems of the New Cuba: Report of the Commission on Cuba Affairs* (New York: Foreign Policy Association, 1935).

5 Truslow Report, p. 442.

6 Ibid., p. 441.

7 Ibid., p. 127.

8 Ibid., p. 13.

9 R. Hart Phillips, *Cuba: Island of Paradox* (New York: McDowell, Obolensky, 1959), p. 259.

10 Carlos Franqui, *Vida, aventuras y desastres de un hombre llamado Castro* (Barcelona: Planeta, 1988), p. 41.

11 Carlos Franqui, *Diary of the Cuban Revolution* (New York: Viking Press, 1980), p. 43.

12 Ibid., p. 44.

13 Rosa Mier interview, Havana, June 19, 2014.

14 Lionel Martin, *The Early Fidel: Roots of Castro's Communism* (Fort Lee, NJ: Lyle Stuart, 1978), p. 84.

15 "Revolución, no, zarpazo!," *El Acusador*, March 13, 1952, FCP.

16 Eugenio Suárez Pérez and Acela A. Caner Román, *Fidel Castro: Birán to Cinco Palmas* (La Habana: Editorial José Martí, 2002), pp. 132–34.

17 Many authors suggest that Castro filed suit against Batista simultaneously at the Court of Constitutional Guarantees and at the Court of Appeals (Tribunal de Urgencia) on March 24, 1952. This is not the case. See FCP (1951–1953), pp. 48–54. Eduardo Suárez Rivas and Pelayo Cuervo Navarro filed suit against Batista at the Court of Constitutional Guarantees, to no avail.

18 Mier interview.

19 This story is recounted with testimony by participants in Santiago Cardosa Arias, "Presencia de Fidel en la Finca Acana, Matanzas," in Matos, ed., *Antes del Moncada*, pp. 165–83.

20 Ibid., pp. 180–83.

21 Ibid., pp. 176–78; 180–83.

22 Franqui, *Vida, aventuras y desastres de un hombre llamado Castro*, pp. 75–79; Suárez Pérez and Caner Román, *Fidel Castro*, p. 144; de la Cova, *The Moncada Attack*, p. 35.

23 Fidel Castro and Ignacio Ramonet, *My Life: A Spoken Biography* (New York: Scribner, 2007), p. 113.

24 "Refuta Pardo Llada a la Juventud Progresista Asegura también que el gobierno está preparando 'nueveas provocaciones,'" *El Mundo*, February 17, 1953, FCP.

25 *El Avance Criollo*, February 14, 1953; *Prensa Libre*, February 15, 1953; Carmen Castro Porta, *La lección del maestro* (La Habana: Oficina de Publicaciones del Consejo de Estado, 2010), p. 74; *El Avance Criollos*, February 17, 1953; *Informacion*, February 18, 1953.

26 Fidel Castro and Ignacio Ramonet, *My Life*, p. 106.

27 Suárez Pérez and Caner Román, *Fidel Castro*, p. 171; de la Cova, *The Moncada Attack*, p. 46.

28 Katiuska Blanco Castiñeira, *Fidel Castro Ruz, Guerrillero del Tiempo: Conversaciones con el líder histórico de al Revolución Cubana*, Tomo II (La Habana: Casa Editora Abril, 2011), pp. 133–35. Castro provides a similar account in Fidel Castro and Ignacio Ramonet, *My Life*, pp. 104–5.

29 De la Cova, *The Moncada Attack*, p. 44.

30 Jules Dubois, *Fidel Castro: Rebel-Liberator or Dictator?* (Indianapolis: Bobbs-Merrill, 1959), pp. 29–30.

31 De la Cova, *The Moncada Attack*, 56–57.

32 Fidel Castro and Ignacio Ramonet, *My Life*, pp. 119–20.

33 Gisela Gallo, ed., *Moncada: antecedentes and preparativos* (La Habana: Editorial Política, 1980), pp. 161–64.

34 Castro quoted in Marta Rojas, *El juicio del Moncada* (La Habana: Editorial de Ciencias Sociales, 2012), p. 32. See also Blanco Castiñeira, *Fidel Castro Ruz,* II, pp. 152–53.

35 Fidel Castro and Ignacio Ramonet, *My Life*, p. 122.

36 Blanco Castiñeira, *Fidel Castro Ruz*, II, p. 153.

37 Suárez Pérez and Caner Román, *Fidel Castro*, 168.

38 Juanita Castro, *Fidel y Raúl, mis hermanos*, pp. 107–8.

39 *Hoy,* June 9, 1953, pp. 1, 8. Raúl's Castro's swing through the communist bloc may be most notable for the company he kept aboard the vessel *Andrea Gritti* on his way home to Cuba. This included Nikolai Leonov, a young Soviet foreign officer headed for a posting in Mexico. The two young men hit it off on the ship. They later reunited in Mexico, where their conversations included Che Guevara. Leonov accompanied Anastas Mikoyan, deputy chairman of the Council of Ministers, on his trip to Mexico, the United States, and Cuba in late 1959–early 1960, where the Soviets eventually struck a deal with Castro to buy sugar in exchange for Cuba purchasing crude oil. Sergei Khrushchev interview, Cranson, RI, April 24, 2015. Leonov's acquaintance with Raúl Castro is recounted in Sergeevitch N. S. Leonov, *Licholetye* (Moscow: Terra Publishing, 1997). For an interesting account of Nikita Khrushchev's awakening interest in Castro and Cuba, see Sergei N. Khrushchev, *Nikita Khrushchev and the Creation of a Superpower* (University Park: Pennsylvania State University Press, 2003), pp. 405–11, 429–37.

40 De la Cova, *The Moncada Attack*, p. 56.

41 Juanita Castro, *Fidel y Raúl, mis hermanos*, p. 116.

42 Naty Revuelta interview, Havana, October 30, 2013.

43 De la Cova, *The Moncada Attack*, p. 72.

44 Suárez Pérez and Caner Román, *Fidel Castro*, p. 188.

45 Fidel Castro and Ignacio Ramonet, *My Life*, p. 168.

46 Suárez Pérez and Caner Román, *Fidel Castro*, pp. 189–90.

47   Ibid.

48   De la Cova, *The Moncada Attack*, pp. xxi, 81.

49   Ibid., p. 100.

50   Ibid., pp. 109, 154.

51   Ibid., p. 156.

52   Ibid., p. 177.

53   Fidel Castro and Ignacio Ramonet, *My Life*, pp. 162–65.

54   Ibid., p. 165.

55   Rosa Mier interview.

chapter seven - GOD AND THE DEVIL

1   Juanita Castro, *Fidel y Raúl, mis hermanos: la historia secreta* (Doral, FL: Aguilar, 2009), p. 108; Enma Castro interview.

2   Juanita Castro, *Fidel y Raúl, mis hermanos*, p. 109; Fidel Castro and Ignacio Ramonet, *My Life: A Spoken Biography* (New York: Scribner, 2007), p. 125.

3   Juanita Castro, *Fidel y Raúl, mis hermanos*, pp. 109–10.

4   Ibid., pp. 112–13.

5   Ibid., pp. 113–14.

6   Ibid., p. 114.

7   Eugenio Suárez Pérez and Acela A. Caner Román, *Fidel Castro: Birán to Cinco Palmas* (La Habana: Editorial José Martí, 2002), pp. 199–201.

8   Suárez Pérez and Caner Román, *Fidel Castro*, p. 201; Antonio Rafael de la Cova, *The Moncada Attack: Birth of the Cuban Revolution* (Columbia: University of South Carolina Press, 2007), pp. 192–93.

9   De la Cova, *The Moncada Attack*, p. 198.

10   Ibid. Casero's account of Castro grew more critical over time after he moved from Cuba to Miami. Compare what he told author de la Cova, in *The Moncada Attack*, to what he told a U.S. consul at Santiago de Cuba originally reported; Arthur W. Feldman to Harold M. Randall, October 5, 1953, *Confidential U.S. State Department Central Files. Cuba: Internal Affairs and Foreign Affairs, 1945–1954* (Frederick, MD: University Publications of America, 1986).

11   Fidel Castro and Ignacio Ramonet, *My Life*, p. 107.

12   Carlos Franqui, *Diary of the Cuban Revolution* (New York: Viking, 1976), 65; Castro to Ramón Castro Ruz, September 17, 1953, FCP.

13   Castro to Mirta Díaz-Balart, August 18, 1953, FCP.

14 Authors disagree about the exact number of soldiers and even defendants present that day. Compare de la Cova, *The Moncada Attack*, pp. 203–4, and Jules Dubois, *Fidel Castro: Rebel-Liberator or Dictator?* (Indianapolis: Bobbs-Merrill, 1959), pp. 40–41.

15 De la Cova, *The Moncada Attack*, pp. 204–5. Some accounts have Castro at the tail of the procession.

16 Marta Rojas, *El juicio del Moncada* (La Habana: Editorial de Ciencias Sociales, 2012), pp. 9–12.

17 Ibid., pp. 54–55.

18 Ibid., pp. 73–74.

19 Ibid., pp. 119–20.

20 Ibid., pp. 129–30.

21 Ibid., p. 201.

22 Ibid., pp. 232–33.

23 Ibid., pp. 245–46.

24 Ibid., pp. 249–50.

25 Ibid., p. 259.

26 Fidel Castro, *History Will Absolve Me* (Secaucus, NJ: Lyle Stuart, 1984), p. 118.

27 Ibid., pp. 115, 117–18.

chapter eight - THE GREAT BOOKS

1 Naty Revuelta interview, Havana, October 30, 2013; José Bell Lara et al., eds., *Cuba: la generación revolucionaria, 1952–1961* (La Habana: Editorial Félix Varela, 2012), pp. 62–63.

2 Naty Revuelta interview.

3 Ibid. For a slightly different account of Castro's and Revuelta's initial encounter and subsequent relationship, see Alina Fernández, *Castro's Daughter: An Exile's Memoir of Cuba* (New York: St. Martin's Griffin, 1999), pp. 60–71. For more on Revuelta, see Carmen Castro Porta, *La lección del maestro* (La Habana: Oficina de Publicaciones del Consejo de Estado, 2010), pp. 123–28.

4 Revuelta quoted in Fernández, *Castro's Daughter*, p. 66.

5 Castro to Naty Revuelta, November 7, 1953, NRP.

6 Castro to Revuelta, December 22, 1953, NRP.

7 Ibid. For a detailed account of the rebels' time in prison, see Mario Mencía, *Time Was on Our Side* (La Habana: Editora Política, 1982).

8 Mario Mencía, *Fertile Prison: Fidel Castro in Batista's Prisons* (Melbourne: Ocean Press, 1992), p. 39.

9 Ibid., p. 36.

10 Castro to Revuelta, December 22, 1953, NRP.

11 Mencía, *Fertile Prison*, pp. 32–33.

12 Castro to Luis Conte Agüero, December 12, 1953, FCP; this letter also appears in Luis Conte Agüero, *The Prison Letters of Fidel Castro* (New York: Nation Books, 2007), p. 1.

13 Castro to Revuelta, December 22, 1953, NRP.

14 Photocopies of Castro's annotated copy of Marx's *Capital* in FCP (1951–1953), pp. 162–77.

15 Ibid. The quote from Marx comes from *Capital*, Volume I, Book I, Chapter 10, "The Working Day."

16 Castro to Revuelta, January 28, 1954, NRP.

17 Castro to Revuela, March 18, 1954, NRP.

18 Ibid.

19 Ibid.

20 Suárez Pérez and Caner Román, *Fidel Castro*, pp. 218–19.

21 Castro to Revuelta, March 24, 1954, NRP.

22 Jenni Maria Lehtinen, *Narrative and National Allegory in Rómulo Gallegos's Venezuela* (Cambridge, UK: Modern Humanities Research Association, 2013), pp. 120, 156–57.

23 Castro to Revuelta, March 1, 1954, NRP.

24 Ibid.

25 Revuelta to Castro, March 5, 1954, NRP. On the Martínez-Solís debate, see *Diario de la Marina*, February 19, 1954, p. 4.

26 Castro to Revuelta, March 8, 1954, NRP.

27 Ibid.

28 Ibid.

29 Ibid.

30 Castro to Revuelta, April 4, 1954, NRP.

chapter nine - TRUE LOVE

1 Castro to Melba Hernández, April 17, 1954, FCP.

2 Ibid.

3 Ibid.

4 Castro to Naty Revuelta, May 3, 1954, NRP.

5 Revuelta to Castro, May 3 and 5, 1954, NRP.

6 Revuelta to Castro, May 6, 1954, NRP.

7 Castro to Mirta Díaz-Balart, May 12, 1954, FCP.

8 Castro to Revuelta, late June 1954 [incomplete], NRP; also in Carlos Franqui, *Diary of the Cuban Revolution* (New York:Viking, 1976), p. 78.

9 Ibid.

10 Castro to Luis Conte Agüero, June 12, 1954, FCP; also in Luis Conte Agüero, *The Prison Letters of Fidel Castro* (New York: Nation Books, 2007), pp. 18–22.

11 Castro to Luis Conte Agüero, June 19, 1954, FCP; also in Conte, *The Prison Letters of Fidel Castro*, pp. 22–28.

12 Mario Mencía, *Fertile Prison: Fidel Castro in Batista's Prisons* (Melbourne: Ocean Press, 1992), p. 138.

13 Castro to Melba Hernández and Haydée Santamaría, June 18 and 19, 1954, FCP.

14 Melba Hernández to Castro, August 1, 1954, FCP.

15 *Bohemia*, July 11, 1954, pp. 60–63, 82.

16 On U.S. policy and activity in Guatemala, see Tim Weiner, *Legacy of Ashes: The History of the CIA* (New York: Doubleday, 2007), pp. 93–104; Stephen Kinzer, *The Brothers: John Foster Dulles, Allen Dulles, and Their Secret World War* (New York:Times Books, 2013), chapter 6; Lars Schoutz, *Beneath the United States: A History of U.S. Policy Towards Latin America* (Cambridge: Harvard University Press, 1998), chapter 17; and Campbell Craig and Fredrik Longevall, *America's Cold War: The Politics of Insecurity* (Cambridge: Belknap Press, 2009), pp. 153–57.

17 Castro to Mirta Diaz-Balart, July 17, 1954, FCP.

18 Castro to Luis Conte Agüero, July 17, 1954, FCP.

19 Castro to Luis Conte Agüero, August 14, 1954, FCP.

20 Ibid.

21 Castro to Lidia Castro, October 25, 1954, FCP.

22 Mencía, *Fertile Prison*, pp. 154–55; Eugenio Suárez Pérez and Acela A. Caner Román, *Fidel Castro: Birán to Cinco Palmas* (La Habana: Editorial José Martí, 2002), pp. 238–39.

23 Mencía, *Fertile Prison*, pp. 143–44.

24 Ibid., p. 158.

25 Ibid., p. 165.

26 Castro to Lidia Castro, November 29, 1954, FCP.

27 Castro to Lidia Castro, December 8, 1954, FCP.

28 Castro to Revuelta, December 23, 1954, NRP.

29 Ibid.

30 Revuelta to Castro, December 30, 1954, NRP.

31 Mencía, *Fertile Prison*, pp. 166–67.

32 Castro to Lidia Castro, March 13, 1955, FCP; Echeverría quoted in *Bohemia*, March 27, 1955, pp. 59, 61–97; *Diario Nacional* quoted in Mencía, *Fertile Prison*, pp. 174–75.

33 Castro to Luis Conte Agüero, March 19, 1955, FCP, published in *Bohemia*, March 27, 1955, pp. 63–94.

34 Castro to Lidia Castro, May 2, 1955, FCP.

35 *El Crisol*, May 16, 1955, pp. 1–8.

36 Juanita Castro, *Fidel y Raúl, mis hermanos: la historia secreta* (Doral, FL: Aguilar, 2009), pp. 124–25.

37 "Pateticas escenas en la Isla de Pinos," *La Calle*, May 17, 1955, pp. 1–7; "Libertados todos los presos políticos," *Prensa Libre*, May 17, 1955, pp. 1–13.

38 "Del Moncada al presidio y a la libertad," *La Calle* May 16, 1955, pp. 1–7.

39 Juanita Castro, *Fidel y Raúl, mis hermanos*, pp. 124–25.

40 *Diario de la Marina*, May 18, 1955, p. 1.

41 Ibid.

42 See, for example, ibid; and *Bohemia*, May 15, 1955, pp. 1, 4.

43 Castro to Revuelta, January 19, 1954, in NRP.

44 "Mientes, Chaviano!" *Bohemia*, May 29, 1955, pp. 95–96.

45 "No debe aprovecharse este momento para exciter el odio, sino para consolidar la paz, dice el PPC," *Prensa Libre*, May 31, 1955, pp. 1–12.

46 "Quieren mi cabeza los hombres de Batista," *La Calle*, June 4, 1955, pp. 1–8.

47 Batista's remarks at the June 5 event are quoted in "Manos asesinas," *La Calle*, June 7, 1955, p. 3, published in Roland Bonachea and Nelson P. Valdés, eds., *Revolutionary Struggle: Select Works of Fidel Castro* (Cambridge: MIT Press, 1974), p. 250.

48 "Estúpidos!" *La Calle*, June 9, 1955, pp. 1–6.

49 "Frente al terror y frente el crimen," *La Calle*, June 11, 1955, p. 3.

50 Fidel Castro, "La censura radial," *La Calle*, June 15, 1955, pp. 1–6.

51 "Al Tribunal de Urgencia de la Habana," June 17, 1955, FCP.

52 "Aquí ya no se puede vivir," *La Calle*, June 17, 1955, p. 1.

53 Armando Hart, *Aldabonazo: Inside the Cuban Revolutionary Underground, 1952–1958* (New York: Pathfinder, 2004), pp. 94–95; Katiuska

Blanco Castiñeira, *Fidel Castro Ruz, Guerrillero del Tiempo: Conversaciones con el líder histórico de al Revolución Cubana*, Tomo II (La Habana: Casa Editora Abril, 2011), pp. 333–34; 441.

54 "Declaraciones a la prensa del Fidel Castro Ruz," July 7, 1955, FCP.

55 Juanita Castro, *Fidel y Raúl, mis hermanos*, pp. 129–30.

56 Naty Revuelta interview.

chapter ten - EXILE

1 Antonio del Conde interview, Havana, Feburary 28 and March 1, 2014. See also Antonio del Conde, *Memorias del dueño del Yate Granma* (Mexico City: Grupo de Amistad con Cuba LXII Legislatura Cámara de Diputados, 2013); and Otto Hernández Garcini, *Huellas del exilio: Fidel en México, 1955–1956* (La Habana: Casa Editora Abril, 2004).

2 Hernández, *Huellas del exilio*, pp. 53–54.

3 Juanita Castro, *Fidel y Raúl, mis hermanos: la historia secreta* (Doral, FL: Aguilar, 2009), pp. 132–33.

4 Armando Hart, *Aldabonazo: Inside the Cuban Revolutionary Underground, 1952–1958* (New York: Pathfinder, 2004), pp. 82–89.

5 Castro to Faustino Pérez, July 14, 1955, FCP.

6 "Declaration to be read at commemoration of July 26," July 26, 1955, FCP; Eugenio Suárez Pérez and Acela A. Caner Román, *Fidel Castro: Birán to Cinco Palmas* (La Habana: Editorial José Martí, 2002), p. 270.

7 "Informe del Agregado Naval a la embajada de Cuba en México, Julio 29 de 1955," in Martha Verónica Álvarez Mola and Sergio Ravelo López, eds., *La Expedición Granma: selección de documentos* (La Habana: Editora Política, 2007), p. 20.

8 "A Los Compañeros de la Dirección," August 2, 1955, FCP.

9 Castro to Melba Hernández, July 24, 1955, FCP.

10 Hernández, *Huellas del exilio*, pp. 65–73.

11 Castro to Melba Hernández, August 10, 1955, FCP.

12 "Manifesto No. 1 del 26 de Julio a Pueblo de Cuba," August 8, 1955, FCP.

13 Castro to Melba Hernández, August 10, 12, and 27, 1955, FCP.

14 "Mensaje al Congreso de Militantes Ortodoxos," August 16, 1955, FCP; Hart, *Aldabonazo*, pp. 102–3; Roland Bonachea and Nelson P. Valdes, eds., *Revolutionary Struggle: Selected Works of Fidel Castro* (Cambridge: The MIT Press, 1974), pp. 68–69.

15   Simon Reid-Henry, *Fidel and Che: A Revolutionary Friendship* (Cleveland: Scepter Press, 2009), p. 118.

16   Ernesto Che Guevara, *Reminiscences of the Cuban Revolutionary War* (New York: Ocean Press, 2005), p. 10.

17   Jon Lee Anderson, *Che Guevara: A Revolutionary Life* (New York: Ocean Press), p. 172.

18   Ibid., p. 171.

19   Marvin D. Resnick, *The Black Beret: The Life and Meaning of Che Guevara* (CreateSpace Independent Publishing, 2011), p. 44.

20   Anderson, *Che Guevara*, pp. 167–81; Reid-Henry, *Fidel and Che*, pp. 116–31; Resnick, *The Black Beret*, pp. 38–49.

21   Castro to Melba Hernández, August 27, 1955, FCP; Naty Revuelta interview.

22   Carmen Castro Porta, *La lección del maestro* (La Habana: Oficina de Publicaciones del Consejo de Estado, 2010), pp. 102–4.

23   Castro to Moisés Crespo, January 2, 1956, FCP.

24   Castro to Melba Hernández, October 4, 1955, FCP.

25   Vincente Caballas Jr., "Mitin Oposicionista en New York," *Bohemia*, November 6, 1955, FCP.

26   "Discurso pronunicado por el Doctor Fidel Castro Ruz en el Salon Palm Garden, en New York," October 30, 1955, FCP.

27   *Bohemia*, November 6, 1955, FCP.

28   "Discurso pronunicado por el Doctor Fidel Castro Ruz en el Salon Palm Garden, en New York."

29   "A los compañeros de la Dirección del M.R. 26 de Julio," November 1955, FCP; *Bohemia*, December 4, 1955, pp. 78–80. The *Miami Herald* coverage was picked up by *Prensa Libre*, November 16, 1955, p. 426.

30   Carlos Franqui, *Diary of the Cuban Revolution* (New York: Viking, 1976), pp. 98–99; Hart, *Aldobonazo*, pp. 109–10; Bonachea and Valdes, eds., *Revolutionary Struggle*, pp. 72–73.

31   "Reglamento Interior de Conducta Para Cada Casa de Residencia," Hernández, *Huellas del exilio*, pp. 153–56.

32   Katiuska Blanco Castiñeira, *Fidel Castro Ruz, Guerrillero del Tiempo: Conversaciones con el líder histórico de al Revolución Cubana*, Tomo II (La Habana: Casa Editora Abril, 2011), pp. 371–76; Hernández, *Huellas del exilio*, 142–43.

33   Hernández, *Huellas del exilio*, p. 150; Heberto Norman Acosta, *La*

palabra empeñada, Tomo II (La Habana: Oficina de Publicaciones del Consejo de Estado, 2005), pp. 22–24.

34   Acosta, *La palabra empeñada,* II, p. 39; Hernández, *Huellas del exilio,* p. 151.

35   Acosta, *La palabra empeñada,* II, pp. 12–13.

36   Blanco Castiñeira, *Fidel Castro Ruz,* II, pp. 363–65.

37   "La condenación que se nos pide," *Bohemia,* March 11, 1956, pp. 59, 69, translated in Bonachea and Valdes, eds., *Revolutionary Struggle,* pp. 309–10; "El Movimiento 16 de Julio," *Bohemia,* April 1, 1956, pp. 54, 70–71, translated in ibid, 310–19.

38   Lucas Morán Arce, *La Revolución Cubana: Una version rebelde* (Ponce, Puerto Rico: Imprenta Universitaria, 1980), pp. 35–37.

39   Hart, *Aldabonazo,* 114; Marco Antonio Ramos, *La Cuba de Castro y despues . . . entre la historia y biografia* (Nashville: Thomas Nelson, 2007), p. 210; Bonacha and Valdés, eds., *Revolutionary Struggle,* p. 78.

40   Morán Arce, *La Revolución Cubana,* pp. 47–48; Ramón L. Bonachea and Marta San Martín, *The Cuban Insurrection, 1952–1959* (New Brunswick, NJ: Transaction, 1995), pp. 77–78; Hart, *Aldabonazo,* pp. 111–12.

41   Electo Pedrosa's account is captured in Acosta, *La palabra empeñada,* II, pp. 62–63.

42   Ibid.

43   Jorge G. Castañeda, *The Life and Death of Che Guevara* (New York: Vintage, 1997), pp. 89–90.

44   Martha Verónica Álvarez Mola y Sergio Ravelo López, eds., *La Expedición Granma: Selección de documentos* (La Habana: Editora Política, 2007), pp. 9–11; Blanco Castiñeira, *Fidel Castro Ruz,* II, pp. 367–85.

45   Acosta, *La palabra empeñada,* 2, pp. 99–100; Hernández, *Huellas del exilio,* pp. 181–83.

46   "Exilados, cambio de política?," *Bohemia,* July 1, 1956, pp. 61–62, in Bonachea and Valdes, eds., *Revolutionary Struggle,* p. 319.

47   Acosta, *La palabra empeñada,* 2, pp. 106–9; "Basta ya de mentiras!," *Bohemia,* July 15, 1956, pp. 63, 84–85, FCP.

48   Acosta, *La palabra empeñada,* II, pp. 106–9.

49   Teresa Casuso, *Cuba and Castro* (New York: Random House, 1961), pp. 92–100. Casuso was hardly the only woman to testify to Castro's sex appeal at this time. See Marita Lorenz interview, LaGuardia Airport, NY, February 11, 2015.

50 Casuso, *Cuba and Castro*, pp. 102–4, 164.

51 Acosta, *La palabra empeñada*, II, pp. 196–97; Hart, *Aldabonazo*, pp. 131–34; Anderson, *Che Guevara*, pp. 192–93; Blanco Castiñeira, *Fidel Castro Ruz*, II, 391–94; Hernández, *Huellas del exilio*, pp. 197–98.

52 Castro to María Antonia Figueroa, August 8, 1956, FCP; Morán Arce, *La Revolución Cubana*, p. 48; Hernández, *Huellas del exilio*, p. 215; Acosta, *La palabra empeñada*, II, pp. 230–33.

53 Franqui, *Diary of the Cuban Revolution*, pp. 106–7; Acosta, *La palabra empeñada*, II, p. 256.

54 Acosta, *La palabra empeñada*, II, pp. 273–74.

55 Suárez Pérez and Caner Román, *Fidel Castro*, pp. 288–89.

56 Blanco Castiñeira, *Fidel Castro Ruz*, II, p. 402.

57 Franqui, *Diary of the Cuban Revolution*, pp. 104–5; Blanco Castiñeira, *Fidel Castro Ruz*, II, 402–3.

58 Blanco Castiñeira, *Fidel Castro Ruz*, II, p. 405.

59 Ibid., 398–99.

60 Enma Castro interview; Juanita Castro, *Fidel y Raúl, mis hermanos*, pp. 144–49; Blanco Castiñeira, *Fidel Castro Ruz*, II, pp. 423–26.

61 Acosta, *La palabra empeñada*, II, p. 355; Franqui, *Diary of the Cuban Revolution*, p. 112; Morán Arce, *La Revolución Cubana*, pp. 48–49. The fluidity of the lines shaping the membership of these groups is suggested in Castro Porta, *La lección del maestro*, p. 160.

62 Del Conde, *Memorias de dueño del Yacht Granma*, pp. 110–11.

63 Del Conde interview; del Conde, *Memorias de dueño del Yacht Granma*, pp. 117–20.

64 Del Conde, *Memorias de dueño del Yacht Granma*, p. 127; del Conde interview.

65 Guevara, *Reminiscences*, pp. 13–14; Hernández, *Huellas del exilio*, pp. 270–74, 280; Franqui, *Diary of the Cuban Revolution*, pp. 121–23.

66 Suárez Pérez and Caner Román, *Fidel Castro*, pp. 291–92.

67 Franqui, *Diary of the Cuban Revolution*, pp. 115–16.

68 Hernández, *Huellas del exilio*, p. 282. See also Blanco Castiñeira, *Fidel Castro Ruz*, II, pp. 434–39.

69 Major General Carlos Tabernilla Dolz to the Army Chief of Staff, October 15, 1956, in Hernández, *Huellas del exilio*, p. 212.

70 Directiva de Operaciones, November 1, 1956, in Hernández, *Huellas del exilo*, p. 207; Directiva Numero 5, November 6, 1956, in ibid., p. 207.

71 Telegrams from Army Chief of Staff to command posts throughout

the island, in Sergio Ravelo López, ed., *La expedición del Granma: selección de documentos* (La Habana: Editora Política, 2007), pp. 101–3.

72 Franqui, *Diary of the Cuban Revolution*, pp. 121–24. See also Blanco Castiñeira, *Fidel Castro Ruz*, II, pp. 440–43.

73 Franqui, *Diary of the Cuban Revolution*, p. 124.

74 Ibid., pp. 118–21.

75 Ibid., pp. 117–18.

chapter eleven - TO WAKE THE NATION

1 Fidel Castro, *La victoria estratégica por todos los caminos de la Sierra* (New York: Ocean Press, 2011), 194–98.

2 Quinteto Rebelde interview, Las Mercedes, January 23, 2014.

3 Ernesto Che Guevara, *Reminiscences of the Cuban Revolutionary War* (New York: Ocean Press, 2005), p. 16.

4 Ibid., pp. 15–28; Ernesto Che Guevara, *Diary of a Combatant* (New York: Ocean Press), pp. 34–35. See also Fidel Castro and Ignacio Ramonet, *My Life: A Spoken Biography* (New York: Scribner, 2007), p. 185; and Eugenio Suárez Pérez and Acela A. Caner Román, *Fidel Castro: Birán to Cinco Palmas* (La Habana: Editorial José Martí, 2002), pp. 299–301.

5 Guevara, *Diary of a Combatant*, 34–38. For a detailed account of the work done by País, Sánchez, and their colleagues in the urban underground, see Nancy Stout, *One Day in December: Celia Sánchez and the Cuban Revolution* (New York: Monthly Review Press, 2013). In January 2014, I interviewed a number of former peasants whose families welcomed Castro to the Sierra over a half century earlier. Most had never heard of Castro when he arrived in the mountains; but virtually all spoke of injustices perpetrated by Batista authorities on the local inhabitants for no apparent reason. See, for example, Juan Gonzáles Castillo interview, Santo Domingo, Cuba, January 23, 2014; Eugenio Medina Muñoz interview, Las Mercedes, Cuba, January 23, 2014; and María Dolores Capote interview, Guisa, Cuba, January 21, 2014.

6 Associated Press, "Cuba Wipes Out Invaders; Leader Is Among 40 Dead," *New York Times*, December 3, 1956, p. 1.

7 Guevara, *Diary of a Combatant*, pp. 53–55.

8 Armando Hart, *Aldabonazo: Inside the Cuban Revolutionary Underground, 1952–1958* (New York: Pathfinder, 2004), pp. 141–48; Stout, *One Day in December*, pp. 143–50.

9   The authoritative account is Anthony DePalma, *The Man Who Invented Fidel* (New York: PublicAffairs, 2006).

10 Herbert L. Matthews, "A Cuban Rebel Is Visited in Hideout; Castro Is Still Alive and Still Fighting in Mountains," *New York Times*, February 24, 1957, pp. 1, 34.

11 Carlos Franqui, *Diary of the Cuban Revolution* (New York: Viking, 1976), p. 143.

12 Ibid., pp. 147–69.

13 Hart, *Aldabonazo*, p. 154.

14 Ibid., pp. 153–56.

15 Guevara, *Diary of a Combatant*, pp. 41, 47.

16 Charles Ryan remembers endless marching in total silence, Castro's band of city slickers completely dependent on their peasant hosts for survival. Charles Ryan telephone interview, October 8 and 9, 2009, and Victor Buehlman telephone interview, October 14, 2009.

17 Charles Ryan and Victor Buehlman interviews. Lucas Castillo and his brother Patrocinio, from the village of Santo Domingo, served as a link in those mule trains. Patrocinio acted as a guide to the rebel command, with Lucas delivering food and supplies to the rebels as his brother directed. Lucas was eventually betrayed and was brutally murdered by Batista's army. Juan Gonzáles Castillo interview.

18 Julia Sweig, *Inside the Cuban Revolution: Fidel Castro and the Urban Underground* (Cambridge: Harvard University Press, 2002), pp. 20, 61; Franqui, *Diary of the Cuban Revolution*, p. 181.

19 For a diagram of the battlefield, see Castro, *La victoria estratégica por todos los caminos de la Sierra*, p. 560.

20 Guevara, *Reminiscences*, p. 119.

21 Franqui, *Diary of the Cuban Revolution*, pp. 175–77.

22 Sweig, *Inside the Cuban Revolution*, pp. 29–32.

23 Castro to Celia Sánchez, July 5, 1957, FCP.

24 See, for example, Stout, *One Day in December*, pp. 143–50; Roland Bonachea and Nelson P. Valdés, eds., *Revolutionary Struggle: Select Works of Fidel Castro* (Cambridge: The MIT Press, 1974), pp. 96–99; Sweig, *Inside the Cuban Revolution*, pp. 20–35.

25 Castro to Celia Sánchez, July 5, 1957, FCP.

26 Ibid.

27 País to Castro, July 5, 1957, in Franqui, *Diary of the Cuban Revolution*, pp. 196–98.

28   País to Castro, July 7, 1957, in ibid., pp. 202–5.

29   Ibid.

30   Castro to Conchita Fernández, July 11, 1957, FCP; Castro to Celia Sánchez, July 12, 1957, FCP.

31   Sweig, *Inside the Cuban Revolution*, p. 31.

32   Sierra Maestra Manifesto, July 12, 1957, FCP; translated in Bonachea and Valdes, eds., *Revolutionary Struggle*, pp. 243-48.

33   Castro to País, July 21, 1957, FCP.

34   Castro to País, July 21, 1957, FCP.

35   Ibid.

36   Ibid.

37   Ibid. Castro repeated this glowing account of the peasants in the Sierra in a note to Celia Sánchez dated August 17, 1957, FCP.

38   Ibid.

39   Espín interview in Franqui, *Diary of the Cuban Revolution*, p. 214.

40   Castro to Celia Sánchez, July 31, 1957, FCP.

41   René Ramos Latour to Sánchez, August 1, 1957, in Franqui, *Diary of the Cuban Revolution*, pp. 218–20.

42   Castro to Celia Sánchez, August 14, 1957, FCP; see also Castro to Sánchez, August 11, 1957, FCP.

43   Fidel Castro, *La victoria estratégica por todos los caminos de la Sierra* (New York: Ocean Press, 2011), p. 20; Guevara, *Diary of a Combatant*, pp. 180–81.

44   Guevara to Castro, August 31, 1957, in Franqui, *Diary of the Cuban Revolution*, pp. 224–25.

45   Guevara, *Reminiscences*, p. 138

46   Ibid., p. 161.

47   Ibid., pp. 161–66; Franqui, *Diary of the Cuban Revolution*, pp. 181–82. Castro discusses the dilemmas of what to do with suspected traitors and runaways in a letter to Celia Sánchez dated August 11, 1957, FCP.

48   Guevara, *Reminiscences*, p. 172.

49   Hart, *Aldabonazo*, pp. 194–98; Zweig, *Inside the Cuban Revolution*, pp. 58–78; Hart to Castro, October 16, in Franqui, *Diary of the Cuban Revolution*, pp. 239–42.

50   The Miami Pact is translated in Jules Dubois, *Fidel Castro: Rebel-Liberator or Dictator?* (Indianapolis: Bobbs-Merrill, 1959), pp. 188–90.

51   Castro to the Directors of the Partido Revolucionario Cubano, Partido del Pueblo Cubano, Organización Auténtico, Federación

Estudiantil Universitaria, Directorio Revolucionario, Directorio Obrero Revolucionario, in Dubois, *Fidel Castro*, pp. 190–206.

52 Zweig, *Inside the Cuban Revolution*, 91–92.

53 René Ramos Latour to Castro, November 4, 1957, in Franqui, *Diary of the Cuban Revolution*, pp. 244–45.

54 Guevara to Castro, August 31, 1957, p. 225; Ramos Latour to Castro, September 15, 1957, pp. 229–31; Ramos Latour to Celia Sánchez, December 5, 1957, pp. 260–61; Hart to Celia Sánchez, December 6, 1957, pp. 262–26; and Guevara to Castro, December 9, 1957, pp. 264–65; all in Franqui, *Diary of the Cuban Revolution*.

55 Guevara to Castro, December 9, 1957, in ibid., pp. 264–65.

56 Guevara to Ramos Latour, December 14, 1957, in ibid., pp. 268–70.

57 See, for example, Ramos's reply to Guevara, December 19, 1957, in ibid., pp. 272–76.

58 Castro to Che Guevara, December 13, 1957, FCP.

59 Castro to Celia Sánchez, August 11, 1957, FCP.

60 Castro to Celia Sánchez, August 14, 1957, FCP.

61 Castro to Sánchez, August 11, 1957.

62 Castro to Juan Rodríguez, November 6, 1957, FCP.

63 Castro to Nancy Reyes, November 16, 1957, FCP.

64 "Parte oficial del Cuartel General de Fidel Castro," January 23, 1957, FCP.

65 "Acta de liberación de prisioneros de guerra," May 30, 1957, FCP.

66 Castro to a local farmer, September 2, 1957, FCP.

chapter twelve - KEEPING ORDER
IN THE HEMISPHERE

1 Armando Hart, *Aldabonazo: Inside the Cuban Revolutionary Underground, 1952–1958* (New York: Pathfinder, 2004), pp. 177–81, 227–29, 268–73.

2 Castro to Che Guevara, January 14, 1958, FCP.

3 Hart, *Aldobonazo*, pp. 231–32.

4 Lee Lockwood, *Castro's Cuba, Cuba's Fidel: An American Journalist's Inside Look at Today's Cuba—in Text and Pictures* (New York: Macmillan, 1967), p. 162.

5 Enrique Meneses, *Fidel Castro* (New York: Taplinger, 1966), p. 62; Armainio Savioli interview, February 1, 1961, *L'Unita* (Rome), No. 32, pp. 1–2.

6 Lucas Morán Arce, *La Revolución Cubana: Una version rebelde* (Ponce, Puerto Rico: Imprenta Universitaria, 1980), p. 126. See also Gianni Mina, *An Encounter with Fidel* (New York: Ocean Press, 1996), p. 118.

7 Memo from Embassy Havana to Department of State, November 17, 1948, in Jack B. Pfeiffer, ed. *Central Intelligence Agency, Official History of the Bay of Pigs Operation*, Vol. II (Berkshire, UK: Books Express Publishing, 2011), p. 1.

8 American Embassy Havana to Department of State, May 31, 1955, in *Confidential U.S. State Department Files, Cuba: Internal Affairs and Foreign Affairs* (Frederick, MD: University Publications of America, 1987).

9 Memo from State Department attaché V. Lansing Collings to Daniel M. Braddock, counselor at the U.S. Embassy, Havana, October 14, 1957, in Pfeiffer, ed., *Official History of the Bay of Pigs Invasion, Volume III* (Berkshire, UK: Books Express Publishing, 2011), p. 3.

10 American Embassy Havana to Department of State, January 31 and February 6, 1956, in Confidential U.S. State Department Files.

11 Ambassador Earl T. Smith to Secretary of State John Foster Dulles, September 13, 1957, *Foreign Relations of the United States*, 1955–1957, Vol. VI, American Republics: mulitilateral; Mexico, Caribbean, No. 294; hereafter *FRUS*.

12 Ibid.

13 Berle quoted in Pfeiffer, ed., *Official History*, p. 6.

14 William A. Wieland to Roy R. Rubottom, Jr., January 10 and 17, 1958, *FRUS*, 1958–1960, Vol. V, Cuba, Nos. 3 and 5.

15 Smith quoted in *FRUS*, 1958–1960, Vol. V, Cuba, No. 6.

16 Department of State to American Embassy, January 22, 1958, in *FRUS*, 1958–1960, Vol. V, Cuba, No. 7.

17 William A. Wieland to Earl T. Smith, February 3, 1958, *FRUS*, 1958–1960, Vol. V, Cuba, No. 10.

18 Assistant Secretary of State for Inter-American Affairs (Rubottom) to the Ambassador in Cuba, February 14, 1958, *FRUS*, 1958–1960, Vol. V, Cuba, No. 13.

19 American Embassy to Department of State, February 20, 1958, *FRUS*, 1958–1960, Vol. V, Cuba, No. 16.

20 Castro to Che Guevara, January 28, 1958, FCP.

21 Meneses, *Fidel Castro*, pp. 63–64.

22 Andrew St. George, "Cuban Rebels," *Look* (February 4, 1958), p. 30.

23 Castro to Sergio Carbó Enero-Marzo, February 23, 1958, FCP.

24 Castro to Chief of the Garrison at Pino del Agua, February 16, 1958, FCP.

25 Franqui, *Diary of the Cuban Revolution*, pp. 284–85.

26 Castro to Ceferino Rodríguez, February 26, 1958, FCP.

27 Castro to Aquiles Chinea, March 17, 1958, FCP.

28 Castro to Teodora Enríquez, March 4, 1958, FCP.

29 Castro to Francisca Isbert, March 18, 1958, FCP.

30 Castro to José Ramón Pérez, March 10, 1958, FCP.

31 Executive Committee of the National Medical Association to the Chief Justice of the Supreme Court, October 28, 1957, in Jules Dubois, *Fidel Castro: Rebel-Liberator or Dictator?* (Indianapolis: Bobbs-Merrill, 1959), p. 186.

32 Meneses, *Fidel Castro*, 72; Julia Sweig, *Inside the Cuban Revolution: Fidel Castro and the Urban Underground* (Cambridge: Harvard University Press, 2002), p. 108.

33 Judges' letter to Chamber of Administration, Court of Appeals of Havana, March 6, 1958, in Dubois, *Fidel Castro*, pp. 220–22.

34 Civic Institutions, March 15, 1958, in ibid., pp. 225–29.

35 Total War Manifesto, March 12, 1958, in ibid., pp. 233–39.

36 Sweig, *Inside the Cuban Revolution*, pp. 97–101, 124–26, 139–40; Hart, *Aldabonazo*, pp. 237–49; Meneses, *Fidel Castro*, p. 76; Roland Bonachea and Nelson P. Valdés, eds., *Revolutionary Struggle: Select Works of Fidel Castro* (Cambridge: MIT Press, 1974), pp. 106–8.

37 Meneses, *Fidel Castro*, pp. 74–77.

38 Castro to Celia Sánchez, April 16, 1958, FCP; Hart, *Aldabonazo*, pp. 282–84.

chapter thirteen - PLAN FIN-DE-FIDEL

1 Fidel Castro, *La victoria estratégica por todos los caminos de la Sierra* (New York: Ocean Press, 2011), pp. 431, 570.

2 Julia Sweig, *Inside the Cuban Revolution: Fidel Castro and the Urban Underground* (Cambridge: Harvard University Press, 2002), pp. 159–63.

3 Editorial note, *FRUS*, 1958–1960, Vol. VI, No. 51.

4 State to American Embassy, February 28, 1958, *FRUS*, 1958–1960, Vol. V, Cuba, No. 22. See also State to Embassy, March 3, 1958, Vol. V, Cuba, Nos. 26 and 27.

5   Smith to State, April 13, 1958, *FRUS*, 1958–1960, Vol. V, Cuba, No. 50.

6   Smith to State, March 14, 1958, *FRUS*, 1958–1960, Vol. V, Cuba, Vol. VI, Cuba, No. 34.

7   Acting Secretary of State Herter to President Eisenhower, December 23, 1958, *FRUS*, 1958–1960, Vol. VI, Cuba, No. 189; Smith to Rubottom, June 16, 1958, *FRUS*, 1958–1960, Vol. VI, Cuba, No. 65.

8   Memorandum of Conversation Between Assistant Secretary of State (Rubottom) and Cuban Ambassador (Arroyo), May 22, 1958, *FRUS*, 1958–1960, Vol. VI, Cuba, No. 58. See also Editorial Note, *FRUS*, 1958–1960, Vol. VI, Cuba, No. 56.

9   Smith to State, June 16, 1958, *FRUS*, 1958–1960, Cuba, Vol. VI, No. 65; Rubottom to Deputy Under Secretary of State for Political Affairs (Murphy), June 26, 1958, *FRUS*, 1958–1960, Cuba, Vol. VI, No. 68.

10 Smith to State, December 2, 1958, *FRUS*, 1958–1960, Cuba, Vol. VI, No. 169; Smith to State, December 5, 1958, *FRUS*, 1958–1960, Cuba, Vol. VI, No. 170.

11 Circular No. 1 (To all commanders, platoon captains, and squadron lieutenants), May 6, 1958, FCP.

12 Castro to Celia Sánchez, April 27, 1958, FCP.

13 Ibid.

14 Castro to Celia Sánchez, May 7, 1958, FCP.

15 Castro to Horacio Rodríguez, June 3, 1958, FCP; Castro to Celia Sánchez, June 5, 1958, FCP.

16 Castro to Celia Sánchez, May 8 and May 17, 1958, FCP.

17 Castro to Ramón Paz, May 8, 1958, FCP.

18 Response to questions posed by Jules Dubois, May 18, 1958, FCP.

19 Israel Rodríguez Serano interview, Buey Arriba, Cuba, January 24, 2014; Castro, *La victoria estratégica*, p. 47. Maria Dolores Capote confirms this account of Castro's way with the locals, as do Luis Angel Seguro Castillo, Leonardo Nieto Cabrales, Damián Medina Antolín, and Israel Rodríguez Serano. Maria Dolores Capote interview; Luis Angel Seguro Castillo interview, Santo Domingo, Cuba, January 23, 2014; Leonardo Nieto Cabrales interview, Buey Arriba, Cuba, January 24, 2014; Damián Medina Antolín interview, Las Mercedes, January 23 2014.

20 Castro, *La victoria estratégica*, pp. 48–57. Such atrocities were commonplace. Luis Angel Seguro Castillo interview.

21 Castro to Camilo Cienfuegos, June 11, 1958, FCP.

22 Castro to Ramón Paz and Pedro Miret, June 12, 1958, FCP.

23 Castro to Paz, June 18, 1958, FCP.

24 Castro to Ramiro Valdés, Juan Almeida, and Guillermo García, June 17, 1958, FCP.

25 Castro to Che Guvevara, June 19, 1958, FCP; Castro, *La victoria estratégica*, pp. 136–37.

26 Castro to Paz, June 20, 1958, FCP; Castro, *La victoria estratégica*, pp. 140–41.

27 Castro to Miret, June 20, 1958, FCP.

28 Castro to Paz, June 20, 1958, FCP.

29 Ibid.; Castro, *La victoria estratégica*, p. 147.

30 Carlos Franqui, *Diary of the Cuban Revolution* (New York: Viking, 1976), pp. 366–67.

31 Castro, *La victoria estratégica*, pp. 241–42.

32 Castro to Colonel José Quevedo Pérez, July 15, 1958, FCP.

33 Castro to Colonel José Quevedo Pérez, July 19, 1959, FCP.

34 Franqui, *Diary of the Cuban Revolution*, p. 382. Castro, *La victoria estratégica*, p. 265.

35 Jules Dubois, *Fidel Castro: Rebel-Liberator or Dictator?* (Indianapolis: Bobbs-Merrill, 1959), pp. 280–83.

36 Smith to State, June 16, 1958, *FRUS*, 1958–1960, Vol. VI, Cuba, No. 65. U.S. military support for Cuba is described in Deputy Assistant Secretary of State William P. Snow to Acting Secretary of State Herter, May 6, 1958, *FRUS*, 1958–1960, Cuba, Vol. VI, No. 55.

37 Rubottom Memorandum, June 26, 1958, *FRUS*, 1958–1960, Vol. VI, Cuba, No. 68.

38 Ellis to Burke, June 30, 1958, *FRUS*, 1958–1960, Vol. VI, Cuba, No. 119. For the full story, see Jonathan M. Hansen, *Guantánamo: An American History* (New York: Hill & Wang, 2011), pp. 214–18.

39 Wollam quoted in Smith to State, July 3, 1958, *FRUS*, 1958–1960, Vol. VI, Cuba, Nos. 125–26.

40 Wollam to Leonhardy, June 4, 1958, *FRUS*, 1958–1960, No. 62; Stewart to Snow, July 24, 1958, *FRUS*, 1958–1960, Vol. VI, Cuba, No. 111.

41 Stewart to Snow, July 24, 1958, *FRUS*, 1958–1960, Vol. VI, Cuba, No. 111; Memorandum on Considerations for Policy Recommendations for Cuba, July 25, 1958, *FRUS*, 1958–1960, Vol. VI, Cuba, No. 112.

42 Smith to State, July 25, 1958, *FRUS*, 1958–1960, Vol. VI, Cuba, No. 113.

43   Dubois, *Fidel Castro*, pp. 299–302.

44   Ibid., p. 314.

45   Castro to General Eulogio Cantillo, August 7 and 10, 1958, FCP.

46   Ibid.

47   Ibid.

48   Castro to Cantillo, November 9, 1958, FCP. See also the undated letter, probably written two days later (November 11, 1958), FCP.

49   Law No. 3, "On the Right of the Peasants to the Land," October 10, 1958, FCP.

50   Castro to Cienfuegos, October 14, 1958, FCP.

51   Ibid.

52   Law No. 4, "Against the English Aggression," October 19, 1958, FCP.

53   Castro to U.S. State Department, October 25, 1958, FCP.

chapter fourteen - FIN-DE-FULGENCIO

1   Smith to State, September 24, 1958, *FRUS*, 1958–1960, Vol. VI, Cuba, No. 133.

2   Hugh Thomas, *Cuba, or the Pursuit of Freedom* (New York: Da Capo, 1998), p. 1014.

3   Castro to Cantillo, November 9, 1958, FCP. See also the undated letter, probably written two days later (November 11, 1958), FCP.

4   Smith, Memorandum of Conversation with President-elect Agüero, November 15, 1958, *FRUS*, 1958–1960, Vol. VI, Cuba, No. 154.

5   Pawley quoted in *FRUS*, 1958–1960, Cuba, Vol. VI, Nos. 164 and 173. See also Anthony R. Carrozza, *The Extraordinary Life of the Adventurer, Entrepreneur, and Diplomat William D. Pawley* (Dulles, VA: Potomac Books, 2012), pp. 225–36.

6   Memorandum of Record, First Meeting of General Maxwell Taylor's Board of Inquiry on Cuban Operations Conducted by the CIA, April 22, 1961, *FRUS*, 1961–1963, Vol. X, Cuba, No. 69.

7   Pepe Echemendía to Castro, December 23, 1958, in Carlos Franqui, *Diary of the Cuban Revolution* (New York: Viking, 1976), pp. 469–70.

8   Franqui's and Castro's responses to the proposal brought by Echemendía in ibid., pp. 470–71.

9   Juanita Castro, *Fidel y Raúl, mis hermanos: la historia secreta* (Doral, FL: Aguilar, 2009), pp. 186–87.

10   Castro to Che Guevara, December 26, 1958, FCP.

11   Circular, December 27, 1958, FCP.

12   Castro to Rego Rubido, December 29, 1958, FCP; Castro to Cantillo, December 30, 1958, FCP.

13   Special National Intelligence Estimate, Developments in Cuba Since Mid-November, December 16, 1958, *FRUS*, 1958–1960, Cuba, Vol. VI, No. 182.

14   Memorandum of Discussion at the 392nd Meeting of the National Security Council, December 23, 1958, *FRUS*, 1958–1969, Cuba, Vol. VI, No. 188.

15   "Cuba," Department of State Publication 7171, Inter-American Series 66 (Washington, D.C.: U.S. Government Printing Office, April 1961), pp. 1, 33.

16   Smith to State, January 1, 1959, *FRUS*, 1958–1969, Vol. VI, Cuba, Nos. 206–9.

17   Castro, "Speech to the People of Santiago de Cuba," Parque Céspedes, January 1, 1959, FCP.

EPILOGUE

1   The interview can be viewed here: https://www.youtube.com/watch?v=DOAXEWXF1jw.

2   Dulles quoted in David M. Barrett, *The CIA and Congress: The Untold Story from Truman to Kennedy* (Lawrence: University Press of Kansas, 2005), p. 426. The rebel victory and its aftermath are covered in, among others, Hugh Thomas, *Cuba, or the Pursuit of Freedom* (New York: Da Capo, 1998), pp. 1072–75; Enrique Meneses, *Fidel Castro* (New York: Taplinger, 1966), pp. 91–92; and Jules Dubois, *Fidel Castro: Rebel-Liberator or Dictator?* (Indianapolis: Bobbs-Merrill, 1959), pp. 362–74.

3   Dubois, *Fidel Castro*, 371. Years later, Castro conceded that the executions had been a mistake. See Fidel Castro and Ignacio Ramonet, *My Life: A Spoken Biography* (New York: Scribner, 2007), pp. 220–22. The number of executed in Cuba in the first three months was small compared to other postwar purges in other nations. See Andrew Rigby, *Justice and Reconciliation: After the Violence* (Boulder: Lynne Rienner, 2001), chapter 2.

4   Richard M. Nixon, Memorandum on Meeting with Fidel Castro, 19 April 1959, Appendix F, Jack B. Pfeiffer, ed., *Official History of the*

Bay of Pigs Operation, Volume III (Berkshire, UK: Books Express Publishing, 2011), p. 340; Herter quoted in Robert Quirk, *Fidel Castro* (New York: Norton, 1998), p. 238; Smathers quoted in Brian Lewis Crispell, *Testing the Limits: George Armistead Smathers and Cold War America* (Athens: University of Georgia Press, 1999), p. 156.

5   Long quoted in Jim Rasenberger, *The Brilliant Disaster: JFK and America's Doomed Invasion of the Bay of Pigs* (New York: Simon & Schuster, 2012), p. 17; Fulton quoted in Crispell, *Testing the Limits*, p. 155: Nixon, Memorandum on Meeting With Fidel Castro, in Pfeiffer, ed., *Official History of the Bay of Pigs Operation, Vol. III*, p. 343.

6   Charles Maier interview, Cambridge, MA, October 18, 2014.

7   "Visitor from Cuba," *The New York Times* (April 25, 1959), p. 20.

8   Fidel Castro, speech delivered before the delegates from the 21 American nations assembled at Buenos Aires, May 2, 1959, in Castro Speech Data Base, Latin American Network Information Center (LANIC), http://lanic.utexas.edu/project/castro/db/1959/19590502-1.html.

9   Eisenhower quoted in Stephen G. Rabe, *Eisenhower and Latin America: The Foreign Policy of Anticommunism* (Chapel Hill: The University of North Carolina Press, 1988), p. 128.

10 Fidel Castro, speech on Marxism–Leninism, December 2, 1961, available at http://www.walterlippmann.com/fc-12-02-1961.html.

11 Fidel Castro and Ignacio Ramonet, *My Life: A Spoken Biography* (New York: Scribner, 2007), p. 282.

12 Max Lesnik interview, Salim Lamrani, Conversations with Max Lesnik (courtesy of Salim Lamrani).

13 José Martí, Dedication to the Statue of Liberty (October 29, 1886), in *José Martí Reader: Writings on the Americas* (Ocean Press, 2016), p. 64.

INDEX

Page numbers in *italics* refer to maps.

PHOTO CREDITS

INSERT 1

Courtesy OAH: 1, 2, 3, 4, 5, 6, 8, 9, 10,
11, 12, 13, 14, 15, 16, 17, 18

J. Hansen: 7

INSERT 2

J. Hansen: 1, 18, 19

Courtesy OAH: 2, 3, 4, 5, 6, 7, 8, 10, 13, 14, 15, 16, 17

Courtesy of Marta Rojas: 9, 11

Courtesy of Naty Revuelta: 12

Getty Images: 20

ABOUT THE AUTHOR

Jonathan Hansen is Senior Lecturer on Social Studies and Faculty Associate, David Rockefeller Center for Latin American Studies at Harvard University. He is the author of *The Lost Promise of Patriotism: Debating American Identity, 1890–1920* (Chicago, 2003) and *Guantánamo: An American History* (Hill and Wang, 2011), along with articles, essays, and reviews on U.S. politics, imperialism, nationalism, and race and ethnicity. His writing has appeared in *The New York Times*, *The Huffington Post*, *The Guardian*, and *Cognoscenti*, among other places.